Many Sisters

WOMEN IN CROSS-CULTURAL PERSPECTIVE

Edited by

Carolyn J. Matthiasson

THE FREE PRESS
A Division of Macmillan Publishing Co., Inc.
New York

COLLIER MACMILLAN PUBLISHERS
London

The Free Press
A Division of Macmillan Publishing Co., Inc.
866 Third Avenue, New York, N.Y. 10022

Collier Macmillan Canada, Ltd.

First Free Press Paperback Edition 1979

Library of Congress Catalog Card Number: 74-2654

Printed in the United States of America

printing number

HC   2 3 4 5 6 7 8 9 10

SC 1 2 3 4 5 6 7 8 9 10

Library of Congress Cataloging in Publication Data

Matthiasson, Carolyn J.
   Many sisters.

   Includes bibliographies.
   1. Women--History and condition of women. I. Title.
HQ1154.M385   301.41'2'08   74-2654
ISBN 0-02-920330-9
ISBN 0-02-920320-1 pbk.

Contents

v

List of Illustrations

List of Contributors

BARBARA GALLATIN ANDERSON

Barbara Gallatin Anderson is Professor of Anthropology at California State University, Hayward. Mother of three children, each of whom was born in a different country, she has been concerned with both the life cycle and culture change and has published on India, France, Italy, and Denmark as well as the United States. Her most recent fieldwork was in Morocco. She is coauthor of *Bus Stop for Paris, The Vanishing Village,* and *Culture and Aging* and has recently completed *The Aging Game.*

JEAN L. BRIGGS

Jean L. Briggs was born in the United States. She received a B.A. from Vassar College in 1951, an M.A. from Boston University in 1960, and a Ph.D. from Harvard University in 1967. She has done fieldwork in Eskimo communities in North Alaska and in the Canadian Arctic, both Central and Eastern. Her special interest is in ethnopsychology, in particular Eskimo theories concerning emotional structure and interpersonal motivation. Her publications include *Never in Anger: Portrait of an Eskimo Family* and "Kapluna Daughter" (in Peggy Golde, ed., *Women in the Field*). She is presently an Associate Professor in the Department of Sociology and Anthropology at Memorial University of Newfoundland, St. John's, Newfoundland, Canada.

GERTRUDE E. DOLE

Gertrude E. Dole received her B.A. at Middlebury College, her M.A. at the University of North Carolina and her Ph.D. at the University of Michigan in 1957. She has done fieldwork among the Kuikuru of Central Brazil and the Amahuaca of southeastern Peru, about both of whom she has published a number of articles. Her fields of special interest are kinship, tropical forest culture history, and the evolution of culture. She is coeditor of *Essays in the Science of Culture* and has published several articles on comparative kinship. She has taught at the New School for Social Research, Columbia University, New York University, and Vassar College.

MAY EBIHARA

May Ebihara, born in Oregon, received her B.A. from Reed College in 1955 and her Ph.D. at Columbia University in 1968. Her primary area of specialization is

Cambodia and Southeast Asia (with a secondary interest in North American Indians), and she is particularly concerned with studies of kinship and social organization. She has published several articles on Khmer village life, religion, and urban-rural relations, and she is currently writing a book about the community she studied. She is Associate Professor of Anthropology at Lehman College of the City University of New York, Bronx, New York.

DORANNE JACOBSON

Doranne Jacobson was born in Ann Arbor, Michigan, and studied anthropology at the University of Michigan and the University of London. She received her Ph.D. from Columbia University in 1970. Her first field research, among the Navajo Indians of Arizona, was a study of the Enemy Way Ceremonial, on which she published two articles. Her chapter in this book is based on 2½ years of fieldwork in India, where she conducted a study of village women. She is currently writing a book on the seclusion of women in India and is Research Associate in Anthropology at Columbia University and Ogden Mills Fellow at the American Museum of Natural History.

HELGA E. JACOBSON

Born in Berlin, Helga E. Jacobson grew up and received most of her education in England. She studied at the London School of Economics and Political Science and received her B.A. and M.A. from London University in 1960 and 1963 respectively. She obtained her Ph.D. from Cornell University in 1969. Her area of specialization is Southeast Asia in general and the Philippines in particular, with a particular interest in urban social organization and development. She has done field research in Cebu City (1965–66) and in Makati (1971–72). Her publications include a monograph entitled *Tradition and Change in Cebu City* and a number of articles relating to Cebu City; "The Family in Canada: Some Problems and Questions"; and—in preparation—her current research, *San Pedro Village Makati: A Study of a Suburban Community in the Philippines.* She is presently Assistant Professor of Anthropology at the University of British Columbia.

ELLI KÖNGÄS MARANDA

Elli Köngäs Maranda was born in Finland and received her *magister philosophiae* (M. Phil.) degree from Helsinki University in 1955 and her Ph.D. from Indiana University in 1963. Her area of specialization is the Solomon Islands, with particular emphasis on myth and riddle. Her publications include *Structural Models in Folklore and Transformational Essays* and *Structural Analysis of Oral Tradition* (both with Pierre Maranda). "Les Femmes Lau,—Malaita, îsles Salomon—dans l'espace socialisé" (*Journal de la Société des Océanistes*); "Le Crâne et l' utérus: Deux théorémes nord-malaitains" (*Échanges et Communications: Mélanges offerts á Claude Lévi-Strauss á l'occasion de son 60ème anniversaire,* reunis par Jean Puillon et Pierre Maranda); "Structures des énigmes" (L'Homme); and "Theory and Practice of Riddle Analysis" (*Journal of American Folklore*). She is presently Associate Professor of Anthropology at the University of British Columbia, Vancouver, British Columbia, Canada.

CAROLYN J. MATTHIASSON

Carolyn J. Matthiasson was born in the United States. She received her B.A. from Beloit College in 1959 and her Ph.D. from Cornell University in 1968. Her area of specialization is Latin America. She has done fieldwork in Mexico and among Mexican-Americans in the Northern United States. She is presently an assistant professor at the University of Winnipeg, Winnipeg, Manitoba, Canada.

EILEEN MAYNARD

Eileen Maynard was born in Newark, New York, and was graduated from Geneseo State Teachers College in 1944. Upon graduation she enlisted in the U.S. Navy. She received an M.A. in anthropology from Syracuse University in 1957 and a Ph.D. from Cornell University in 1963. Her research projects have centered around American Indians, both in Latin America (Guatemala and Ecuador) and in the United States (South Dakota). She is coauthor of *That These People May Live, Conditions among the Oglala Sioux of the Pine Ridge Reservation.* She also edited and contributed to two monographs on the Colta Lake Indians of Ecuador: *Indians in Misery* and *Essays on the Colta Lake Zone.* Dr. Maynard is an associate professor at Rhode Island College, Providence, R.I.

SAFIA K. MOHSEN

Safia K. Mohsen was born in Cairo, Egypt. She received her LL.B. from the University of Ein Shams in Cairo in 1959, her M.A. from the University of Michigan in 1962, and her Ph.D. degree from Michigan State University in 1970. Her area of specialization is the Middle East and North Africa, with particular emphasis on the legal and judicial processes. Her publications include "Aspects of the Legal Status of Women among Awlad Ali of the Western Desert of Egypt." Currently, she is an assistant professor at the State University of New York at Binghamton.

CARA E. RICHARDS

Cara E. Richards was born in Bayonne, New Jersey. She received her B.A. from Queens College, Flushing, New York, in 1952, and her Ph.D. degree from Cornell University in 1957. She has done fieldwork with the Onondaga and Navajo Indians and in Peru. Publications include *Man in Perspective: An Introduction to Cultural Anthropology; Presumed Behavior: Modification of the Ideal-Real Dichotomy; Huron and Iroquois Residence Patterns, 1600–1650;* and *City Taverns;* among others. She is presently an associate professor at Transylvania University, Lexington, Kentucky.

AUDREY SMEDLEY

Audrey Smedley, born in Detroit, Michigan, received her B.A. and M.A. degrees from the University of Michigan and her Ph.D. from the University of Manchester, England, in 1967. She did two years of field research in Northern Nigeria under a Ford Foundation Foreign Area Fellowship. Her interests include studies in cultural ecology and the history of anthropological theory. She has written several articles and three booklets on *The Meaning of Race and Racial Differences,* on *Slavery,* and on the *History of Man in Africa.* From 1971 to 1973, she was a Fellow of the Radcliffe Institute where she prepared a major work on the Birom. Currently, she is Associate Professor of Anthropology and Afro-American Studies at the State University of New York at Binghamton.

LOUISE E. SWEET

Louise E. Sweet was born in southern Michigan. She received her B.A. from Eastern Michigan University in 1937 (in English literature) and her Ph.D. in anthropology and Near Eastern studies in 1957. Her areas of specialization are the Middle East and ethnic groups in North American societies, with an emphasis on cultural ecology. Her publications include *Tell Toqaan: A Syrian Village,* and *The Middle East: A Handbook of Anthropological Research.* She is presently Professor and Head of the Department of Anthropology, University of Manitoba, Winnipeg, Manitoba, Canada.

ALINE K. WONG

Aline K. Wong was born in Hong Kong. She received her B.A. from the University of Hong Kong in 1962 and her Ph.D. at the University of California, Berkeley, in 1970. She was Head of the Department of Sociology at United College, The Chinese University of Hong Kong but is currently with the University of Singapore. Her areas of specialization are the sociology of the family and social change in Asia and Southeast Asia. Her publications include various articles on the marriage and family institutions in Communist China, social and political changes in Hong Kong, and a forthcoming book on *The Kaifong (Neighborhood) Associations and Community Leadership Structure in a Colonial Setting.*

Preface

In the production of any book, much assistance is needed before it reaches completion. There are many people to whom I owe thanks. I very much appreciate the many useful suggestions made to me by the contributors and their patience with their editor. I am especially grateful to Dr. Louise Sweet for her advice and encouragement.

Much of the inspiration for the book I owe to two former professors of mine, Dr. Joan P. Mencher, and Barbara E. Ward. Both were also very helpful in suggesting contributors. Instrumental, too, in encouraging me to begin the undertaking were Dr. Robert Ritzenthaler and Dr. Edward Wellin.

Above all, appreciation is due my husband, Dr. John S. Matthiasson, for his enthusiasm, assistance with the manuscript, and tolerance of the disruption of the household that the project entailed. And finally, I wish to thank Mary Putnam for diligently typing and proofreading the manuscript.

Carolyn J. Matthiasson

Introduction

Carolyn J. Matthiasson

"Women's lib" is not a new phenomenon. Feminism as a topic of contro-
versy in Europe and North America dates back to the middle of the past
century—although women have, of course, been of interest ever since Eve.
However, in the past hundred years attention to "women's causes" has risen
and ebbed like the tides. The 1960s brought a new peak in interest in
feminism, and with it came a whole flood of books on women. Some recent
feminist writers, in their attempts to attack the enemy "man," emphasize
the myth that women are universally oppressed. In their strident efforts to
make their point, these writers do womankind a great disservice by creating
and perpetuating a false stereotype. Some feminists seem to forget that it is
women who bear the sons and have the major role in their upbringing. An
excellent discussion of how women raise their sons to exploit younger
women and are themselves exploited is found in Eileen Maynard's chapter,
"Women under Two Types of Patriarchy." In this chapter we are given a
fine example of how women in some societies—here the Ladinos—are at
fault in creating their own "oppression." However, it will be clear to the
readers of this book that mothers in many societies rear their sons to regard women as equals.

The essays in this volume should make it clear that the stereotype of
women as universally submissive and oppressed has no basis in fact. Women
in many societies share equal rights and prestige with men. Even in those
societies in which females are treated as inferior to males and in which they
believe themselves to be of lower status, women use their ingenuity to lessen
the impact of male dominance upon them and to achieve at least modest
aims.

In 1966, I taught an adult education course on the status and role of
women in societies around the world. At that time, there were two excellent
books on women's lives, Denise Paulme's *Women of Tropical Africa* and

Barbara Ward's *Women in the New Asia,* but no book that told the reader what life is really like for millions of women in the rest of the world. On the other hand, from Victorian times to the present, much misinformation has been published about women. The Victorians postulated theories about primitive matriarchies, group marriage, and other "barbaric" practices which have never been validated by facts. Many modern popular writers and anthropologists have looked at women from a largely ethnocentric point of view, stressing their subservience and oppression. It seems worthwhile, then, to provide the average reader with accurate information on the activities of women, including their status. The essays in this book have been written from the point of view of women themselves in several societies. Each contributor gives the reader a feeling of what it is like to be a woman in the culture about which she has written.

In order for the lay reader to be able to understand the information in each chapter, the contributors have eliminated as many technical terms as practical and have defined necessary terms as simply as possible. Simple definitions of basic ethnological terms have been included in the final section of the Introduction for the benefit of readers who may not be acquainted with them. Readers with a knowledge of anthropology will wish to skip this section.

CONTRIBUTORS

Each essay in this book is the work of a woman anthropologist or sociologist who has spent considerable time intimately observing life in the culture about which she has written. The authors are able to gain insights into aspects of women's lives not usually open to male ethnographers. Many anthropologists have encountered difficulties in obtaining data on members of the opposite sex. This is as true of women who interview men as it is of men who interview women.

Formality and reserve are the customary behavior patterns between unrelated men and women both in Western societies and in the rest of the world. William F. Kenhel has studied the impact of the sex of the observer on the behavior of wives during joint husband-and-wife interviews in a Midwestern state. He found that when the couple was interviewed by a female researcher, wives responded more frequently and reacted more freely to the discussion than did wives who were interviewed by a male researcher (Kenhel, 1961, p. 185). It is even more difficult to get the woman's point of view in societies which have taboos against the contact of males with females who are not related to them. Many of our male colleagues would contend that those areas which are too intimate for a man to discuss with a woman informant can be covered by a wife or by a female field assistant. This is true when the ethnographer is fortunate enough to have a wife or female assistant with him. However, this has not always been the case; male anthropologists often do fieldwork alone.

Further, while many male ethnographers do understand women's roles, few have been interested enough in the topic to write down their insights. This is partly due to the fact that the topic of women's role has been in vogue scientifically only for the past several years. Women as a subject of inquiry fell out of favor at the end of the Victorian period, possibly as a reaction to the unscientific nature of the studies done by early anthropologists. Scientific studies of women in the 1960s and 1970s owe their stimulus to renewed public interest in the women's movement.

ORGANIZATION

In organizing this book, I tried to achieve a worldwide distribution in the societies represented, to include societies at all levels of technological and political complexity, and to have a variety of types of kinship organization represented. Therefore, included are an example of a hunting and gathering band—the Eskimo of the high Arctic; several tribal groups—the Amahuaca of the Peruvian jungle, the Birom of the northern plateau area of Nigeria, the Lau of the Solomon Islands, the Onondaga of Eastern United States; and peasants and urbanites within national states such as China, Cambodia, Egypt, the Philippines, Syria, Lebanon, France, Guatemala, and India. North American society is not represented because of the difficulty in finding a woman scholar who could discuss North American society from an anthropological point of view. There are a number of other societies which I had hoped to include in this volume. These would have given an even broader perspective to the book. Unfortunately, several potential contributors who had wished to do so were unable, for a variety of reasons, to contribute essays.

Originally, I had planned to organize the chapters in a hierarchy, beginning with the society in which women were the most inferior. Such a ranking proved to be impossible. First of all, the societies did not line themselves up in a tidy progression, but also—more importantly—such a ranking would do violence to the realities and complexities of life in some of the societies. In many societies, both men and women are subordinated. Some subordinate themselves to the needs of larger kin groups such as lineages or to the state. In other societies, castes or castelike groups are politically and socially dominant over both men and women of the lower castes or classes. In still other societies, men and women are subordinated by exploitive outside influences. Therefore, while the arrangement of societies in this book basically reflects the relationships between men and women, the order of the chapters is not based on a progression of status from low to high. The reader should keep in mind that in at least eight of the thirteen societies, men also feel the effects of the dominance of others upon them.

ARRANGEMENT OF CHAPTERS

The chapters are grouped into three broad categories. Within each of the three, the relationships between men and women follow similar patterns. In order not to imply a ranked hierarchy within each of the categories, the chapters have been arranged alphabetically within categories by tribe or national state.

The first category is headed "Manipulative Societies." It includes societies in which women feel that they are inferior to men and resort to deceit, withdrawal, artifice, or circumvention to attain their own desires. While subterfuge and withdrawal are human traits which are used by both men and women, these modes of behavior are not as necessary to women in the achievement of their own ends in the remaining societies.

The second category, "Complementary Societies," is composed of cultures in which women are valued for themselves and the contributions they make to society. In these societies, women are neither inferior nor superior to men, merely different.

The third category, "Ascendant Societies," is represented in this book by only one society, although there may be a few others of this type in the world. An ascendant society is one in which it may be an advantage at times to be a woman. Being a woman is an advantage at times in other societies; however, the difference is one of frequency. In an ascendant society the basis of the advantage is institutionalized. Ascendancy does not, however, imply matriarchy. There is no evidence that any society has ever been truly matriarchal in structure.

DEFINITION OF TERMS

Throughout the book, a number of technical terms are used. This is unavoidable since social scientists, of necessity, have developed a vocabulary to describe the data they use. Unfortunately, many of these words have other meanings to the layman. This can lead to some confusion. The words *status* and *role* are two such words which have come to have a variety of meanings both in the technical sense and to the layman.

STATUS AND ROLE

The word *status* is used in two ways throughout the book. It sometimes refers to a person's relative rank or prestige in relation to others in a society. That is, a person may be inferior to, superior to, or equal to others in a hierarchy. For example, in her discussion of women in North and Central India, Doranne Jacobson refers to women's status in relation to men.

Status is also used in another more technical sense by social scientists to refer to the position a person has in relation to others in a social network. Every society has a system of positions which may or may not be occupied at a particular time. In any given society there may be kinship statuses—mother, father, son, daughter, etc.; occupational statuses—doctor, lawyer, housewife, merchant, etc.; political statuses—elder, headman, chief; and many others. One individual may occupy several statuses simultaneously. A person may be a father, bank president, and Rotarian at the same time. These relationships to others provide the focal point at which the social scientist can begin to examine the ideal and actual behaviors associated with each particular status.

The term *role* is used to refer to the various behaviors, actual or ideal, which are appropriate to particular social positions or statuses. The status "wife" occurs frequently throughout the book and is the focus of a variety of activities and social behaviors. The role of wife in some societies may mean that such a person cooks, cares for children, and manages a variety of household activities. In other societies, a wife's role may include trading, folk healing, weaving, and working in the fields. Society has a framework of ideas about the expected behavior of persons filling certain roles. These expectations vary from society to society, as will be apparent to the reader on reading the chapters in this book.

KINSHIP ORGANIZATION

Societies have developed a multitude of arrangements to carry out domestic life and to relate one domestic unit to another. A number of technical terms have been developed and refined to define and describe these relationships. To help the reader with no previous knowledge of anthropology to understand some of the terms used in the essays, a brief and extremely simplified discussion of some of the kinship terms which occur commonly in this book follows.

Human society has organized domestic life around two universal principles. The first is the principle of affinity, that is, relationships established with in-laws or step kin. The second is the principle of descent, or relationships with blood relatives. All persons who are bound together either by affinity, descent, or both may be considered to be kinsmen. The totality of behavior and expectations that kinsmen share with each other is called kinship.

SYSTEMS OF DESCENT

Many of the chapters in the book mention a particular system of descent used by the members of that society. Stripped down to their basic components, systems of descent are either unilineal or cognatic. The two varieties of unilineal descent which are represented in this book are patrilineality and matrilineality. The basis of patrilineality is descent in the male line only, so that all children belong to the kin groups of their fathers and a son gains his identity and succeeds to both secular and ritual offices through the male line. Matrilineality is based on descent in the female line only, so that all children belong to the kin group of their mothers and secular and religious offices descend through the female line. Membership in a unilineal descent group is lifelong. One cannot marry out of or into this type of kin group.

The particular type of cognatic descent practiced by societies in this book is bilateral descent. In this type of descent, kinship is traced symmetrically along maternal and paternal lines in ascending and descending generations through individuals of both sexes.

INHERITANCE

Inheritance of property in a society usually follows the system of descent. Therefore, property may be inherited unilineally by males only through the male line, by females only through the female line, or bilaterally by both male and female siblings.

RESIDENCE PATTERNS

The societies in this book also follow a variety of residence patterns. They are patrilocality, in which males remain in the same domestic unit as their fathers and wives are brought into the household; matrilocality, in which women remain in the domestic unit and husbands live with their mothers-in-law; virilocality, in which a wife moves to the residence of her husband wherever it may be; uxorilocality, in which a husband moves to reside with his wife wherever she may live; and neolocality, in which both husband and wife set up a joint residence. Residence patterns are not necessarily fixed for life but may shift about depending on circumstance, especially among groups practicing virilocal, uxorilocal, or neolocal residence.

The societies presented in this book that follow patrilineal systems of descent also practice patrilocal residence. They are the Arabs of the Middle East, the Muslims and Hindus of North and Central India, the Birom of Nigeria, the Lau of the Solomon Islands, the Guatemalan Indians, and the Chinese in the traditional period. The traditional Onondaga is the only society in the book which followed matrilocal residence and matrilineality. The French, the Ladinos of Guatemala, the Khmer of Cambodia, the Eskimo, and the majority of Filipinos all have systems of bilateral descent and reside neolocally.

BIBLIOGRAPHY

Kenhel, William F.: "Sex of Observer and Spousal Roles in Decision Making," *Journal of Marriage and Family Living*, vol. 23, no. 2, pp. 185–186, 1961.

Paulme, Denise: *Women of Tropical Africa*, Routledge and Kegan Paul, London, 1963.

Ward, Barbara: *Women in the New Asia*, Paris, UNESCO, 1963.

Manipulative
Societies

The Marriages
of Pacho:

A Woman's Life among
the Amahuaca

GERTRUDE E. DOLE

THE WORD *pacho* in the Amahuaca language refers to a kind of wood that is used for canoe paddles. Like many other terms that refer to objects in the physical environment, it is also used as a personal name. When I first knew her at Varadero,[1] Pacho was a small girl of about twelve. She was pleasant and basically attractive by the standards of Amahuaca men, having a short round face and a thick waist. But she had not yet developed any of the traits that are thought to distinguish a beautiful woman (large breasts, broad hips, and stout thighs). As a matter of fact, she paid little attention to her appearance. Although she wore the traditional metal disk suspended from the septum of her nose, her necklaces were unusually short and were made mostly of plastic trade beads rather than the long strands of tiny black seeds alternating with monkey teeth that are worn by most Amahuaca women. Her hair was short and uneven, the black designs painted on her face with indelible dye from a wild fruit were crudely executed, and she wore only a tiny skirt that was grayed with long use.

Moreover, Pacho had not shown herself to be a good worker, which is

---

I have chosen to narrate the sequence of events that led up to the marriage of a particular girl because I believe these incidents make more understandable the role of a female as a child, a wife, and a mother among the Amahuaca than would generalizations alone.

3

Pacho and her playmates.

the most important criterion in the choice of a wife. She spent much of her time at play with her younger siblings and her pets, a fledgling macaw and a litter of puppies. Certainly she was not mature enough to take on the responsibilities of marriage and housekeeping. It is true that her mother had begun to teach her the duties and skills of womanhood, but when she was asked to prepare food she did the work only with assistance and coaching. It would be difficult to imagine her performing the other minimal duties of a wife, such as planting and harvesting corn, cutting and carrying firewood, making pots and hammocks, or rearing children of her own.

Amahuaca women go to their granaries on the hills every few days to fetch corn and other garden produce. The loads they carry are very heavy. A basket filled with up to 175 ears of corn may weigh 70 pounds, and in addition a mother may have to carry a young child on her hip. Only by carefully choosing footholds for her bare feet, stepping slowly with her toes first, and taking advantage of tree trunks and other live vegetation to grasp and keep her balance is she able to carry these heavy loads down the steep slope, where the clay soil is wet and slippery. Although women do not complain about it openly, these burdens, carried by tumplines across their foreheads, are sometimes so heavy that their necks ache for hours afterward.

Women also spend from one to three hours daily toasting and grinding corn with an enormous rocker pestle that weighs up to 60 pounds. In addition, it is the work of women to cut firewood and carry it in equally heavy loads from the garden plots to their houses.

Men's work, too, is strenuous. Every man cuts trees for a new garden each year and often builds a new house in or near the garden. Men also hunt and may travel many miles before finding game, after which they must carry the game the same distance back home. But the work of men occupies less time than that of women. Whereas men are often seen resting in their hammocks or talking idly together, women have less free time for relaxing and visiting.

However, Pacho did little of such work. She was still a child in behavior as well as appearance—and yet she already had been married twice, once to Francisco and later to Coyaso. This chapter will relate the story of these and subsequent marriages of Pacho.

Coyaso was a distant cross cousin of Pacho and therefore an eligible mate for her. Many Amahuaca consider it best to marry a cross cousin, especially one from another local family group. Until recently Coyaso had lived in a separate group. Since he had joined the growing settlement at Varadero, however, he was a member of the same community as Pacho, living in a separate household about half a mile from hers. He had taken Pacho as his wife, but the next morning she had cried, and—as Coyaso related the incident—he became angry and sent her away. One reason for the failure of this marriage may be that Coyaso himself, although very intelligent, was not an ideal partner. He was an unusually small man and a poor provider. He seldom went hunting and even more seldom shot any

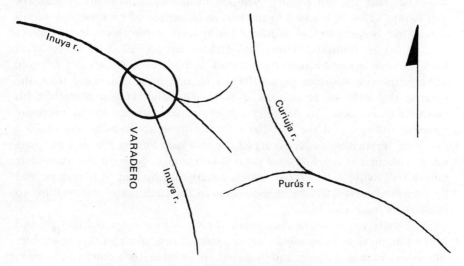

Map 1 *The location of Varadero and nearby streams.*

Amahuaca woman carrying firewood.

game. In fact, he walked with a stiff limp because of a slight deformity that he had inherited from his mother.

Francisco, on the other hand, was a very industrious man and also—when he wore his tall painted bamboo headband, ornaments of feathers, and strings of beads inserted in the perforations around his nose and mouth —very handsome. He had acquired his Spanish name through his contact with Peruvian pioneers. After the death of his second child a few years back, he had gone downstream to work lumber at a Franciscan mission, leaving his wife with her people. When he had been gone some time, she became the wife of Francisco's own first parallel cousin Shanchí,[2] his mother's sister's son. An Amahuaca refers to parallel cousins by the same terms as siblings, and the social ties among them are usually very close.

When Francisco finally returned, he did not contest the new arrangement, although it left him at a great disadvantage. None of his immediate family was living at Varadero, which meant that he had to live alone and be completely self-sufficient unless others in the community were willing to share their food with him.

The daily staple of the Amahuaca is corn, which is toasted and ground into a fine meal to be eaten dry or in a soup. Corn, like all other vegetables and fruits except manioc and bananas, is planted by women. Moreover, women's role in harvesting and preparing these foods for daily meals is

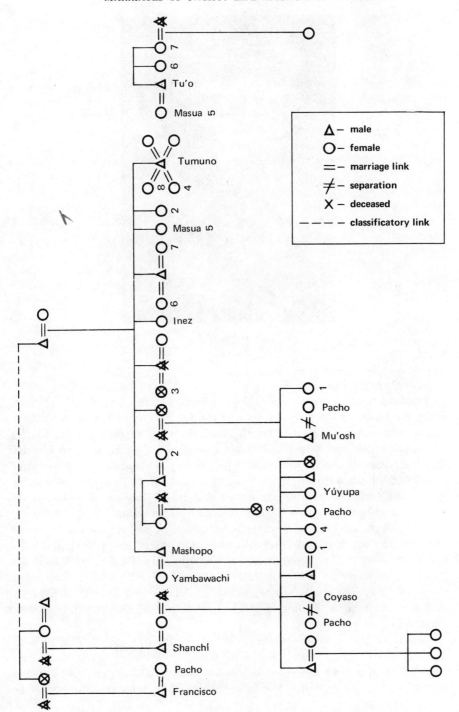

Figure 1.1 *Marital exchanges related to Pacho's marriages.*

Coyaso.

very important. This fact was emphasized by the attitude of others in the community when a young woman visited her parents and remained away from her husband for several days. On the fourth day of her absence some of the other women heard the rhythmic beat of a corn grinder in the husband's house and began to talk about it. Two of them spoke in lengthy and animated simultaneous monologues, as is the custom when discussing a problem of mutual concern. The speakers did not look at or answer each other, but each expressed her opinion that it was bad for the man's wife to remain away so long that he had to grind his own corn.

Since Francisco had no woman in his house, he had no corn of his own. However, he was a good hunter and often had game, which he shared with other members of the community. He had also helped other families make gardens and harvest their corn. In return, he received prepared corn from his aunt; from his cousin's wife, whose garden he had helped to harvest; and from women in the family of his cross cousin Mashopo, whose garden he had helped to prepare.

Mashopo had two wives, the older of whom was called Yambawachi (literally "No Skirt"). Yambawachi lived with her three youngest children in a house about 30 feet from the one occupied by her husband and his second and younger wife. Yambawachi's people lived on another river many days' walk from Varadero. Her father had been killed by a Peruvian pioneer and her mother had died when Yambawachi was about five years old. Orphans and small children who have lost one parent are often taken as wards by their grandparents. Yambawachi was taken to the home of her mother's parents, who were Yaminawa.

The Yaminawa are enemies of the Amahuaca because they have killed many Amahuaca. They even killed a brother of Mashopo as recently as two years past,[3] and in retaliation another of Mashopo's brothers killed one of the Yaminawa raiders.

Although Amahuaca and Yaminawa groups feud with one another, Mashopo himself was friendly with Yambawachi's group and had visited their settlement when she was eight or ten years old. Because of the scarcity of marriageable women among the extremely sparse population of Amahuaca, it is not unusual for men to seek out orphaned or adopted girls as wives. When Mashopo returned home, Yambawachi's brothers "took her by the hand" to his home and gave her to him.

It is said that formerly there were enough women, but that killings by pioneers and epidemic diseases have drastically reduced the numbers of Amahuaca, who are now settled in widely separated extended family units of from one to four nuclear family households.[4] Of the very sparse remaining population, a significant number of women have been taken by other tribes and several have been taken away from their homeland by Peruvian

Francisco.

Mashopo.

soldiers. About fifteen years earlier, the Peruvian government had sent troops to the area to guard its border with Brazil. Varadero is many days' travel from any Peruvian settlement. While the garrison was stationed there, the soldiers attracted natives to their barracks, were intimate with some of the women, and took them away when they left the area.

Of these women some died and others drifted from one man to another in riverine pioneer settlements. One girl apparently served as a prostitute for the soldiers at the army post. She had been taken to the barracks by her father and given to the soldiers. When they left she was taken by one of them to the city of Iquitos but was later discarded. She has returned to Varadero, but in spite of her open flirtation with native men, none of them has taken her as his wife.

Because of general depopulation and the loss of women in particular, the extended family local groups of Amahuaca are now too small to ensure a supply of girls as mates for maturing boys in neighboring groups. Moreover, mature men frequently take from two to four wives. In some instances a man takes a second wife to replace an old or ailing woman. A large proportion of the co-wives are widows. A dying man may ask his brother to take his wife in order to make certain that his children will be cared for. Nevertheless, these instances of the levirate also take marriageable women out of circulation and make the scarcity of wives for adolescent boys more acute. Hence it is sometimes necessary for a young man either to marry an old woman or to seek a wife in a settlement far away on another river, perhaps among an enemy group. Occasionally a man takes a woman by force if she is reluctant to accompany him, and he may even kill her father and brothers if she is a member of an enemy group and her people are unwilling to give her away.

Because of the scarcity of eligible women, girls are married while very young, frequently before puberty at nine or ten years of age; many are betrothed in infancy by their parents. In fact, Coyaso's brother's daughter of about two was promised to a distant cross cousin who was approaching puberty. The teenage boy also had two younger brothers, with whom the two-year-old girl played. She was encouraged to tease one of them, a boy of about seven, by calling him bawdy names and pulling his penis from under the tight bast belt with which the prepuce was secured. Such behavior is customary between youngsters of the opposite sex who are cross cousins and therefore potential mates.

When youngsters are betrothed before puberty, their parents may exert pressure on them to live together. However, the Amahuaca say that marriage occurs only if the girl wishes it. In any case, a marriage ordinarily is not consummated for some years, at least not until the girl's menarche. There is ample opportunity for youngsters to observe the act of intercourse,

Yambawachi and two of her children.

which may be performed in the hammocks and is sometimes the subject of much joking among other members of the household. Sometimes youngsters engage in sex activity secretly in the forest, but it is thought improper for preadolescents to have intercourse and it is said that their parents would punish them if they knew about it. Nevertheless, an adolescent boy may associate very closely with his young sister and may introduce her to her first sexual experience.

In general, men exert considerable authority over women, and in the presence of men a woman does not conduct herself in a casual or relaxed manner but is quiet, decorous, and usually busy at housework. If a woman is not working, she usually withdraws when men come on the scene. If, for example, a woman is sitting on a bench, she leaves the area or moves to a mat on the dirt floor when men approach. Log benches are the traditional sitting places for men, whereas women sit on the floor. When a woman who was lounging on a bench heard male voices in the vicinity, she arose quickly and with some apprehension, adjusted her headband and skirt before they appeared, and moved away from the bench to a palm leaf mat.

Men's attitude toward their sitting places may be illustrated by an incident in which Coyaso ordered his sister-in-law off a bench. This young woman was sitting on a bench outside her house, holding her twin infants in her arms, when Coyaso approached. He picked up a piece of roasted meat, tossed it onto the bench and said to the woman, "Move away; I am going to eat." She moved away while he went into the house to get a bowl of cornmeal and prepared to sit down on the bench to eat it. He had given the command in a relaxed manner, without anger but with authority; the woman obeyed him immediately without other visible reaction.

Dominance of men over women is exerted most strongly in the context of marriage. Once married, a man may instruct his wife in such things as gardening, carrying house posts, and helping him thatch their house. If she declines to perform some task, he may undertake to cure her of what to him appears to be laziness with a medicinal infusion of snuff. If this is not effective, he may beat her on the shoulders, arms, legs, buttocks, or back with a special hardwood club that has a flat blade with sharp edges. Although the club is shorter, it resembles in shape the clubs used in war and in avenging adultery among other peoples of western Amazonia. It is very neatly carved out of hardwood, as if softer wood, which of course would be much easier to carve, would not be efficient enough for the job. A beating with such a club may be so severe that the woman is barely able to walk for a few days afterward.

A woman may be beaten for annoying her husband in a variety of ways, such as not preparing food when he wants it or putting too much salt (a recently acquired trade item) in his food. One elderly woman, who had been beaten for not wanting to carry a load of bananas, willingly answered questions about the incident and even laughed about it without shame.

Another woman was beaten occasionally because she did not become pregnant but continued to menstruate.

Some Amahuaca men consider themselves more gentle than neighboring people, who are said to beat their wives on the heads also. But other Amahuaca men said that this is done among the Amahuaca, too, and that men sometimes punch their wives in the face when they are angry. A man may even kill his wife with his bow and arrow. Men reported, understandably, that the wife is afraid and does not hit back at her husband, nor does she run away.

If a man is thoroughly dissatisfied with his wife for having a bad temper, for being lazy, or for repeatedly committing adultery, he may get rid of her, literally "casting her away." He throws her hammock and other personal belongings out of the house and makes her leave. This is what occurred when one man wanted to go downstream to cut wood for a lumber boss and his wife refused to accompany him with his two children. In another instance women who were married to two cousins were exchanged by them, and the newly constituted couples remained on very friendly terms with each other.

It is little wonder, therefore, that young girls among the Amahuaca are sometimes reluctant to marry and may run away. Yambawachi herself had been a reluctant bride. She recalls that at first, when she was taken away from home and given to Mashopo, she was afraid at night. But she was very young at the time and her grandparents' home was downriver, far from Mashopo's. She remained with him and raised a large family.

However, Mashopo disclaimed some of her children. He believed that her two oldest had been sired by one of his brothers. He also believed that her youngest child, a newborn infant, had been sired by Tumuno, another of his brothers who lived with his father about half a day's journey from Varadero. Amahuaca men do not permit open polyandry. ("It would make them angry," as one man put it.) Nevertheless it is not unusual for a man to allow, tacitly, an unmarried younger brother to consort with his wife when they live in the same household. But Mashopo's brothers lived in another settlement.

When a woman is unfaithful, as Mashopo believed Yambawachi had been, her husband may beat her or leave her, or he may cut the scalp of his rival with a bamboo knife. But when the rival is a brother, a man may choose not to make an issue of it. There was, however, some obvious coolness between Mashopo and Tumuno. When that young man visited at Varadero, he wore elaborate ceremonial body paint and headdress and sat with his back to Mashopo's house. This practice is said to be observed as a precaution to ensure that one will not be ambushed and killed from behind. Such is the tension and fear of hostilities among kinsmen as well as nonkin who live apart from one another.

Ordinarily all the members of a polygynous family live in a single

Tumuno visiting Mashopo wearing body paint.

house, each wife having her own corner. The fact that Yambawachi lived in a separate house was somewhat exceptional. When a man has more than one wife, he may favor the younger one and prefer to live with her only. Moreover, plural wives do not always live amicably together. One woman, for example, admits to having poisoned her co-wife, probably by putting the juice of a toxic wild fruit in her soup. At any rate, Yambawachi was in effect rejected by her husband now, although he still provided her with meat and made a very large garden in which both his wives planted corn.

In spite of her somewhat anomalous situation, Yambawachi was a hearty, friendly woman and did not appear forlorn. She was a permissive mother and showed no compulsion to be a good housekeeper. For instance, she made fewer pots and other utensils than did other women, her corn soup was always full of hulls, and both her skirt and her hammock were skimpy, old, and ragged.

Pacho was a daughter of Yambawachi and Mashopo. She and Francisco had associated together for some time, and Pacho finally went down to Francisco's house in the valley several rods from her own for a time. At that time her father tacitly consented to the marriage and told Francisco and his cousin that he was not angry about it. But he complained later that it was bad that Francisco should take Pacho. In any case, Pacho did not really want to be married yet, and she left without planting corn or any other vegetables in Francisco's garden. It was soon after this incident that Coyaso had—so briefly—taken Pacho as his wife.

But Francisco was patient. After his failure to keep Pacho, he did not immediately press his suit but instead spent much of his time with his cousin Shanchí, his former wife (now wife of Shanchí), and her two sons. His continuing interest in Pacho did not become apparent until another young man appeared in the community a few months later. That young man was Mu'osh, a nephew of Mashopo.

Mu'osh was an orphan who lived with his grandfather, Mashopo's father, on the Curiuja (pronounced Kuriúha) River about half a day's journey from Varadero. He came to Varadero with his grandfather's family on the day of a corn harvest festival. Although that family had apparently not been invited, they attended the festivities. The visiting men engaged in initial monologues, formalized and simultaneous, with several men of the host group, and then they remained standing for about an hour. When they finally sat down on the log bench at their feet, they faced away from the assembled group even after being presented with a bowl of ceremonial corn soup.

Mu'osh.

Mu'osh's sister carrying firewood.

After the ceremony, Mu'osh remained for a time at Varadero and was lodged in the house of his sister, who had recently been given to Pacho's brother, Yambawachi's oldest son. Mu'osh and Pacho's brother did very little hunting or any other work during this extended visit. Instead, they spent a great deal of time reclining in their hammocks, which occupied virtually all the space in the tiny hut of Mu'osh's sister and her husband, the first one that young man had ever built. His wife's ragged little hammock was untied from its usual place and tossed onto the dirt floor to make room for her brother's.

Mu'osh's sister was a small, slight girl of perhaps thirteen. Most of her time was spent in chopping and carrying firewood, fetching corn from the garden granary and grinding it, and in cooking corn soup for the boys and herself. She appeared oppressed and unhappy as she worked. Undoubtedly Pacho would have been equally unhappy in a similar situation.

Mu'osh himself was only a boy of about fourteen, still very undeveloped and wearing a ragged piece of trade cloth around his loins, seemingly to conceal his sexual immaturity. About two weeks after his arrival at Varadero, people in the community began to talk about a marriage of Pacho to Mu'osh. In fact, the boy said he was marrying not only Pacho but also her little sister Yúyupa, who was five or six.

The match between Pacho and Mu'osh was a technically correct one according to Amahuaca custom, since her father was brother of Mu'osh's dead mother and the two youngsters were therefore cross cousins living in separate settlements. Moreover, Mu'osh had proved his eligibility to marry by clearing a patch of forest for a garden, and it was said that he hunted for his grandfather, who was an old man and no longer hunted much. Still, even though it is not unusual for a man to take two sisters as co-wives, the possibility that this boy could attract and support two wives clearly seemed remote to some members of the community, and the events that followed made it clear that his claim to Pacho was not regarded as secure by everyone.

After Mu'osh's arrival, Francisco began to wear a tall headband and other finery. He joined with Coyaso and two other men in drinking the hallucinogenic drug ayahuasca (yage). Ayahuasca is used by the Amahuaca to help them see spirit beings, especially deceased relatives, to talk with them and to enlist their help in learning about the unknown. As he chanted under the influence of the drug, Francisco was observed embracing and stroking the face of one of his drinking companions. He was the only one of the four men who did this. In his chant he mentioned his relatives' frequently and later reported that he had seen spirit people dressed in ceremonial garb and naked women. In the light of subsequent events it is significant that sorcery was mentioned also in the chants of some of the men.

Pacho's behavior showed signs of an increasing awareness of her impending marriage. In her play with Yúyupa, for example, they simulated intercourse with each other and called attention to the act with unashamed delight. Pacho also began wearing a cotton cord around the top of her tiny skirt, a custom that is associated with the inception of intercourse. About the same time she began to wear a rag around her chest, as did Mu'osh's sister, covering her undeveloped breasts. She and her sister-in-law spent some of their free time dancing together and chanting fertility songs. They walked forward and backward hand-in-hand, chanting ditties that are thought to induce pregnancy. These two girls also made sun-dried clay dolls, complete with incised lines to represent painted facial designs. Seeds were pressed into the clay to represent eyes and necklaces, and the dolls' heads were topped with some of the girls' own hair. These dolls are also said to help cause pregnancy.

About a week later Mu'osh's grandfather came again to Varadero, and it was said that Pacho would go with Mu'osh and his grandfather to their home on the Curiuja river. It is customary for a woman to live in her husband's community when a marriage unites families who live some distance apart. Usually, however, the groom lives initially with his bride's family for a period that varies from a few weeks to a year, helping his father-in-law in such tasks as land clearing and hunting.

During the night following the second appearance of Mu'osh's grand-father, Coyaso's brother was heard chanting by himself in his house. This type of individual chanting or "singing" is done privately for the purpose of curing oneself, and in fact Coyaso said that Francisco was working black magic on his brother with a sorcerer's thorn arrow. On the following even-ing Francisco again drank ayahuasca, this time with a larger group of men. In addition to Francisco, the group consisted of Mashopo, Mu'osh and his brother-in-law (Yambawachi's son), and Coyaso and his brother—that is, all the men who were directly concerned with Pacho's marriage except Mu'osh's grandfather. The absence of Mu'osh's grandfather is easily under-standable, since old men do not drink ayahuasca.

As was expected, Mu'osh took Pacho as his wife when he returned to his home. This meant that his period of residence with his wife's family was minimal and that he would not perform bride service. It was rumored that he had given Mashopo some money in lieu of bride service. Since Mu'osh's community had already given a girl, his sister, to Yambawachi's son, it may have been felt that Pacho had been paid for in advance, thus obviating the necessity of both extended matrilocal residence and bride service. However, the exchange of Pacho for Mu'osh's sister was not the only marital ex-change that had taken place between these closely related families.

Mashopo's younger wife's brother had taken an aunt of Mu'osh as his wife, and that man's niece, Mashopo's wife's daughter by a previous mar-riage, had been given to an uncle of Mu'osh (see genealogy, Figure 1.1). Later Pacho's oldest sister had been given to Tumuno, another uncle of Mu'osh. In payment for this girl, Tumuno had lived with his parents-in-law for a time and had made a grinding trough, among other things, for Yambawachi. Hence Mashopo's family could claim that they had given as many women as they had received and therefore did not owe a woman to Mu'osh.

The alliance was complicated by the fact that when Mashopo had taken his little bride from the Yaminawa over fifteen years earlier, he had also taken Tu'o, a young orphaned boy. Among the Amahuaca and neighbor-ing peoples, both male and female orphans are often given aways as servants by their guardians. As Tu'o matured, an argument with Mashopo de-veloped and Tu'o left his guardian-master. He participated in a revenge raid on which a brother of Mashopo was killed, and he later married Mashopo's sister Masua, an aunt of Mu'osh.

Tu'o and Masua ultimately returned to Mashopo's community, and it was at his house that Mu'osh's family stayed on their visits to Varadero. That marriage was one of several that united Tu'o's family to Mu'osh. Tu'o's two sisters had married a third uncle of Mu'osh, and a daughter of one of these women by a previous marriage was also taken by Mu'osh's uncle Tumuno before his marriage to Pacho's older sister. Hence even if Tu'o were still regarded as a member of Mashopo's family, the marriage of these women had amply compensated for the woman that Tu'o had obtained.

In spite of Pacho's apparent interest in marriage and the general understanding that Mu'osh would take her, when they set out for the Curiuja river she was very reluctant to go with Mu'osh and again cried in protest. Nevertheless, she was compelled by her family to go. Mashopo and several others of his family, including Pacho's mother, accompanied her, reminding one of Yambawachi's account of her own marriage, when her brothers "took her by the hand" to Mashopo's home. On this trip to the Curiuja, Yambawachi carried her infant daughter in a sling over her hip in spite of the fact that the baby was ill at that time. Francisco also went along, as did his cousin Shanchí and the latter's mother.

Although no ceremony had taken place, it was understood that Pacho was now Mu'osh's wife, and the couple was expected to live with the groom's family. The manifest purpose of the bridal party accompanying Pacho seemed to be to settle Pacho's marriage to Mu'osh, but the reasons for making the journey given by some members of the group suggest that those individuals had other motives. Francisco, for instance, said he wanted to visit his "uncle" (his mother's classificatory brother), Mu'osh's grandfather. Mashopo indicated that he went along to see his mother, who was ill, as did Francisco's aunt, a distant affinal relative of the sick woman. The reason that Yambawachi gave was that her daughter's child was ill and she wanted to see her as well as Mashopo's sick mother.

There was some irony in Yambawachi's expressed reason since she was traveling with her own sick infant. The fact that she undertook to walk half a day's journey with the sick baby and return the next day is an indication that the trip was quite important to her. In fact, the course of subsequent events tends to support the suggestion that at least some of the people involved may have been motivated by other interests than those of which they spoke and that in reality they wished to assess for themselves the factors involved in Pacho's marriage.

When her family returned to Varadero the next day, Pacho was with them. In spite of the pressure exerted by her relatives in accompaying her and unlike her mother a generation earlier, she had left Mu'osh and refused to marry him.

Running away is, however, only a negative expression of choice. An Amahuaca girl has little positive choice in determining who her first mate will be or when she will be married. I have already mentioned that many girls are betrothed as infants and are married before they reach puberty. At that time they are too young to actively want a husband. Moreover, they are often reluctant to marry because they know they will be required to leave their local kin group and become the drudges of other groups, for whom they will have to plant and harvest crops and prepare food.

Hence the decisions about initial marriages are made for the most part by adults, a girl's parents and her prospective husband or his parents.

The initial decision about the first marriage of a young man is made by his parents or guardians. The young man is then coached to prepare a garden plot and urged to ask for the girl that has been selected for him. In proposing, a man first "asks" the girl. But even the form of his proposal is coercive: "I am going to take you." Again, if she agrees to the proposal, according to custom she makes no reply, and he then discusses the matter with her father. Running away is, therefore, a girl's only means of expressing her negative feeling effectively. It is a way of vetoing—by withdrawing from an intolerable situation—a decision about her life that has been made by others.

Withdrawal is not restricted to women, but it is perhaps the most important device used by the Amahuaca to avoid confrontation and conflict, as we shall see later.

When a girl runs away from her husband, he usually follows and takes her back to his home. She may run away several times, and each time the man goes to retrieve her. The Amahuaca say that after being taken back several times, the girl becomes accustomed to her husband and will be "tame." In this instance, however, Mu'osh did not follow Pacho to take her back—not immediately, at least.

After returning to Varadero, Francisco again spent most of his time with Mashopo's family and did a considerable amount of labor for them. Very soon he and Mashopo went into the forest to select a large cedar tree to be cut for a canoe for Mashopo. In felling the tree and in the initial stages of cutting the canoe, he was helped by Coyaso and his brother as well as by Mashopo. But it was Francisco who, during the next three weeks, did most of the work of cutting and shaping the 30-foot canoe, a skill that he alone has mastered while working lumber downriver.

About this time Francisco began to flirt openly with Pacho, and the community seemed to accept his right to woo her. Nevertheless, the matter of her proper suitor apparently was not entirely resolved. Latent anxieties continued to be expressed in terms of fear of witchcraft. When Coyaso and his brother heard the cry of a carrion eagle, for example, they commented that its spirit is bad because it kills people by witchcraft.

Cutting of the canoe was unexpectedly interrupted by the death of Yambawachi's infant, who, it will be recalled, had been ill since before the trip to the Curiuja river. A week after her return the baby was still very ill. It had a fever and the mother complained that the area of its spleen was swollen. She kept the infant wrapped tightly from head to foot, permitting it very little freedom to breathe. At this time Mashopo, who disclaimed paternity of the baby, seemed to be unaware that it was ill.

The death of the baby was discovered at dawn, and Yambawachi immediately began to wail. The corpse was buried by Francisco, who first wrapped it in an old skirt and tied it in a compact bundle with freshly cut bast. Before long the adults and most of the children from all the other households in the community, on hearing Yambawachi's wails, came to pay their respects, some of the women dressed in their best skirts and fresh body paint. It was the women especially who consoled the mother, commenting sympathetically about the child's illness. Yambawachi showed no resentment toward any of those present, and there was no indication that she felt they should be blamed for the infant's death. She seemed at times to be clearing herself of blame as she recounted details of the baby's illness in affectionate terms. Repeatedly she chanted that the child had been very sick and that she had notified others of the fact.

As Yambawachi, seated on the floor, wailed over the corpse, the children of both of Mashopo's families wandered in and out of her house at will. Francisco dug away the packed earth in the middle of the dirt floor. When he tired, Coyaso took over the digging. Then Mashopo, who had been smoking nearby, gave his pipe to Francisco, and the two men sat together on a log bench. Soon, however, Francisco resumed the digging, now lying on the ground and reaching down into the deep hole with one arm to remove the dirt.

Finally, when they were satisfied that the hole was large enough and deep enough, the older women who were sitting near the mother spoke to Francisco about a burial pot. One of them suggested using a nice big one, whereupon Francisco picked up one of Yambawachi's earthen cooking pots. His aunt indicated that a larger and finer one should be used, and he readily followed her suggestion. Then, seating himself on the ground in front of the wailing mother, he quietly inspected the corpse on her lap. When he had determined which end of the body was the head, he addressed the bereaved mother, speaking quietly in a ritual manner for some time while she continued to wail. Finally he took the bundle from her and gently placed it upright in the burial urn and fitted another cookingpot upside down over it. After covering the pots carefully with palm leaf mats to prevent dirt from falling into them, he packed some of the loose dirt into the hole around the pots and leveled off the area.

When Francisco had finished the burial to the satisfaction of the older women who had been coaching him, Mashopo invited him into his own house—that is, the house he occupied with his younger wife. There they ate some ripe bananas, while Pacho helped her mother burn the wrappings and an old hammock that had been soiled by the infant. Then, after two hours of work, Francisco took up his bow and arrows and left to continue working on the unfinished canoe.

Yambawachi, still sitting on the ground by the grave and wailing, picked up a pebble from the dirt floor and with slow, ritualized movements pounded the dirt of the grave area to make it smooth and firm. Francisco's aunt suggested that the floor should be swept. In this and other suggestions the older women were acting as custodians of cultural norms as well as comforters. They stayed longer in Yambawachi's house and remained closer to her than did others, supervising details of the ritual. Far from resenting their comments as being interference, the participants in the ritual seemed to appreciate their help.

Much of the behavior during the burial, as in other aspects of daily life, occurred in response to casual comments in conversation. However, when Yambawachi suggested to Pacho that she clean the floor, her daughter did not take this suggestion but continued to play aimlessly and eat bananas. When Yambawachi had at last finished pounding the surface of the grave, she herself set about sweeping away the debris left by the burial. By then she had wailed continuously for over eight hours, since early morning, and she would wail intermittently for about ten days more.[5] During that period Pacho accompanied Francisco much of the time while he shaped the canoe, staying with him when all others left the site. She had, in fact, taken corn soup to him at work and had been his close companion since before the death of her infant sister, and it was clear that she had become very fond of him.

In the meantime the subject of witchcraft continued to concern some of the relatives of those involved in Pacho's marriage. When, for instance, Francisco's cousin Shanchí became ill, Coyaso and his brother said, although jokingly, first that a young boy who happened to be smoking a pipe was working witchcraft and later that they themselves had caused Shanchí's illness by sorcery. They added more seriously that Francisco's aunt's husband was a sorcerer.

In spite of the anxiety expressed about sorcery, relations among all the men of the community remained cordial. On the day following their return to Varadero, they had begun to hold dancing and singing sessions in the evenings for the purpose of causing bananas to ripen for a harvest festival, of which Mashopo was to be the principal host. Francisco was the best singer and knew more harvest songs than the other men, and it was he who led the singing. Moreover, when the canoe was ready to be launched on a nearby stream, Francisco, Shanchí, Coyaso, and Coyaso's brother did the job together.

The same four also performed together the arduous task of cremating Yambawachi's dead child. About a week after the burial, when the infant's flesh had decayed and after Mashopo's mother-in-law had been summoned to come from her home half a day's journey downstream on the Inuya River, the burial urns were disinterred and the cadaver cremated. Again it was Francisco who took the lead and did the greater part of the work. Early in the morning he and his cousin, together with Coyaso and his brother, decided among themselves to cremate the body. (It is worthy of note, in passing, that this decision was made by the young men and not by the baby's mother.) They and the oldest son of Yambawachi cut up a dead tree, chopping and splitting off a large quantity of dry firewood for the funeral pyre. Mashopo, who sat nearby during this procedure, ordered one of his younger children to bring some cornmeal for the workers and gave them some of his tobacco to smoke.

After a large pile of wood had been cut, Yambawachi's trough for grinding corn was also cup up and added to the pile, although there was certainly no need for more firewood than the dead tree yielded. This gesture of mourning left her without any means of preparing corn, and her family would be entirely dependent on others for their staple food until her son cut another trough for her.

Again during the cremation as during the burial, women from other households, including Mashopo's mother-in-law, came to sit in Yambawachi's house to pay their respects and console her. Francisco lit the funeral pyre and then went to Yambawachi as she wailed over the grave. She moved aside and Francisco and his cousin opened the grave. Francisco put the burial urns into Yambawachi's arms and she wailed over them, tenderly caressing the lower one.

At this point Mashopo finally approached his grieving wife, placed one hand on the urns, and wailed with her. After some minutes Francisco removed the urns from Yambawachi's arms and placed them on the funeral pyre, taking care to knock a small piece out of the bottom of the lower pot for a flue. Yambawachi appeared reluctant to release the pots and rose to follow them but was gently restrained by Mashopo's mother-in-law.

The men who had cut the firewood also wailed in a huddle with the bereaved couple for some time, while all the younger members of the family, including Pacho, went about their business of playing as usual. The men tended the fire with long green saplings but were forced by the intense heat of the fire to withdraw now and then. They perspired profusely and one by one, as the cremation proceeded, went down the hill into the forest to wash off the perspiration in a small stream.

After some two hours of burning, Francisco judged the little corpse to be sufficiently burned and removed the pots from the fire with Mashopo's help. As they did so some material fell through the broken base. Mashopo called Yambawachi's attention to this fact and directed her to sweep it up, whereupon she picked up the fragments with her fingers and a splinter of wood, still wailing and weeping copious tears.

Mashopo now ceased to wail and began to chat in his ordinary manner. He asked his daughter Pacho about her newborn puppies and directed her to bring them for him to see. Pacho's old bitch had given birth to three pups in the chamber that had formed within a tall, rotting stump of a large tree near the house. Pacho, Yúyupa, and their young sister-in-law entered the tree chamber and attended the dog while other pups were born.

Holding the dog down on the ground when it attempted to raise itself, they occasionally pressed its abdomen to assist the births. As each pup appeared the girls discussed among themselves whether or not it was alive. Then Pacho pulled it away from the placenta and dug and pulled mucus from the nose and throat with her fingers. She immediately bathed the pup in a bowl of water that was green with algae, having been dipped from a stagnant pool of rainwater near the house. After washing each pup carefully, she put it back with its mother. These techniques are essentially the same as those used by Amahuaca women at the birth of their own infants and were undoubtedly learned more through observation than formal instruction.

As Mashopo sat and chatted, he directed Pacho's sister-in-law to roast some plantains for him, which she did, using coals from the cremation fire. Again, as when he directed his wife and daughter, his request was phrased as an order.

In general, among kin and household units, men's wishes are directed to women in the form of orders, whether those women are wives, sisters, sisters-in-law, daughters, or daughters-in-law. By contrast, all the prompting by women, whether kin or not, was phrased as suggestions. Commands are also given by males to their younger male kin. In the family pecking order the position of women and youngsters is relatively low, and the status of young females is the lowest of all. In addition, because of the solidarity of the patrilocal consanguineal kin, the position of a young wife as an in-marrying daughter-in-law is the lowest among all adults.

Finally, about four hours after he had begun to cut the firewood, Francisco stirred the coals in the cremation urn as it lay cooling on the ground. He picked up a fragment of bone and spoke to Yambawachi, whereupon she approached the pot and picked out a few more bones with splints of bamboo, the ashes being still too hot to touch with her fingers. She managed to enlist Pacho's help in separating bone fragments from the ashes for a time, although Pacho's mind was quite clearly not on the work. Instead, she was listening to the conversation between Mashopo and Francisco, who were sitting together on the log bench, talking and laughing in a relaxed manner and eating toasted cornmeal. They talked and joked about how they had hunted and killed certain animals, about their food, about making corn soup. Meanwhile Yambawachi continued to sort out bits of bones and teeth, a tedious and painstaking task that required about four hours.

Before this task was completed, Mashopo's mother-in-law commented that Francisco must be hungry. Yambawachi then directed her daughter to light a cooking fire and make some corn soup. This Pacho managed to do only with coaching and help from her mother. After making a fire she filled a cooking pot with water and mixed with it some ground corn, which she boiled to make soup. She also roasted an ear of corn, the kernels of which she masticated and spat into the boiling soup. She gave a bowl of this soup to Francisco, and soon she and Francisco disappeared together, leaving by the path that led toward Francisco's house.

All this time—seven hours after the beginning of the cremation operations—Yambawachi had eaten nothing. She now began to show signs of fatigue, yawning occasionally between wails. Finally she set aside the bowl of bone fragments and gathered up charcoal from the funeral fire. She put the broken cremation vessels and other debris into the open grave and swept into it the loose dirt, thus completing the funeral ceremony except for the last step of taking the charcoal to the river and placing it in the swift stream. (The charred bits of bone were to be ground up and the bone powder consumed by Yambawachi in corn soup later, when she had a new grinding trough.)

In the following weeks Pacho's manner toward Francisco became more intimate. They bathed together in the river and Pacho openly showed affection for Francisco even in the presence of Mashopo. Several people in the community said that they were married and that Francisco had paid for Pacho by cutting the canoe. Francisco was living in Mashopo's house and Pacho herself said that Francisco was her husband. A few days later the couple moved to Francisco's house. Only Pacho's brother, who had been the constant companion of Mu'osh during the latter's visit to Varadero, seemed reluctant to recognize the marriage.

Shanchí's illness lingered on. He became very agitated and complained that his whole body was "bad." He believed that some boils on his face had been caused by a sorcerer, who had shot a thorn arrow into his hand. He was convinced that someone had worked black magic on him also by taking red pigment seeds from a plant in his garden and by drinking an infusion of those seeds and of some medicinal plants. He declared he would smoke to learn who was causing his illness and would kill the sorcerer.

On the day after Shanchí made this statement, the rising tension among the young men of the community was finally made explicit in a set of simultaneous monologues. Francisco, Shanchí, and Coyaso and his brother, along with Pacho's brother, sat down together and held this ritual conversation. All the men talked at once, each one looking ahead into space or at the ground rather than at any of his companions. Shanchí in particular seemed to be talking to the air with no one listening. However, each man apparently did hear at least some of what the others were saying, for occasionally one responded specifically to another's comments. They all spoke in low voices, and the purpose of the ritual conversation seemed to be to reassure one another of their sympathetic feeling rather than to voice antagonism.

Now, two weeks after the cremation, plans were made to resume singing in preparation for the banana festival. Mashopo organized a singing and dancing session to be held at Shanchí's house, where the men intended to dance all night. He also expressed his intention to go downstream in his new canoe to fish and hunt tapir to obtain fat for use in preparing body paint. He and other members of his family planned to remain there "ten or twenty days," or until their supply of cornmeal was exhausted. There was considerable enthusiasm for the projected festival. Yambawachi especially, who had ceased to mourn for her child only a week before, spoke of it with a great deal of pleasure. She said that women as well as men would dance all night. They would not sleep at all and their feet would be sore from dancing. Many, many other relatives would come to join in the festivities from far away on the Purús and Curiuja Rivers (she had lived with her Yaminawa grandparents on the Purús), and people would drink a great deal of ayahuasca during the festival.

Late in the afternoon of the very day that these plans were being discussed, while people from several families were chatting together, Mu'osh and his family again appeared at Varadero. This time not only his grandfather and one uncle but a second uncle and the entire extended family of about fifteen people accompanied him.

On their arrival the visiting men stood erect for some time, assuming a very serious manner, while the women sat down on palm leaf mats. Soon Pacho's brother approached Mu'osh and stood silently beside him. Mashopo came to the group and greeted the visitors, pointing out his kinship relation to each of the men. Mu'osh's sister chatted freely with the visitors, who of course were related to her as brother, aunts, uncles, cousins, and grandparents. By contrast, as the group from the Curiuja settlement approached, Coyaso and his brother and the latter's wife hid from them by going behind the house, where they listened in tense silence. Coyaso's sister-in-law clutched at me and remained very quiet except for the whispered comment, "A lot of people came." Before long she left the group and went to her home.

A short time after the arrival of the visitors from the Curiuja, two men who were related to Mu'osh as his mother's classificatory brothers came to chat with Mu'osh's grandfather. One of them, Winá, invited all the men present, including Coyaso and his brother, to his house. There he himself served to all the men entrails of the tapir he had brought home, a delicacy which his wife had just boiled. The visitors, as well as Coyaso, his brother, and Mashopo, were all invited back to the same house to sing and dance in the evening. Both the host and Mashopo appeared very anxious to establish good relations with the visitors.

The women were not invited to eat the tapir meat. Mashopo's wives had stayed to chat with them, and as they left to go home before dark, the younger of Mashopo's wives cordially invited the visiting women to go to her house the next day. Both she and Yambawachi had planned to go downstream with Mashopo on the following day, but the arrival of Mu'osh and his family apparently changed their plans, for Yambawachi now told me that she would not be going.

After the departure of Mashopo's wives and children, the women from the Curiuja began to ask where Pacho was. None of them went to Mashopo's house to look for her, however. All the visitors, including Mu'osh, who had stayed at Pacho's brother's house on his previous visit, spent the night with Mu'osh's aunt Masua, who had married Tu'o.

In the evening Shanchí's family came to speak with the visitors. Their demeanor was unusually reserved and proper. Although the singing had originally been scheduled to take place at his house, Shanchí did not join the singers at Winá's house, indicating that he had not been invited. After perhaps an hour of singing and dancing, however, Mashopo sought out Shanchí and invited him to join the singers. In an unusually cordial manner, he took Shanchí by the hand and led him to Winá's house. The singing lasted only about an hour and a half on that occasion.

Early the next morning Mashopo and his extended family went downstream, leaving word this time that they would spend "a month" hunting tapir and other game and getting cane for arrows. Pacho, however, was left behind.

This move seemed to represent a hasty change in plans. For one thing, Yambawachi did not remain as she had said she would, and her co-wife, who had invited the visiting women to her house so cordially on the previous day, would not be there to receive them. Moreover, the period of the projected trip downstream had been lengthened from ten or twenty days to a month. From this turn of events it was obvious that the presence of Mu'osh's family made Mashopo uneasy and that he wished to avoid the necessity of discussing Pacho's marriage with them. The early disappearance of Mashopo's family is another example of withdrawal to avoid a confrontation that might result in conflict among kin. In this instance Pacho was left entirely without support and was merely a pawn in the transactions among men.

When Francisco was asked about his wife he said cryptically that she was no longer his wife and that Mu'osh would be taking her. That evening Francisco led singing and dancing again, but this time the session was even shorter than on the previous evening. Later during the night Shanchí was heard chanting a curing song for a long time at his house.

On the following day the visitors, except for Mu'osh and his grandfather, also went downstream, saying they intended to visit a sister of

Mu'osh's mother. Meanwhile he and his grandfather took Pacho against her will to the house of Mu'osh's aunt Masua. Pacho was crying because she did not want to go with them. Soon Winá's brother went to the house where Pacho was being held and was joined there not long afterward by Coyaso and his brother. Coyaso had recently spent considerable time with Mu'osh rather than with Francisco as previously, and he had clearly allied himself with the Curiuja family in the question of Pacho's marriage. On one occasion he had even expressed some resentment toward Francisco and Mashopo, which is significant in the light of the fact that words of discord and criticism are rarely heard in the Amahuaca community. Ordinarily people speak of others only with approval, sympathy, or humor.

In general the Amahuaca are extraordinarily peaceful. There is no argumentation and no ritualized mock combat. Outside the family unit, conflicts are solved by withdrawal or murder. In the view of the Amahuaca, such homicides are committed in self-defense and not as acts of aggression. They are committed to prevent further sorcery, a common motive, or to do away with someone who is suspected of intending to kill.

In spite of the peaceful nature of the interpersonal relations, Pacho was under tremendous pressure. With Winá's brother and Coyaso and his brother—in addition to Tu'o, Mu'osh, and Mu'osh's grandfather—Pacho was surrounded by males who supported her marriage to Mu'osh. It would have been impossible for her to resist the pressure created by their mere presence. Among the Amahuaca, the role of women in interfamilial and intergroup relations is generally passive or integrative. It is men who act out hostilities among communities as well as in the family. For this reason men are feared by one another and by women.

About midday Mu'osh and his grandfather left for their home, taking Pacho with them. Coyaso and his brother accompanied them with the expressed intention of conducting Pacho halfway to her new home.

About midafternoon, Francisco sat down to chat with Winá's wife, who was his classificatory sister. He talked of marriage and of his payment for Pacho, of the gardens he had helped to make and the canoe he had cut while Mashopo had sat and watched. He expressed great frustration and resentment and said he was going to go away. In the course of the conversation he became very agitated and looked not at his "sister" but into space as he talked. She listened quietly and from time to time answered him with sympathy.

Late in the afternoon Francisco was still talking with Winá's wife and had been joined by Shanchí and his wife (who, it will be remembered, was both Francisco's former wife and Coyaso's mother). When Coyaso and his brother returned from accompanying Pacho, they remained outside the house where these four people were talking together, entering only after they had left. This behavior emphasized the tension that had arisen between Francisco and the parties to Pacho's marriage to Mu'osh.

In the evening of that same day people in the community were surprised to see Pacho herself appear at Varadero and go toward her home. She had gone through a considerable ordeal. After spending the previous night without her family, she had walked to the Curiuja settlement, ordinarily half a day's journey, and had hurried back through the forest alone, reaching home at nightfall. This was a feat that surely required a great amount of strength and determination. It also showed courage, as the Amahuaca have great fear of traveling in the forest at night.

Pacho's behavior emphasized the great amount of physical strength that Amahuaca women must have—which had already been demonstrated by Yambawachi's lengthy mourning, by the heavy burdens the women must carry, and by other household chores such as chopping firewood and grinding corn.

The next morning brought another surprise. Francisco and Pacho had disappeared without taking leave of others and had thus withdrawn from a situation that would undoubtedly have resulted in further tension and perhaps conflict with both Mashopo's and Mu'osh's families. People at Varadero surmised that they would go to an old house on the Purús river, where Francisco had formerly lived with Shanchi's wife.

Except for the clothes they wore, they probably took with them little more than hammocks, bow and arrows, an axe, and a machete. It is unlikely that they could have taken much food with them, since Mashopo's families would have taken all their supply of prepared food. Unless they found some ripe bananas in an old garden, they would have been hungry for a while. Francisco was a good hunter and would provide plenty of meat, but to supplement this the couple would have to find wild fruits, palm nuts, roots, and perhaps even tree fungi. Even if they found an old house still standing and a grinding trough in it, there would be no corn to grind.

If, on the other hand, they did not find a house, they would have to put one up immediately. They might seek shelter under a simple frame of saplings covered with palm fronds while Francisco cut house posts, poles for the roof, and thatching leaves. Once these materials are cut, an Amahuaca house can be erected in one or two days by a man with help from his wife. Pacho would help in carrying posts and thatching leaves to the house site, and she would fold the palm leaves for thatch and hand them to Francisco as he lashed them to the house frame. Amahuaca houses are small and very simple. It is these simple living habits, together with their dependence on game, that make it possible for families to live apart from one another and to move so frequently.

Pacho would also have to make palm leaf mats and baskets and pots for cooking.

It was near the end of the rainy season, in a "month" of the Amahuaca calendar when the Pleiades are at the horizon just before dawn. Cold winds often whip up black clouds that "spider" in the sky. After a storm, the streams rise as much as 10 feet and the current becomes treacherously strong, making the streams impossible to cross. Thus, although it is possible for a couple to live alone, it would be difficult in this season. However, other Amahuaca families live on the upper Purús, and Francisco and Pacho would find hospitality with them if they needed it.

At Varadero, Coyaso's surprise in learning that Pacho had come back a second time was less evident than his scorn. He immediately surmised that she had run away because she was afraid to marry Mu'osh. When it became known that she and Francisco had eloped, people in Coyaso's household began to talk against both Francisco and Pacho. They reaffirmed that Mu'osh and not Francisco was Pacho's rightful husband, and that she had been paid for by the marriage of Mu'osh's sister to Yambawachi's son. They contended also that Francisco had not paid for Pacho, and that his work of cutting the canoe and conducting the burial and cremation for Yambawachi was given without implying obligation.

In answer to these opinions, Winá's wife, who had sympathized with Francisco's complaint, suggested that Pacho was still young and did not really want to be married. But Coyaso's brother's wife answered with a scathing condemnation of Pacho's behavior, in which she said that Pacho was "bad" and that the Amahuaca were disowning her because she was afraid to marry Mu'osh. In her contempt she now referred to Pacho as a Yaminawa, calling attention to the fact that Pacho's mother had come from that enemy group. According to her, Amahuaca women are not afraid of getting married and they do not run away. As might have been expected, her husband and his brother (Coyaso) agreed with her at each step of the indictment.

It is significant that the woman who delivered this indictment had married into the community from a distant river when she was very young and had no close relatives at Varadero. She was now perhaps seventeen years old and already had three small children. One of her children was between two and three years old; the others were twins of about four months, which she carried in crossed bandolier slings, one on each hip. She took them all with her wherever she went, and because the hills at Varadero were steep and slippery, it was often necessary for this little mother to carry all three children when she went to the garden or crossed the river. The twins were carried in slings and the other child was lifted by the hand, like an infant ape, as she climbed up and down the steepest hills.

The difficulties of moving about were not the only ones involved in

Amahuaca mother with twins.

caring for her three infants. In this instance one of the twins was unusually small, being weakened by constant diarrhea for several months. The little mother often appeared not to want the sickly baby to live. She frequently ignored its crying or shoved it impatiently away from her breast. Although infanticide is not a general practice among the Amahuaca and in this instance the parents had explicitly decided against it, one can easily see that closely spaced babies may burden a young mother excessively in the hilly terrain of the Inuya headwaters. For this reason among others, parents occasionally kill a child in infancy. In the light of the difficulties in her own life as a wife and a mother, it is not surprising that Coyaso's sister-in-law expressed anger at Pacho's refusal to accept such responsibilities.

Coyaso's own basic interest in the affair soon became apparent when he said that if Mu'osh had succeeded in keeping Pacho he would have had to make a payment to Coyaso himself, since the latter had no wife and was also a potential mate for Pacho. He would have expected Mu'osh to make a small garden for him and would have given some arrows to Mu'osh in return.

Francisco's marriage to Pacho was, in fact, somewhat irregular. First of all they lived in the same community. Settlement exogamy has been both customary and necessary among the extended-family groups of Amahuaca.

Traditionally Amahuaca settlements have been very small—no larger than twenty persons—and each comprised a single extended family. Ideally such a group included an elderly couple, their unmarried children, and the families of their married sons. Because the groups are very small, there are often no marriageable females in the group when a young man reaches marrying age.

If men take their wives from other communities for demographic reasons and remain at home after marrying, their sons' cross cousins (that is, their mothers' brothers' daughters or fathers' sisters' daughters) will be members of other communities than their own. Like most primitive societies, the Amahuaca prohibit marriage between parallel cousins—the offspring of two brothers or of two sisters. Thus both for demographic reasons and to avoid incest, Amahuaca men have customarily taken their wives from other local kin groups.

To a certain extent the rivalry of Mu'osh and Francisco can be attributed to the fact that several previously separate local kin groups now live together at Varadero. Francisco, for example, had formerly lived at some distance from Mashopo's family. Since he had come to Varadero, however, he was in daily contact with Mashopo's family, and a marriage with Pacho that would have been exogamous previously now became a locally endogamous match.

An additional objection to this match was that Francisco was of a generation above Pacho's, being her father's cross cousin. Coyaso held that it was bad for a man to marry his cousin's daughter, but his principal complaint was that Francisco had not paid him a machete, to which he felt he was entitled. According to Coyaso, when a man takes a woman other than his cross cousin, he should pay to each of her potential husbands a machete, a belt of seed beads, a headdress with woven cotton bands, or all these things.

Moreover, Coyaso's brother maintained that cutting the canoe and conducting the burial services were not payment to Yambawachi. When asked what this work had been in payment for, he said, "Inez later." Inez was the sister of Mashopo who had gone downriver with the soldiers and had returned to the Curiuja settlement. The implication was that Francisco might marry her sometime later. The brothers said that payment to Mashopo and Yambawachi for taking Pacho would have consisted of a machete, an axe, a hammock, a blanket, a knife, cutting a garden plot, a log trough, a pestle, and making a house in addition to the canoe.

Another instance of suspected witchcraft now became apparent. Tu'o, the husband of Mu'osh's aunt Masua, said his entire body hurt and he accused Francisco of being a sorcerer and of sending a foreign object into his wrist, making it lame. Although it had been said earlier that there were no sorcerers at Varadero, Coyaso now agreed with Tu'o that Francisco was a sorcerer. This instance of suspected witchcraft caused considerable anxiety, because Masua believed her grandfather had died in this way. Putative killing by sorcery is not uncommon among the Amahuaca. In fact, ten murders had been committed among the various groups of Amahuaca in the vicinity of Varadero in the previous seven years, some of them for the purpose of avenging deaths that were attributed to sorcery. Mu'osh's grandfather himself claims to have killed five people through sorcery. Moreover, his son-in-law, the father of Mu'osh, had been killed by a raiding party of which Tu'o had been a member.

It is true that Francisco was a chief repository of harvest festival lore, as the community had depended on him to lead the others in singing the harvest songs. But he had not been spoken of before as a sorcerer. Now, with Francisco gone, there was no more singing and dancing, which meant that the celebration of the banana harvest would not take place. For this reason, and perhaps also because of the polarization of the little community, with one faction for Francisco and the other faction against him, people in the Varadero community were deeply concerned about his elopement with Pacho.

Shanchí's stepfather, the husband of Francisco's aunt, expressed his concern by urging that the missionary who had been living among them should "write a letter to Francisco" to convince him to return to Varadero. He and Shanchí's mother also took a quantity of tapir meat from his hilltop house down to Francisco's empty house in the valley and invited others in the community to join with him to eat it there. Undoubtedly this gesture was meant to improve rapport with other members of the community after Francisco's elopement had caused a rift.

Shanchí and Coyaso soon turned their attention toward improving their own lots. Shanchí, whose wife was getting old, said he would soon go to the Purús, where he had relatives, and get another wife for himself. Coyaso also expressed his intention of going to the same area to find a wife. Interestingly enough, he said there would be no payment and no bride service for that woman. As a matter of fact, an alliance had already been initiated that would unite his family with a family from the Purús. As I mentioned earlier, Coyaso's niece had been spoken for as the future wife of Coyaso's classificatory sister's son, who had come to Varadero from the Purús river only a few months earlier.

These intentions are another instance of the role of males in initiating marriage plans. It appears to be relatively rare that women, especially young women, initiate plans for marriage, and the role of males in planning marriage is an example of the generally dominant role of males.

Amahuaca society is relatively egalitarian, and women appear to be accorded moderately high status by comparison with many strongly lineal societies. This impression is supported by the attitude of women themselves, who do not generally express resentment about their treatment by males or protest their lack of control over their lives. Nevertheless their role in decision making is a relatively passive one, and nearly every aspect of their lives is dominated by males.

Moreover, the incidents narrated here show that in many instances women are thought of as possessions "to have and to hold." The frequency of wife capture from unfriendly groups, infant betrothal, child marriage, and coercing girls to marry against their wishes all belie the statement of male informants that marriage does not take place unless the girl is willing.

It is interesting that, in the instance narrated here, when a girl behaved in a manner contrary to tradition and exerted some degree of positive choice in selecting her mate, her unorthodox behavior threatened to split the community.

From the data presented here it may be concluded that tension between local groups and even among close kin is fostered by both the infrequency of intergroup contact and the keen competition for wives among the small and very sparsely settled Amahuaca population. Moreover, by allowing such tension to generate factions that split local groups, very small communities run the risk of culture loss, as is illustrated by Francisco's absence. With his elopement, the community lost its capacity to hold a harvest festival.[6] In addition, frustrations such as those developed by Pacho's marriages tend to lead to suspicion of sorcery and thus to homicides.

Fortunately for the Varadero community, Francisco and Pacho, after living for some months on the Purús river, returned to the Inuya and established a new household near that of Francisco's aunt and her husband across the stream from the households of Shanchí and Coyaso's brother. Coyaso then lived a short distance away, and Mashopo's families remained at their previous location somewhat farther upstream. Thus the settlement plan continued to express the social distance that separated the principal characters involved in the drama of marriage.

NOTES

1. Varadero, a Spanish term meaning "crossing" or "portage," is the name given by Peruvians to an Amahuaca settlement at the headwaters of the Inuya river near the height of land between the Inuya and the Juruá-Purús drainage in Southeastern Peru. In 1961 the community of Amahuaca there comprised seven loosely aggregated household groups that had been gradually attracted to the site by Robert and Dolores Russell, missionaries affiliated with the Summer Institute of Linguistics. I am indebted to Robert Russell for some of the information contained in this narrative, especially population data, information about events that occurred previous to the date of my fieldwork in 1960 to 1961, and translations of some native terms.

2. Some of the Amahuaca phonemes do not occur in English, and the symbols used by linguists to represent them have other meanings in English. Hence in this paper I shall use a simplified anglicized spelling of Amahuaca names that roughly represents the native pronunciation.

3. The time mentioned here refers to the ethnographic present of 1961.

4. The events related in the present paper involved people in one such extended-family group and the rather artificial and somewhat larger community at Varadero, a loose and unstructured aggregate of previously separate families.

5. For other details of this incident, see Gertrude Dole, "Endocannibalism among the Amahuaca Indians," *Transactions of the New York Academy of Sciences*, ser. II, vol. 24, no. 5, pp. 567–573, 1962.

6. I have discussed the relation of community size to social complexity in an unpublished manuscript, "The Influence of Population Density on the Development of Social Organization among the Amahuaca of Eastern Peru," n.d., a paper presented at the Annual Meeting of the American Anthropological Association, Philadelphia, 1961.

The Egyptian Woman: Between Modernity and Tradition

SAFIA K. MOHSEN

Introduction

In recent years, Egyptian writers have emphasized the impact of Westernization on the traditional way of life. Specifically, writers have paid attention to the effects of Western ideas on the traditional conception of the role of women and on the various areas of conflict which the introduction of these ideas has created.

The conflict between the traditional and the modern role of the Egyptian woman finds its most obvious manifestation in the domain of family relations. Legally, these relations are set by rules based on the Islamic laws of personal status and family. These rules, in turn, support the traditional aspects of the family relations which recognize a certain degree of inequality in status between men and women, with women commonly being put at a disadvantage.

Because of their recognition and support of such inequality, the law has come under attack by those advocating a more modern role for women, a role based on legal and social equality. Pressure for reform has resulted in a number of proposals aimed at freeing women from the restrictions placed on them by present laws and from the traditional roles that these laws support. The aim of this chapter is to show that in their eagerness to improve the status of women in Egyptian society, the advocates of women's rights have tended to neglect the fact that the traditional role of women is supported by much more than a set of formal legal rules. Despite the appearance of modernity, the attitude toward the role of women in public life—as well as in private—still remains a fairly conservative one. This conservative attitude is held by both men and women.

It is interesting to note that women's equality in public life seems to be more readily accepted than their equality in the domain of personal relations and family matters. It is one thing for a woman to become a member of the Arab Socialist Union or to hold a cabinet office, but it is another for that same woman to have the same right of divorce or custody of her children as her husband.

Legal reform may change the formal aspect of the inequality, but only changes in the attitude of Egyptian society will ensure the actual equality of men and women. This does not imply that legal reform is useless, for it is important. It means simply that legal reform is not enough. In addition to its practical and symbolic value, legal reform might, in the long run, effect changes in attitudes by creating norms supportive of the new role of women. But until such changes in attitude are evident, no legal reform, however substantial it may be, can result in a magical transformation of the traditional role of the Egyptian woman into a modern one.

Evidence of such changes is not lacking. The high cost of living, which makes for cooperation of both the husband and wife in the financial support of the family, has already created support for the working woman. The increased dependency on the income of women as a source of family support might prove to be one of the most important factors in changing the role of the woman. Increased education of women, especially university education with its coeducational atmosphere, may also dissolve the barriers between the sexes and create a wider basis of cooperation and mutual respect between them. Increased education and employment for women would further result in less dependency on their families and consequently would give them relative freedom from the control of their families. But these and other factors influence the role of women gradually, over a long period of time. Although they might not be as obvious or as immediately observable as legal reform, their effect on the changing role of the Egyptian woman is equally or perhaps even more significant.

WOMEN'S RIGHTS AND THE LAW OF MARRIAGE AND DIVORCE

Personal status and family law are the only aspects of Islamic law, or *Shari'a*, still formally applied in Egypt. Until about a century ago, Islamic law reigned over the entire Middle East. This does not mean that all aspects of that law were equally applied, for parts of it, especially administrative and constitutional law and even criminal law, required rules of evidence or procedure which were incompatible with certain aspects of modern life. The commercial law was equally anachronistic, for the Islamic prohibition of usury and of speculative contracts was too restricting for the requirements of the highly developed market economy. But the *Shari'a,* or Islamic law, remained in the background as the ultimate guide for social interaction.

The basic shift from Islamic law came with the establishment of secular courts and laws to function side by side with the *Shari'a* courts. Thus the Ottomans enacted the commercial code in 1850, the penal code in 1858, and the code of maritime commerce in 1863. All these codes were based on European models, especially the Napoleonic Code. Secular courts, mixed courts for cases involving foreigners, and *nizami* courts for cases involving only Ottoman subjects were established for the application of these laws. The *Shari'a* laws were applied by the *Shari'a* courts and were restricted to cases of personal status and family affairs between Muslim subjects.

This was the case in Egypt. Egypt attained its judicial independence with the establishment of the mixed courts in 1873 and the native courts in 1883. Two civil codes and a criminal code, all based on the Napoleonic Code although they included certain sections based on the *Shari'a,* were enacted for application by these courts. The *Shari'a* courts were restricted to the personal status and family cases. It was only the family law in its widest sense that was still applied in the old courts from the old books and by the old *Shari'a* personnel.

Although the *Shari'a* courts were abolished in 1956 and cases of personal status for both Muslims and non-Muslims were transferred to the civil courts, these cases continued to be judged according to the rules, procedures, and principles of *Shari'a* law. It is these laws, especially those regulating marriage, divorce, and the custody of children, that are the main targets of attack of the feminists and supporters of women's rights in Egypt; and it is within the domain of these laws that the conflict between the traditional and modern role of the Egyptian woman is evident.

Let us examine briefly some aspects of the laws of marriage and divorce. According to Islamic law, marriage is a civil contract between a man and a woman begun by the request of one party to the marriage and the acceptance of the other. Marriage may be contracted only between a man and a woman who are both of age and both of sound mind and of free will. If they are related by kinship, this relationship must be of a degree that is not prohibited by law. Mentally retarded persons or those who are under age (sixteen years for the woman and eighteen years for the man according to the·law as applied in Egypt) can be married only by permission of their guardians. The presence of two credible witnesses is a prerequisite for the validity of the contract.

For the contract to be effective, a certain amount of money (*mahr*) is paid by the groom to the bride. Part of the *mahr* is paid at the writing of the marriage contract. This part is called *muquaddam*, or the advance *mahr*. The other part, the *mu'akhar* or delayed *mahr*, is due either on the death of the husband or in the case of divorce. The amount of *mahr*, as well as the proportion of *muquaddam* to *mu'akhar*, varies from case to case. The law leaves the amount of *mahr* to the bargaining power of the two parties, although it requires that the *mahr* be suitable for the woman to be married, taking into consideration the social position of her family.

The *mahr* is not a price for the wife; it is a compulsory gift which becomes the private property of the wife. She usually uses all or part of the *mahr* to outfit herself and furnish the house. For this reason, many prefer that the *muquaddam* or advance part of the *mahr* be greater than the *mu'akhar*. Others prefer it the other way around, keeping a large amount of *mu'akhar*, or delayed payment, as a deterrent to the husband should he think of divorcing his wife.

The marriage contract gives the couple certain rights over one another.

1. The first and most important is the right to have sexual access to the other person. The husband has an exclusive right over his wife's sexual activities. The woman's position, however, is quite different, since Islamic law gives the husband the right to have up to four wives. Islam holds marriage in high esteem, regarding it the only way of perpetuating the species. Therefore some jurists (Maliki and Hanbali schools of Islamic jurisprudence) consider the right of sexual access a mutual one for both husband and wife. Others (Shafi'i and Hanafi schools of jurisprudence) believe it to be the right only of the husband and the duty of the wife. According to these schools, the marriage is effective if the man has had sexual relations with his wife only once. The wife has no right to divorce or annulment if the husband fails to play his sexual role after the initial consummation of the marriage.

2. The right of obedience, or *habs*, belongs only to the husband. The word *habs* means "detention" and implies the right of the man to keep the woman in the marital house. The right of *habs* has its basis in a paragraph in the Qor'an which reads: "They [women] should not go out of the house lest they commit a grave sin" (*Sura* IV:33). The wife may leave the marital house without the permission of the husband only to visit her immediate relatives, especially her parents. (She may visit her parents once a week without the husband's permission.) Relatives other than the parents are not covered under that license and she is entitled to visit them only once a year

without the permission of the husband. These visits do not include staying overnight, however. If such a stay is planned, even with her parents, she has to obtain the husband's permission.

Habs entitles a man to prevent his wife from going outside the house to, for example, work or attend school. According to the majority of Islamic jurists, when a woman goes out without the permission of her husband to work or to school, she undermines his right of *habs*. A woman who violates that right is defined as disobedient (or *nashis*) and, therefore, not entitled to financial support by the husband. On the other hand, some jurists restrict the husband's right to detain his wife to instances of direct conflict, as when a job would take her away from home for long periods of time.

The right of *habs* was later developed into the right of the husband to force the wife to live with him even against her will. This practice came to be known as *bait el- ta'a'*, (or "the house of obedience"). According to this procedure, a man can, under certain circumstances, ask the police to arrest his wife and bring her home to live with him. This practice was introduced into the Egyptian personal status and family law in 1897, after an interpretation of the Islamic right of *habs*.

3. Divorce, according to Islamic law, allows a man to dissolve a marriage merely by pronouncing the dismissal formula "I divorce you" in the presence of credible witnesses. The husband need have no grounds for the divorce. A husband who has divorced his wife can reverse the process merely by living with her again as a husband if he does this during the *'iddah* or waiting period of three months following the divorce. No new contract is needed in this case.

The *'iddah* is a period during which the woman cannot marry another man. Its main purpose is to make sure that, if the woman is carrying a child fathered by the husband, there will be no conflict regarding paternity. If the husband does not take back his wife during the *'iddah* period, he cannot thereafter do so without a new contract. The divorce in the latter case is called *ba'in*, or absolute, in contrast to the *rag'i*, or temporary divorce during the *'iddah* period. If the husband exercises his right of absolute divorce three times, he cannot remarry his wife unless the latter is married first to another man, or *muhallal*, and then divorced by him.

The woman does not have the same right of divorce as the man. She cannot divorce her husband except by establishing adequate grounds for divorce and obtaining a court decision. The grounds specified by Islamic law for divorce are

Inability or unwillingness of the husband to support his wife.

Incurable illness of the husband. This applies to both mental as well as physical illness.

Social inconvenience, defined vaguely as any conditions created by the husband which put on the wife a heavy burden to which she is not accustomed.

The absence of the husband for more than a year without good reason.

The imprisonment of the husband for more than three years.

With the exception of the case of divorce on the basis of lack of financial support, the divorce by the court is always *ba'in*, or absolute. Whether the divorce is initiated by the husband or the wife, the wife is—theoretically—entitled to alimony for the period of *'iddah*. This is not always the case in practice, however. In many instances, the husband will make the wife forfeit her right to alimony as a condition of granting her the divorce. In certain cases, a wife or her parents may even pay the husband a sum of money to obtain the divorce, especially when the wife does not have adequate grounds, thus avoiding going to the court.

Custody of children is given to the mother until age seven for boys and nine for girls. Upon petition to the judge and if the judge finds it in the best interest of the children, the period of maternal custody can be extended to the ages of nine for boys and eleven for girls. After they reach these ages, the father has an undisputed right to the custody of his children. At this point the relative merits of the parents are not taken into account, nor are the best interests of the children.

Women's legal inequality in matters of marriage and divorce has been challenged for a long time. But it was not until the feminist movement in Egypt became organized that this challenge became a serious one. Its origin in Egypt can be traced to the efforts of a number of men and women, notable among whom are Rifa'a El Tahtawi, Mohammad 'Abdu, Qasim Amin, and Huda Sha'rawi.

In his book entitled *The Honest Guide for Boys and Girls,* published in 1873, Rifa'a El Tahtawi pressed for the education of women. Education, he maintained, was important not to qualify the woman for a public office or a profession but rather to improve the condition of the family and to make the woman a better companion to her husband and a better mother to her children.

Sheikh Mohammad 'Abdu concentrated his efforts on the question of polygyny. He argued that Islam gave a high status to the woman and that polygyny was permitted in Islam because it served the need of the Muslim community at the time of the Prophet. It is the interests of the community that Islam protects, and if a certain practice is proved disadvantageous to the community, then there is no religious restriction on abolishing it. Polygyny, according to him, is such a practice and should therefore be abolished.

To support his views, he cited various examples in which a practice, though permitted by Islamic law, was suspended or forbidden to safeguard the interest of the society. One of these examples is the case of the members of the diplomatic corps being forbidden to marry foreigners, even if they are of the same faith—a restriction that is not recognized in Islamic law. In addition to opposing polygyny, Mohammad 'Abdu also argued for the transfer of the right of divorce from the husband to the court, with equal recourse for men and women.

Qasim Amin's target was the veil. He advocated the removal of the veil on the grounds that it had no basis in Islam and that it degraded the woman. Like both El Tahtawi and 'Abdu, Qasim Amin insisted on the need for allowing women more opportunity for education, referring to certain passages in the Qor'an that call upon believers, with no specification of sex, to acquire knowledge and to seek education. At first Amin, like Mohammad 'Abdu, thought that reform could be achieved simply by reinterpreting the Islamic law rather than by abolishing it and replacing it with a new and secular law. By 1900, however, he changed his position. In his second book, *The New Woman,* he insisted on the separation of religion and secular life and held that women should be treated as equal to men in all respects, something that is achieved best by instituting secular laws to replace the religious ones in dealing with personal status and family.

It was Huda Sha'rawi, however, who started the active fight for women's rights in Egyptian society. The wife of a famous political leader, she was highly respected in Egyptian high society as well as by the public. In 1923, after attending a conference in Rome and upon her arrival in Alexandria, she shocked the receiving crowds by taking off her veil. Until that time, the veil had been commonly worn by women in Egypt. Veiling was not the practice among all segments of the society, however. It was, for example, not compatible with the economic activities of women among the nomadic and seminomadic groups in Egypt, nor did peasant women wear it while helping their husbands in the fields, although they did use veils in the presence of male strangers. The veil was mostly worn by urban women and was considered to some extent a symbol of aristocracy, although it was not restricted to the women of aristocratic families. Women who dared to go unveiled in public were ridiculed, sometimes even spat upon, and were generally considered as being cheap and unworthy of respect. Huda Sha'rawi's action changed this image—it offered respectability to those who were bold enough to follow her lead. Within a few years, unveiling became the practice of the majority of women in the urban areas of Egypt.

Huda Sha'rawi went beyond this symbolic fight for the rights and equality of women. She organized women's groups and used her influence to achieve actual reform in the status of women. Since the time of Sha'rawi, the number of these groups and their memberships have increased substantially. At the present time, their memberships include women and men from all segments of the Egyptian society; their demands have become bolder and their methods more explicit and sophisticated. After 1952 and with the Egyptian revolution calling for the cooperation of all Egyptian men and women to build the new socialist society, there has been more awareness of women's problems, and the government has been supportive, at least verbally, of most of the goals of women's rights.

The goals of the movement centered around three main points:

1. More opportunities for formal education for women

2. Political reform and, more specifically, the right of women to vote and run for political office

3. Drastic legal reform, especially in the area of personal status and family law

The cry for educational reform met relatively little public resistance, and that was reflected in the rapid increase in the number of females in Egypt's educational institutions. This was an increase in actual numbers as well as an increase in proportion to the percentage of males. In 1921 to 1922, the number of females in government schools was 24,316, and only 43 of these were in secondary schools. In 1962, the number of females in government schools had risen to 1,154,454, with more than 100,000 in secondary schools and 20,000 in postsecondary institutions. In relative terms also, the education of women has expanded. In 1953 to 1954, female students accounted for only 23 percent of the total student population in elementary schools and 14 percent of the secondary schools' student body. By 1961 to 1962, the percentage had increased to 40 percent on the elementary school level and 24 percent on the secondary school level.

Political reform was not as rapid or as easy to achieve. The right of women to vote was opposed by religious groups as well as by a sizable percentage of the secularly educated elite (not to mention the uneducated majority). On June 11, 1952, under pressure from the group working for women's right to vote, the Commission of Fatawi of Al Azhar, the highest authority on the interpretation of Islamic law and doctrine, issued a definitive *fatwa*, or legal statement. This statement criticized those who believed that Egypt could enter the twentieth century only by imitating other countries and doing what those countries have done. Such individuals, according to the *fatwa*, were undermining the national dignity and basic moral values of an Islamic society. The writers of the *fatwa* rejected the right of women to vote and to serve in Parliament as incompatible with the spirit of Islam. They referred to the passage in Qor'an which reads: "Remain in your homes, and do not exhibit yourselves in public the way women in the time of ignorance did."

The *fatwa* maintained that although the directive quoted above was addressed to the Prophet's women *(het)*, it should apply to all Muslim women; that women should remain at home to protect their honor and to avoid tempting others; and that participation in public affairs exposes the woman to indecencies. On the other hand, the *fatwa* did not object to women working in the private domain as doctors, teachers, or nurses. To support their views of excluding women from public participation, the writers of the *fatwa* drew upon historical records which showed that when Abu Bakr was confirmed as successor to the Prophet, only men made the decision. The reason for the exclusion of women from participating in that decision, they held, could be found in the Qor'an's description of women as weak creatures created for specific tasks and fit to function only within the domain of the family.

Although the Commission of Fatawi was forced by the Egyptian government to accept the reform and women were given the right to vote in 1956, this conservative attitude still exists in Egypt. Only a few years ago, Sheikh El Ghazali argued in the General Assembly for the seclusion of women in their houses, the reinstatement of the veil, and public prosecution for those who dared to go without it. Despite this opposition, women's participation in public life has been quite noticeable in the last few decades. A number of women have been elected to the National Assembly of the Arab Socialist Union; two have become cabinet members; and numerous others are occupying leading positions in the government and the political structure in Egypt.

It is true that some professions are still restricted against women (e.g., judgeships and district attorneys' positions), but in most fields women seem to be accepted at least in principle if not in actuality. An example of the latter case is the diplomatic corps, where women are not in theory barred from holding diplomatic office. Hiring for these positions is done on the basis of public competition which is open to both men and women. In actuality, however, very few women ever pass the examinations for these offices. But in general, women seem to be fairly well accepted in the public domain.

It is interesting to note that women generally find relatively little resistance with regard to employment from men, less than might be expected in a male-dominated society. Curiosity might be one of the factors influencing this phenomenon. For a long time men have been used to finding women in a certain role, and they are curious to see what a woman can do in a traditionally male occupation. Instead of resistance and jealousy, women frequently meet encouragement from male colleagues. Besides, women are not considered important enough to be part of the competitive structure —to be dangerous as rivals. Another factor is that in a highly competitive male-dominated occupational structure, the choice of a woman sometimes serves as a compromise in a deadlocked situation. Women are still excluded from the power struggle, and this, in many cases, works for them, since they are rarely the targets of the political plots so commonly devised by their male colleagues against one another. It is within the domain of legal reform, however, that the advocates of women's rights are concentrating their efforts. The reforms sought center around the following five main demands:

1. Abolishing or at least restricting polygyny. Apart from being a symbol of women's inferiority, polygyny, the reformers argue, is incompatible with the social policy of birth control. According to some of the Islamic jurists, polygyny could be abolished by simply reinterpreting Islamic law itself. They maintain that closer examination of the Qor'an would reveal that Islamic law in fact did not permit polygyny. A man could have up to four wives, according to Islamic law, only if he could be "absolutely just towards all the wives." This justice requires total impartiality not only in the form of treatment but also in feeling, something that the Qor'an in the same *sura* specified as impossible. ". . . but if you fear being unjust, then marry only one . . . and you know you can never be totally just" (*Sura* IV:38). The legal interpretation is that when a license is attached to an impossible condition, the license is in fact nonexistent, and polygyny was attached to such an impossible condition. But those who hold these views are a small minority.

The majority of Islamic jurists today maintain that polygyny is an undisputed right according to the Islamic law. To them, polygyny fulfills an essential social function first of all because it prevents immorality by giving the married man the chance to marry the woman he desires instead of having her as a mistress. They further argue that polygyny enables a man to continue to support a wife who is sick or unable to fulfill her marital obligations for reasons that are not her fault while having a normal marital relationship with another. As such, according to this reasoning, polygyny serves to protect the woman and not to ensure the man's pleasure.

So basic is this right to polygyny, according to these jurists, that a man retains it even if it was specified in the marriage contract that he is not to have a second wife. For this reason, the feminists hold the direct interference by the legislators to be essential. They insist on restricting polygyny to special cases in which the judge may permit it and for legally specified reasons, such as the sickness or sterility of the first wife. Such permission would give the first wife an automatic right to get a divorce. Opponents of restricting the right of polygyny oppose this proposal on the basis that it exposes the secrets of the families to public discussions, thus undermining the dignity of both husband and wife.

2. Abolishing the procedure of *bait el-ta'a*. The right of *habs* and the

associated institution of *bait el-ta'a* should be abolished. *Bait el-ta'a,* the reformers argue, is not even Islamic. In a speech to the National Assembly in March 1965, Shiekh Zakaria el Berri, Professor of *Shari'a* at Cairo University School of Law, maintained that "the relationship between husband and wife in Islam is a contractual one based on the rights and duties given to each by the marriage contract, and on mutual respect and consent of both parties." No provision in the *Shari'a,* he held, gave the husband the right to detain the woman against her own will. On the contrary, it emphasized the goodwill between the husband and wife when it called upon the husband to "keep them [wives] with charity, or let them go with kindness" (*Sura* IV:35). Dr. Kamal El 'Eteifi, a professor of law, went further, considering *bait el-ta'a* as equivalent to statutory rape, since it involves having sexual relations with the woman against her will.

In March 1967, the Minister of Justice at the time drafted a proposal to stop the practice of coercion in the exercise of the procedures of *bait el-ta'a.* Although relatively few sentences of *bait el-ta'a* are actually carried out by the police (230 out of 1,266 cases in 1966), the practice is so outrageous that its abolishment is at the top of the list of demands for reform.

3. Redefining the right of *habs* so as to give women freedom to work and pursue education without arbitrary control by men. In 1967, a committee was formed to draft a new proposal for reform in the personal status and family laws. In that proposal, the working wife was regulated under Article 85, which reads as follows: "A wife may go out of the house in the case of necessity and in cases permitted by custom.... Her going out to work is not considered a violation of the right of *habs* if she specifies going outside the house for work as a condition in the marriage contract."

The wording of this article makes it clear that the normal condition is one in which the woman stays in the house and that work is the exception rather than the rule. The justification that the committee gave to specifying work as the condition in the marriage contract before it is considered legal is that the man has to know what he is getting into from the beginning, and therefore has the chance to refuse marriage if the woman feels very strongly about her right to work or to education. Even when such condition is included in the marriage contract, the husband, according to the new proposal, has the right to violate that condition and prevent his wife from working if her working "puts unnecessary hardship upon him." The definition of what constitutes an unnecessary hardship is left to the husband.

The proposal was understandably rejected by the feminists.

4. Redefining the right of divorce, making it equally available to both

husband and wife. As in the case of polygyny, according to the reformists, discrimination in the right to divorce reflects the inferior status of women under Islamic law. In justifying this discrimination, Islamic jurisprudence refers to the difference in temperament between men and women. Women, by the very nature of their role as mothers, it is claimed, are more emotional and thus less capable of making rational decisions. Therefore—according to Islamic jurists—to base the stability of the family upon their impulsive decisions would be to undermine the whole institution of marriage. These conservative jurists also believe that giving a judge the right to make decisions regarding divorce (rather than to either the wife or the husband) is unacceptable since this would expose family secrets to public examination. Besides, they maintain, though the right of the husband might appear unchecked, there are many social and practical considerations that impose severe restrictions on such a right.

Advocates of women's rights reject this argument. First, they hold that there is no proof that one sex is inherently more (or less) emotional than the other. Second, they say that if exposing the family secrets is the main reason for not requiring the husband to go to court for a divorce, why is it not a consideration in the case of the wife seeking a divorce, since in the latter case the family secrets are equally exposed?

5. Changing the laws regulating the custody of children to take into consideration the welfare of the children. This represents another area of required legal reform. According to the Egyptian law of family affairs, a divorced man gets automatic custody of his children after the boys reach age seven and the girls reach age nine. No consideration is given to his fitness to care for the children or to the welfare of the children themselves.

To bring pressure upon the legislators, the reformers presented an actual case on public television. It involved an educated woman who was forced by her parents to marry a rich and uneducated man twenty-five years older than she was. After they had had two children, he divorced her and sent her and the two infants to live with her mother in Cairo. For twelve years she never heard from him, nor did he send any money for child support. Then, when the children were in high school, he showed up demanding his children. He planned to take them back to the village where he intended to force his daughter to marry an uneducated relative. The mother tried all legal avenues without success, since the law was clearly on the father's side. His was an undisputed right of custody—due him by virtue of his biological paternity.

The case stimulated a great deal of discussion by laymen as well as jurists and created public sympathy for a reform of the custody laws. Those who were for reform argued that paternity was a legal concept, defined in terms of rights and duties, and not a biological one. If the duties of the father were not fulfilled, as in the above case, then the father should lose his eligibility (*ahliya*) for custody of the children. They maintained that this was the original goal of Islamic law—to safeguard the interests of the children and to protect their rights, rather than to give absolute control over them to the father. It was the ambiguity in the writing of the law, they held, that led the courts to interpret this right in a rigid manner, giving the man automatic custody of the child at a given age. They urged the revision of the law in such a way as to eliminate this type of interpretation.

6. The final demand for legal reform was related to the above right. According to the law, a parent who did not have the custody of the child had the right to see the child periodically, the specification being that such visits were to take place at the police station when the parents could not agree on another location. Reformers argued, with good reason, that a police station is not a proper place for children to see their parents and that the police station is usually chosen by one parent to humiliate the other, with no regard to the feelings or the welfare of the children themselves. The practice was abandoned by a decree issued on February 27, 1967.

THE ROLE OF WOMEN: THE SOCIAL REALITY

It is difficult to talk about the role of "the Egyptian woman" without reference to a particular segment of Egyptian society. The role of women in rural areas differs from that in urban areas, and both roles differ from those of women among the nomadic and seminomadic groups. Even within urban areas, we find differences in the roles of women of different social classes and ethnic or religious backgrounds. For the purpose of this article, I will concentrate on practices and attitudes relating to the role of urban middle- and upper-middle-class women.

There are two main reasons for selecting this particular segment of the society. The first is that the active feminists and supporters of women's rights come from this particular group. It is women from this stratum of Egyptian society that make the loudest complaint against the present legal treatment of women. The other reason is that it is this particular stratum of society with which the writer is personally familiar. Whenever it is feasible and material is available, I shall try to draw comparisons between the practices and attitudes of individuals belonging to different generations in order to show the extent to which these practices and attitudes might have changed.

The traditional pattern called for the girl to stay at home before marriage. Forty or fifty years ago the girl was expected to help with various activities within the home, including housework and the care of younger brothers and sisters. In well-to-do families where such help was not needed, she was supposed to occupy herself with activities that would prepare her for the role of successful wife and charming hostess. Private tutoring in French and music was usually provided by those who could afford it. Traditionally, formal education was discouraged, and when permitted, it was viewed as a temporary thing until the right man came along and the girl was taken out of school. Among women who are forty-five years of age or older, it was a common experience in girlhood to be forced to leave school, regardless of how successful they were, to comply with parental marriage plans. Completing one's education was unimportant if the "right man" came along.

Most girls seem to have accepted this pattern submissively, viewing it fatalistically as the result of some kind of inevitable and inexplicable law and trying to adjust their lives to fit their circumstances. Others resented being forced to leave school to marry someone who, in most instances, they did not know and sometimes had never even seen. The writer has had a personal experience with a case in which the woman was forced to leave her studies one month before graduation to marry someone whom she had never met. This woman, whom I shall call F, is now fifty-five and has a married son.

> I was in the last year of my high school at Sania school for girls. My grades were the best in class, and I was recommended by the headmistress to be sent to England after graduation to continue my education at government expense. Suddenly a disaster happened in the form of a suitor. He wasn't very rich, but he had a good position in the Ministry of Justice. He was about fifteen years older than I, and when I met him in the family gathering, I didn't like him at all. But that was not why I pleaded and begged my parents not to force me to marry him. I just was not interested in marriage, and I was interested in nothing more than completing my education. But pleading with my parents didn't work, and I was forced to leave school one month before graduation. I never forgave my husband for that, although it was not exactly his fault. I felt miserable and never liked my married life. Every time I open a newspaper and see some of the names of those lucky girls who were not stopped by their parents and who now occupy prominent positions in the government, doing great things with their time, I feel terrible and hate my parents for what they did to me. They couldn't understand why I would want to complete my education. "What for? Work? Do you want to scandalize us in front of our friends? Do you want them to think we can't feed you? . . ."

(Interview, August 27, 1971)

Of course, not every woman reacted to the restricting of her studies the way F did. Many accepted the restriction with a great deal of fatalism:

> After all, marriage is the ultimate goal of any woman. What else could I have done—argue with my parents? They would have killed me. They might have thought I had another man in mind and that I was taking the education as an excuse for refusing the man of their choice. I couldn't have done this to them after all their efforts to raise me as a respectable girl.

> (Interview, August 27, 1971)

The above responses were given by two urban upper-middle-class women in their fifties. Neither had completed her high school education. But at that time, university education for women had not yet been accepted by many. Very few women, in fact, did attend college.

By the time the writer attended college in the late 1950s, higher education had become an acceptable pattern among middle- and upper-class families in Egypt. Also, work had become more acceptable for the woman with a college degree. Yet college was viewed by the majority as the place for the girl to meet the right man, and once that goal had been achieved, the girl would not normally hesitate to leave her university studies. This pattern, of course, had many exceptions, but the predominant attitude of the female college student was to "capture" a suitable husband—and the sooner the better.

"What would you do with a degree?" was the response the writer got when, in her freshman year in college, she turned down a marriage offer in order to continue her education. "Get a job that pays you £15? ... you surely don't need it—you spend three times that much on a single dress. K is a great man; any girl would dream of having him as a husband. Do you think the degree will bring you a better husband? By the time you graduate you will be older, and who knows, you might not find someone as good as K."

This type of response was encountered not only from older relatives but also from friends, many of whom married and left college without getting a degree. Such an attitude was reflected in the importance put on wearing stylish and expensive clothes and the most elaborate makeup. A visiting professor from the United States remarked that the girls at Cairo University looked like they were on their way to a cocktail party rather than to a classroom. Families barely managing to sustain themselves financially made a deliberate effort to outfit their daughters in college with fashionable clothes.

I remember that the first day of each academic year was considered a review day. The male students waited on both sides of the corridor leading

to the classroom hall to look at the faces of the new female students entering the university. Females in the second, third, and fourth year classes
also watched the newcomers, sizing up the possible competition. The more
attractive female students received a great deal of attention from their male
classmates, but their goal was usually to attract a young member of the
faculty or at least a wealthy student.

Romantic ties were known to exist, although those involved generally
managed to keep their relationships secret. Rumors about who was going
out with whom were the favorite items of gossip during my college days.
Respectable girls were not supposed to go out with men. The main strategy
was to attract the suitable bachelor, and the next move was for him to ask
her parents' permission to marry her. When this was accomplished, and if
the man was considered a "good catch," the girl left college to prepare for
marriage. Leaving college for marriage was much more common during the
first two years of school than during the last two (where the pattern consisted of an engagement before and the wedding after graduation). But
marriage remained the most important goal for the majority of the college
girls.

Although university education was an acceptable pattern, many parents
discouraged their daughters from pursuing it. The main reason was that
it was not necessary and that the girl's interests might be distracted and
diverted elsewhere. Besides, the university gave the girl an opportunity to
associate with men without proper supervision. Some families feared that
a university degree might reduce a girl's chances of marriage by scaring off
suitable males who might distrust educated women. Some families preferred
that their sons marry a fairly uneducated girl on the theory that educated
women were harder to manage and that they tended to control their
husbands and their families.

At the present time, attitudes are not too different from those described
above. It is true that university education has become an acceptable pattern
for women in Egypt. It is also true that work—gainful employment—for
women has also been accepted because of the increase in the cost of living,
which requires the cooperation of husband and wife to support a household. Although a working woman with an income is frequently sought
after as a marriage partner, many people still look with suspicion on educated women and seek uneducated women for marriage.

In an article entitled "The Flesh Market" (*Hawwa'*, January 1972),
Amina El Said, one of the leading figures in the women's liberation movement in Egypt, discussed two cases that came to her attention during the
last few months. The first of these concerned a woman in her early thirties,
very attractive and from a respectable family. Upon the completion of her
college degree, she decided to continue her studies in England, where she
obtained a Ph.D. in educational psychology. She now occupies a good posi-

tion and earns a very comfortable salary. Her main complaint is that since she completed her graduate degree, no one has shown any interest in marrying her. Before she went to England, several marriage proposals were offered her, but she had turned them down to finish her education. Since her return to Egypt some years ago, several men had shown initial interest in her, but their interest soon disappeared. When she insisted on knowing the reason, one of the men told her that he liked her but frankly did not know what to do with a highly educated woman. He told her that marrying her meant to him that he would have no control whatsoever over the affairs of the house and that he would rather marry an uneducated woman with whom he felt more comfortable.

The second case involved an educated man of thirty-six. After completing his college education, he migrated to Australia where he found a good position and acquired a great deal of money. Last summer he came back to Egypt on a two-week vacation to look for an Egyptian wife who would accompany him back to Australia. Since he had no relatives left in Cairo, he asked Amina El Said—a leader of Egyptian feminists—to look for a wife for him. He had a number of requirements of the prospective bride. The first and most important was that she should not be educated. A high school diploma was the maximum. Other specifications pertained to the appearance of the woman: tall, slim, brown eyes, thin lips, and a small nose. Apart from these, he did not care. He was even willing to leave for Australia without seeing the prospective bride. She was to be sent to him with his prior agreement to marry her as long as she met the above specifications (*Hawwa'*, January 22, 1972).

Amina El Said's conclusion was that Egyptian society put too much emphasis on the physical aspect of marriage—to the almost total neglect of companionship, cooperation, and communication between husband and wife. Emphasis on a physical relationship would not by itself lead to the inferiority of women if both the man and the woman had equal say in the selection of the marriage partner. This is obviously not the case in Egypt. Men have, by the fact that they are the ones to initiate the marriage request, a much greater role in the selection of their partners than do women, although men and women both are under the influence of their parents in the selection of their marriage partners.

Traditionally, arranged marriages have been the rule. The girl is suggested to the man as a marriage partner by one of his female relatives or by friends of his mother. In some instances, the prospective groom would have seen the girl in the street, in the house of a friend, or at work. He then tells his mother of his desire to marry that particular girl. Upon discussing the matter with the father, both parents proceed with the investigation of the prospective bride, her family, their reputation and wealth, and her reputation. Once satisfied with their investigation, they (especially the woman) would pay a visit to the girl and her parents to meet the girl and examine such things as her beauty, her voice, the way she walked, and how accomplished a hostess she was—judging from the way she served the tea and presented the cookies.

In 1964, I was a participant observer at such a meeting. The prospective groom was a judge in his middle thirties, never married before, and the prospective bride was a law student from a well-to-do family. The initial investigation of the girl's reputation—as well as that of her family—had been previously undertaken, and the final review was to be made. I went with the parents of the man, his two sisters, and his younger brother. We were received in the guest room by the girl's father; then the mother appeared. Half an hour later, the girl appeared. For more than fifteen minutes she sat motionless and did not speak. Then her mother ordered her to go to the piano to entertain the guests, which she did. The evening was pleasant enough and not as embarrassing as I had thought it would be.

Later, in the prospective groom's house, the conversation centered around what each one of the visiting team thought of the appearance as well as the behavior of the girl and her parents. For a while the question centered around whether or not the girl was wearing padded undergarments, and that seemed to be a very important point as far as the man was concerned. In general, the girl was acceptable, but all members of the suitor's family decided that she was not the right girl for him because her mother seemed too assertive and carried on the conversation, while her father was not assertive enough. They decided that a girl raised in such an atmosphere would be hard to control—might have the same attitude toward authority within the family that her mother had.

The experience must have been quite distressing to the girl herself, although she did not seem to mind it. Describing her first encounter with her in-laws, a friend of mine once told me that she was terrified of meeting her husband-to-be's mother. She said that at the first meeting she could not do anything right. She spilled the tea and broke the teacup. "It was a mess. She thought I was clumsy . . . she still thinks so. You just feel like an actress or worse, like a slave in a slave market. . . ."

The above pattern is still the rule among more traditional families, but it is being slightly altered among more liberal families where more freedom of choice in marriage partner is given to both men and women. Now we hear more about the need to select one's future wife without interference from the family. In reality, however, this does not happen very frequently.

The conflict between the old pattern and the new attitude is reflected in the letters to the editor of *Hawwa'* and *El Musawwar*. Of 336 letters to the editor in both *Hawwa'* and *El Musawwar* during the last three years, more than 75 percent of the problems centered around the conflict between the desire to marry on the basis of personal choice and the need to please parents by marrying the woman or man the parents prefer.

But the problem goes beyond the need to please the parents. There are other things to take into consideration. In the case of the man, the possible severing of kinship ties (which might carry along with it disinheritance) is a main deterrent. When a young man is financially dependent on his parents, he will, in most instances, choose to comply with their wishes in his choice of a mate. For her part a woman will, in marrying a man of whom her parents' disapprove, risk losing their support should she be mistreated by her husband. This means that she will also lose any kind of insurance or security in case of divorce, a form of insurance that is particularly important where the woman is not gainfully employed and her parents represent her only other means of support. Moreover, a woman who takes the liberty of becoming acquainted with a man before she marries him is subject to the mistrust not only of her parents and friends but also, in many cases, of the man himself.

Today, despite the relative lack of restriction on women with regard to obtaining an education and working, the concept of dating remains foreign and unaccepted. With few exceptions, parents do not permit their daughters to go out with men even under the most innocent circumstances, and men themselves look down upon the woman who does so. It is within this area that the conflict between the old and the new values in the selection of the marriage partner comes into play. One of the letters to Amina El Said illustrates this point quite clearly:

> I am a student in the School of Engineering at Cairo University in my senior year. All my life I thought that if I am ever to marry it would be someone I personally knew and loved and not someone picked for me by my parents. Then I met this girl in the cafeteria and it was love at first sight. I asked her to go out with me and she agreed. I have known her now for more than two months; during that time she let me kiss her. I love her very much but I am torn by a deep feeling of suspicion. If she went out with me, then she must be an easy girl, and who would guarantee that she would not go out with other men after we were married. In fact, how can I be sure she hadn't gone out with men before me? What can I do? I cannot marry a girl without knowing her first, and those who let me know I can't trust.

This theme is also found in most of the letters sent by girls who are always asking what to do if a man they like asks them to go out. A university graduate complained in one of the letters that her chances of marriage have been ruined because of a romantic letter she once wrote to her next-door neighbor. The neighbor had been showing the letter to anyone who might be interested in marrying her, and that by itself sufficed to scare the suitors off.

While women suffer from the slightest hint of a relationship with a man, no matter how innocent this may be, men boast about their premarital escapades with women. This double standard is reinforced by

women's implicit acceptance of it. Even the leaders of the feminist movement tacitly accept it. While Amina El Said is militant in her demands for
the equality of women, she has recognized the old views. In her responses
to women who have asked whether they should go out with a man before
marriage, she has reminded them to beware of what might happen to their
reputations. She has told them to be sure of the man's intentions, that he
is not just passing time with them. Replying to a letter from a Cairo University student who asked her advice about what to do about a classmate
whom she liked and who had asked her to go to the movies with him and
to see him outside the University, Amina El Said wrote:

> Beware of that kind of irresponsible young man who thinks that because
> a woman goes to the University, that she is an easy prey for his irresponsible
> appetite. Be sure of his intensions, and that he would not drop you after
> he has had what he wanted. Tell him that if he likes you enough, there
> is an acceptable way of seeing you. Otherwise, don't waste your time with him.

The importance of these responses lies in the fact that they come from
one of the leaders of the feminist movement in Egypt. They reflect the fact
that despite all the steps the country has taken toward modernity with regard to the role of women, Egypt is still very conservative. These responses
also show that while the advocates of women's rights demand such obvious
reform as legal and political equality, they never go deeper to the roots of
the problems.

Some may find ways of using an unjust law to their advantage, but even
an equitable legal position will not automatically ensure equality in the
status of women or even improve it. Divorce laws are an example. It is
true that it is easier for the man to obtain a divorce than it is for the
woman under the present Egyptian law of personal status and family law.
But it is also true that a woman can obtain a divorce fairly easily. Although
she has to go to court to obtain the divorce, all she really needs is a witness
who will say that her husband has mistreated her in a way that is prohibited by law. This is easy to do. It is commonly known throughout the
judicial system that there are individuals who are willing to provide such
testimony in court whether or not they had known the disputing parties.
The fees for such services range from £.5 to £2 or £3.

But a wife who desires a divorce does not have to use illegal means; in
most cases, the husband can be pressured or bribed to divorce his wife.
There is usually no problem about this if the woman will promise to forfeit her right to the *mu'akhar* and alimony or even offer the husband some
financial or other form of compensation. Yet very few women who are un-
happily married ever resort to divorce. Economic factors are the most important deterrent. These are particularly important in the case of women
who have no financial means of their own and have to rely on their parents.

Such women are usually under considerable pressure from their parents not to ask for a divorce, especially where there are children who would accompany the women to their parents' homes after the divorce.

Even if a woman has an independent source of income, the social stigma suffered by a divorced woman in Egypt is still so strong that she will think twice before she ever resorts to this, no matter how miserable her marriage may be. Many of the letters to Amina El Said from divorced women describe how friends avoid them and how male colleagues in their offices begin to make obvious advances and treat them as potentially easy sexual prey. Many of them also describe their loneliness and the difficulty of finding a second husband. Those available to them are usually a great deal older and less desirable than their first husbands.

Another aspect of the conservative attitude toward the role of women in contemporary Egyptian society is reflected in views of housework. During the last few years, a debate has been going on between those who advocate cooperation between husband and wife in doing domestic work and those who think that women, and only women, should have this responsibility. Some feel strongly that the Egyptian male loses his manhood if his wife works, forcing him to help with housework, cooking, or child care. They argue that the family does not benefit when women work. On the other hand, those who advocate employment for women outside the home insist that men will not be degraded by doing some of the domestic work; after all, they live there too.

The question was opened to public discussion a few years ago, and television polls of men and women in all segments of society were taken. The exact distribution of responses was not announced, but the general findings indicated that the majority of responses were against domestic work for men. The most interesting aspect of the poll was that women as well as men opposed male participation in domestic work. The view of some was that housework is the woman's domain and the one in which she has the upper hand. Should the man participate in this facet of married life, the woman might lose her usefulness to the man and become dispensable. Others argued that the man, to them, implies a certain image involving a set of traditionally defined activities that do not include housework, and that they would not respect a man who washed the dishes or changed the diapers. Still others maintained that men would simply stand in their way and create confusion around the house rather than provide help.

Conclusions

The process of modernization in Egypt calls for a new conception of the role of women, one based on equal participation and equal rewards for men and women. To achieve the necessary reforms, supporters of women's rights have concentrated their attack on the laws of personal status and family relations, seeing them as the main obstacle to equality. By concentrating their efforts on legal reform, however, the feminists have tended to neglect the roots of the problem, which lie not in a set of formal rules but rather in a number of cultural practices and attitudes that stand in the way of total equality. These conservative attitudes are held by both men and women.

Men's conservatism stems from the need to maintain the status quo, which is to their advantage. Women's conservative attitude stems partly from the fear of having to compete in areas for which they have not been culturally trained. The home for the woman is the domain of her authority and the source of her security. Some women view equality (especially if it entails cooperation between husband and wife in domestic activities) as a sacrifice of the woman's only stronghold. It will take more than legislation to change some of these attitudes. It might take a few generations for women to achieve the self-confidence needed to compete in the man's world. But until this happens, any attempt to change the role of women by mere legislation is bound to effect minimal results.

BIBLIOGRAPHY

Amin, Qasim: *Al ma'ah el gadida* [*The New Woman*], Cairo, 1900.

Badran, B. A.: *Ahkam al zawag waltalaq fi el Islam* [*Islamic Rules of Marriage and Divorce*], Cairo, 1965.

El Khatib, A.: *Al ahwal el shakhsis* [*Law of Personal Status*], Cairo, 1964.

El Tahtawi, R.: *Al murshid el amin lil banat wal banin* [*The Honest Guide for Boys and Girls*], Cairo, 1873.

Zeidan, G.: *Tarikh el tamaddun el Islami* [*History of Islamic Civilization*], 6th ed., 1954, parts 1–5.

The Changing
Frenchwoman:
Her Challenged World

BARBARA GALLATIN ANDERSON

For the Frenchwoman, regardless of class, life has always been a battle of the sexes that she will lose. But she will lose by a margin of her own choosing, a narrow but comfortable margin in which in many ways the obscurity of second-best status has proved, in her judgment, advantageous. The Frenchwoman *thinks* from the basis of this "disadvantage," and it has been the major impetus to the evolution of a distinctive pattern of living. She does not think "defeat," since she has never been geared to victory. And her pleasure is not—has never been—in winning, but in the masterful manipulation of the players to the achievement of her own ends, a perhaps greater triumph since it is the more demanding. Like the football player who excels at passing, she exerts all her efforts to make it easy for men to score—to shine in the public eye. The roar of the crowd is for him—for her French husband, father, son, or lover. Visibility, overt confrontation, and obvious pace-setting are liabilities in a world where she has for centuries coped with massive social inequities by deflecting their impact. From bedroom to political arena, she has through the years perfected techniques for unobtrusive but telling influence and sometimes actual control.

A MODEL MATRON—MADAME GAUTIER

My first unwitting tutor on the Frenchwoman was "Madame," who had been hired as our housekeeper and was to rescue us from the devastation of my flagging efforts to cope with daily life in a rural French community. We treated her with no less deference than is due any reigning monarch. And in her no-nonsense approach, Madame very soon had us under control. The mother of ten children, she had developed a quiet efficiency which extended into any encounter.

Our children spent as much time in her home as ours except on days when "Monsieur" was home. It was the time when Monsieur "recharged" himself, and with his presence the maelstrom of daily activities in the home congealed to a level of eerie calm. Then our children stayed in their own home and waited impatiently for the visit of Madame's youngest, Georgette, who at fourteen was already a miniature of her mother and boundlessly talented.

I remember one April afternoon when Georgette did not appear. It had been raining for several days and our housebound little girls were sick with disappointment. They had talked of Georgette's coming all morning long. She had said she would make for their afternoon *goûter, crêpes*— thin little pancakes to be rolled with jam and devoured from the stove with hot mugs of the fragrant French chocolate.

"But she said she would come! She *promised*," they protested late in the afternoon to her mother.

"Ah, yes," said Madame, smiling but without apology, "but we did not think then that Monsieur might have need of her. However, her father is at home this afternoon. He did not have to work after all. No. She will not come today. It is not possible." It was a flat, quiet statement of irritating finality.

The children walked to the window and together we looked at the field where the muddy earth was already sprouting green shoots. The children looked at one another. The words were unspoken but unmistakable. Monsieur Gautier. Always Monsieur Gautier. How different it was to be a French child. How wretched a fate to be born a French *girl*. Georgette had to remain at home for the sole purpose of waiting on her father: to be there if he should have need of something, to run an errand if he should want an errand run. Of course, in so smoothly run a household as Madame's, where all his needs would in any case have been anticipated, there was seldom anything for Georgette to do. But she had to *be* there all the same.

Our daughters suffered vicariously Georgette's distressing vulnerability in a male-oriented household and a male-dominated world. At fourteen she was already well initiated into her subservient place in the hierarchy of French family life.

We were, in a matter of weeks, quite fed up with Monsieur Gautier's tyranny, and ready—in the best tradition of American womanhood—to close ranks and *help* Madame and Georgette. Minimally, we wanted to console them. We had private fantasies of the revolt of the Gautier women, who outnumbered the men in the family two to one.

We never witnessed the feeblest indications of discontent in the ranks. As husband and father, Monsieur Gautier was head of his household. No familial activity excluded a consideration of his preeminence. He was deferred to and respected, a prepossessing figure, imperturbable and confident. No conversation could be launched at the dinner table without his consent, and our children came home with awesome reports of a frayed whip that hung conspicuously close to his armchair. Yet he was loved! That gave us pause. It was a long time before we could put Monsieur into the perspective of French life and, with that, comprehend Madame Gautier's position as wife and mother—and as Frenchwoman.

Monsieur Gautier's attitude toward us was one of benevolent tolerance. We lived in fear that he would take Madame from us. She ran our winter-cold house with amiability and a startling efficiency, breathing a special life into it, producing fabulous meals of omelets, rabbit stew, and the great pot-au-feu of meat and vegetables that simmered through the day on the back of an old stove that would—we were convinced—produce heat for no other mortal. What I blundered through for hours she accomplished almost as a minor diversion, so that we had bright sheets, boiled white in a giant kind of percolator; blankets and bedspreads and rugs beat clean in the sun; cupboards made to shine with mysterious mixtures of oil and lemon. And not the least of her talents was her careful and sustained attention to the deportment of our children who, she made it gently known, lacked some of the basic French graces. Under her supervision they learned to bow and extend their hands in greeting whenever adults entered a room, to keep their clothes on their proper hooks, and not to add to the work of a well-run home by what seemed to her self-indulgent demands. A bath a day—"*Dis donc!*" Any French child can wash from head to toe with a basin of water. Ours learned how and passed the most meticulous inspections. And all of this with kindness and a readiness to take time to hear a recitation of a poem memorized for school, explain the names of herbs in the garden, or give a minute to Kiki, the vicious dog who completes any well-organized French household. Kiki too had things to learn and could go about unmuzzled as long as he limited his bites to those who trespassed our premises.

Monsieur Gautier was far from committed to his wife's working outside the home. It was her first such undertaking, and she had accomplished it by placation and the tactical circumvention that is second nature **for** Frenchwomen. Madame, at forty-four, with twenty-three years of marriage and ten children behind her, was a master of the art and marvelous to behold in action.

"He is not happy about it," she told me. "But he is not eager to bring it to the point where it is an issue between us. We have our little truces though he does not always like to think it."

When I expressed some surprise that he had consented to her working in the first place, she smiled at my naïveté.

"One never poses to a man a question or suggestion to which 'no' is a possible response," she said. And then, after the briefest pause, "Unless, of course, she wants a 'no' answer."

"I never asked Monsieur if I might work. I simply assumed his approval in a way that would make his opposition seem unkind, un-Christian, and absured." She waved her hands in a typically French gesture, meant to soften the implication of words that might otherwise seem too harsh.

"After that first afternoon, do you remember, when I came to your home, I knew I should have to speak to my husband of it that evening. For him to have found out from another source would have been unwise," she said, in one of her usual understatements. "Of course, the children knew, but they do not speak ever about the behavior of adults."

"When the time was right, I gave a great sigh and told him that I had grown weary of the priest's urging and had gone at last to see what needed to be done for the American family."

She gave me a long look.

"I did speak to Father LeBihan," I protested.

"I *know*," she said simply.

And Monsieur Gautier *knew*, it was obvious, what was coming. It was a period of mutual reconnoitering, as I was later to realize, in which French men and women, husbands and wives, assess respective assets and the terrain being called into review.

"I gossiped a little," Madame said, "in a light vein, so he would know I considered the afternoon one of diversion and not of work. I said that the next day I should pick up a cake from the bakery near you where I had seen the first strawberry tart of the season—he adores them. And I told him that I had made it clear that I should not be able to devote more than a few hours a day to getting you settled."

"What was his response?" I asked.

"But you have missed the point entirely, my dear woman," Madame said, lifting her shoulders to her ears and spreading her arms in mock despair. "I never raised a question."

And Monsieur was no more eager than Madame to foster an exchange where an unnecessary and perhaps unenforceable ultimatum would be forthcoming. The price was too high; the jeopardy to a cherished order premature. They would wait and see, both of them. And there would be some extra cash for family expenses.

In the traditional French home there exists an unspoken consensus that familial, communal, and even national stability depends upon the French husband's continuing authority. And by virtue of this consensus the authority persists—*as long as it is not abused.* Where personal interests may place familial integrity in jeopardy, the husband provides a monitoring caution. Even the inevitable must be slowed to a decorous pace. The father arbitrates the outer limits of change, and the mother—with seldom a gesture of defiance—forces the pace, sustaining a hierarchy in which she has a distinguished if not preeminent place. Children essentially await their turn and, in the process, learn the rules.

Monsieur Gautier looked the other way when his older daughters began wearing makeup. He did not like it, but grumbled importantly only if its obviousness forced his acknowledgment. On their way to Paris, in a metro station or cafe, they added yet more mascara and a deft touch of eyeliner. But by the time the family had gathered again for supper, these would have disappeared. Little by little change intensifies within the broad somewhat forced bounds of what is considered good taste. It is the father who sets the limits. The game for the girls is to push the limits without forcing confrontation. Sometimes they succeed, sometimes not. It becomes the game of life for Frenchwomen.

The totally capricious or willful application of power on the part of the father is normally controlled by the potential consolidation of—in the case of the Gautiers—eleven family members in subtle but pervasive displays of retaliation. They can disrupt the harmony of home which Frenchmen prize.

Monsieur Gautier looked archly at Madame's newly acquired fashion magazines, but "he would not forbid me my little diversions." He took a harsh but defensible stand when his oldest daughter married without his approval. But while he would not at first permit her and her husband to join in the holiday festivities of the family, he did not forbid her the continuing privilege of visiting her mother and sisters and brothers— though she must use the good manners to come when he was away.

Monsieur Gautier is his family's symbolic link with the ideals of familism and sexual dichotomy which give French life its special quality and meaning, but his family is not expected—even by him—to be slavish in embracing these ideals in too pure a form. The Madame Gautiers of France see to that, though increasingly the sentiment of many of France's younger women is that the price is too high.

CHANGING LAWS, CUSTOMS, AND ATTITUDES

Madame Gautier was the first of many Frenchwomen we were to come to know well over twelve years of intermittent travel and research in France. Daily living is easier for us now, with the children older, and since we have moved from the village to a city apartment with hot water, a bathtub, and a private flush toilet—luxuries still not available to many of the residents of the working-class neighborhood in Paris' "red belt," where we now live. Yet more and more, high-rise apartment houses are intercepting the peeling facades of ancient flats, and bourgeois housewives look down from their modern balconies to watch the smoke rise from a brick factory, an immense pork-processing house, or a distillery. Paris, like most of France, is undergoing dramatic change.

When I meet Madame Maurice, my neighbor, on the street and inquire, "How are things?" she responds, "Not too bad" (literally translated, "One defends oneself"), then I know that, whatever the terrain, women are as busy as ever with the intricacies of survival, French style.

Today the Frenchwoman is facing an awesome dilemma. Somebody is changing the rules. Shortly after the termination of World War II, in 1946, Frenchwomen finally acquired the right to vote. Through a gradual but massive reappraisal of the ancient civil code, they were, by 1965, permitted to dispose of their own money as they chose, to work, and to open a bank account without their husbands' permission. Moreover, they were freed from inequities of the law that made a wife subject to up to two years of imprisonment (plus the dissolution of their marriage and the loss of their children) for marital infidelity, while her husband could not even be accused of infidelity unless he had moved his mistress into their home and there had sexual intercourse with her—in which case he was subject to a fine. Male supremacy, so long entrenched in French law, has been significantly diluted, both through new legislation and through more relaxed interpretations of existing statutes, so that the French wife now must at least be consulted in decisions seriously affecting the welfare of home and children. France's archaic 1920 anticontraceptive law, assailed in 1956 by the French Movement for Family Planning, was finally reformed in 1968 to permit druggists for the first time to sell contraceptives of all kinds to women over eighteen, though only on medical prescription. (The sale of condoms as a deterrent to the spread of syphilis had always been legal.) Most recently, the paralyzing student and worker revolts of 1968 brought in their aftermath still other concessions affecting the educational and work opportunities of women.

She can win at this game of life, the Frenchwoman is now being told. She has a fighting chance for equality. But she is not sure she wants that. Her few feminist sisters often seem more a threat than all the dominant males and national inequities put together. And it is a source of some consternation (to the majority of Frenchwomen, I think) that the feverish enthusiasm for "freedom for the bondaged sex"—as one subway banner reads—should have taken so practical a turn.

In some areas, reticence and suspicion have resulted in backtracking. Fewer Frenchwomen work today than did in the first quarter of the century (a reduction from 38 to 34.9 percent of the work force). And those who do work are older. Young women continue typically to leave their jobs with marriage and do not resume work—if at all—until after their childbearing years, when their absence presents the least disruption to the home. Eighty percent of today's male university students (France's future husbands and fathers) express a preference for women who will remain at home after marriage. In other words, the old image of an inevitable role dichotomy as the logical basis for male-female interaction is still powerfully and persistently operating in contemporary France—despite much loud shouting and pushing outside the fortress walls.

Where social legislation has provided women with new privileges, these have been almost reluctantly absorbed and rarely fully exploited. Women's hard-gained right to vote has produced no dramatic political change. On the contrary, in the political arena it was followed by a loss of ground. In 1946, at the time of the enfranchisement of women in France, 40 of the 630 national deputies were women. In 1967 only 11 held office, and by 1970 the total was further reduced to 8. In the Senate, the last decade has seen the number of women delegates cut in half. And diminution on the critical level of local politics, notably on communal councils, has been comparable.

There is something suspect about the woman voter, something unfeminine about social initiative in women who wish—now that a benevolent state has provided them with that advantage—to intrude into politics.

On a 1972 woman-on-the-street interview show, only one woman in five said she felt "prepared to vote." Among the problems pleaded were absence of time for reflection, no familiarity with the issues, no personal stance on social problems, a general discomfort, or the explicit conviction that it was basically none of her business. As one woman said: "The woman for the interior; the man for the exterior." Another ventured smilingly that "women's life is lived in little pieces" ("crumbs," literally), and she must depend on "those who can see the issues whole." "It is not her function," she said. The commentator called attention to the repeated evidence of moral brakes formed early in life on involvement in social and political issues, to fear of shocking the established order, and to a concern that they might in some way lose rather than gain advantage. One in three simply responded that she either left that to her husband or that she voted as he instructed her to vote.

The Frenchwoman is as yet uncomfortable with the new promise of equality. She has not rejected it, but seeks first to find substantial substitutes for her home-tested policy of nonevident control. She fears the excesses of well-meaning women more than those of men and society. To risk the traditional rapport between man and woman or to threaten satisfactions (however circumspectly acquired) for promised benefits is basically imprudent. The voluble minority who do not agree with her have in some ways forced her overreaction.

FOUR WOMEN OF FRANCE

But what about the minority who do not think as she does, who reject the inequities of conventional French life and who feel a drive to change things and to map out—for their own lives at least—what they consider a less archaic, uneven, stultifying pattern of life? What of those who want a new basis for love and sex and living?

The challenge to them is great, even in France's burgeoning cities and suburbs, where the push of mass media, of anonymity, and the visible dividends of change can be potent incentives. Perhaps the fairest way is to present, however incompletely, the stances of a range of Frenchwomen, each of whom struck me as being vividly contemporary. Together they blend and mutate, question and refine some major themes. And they are struggling, some of them, with brand new directions in identity.

Michele lives, unmarried, with the father of her three-month-old son. Stephanie works as a secretary while her unemployed husband copes daily with their tiny apartment in a large, soulless high-rise. Jacqueline at fifty is considered "vulgar" even by the indulgent standards of a community geared to looking the other way in social activities that do not concern them. And lastly, Henriette—like Madame of our French village—strenuously defends classic patterns of French family life, carrying forward unsullied and precious the old sexual priorities.

Michele

It was during Michele's pregnancy that she and Philippe found their little flat on the outskirts of Paris. Both had lived in single rooms in Paris. They met when both were involved in the 1968 student uprising at the Sorbonne. Neither wanted marriage. Now, since little Christian's birth, Philippe speaks of it but Michele is reticent.

Well-educated, Michele dreamed only of becoming a physician and eventually took a nursing degree. Her family was poor and her mother, who continues to live in a small Norman town, does factory work still. Four years older than Philippe, Michele has a fragile brunette beauty and her small wardrobe is modern, casual, and very understated.

Under present regulations to safeguard the job security of working women who become pregnant, Michele was entitled to twelve weeks of maternity leave at two-thirds of her normal wages, with free medical aid and a special money grant. By adding earned Christmas vacation and accrued leave, her time at home was made to last almost three and a half months. Thereafter little Christian was placed in a state-owned nursery (crèche) for the infant children of working mothers. Crèche space is scarce and reservations must be made far in advance. "Before conception!" Michele complains facetiously.

The cost varies from 100 to 500 francs ($20 to $100) per month and is low for her since she is single. This will change if Philippe should officially recognize his child. It is Michele who has fought this recognition, since it would permit his custody of the child in the event of separation and requires a trip to the police station (rather than the town hall, as in the case of official marriages) with proof of cohabitation in the form of the corroborative, sworn statements of three local merchants or businessmen.

"Can you see yourself asking the butcher to swear that you sleep with the man whose steaks he sells you?" Michele asks. "How absurd. I could never do that."

She shrugged her shoulders. "It is the government's way of passing a law they don't like by making its advantages in fact either unattainable or humiliating."

Michele's mother, who visited after Christian's birth, is critical of the nonmarriage arrangement by which her daughter and Philippe live. What a joy to have a grandchild! What shame to be able to speak of it only guardedly in the small, gossipy community in which she lives.

A month later Michele spoke furiously of her mother's resolution of "this great problem."

"She told them all that I had gotten married. She says it is necessary if one is to remain there. But I *know*. I *know*. She did not do it to appease the neighbors. That is no reason. She knows it. They must always have something to say. She did it to appease herself. She tells herself and she soon will really believe, that I am married."

Michele will not go along with the fabrication.

"When I go back in summer—*if* I go back, I shall not say I am married if I am not."

Her love for Philippe is real and intense and she takes as scrupulous care of him and their little home as her demanding schedule permits, scrubbing things clean—the floor on all fours since it gets cleaner that way —and with a more serious concern for cooking now that they have a real kitchen.

She had to be assured by the butcher that the hamburger was "*very* fresh!" And her threshold of concern is no lower than that of the most established French housewife. Even supermarkets have special buttons to push so that the butcher can come out and grind beef or lamb to order in full view of his customer.

Before Christian's birth, Philippe had teasingly said he would not change diapers or fix bottles, and Michele had teasingly worried about his ability to do so in any case. But he seemed more nervous than chauvinistic in his reticence, and Michele heaped diplomatic encouragement on his efforts to do things around the house: put on the vegetables, fold a wash, help dry the dishes. Alone with little Christian on the rare Sunday when Michele must work and the crèche is closed, "he manages." Michele hides her apprehension.

"He wants to make concessions, to be less demanding, to tell me that ours can be a different home from the tight little ones we both knew. And he tries," she says. "When you see us together we are casual and easy and there are no lines drawn. But it is not easy for either of us. In his secret heart he holds back. He is not sure how far he can concede and still remain a man."

She laughs. "But it is I who am the most difficult. I am not sure how much I can concede and be a *person* still. You understand? I have worked too hard and too long to be myself. We want to give everything to one another, and in a way we do, but sometimes I feel fiercely apart."

Philippe speaks of their getting married during Easter vacation. "I have not agreed—but this time I have not yet said no."

Michele's small flat, linked by a long alley to the street, has the charm of a Utrillo. From the kitchen window is visible what is never apparent from the street: an intense proliferation of ancient dwellings, butted almost haphazardly one against the other but judiciously divorced by high garden walls. And encircling the fat maze are the giant new apartment houses, which are multiplying constantly. From the highest street one morning I counted eleven cranes on as many construction sites.

Stephanie

Stephanie and Jean-Pierre consider themselves fortunate indeed to have found a large ground-floor studio apartment in one eight-story building, now six years old. With only twenty-eight units, the complex is smaller than most, and they were attracted by the inner patio, where four-year-old Claude can run and play just two steps from his doorway.

Three months pregnant, Stephanie had as magnificent a wedding as her father, a government clerk, could give her. She shakes her head when she points to the elaborate photo album, the gold-trimmed china with a center of rotund cherubs floating over a field of roses, and a large chest of linens including a great hand-crocheted tablecloth she has never used.

"When I think what we could have done with the money. We had sixty guests for the wedding banquet at a time when Jean-Pierre and I didn't have $100 between us."

In a national survey, 72 percent of France's married women under thirty insisted they were virgins when they married, a statistic to which Stephanie lifted her eyebrows, smiled, and puckered her lips in a gesture of disbelief.

"It is true that the French are not nearly so casual about sex as you Americans seem to think. You look at Montmartre or some Bohemian section of Paris and think it is France. Besides you read too much into appearances.

"It is somehow natural for us to be 'sexy.' We learn early to keep reminding men that they are men and we are women—and that is basically what sex is all about, I guess. But the majority do not leap in and out of bed with men who are not 'serious.' We have been taught too long to take care of 'our little treasure.' "

She shook her head. "But even so, 70 percent or more virgins—that is too high. Unless they are really terrified of their parents or all hung up on religion, French girls sleep with the men they love and will probably marry —if they have the chance. There is more sex than there used to be. Parents know. Basically, 'it's normal.' Most are offended only by indiscretion."

Stephanie's mother was conventional in not letting her daughter's growing sexual independence interfere any more than necessary with her own conventional image of a proper courtship and marriage.

"Jean-Pierre and I had been going together since we were fifteen. I would slip away on the pretext I was with some relative or girlfriend.

"We would not have married when we did except for my pregnancy. We are not unhappy about it, but it pushed us into a kind of life we would have delayed longer. I was just seventeen when Claude was born."

Six months after her marriage "my mother talked as though the baby was premature. I don't think it was a question of shame or anything like that. But her mind cannot really *think* except in terms of the way things *should* be."

Like little Claude, 30 percent of France's babies are conceived out of wedlock, a figure that can be reconciled with those on virginity only if one concedes an impressive fertility among the remaining Frenchwomen.

A good stenographer, Stephanie has had little trouble finding work, despite a worsening employment situation that cost her young husband his job with an electrical contracting firm.

"My problem is *keeping* a job," Stephanie told us. And predictably every month to six weeks she would appear at our door, want ads under her arm, to take advantage of a standing offer to use our phone.

"What can you expect?" her husband said, speaking to the world at large, so it would not seem too personalized a censure. "Women are particular. Too particular."

Stephanie disagreed. But she turned to me, not to Jean-Pierre when she said: "No, it is not that, unless it is wrong or 'particular' not to want to ... suffocate. You should spend a day with me in one of those crumbling firms. After three months you are still on ceremonial terms with the janitor."

"She is 'nervous,' " amended Jean-Pierre with some pride, using a word which, in this context, suggested a rather admirable if penalizing sensitivity. Distinctively feminine.

Stephanie went on: "Even in the new offices with the modern furniture and piped music, they are unfair. In one place, a publishing house, I was given the assistant manager's job when he left, but not his title. That way they could give me only two-thirds what he got. The law says now that they must give a woman the same pay for the same job, but there are ways around it."

For almost a month neither was employed. A steady stream of concerned relatives made their way to their door. And then Jean-Pierre found work with an industrial parts company.

A few days later I met Stephanie on the street and asked about her latest job.

"I don't think I'll be working for a while," she said, "though we need the money. As long as we can get by, Jean-Pierre doesn't want me to take a job unless I am happy in it. He would rather have me at home than nervous and upset at work—and to tell you the truth, that does not make me too unhappy."

Jacqueline

Jacqueline's little neighborhood restaurant is a reflection of her own personality: intimate, in some ways studiously correct, but with a kind of jarring earthiness. The six small tables which constitute the entire dining room are especially sought after at lunchtime, and Jacqueline accepts or rejects guests according to the vagaries of her mood and her assessment of her customers.

On one side is the dining room, meticulous with its starched table linens, cut flowers, and service plates at each table; on the other, a worn stand-up bar banked with a curling collection of risqué postcards.

Barelegged in mules with a nondescript sweater and a billowy skirt to cover her ample hips, Jacqueline at fifty has an enormous contempt for peers of her sex.

"Cows, all of them. They lead safe, dull lives in the same dull pastures into which they were born. They have neither the sense nor the spirit even to be good in bed.

"Their husbands come in and play footsies with their secretaries. The women close their eyes, or they moan—but not too loud. It is the way men are, they say.

"Oop-la! They are afraid for their little worlds and their little pocket-books, that's all. Not a one could support herself for a week if she had to."

For the young she has more respect but considerable ambivalence. "They have courage and I am with them in that. They are not afraid to challenge life as a person first and as a woman second."

A thumbs-up gesture to show agreement. "To wait around for the magic of marriage makes it possible for them to begin to function as human beings. Ri-di-cu-lous. Anyway by that time most have forgotten how."

What outrages her, however, is the feminist stance that their struggle for women's rights in France is somehow innovative.

"A lot of us are battle-scarred. We were fighting the good fight when they were still in wet diapers. And *then* there was no sympathy—least of all from other women. I remember my own mother, how she wrung her hands and implored me to go back to my husband when she knew what a hell life was for me with him."

It was 11 A.M., but Jacqueline turned from the bar, pulled a bottle from the shelf, and poured us both an aperitif. She was warming to her indignation. A man stuck his head in the door; "One o'clock? Is there place for two?"

"Filled," said Jacqueline, the bottle still poised in midair. "Nothing left. Nothing. Nothing." And to me, when the door closed: "He scolds about the house wine and will not pay the price of anything better."

We sipped the Martini.

"I was twenty-five with five children. When we were first married he was in the Army and he had planned to make it his career. We didn't really want for very much and life could have been good, except that it was considered normal that I should have a baby every year and, innocent that I was, I didn't know or *think* to do anything about it. The nice girl was a stupid, dutiful girl. Besides, at that time you could buy an elephant easier than a contraceptive. Nothing. Nothing. My husband would not spoil his pleasure by getting anything for himself.

"Then, all of a sudden, he decided to leave the Army and go into business. He invested our savings in a business he bought from someone who was going *into* the Army. A grocery store!"

She clasped her hands together and raised her eyes in mock prayer.

"From eight in the morning until eight at night. A man can't do it alone. And the oldest child seven years old. Sometimes he would just disappear for three or four days and I was not to ask why. I did everything. Finally, to add to our little income, I began to prepare hot dishes to sell over the counter at lunch. People were pleased and came back."

She was silent a moment. Reflective.

"Most marriages reach a kind of truce, but even so lines are drawn beyond which even men cannot go. That is a deep and special knowledge we do not talk about. But *we* know. And *they* know."

Jacqueline fled with the five children, spending her remaining resources ("I was not so absurd as not to have something hidden away") to get the shrewdest lawyer she could afford.

"A divorce was out of the question. At that time I would have cut my own throat. But a legal separation. Ah, that protected my future earnings, and even a French judge would not give the children to so abusive a man."

She smiled. "Now you can get a divorce in three months for $800—if you know how."

"This is my third restaurant. I had one in the Midi, one on the other side of Paris, and when I found this place it was a beat-up hangout for the drunks who wandered down from the flea market. It took me two and a half months of work, night and day, to remodel it. Most of the work I did myself, even the carpentry."

Jacqueline's cook came out of the kitchen. "We need more lemons for the veal." Jacqueline grabbed change from the till. The grocer was next door, a three-minute trip.

"The baby is twenty now. A soldier like his father. I am *Mademoiselle* Jacqueline. And I shall die Mademoiselle Jacqueline. I pick my friends and I pick my clients. From time to time there is someone—perhaps more special." Her voice trailed off.

"I am not averse to good company, good evenings, and I could not endure a world without men. But while I do not play the juvenile, my heart is with the young women of France who are not content to take as long as I did to find out what *real* femininity is all about—so long as they don't insist they invented it."

Henriette

Madame Henriette Beaulieu, on the other hand, looks as though she were born Madame Beaulieu and can never have had a girlhood, though I have seen girls in my daughter's class in the local school who, at twelve, have the same no-nonsense, perpetually middle-aged attitude of competence. The precision of body movements, the purposeful gait, even their smiles seem somehow controlled. They are not unfriendly. They are "ahead of you"—prepared.

My son was in awe of Madame Beaulieu and her house, which he much admired. It was, like most French homes, considerably smaller in scale than American ones.

"You never have to *look* for anything," Scott said. "You reach out a hand and it's there."

The placement of furniture, the precise fit of the shutters, the patch-work of rugs, and the relatively low ceilings gave everything a contained look of inevitable, almost ordained order.

Once, when I asked Madame Beaulieu if she had ever rearranged the furniture, she gave me an almost startled look, and I watched her eyes move about the room, trying to see it differently.

"I can't imagine what it would be," she said. And I could not either.

Her two sons, Paul and Thierry, have "good friend" status with Scott. But he was weeks learning *how* and *when* they were expected to play to-gether. Madame Beaulieu ran her home with a measured cadence to which the entire household reacted with the easy confidence of a ballet troupe who have danced to the same music a thousand times and respond with-out thinking.

In the courtyard was a small workshop, exquisitely outfitted, where the boys oiled Scott's skates so they would not rust, repaired his belt buckle, and even tacked a loose heel back in place. Play was rather grudgingly permitted as something interstitial to fixed hours for homework, meals, rest, chores, limited TV viewing, family excursions, haircuts, movies (every Thursday afternoon), and personal shopping (Saturday afternoon). Ram-bunctious activities were regarded as unacceptable, and the two brothers had an effortless way of playing—and enjoying—anything from tag to rugby without seeming to get dirty or even untuck their shirts.

Henriette Beaulieu knit all their sweaters, which were handsome, and as the seasons changed the boys acquired the appropriate wardrobe changes. Their rooms had everything: small radios, a phonograph, an encyclopedia, Thierry's collection of miniature racing cars, and photographs of summer outings.

Henriette has no women friends in the neighborhood. The person she sees most, outside of her immediate family, is her sister, who lives fifteen minutes away.

Monsieur and Madame Beaulieu have an easy, warm relationship with a clear division of labor: she cooks, keeps house, makes minor purchases without consultation, and has the running responsibility for the proper development of the children. Monsieur Beaulieu, a master electrician, does not unilaterally decide major undertakings but retains veto power. He handles minor household repairs but is otherwise without burdensome obligations at home. Pervading all thought, activity, and planning, how-ever, is the implicit consensus that familial happiness must be built around Monsieur Beaulieu's physical and spiritual contentment. To this end Madame Beaulieu has shaped her own identity.

She refused to generalize about Frenchwomen. "How can one speak for others whose lives one does not know at all? I have no daughters, only sons. Two children. That is enough if you want to do anything for them at all. So I do not much know how other women think or what they want, but from what I read and see on TV, I am not sure they do either.

"We have the vote—and it was about time. But what does it mean? The issue is either important for your family or your business or your neighborhood, so—of course—you cannot decide it alone anyway."

Her voice trailed off with the little sputtering sound and jut of chin which suggest that an alternative view is indefensible.

"Women want more education and better work opportunities. So much the better. But, however you shift things, it is to the women that the babies will be born, and I have never seen the sense in making a tragedy of the obvious."

She stopped, reluctant to be misinterpreted.

"It is true that today in France it is not easy with one income. But this should give *men* incentive. And at night when my husband comes home, I am here and as much a woman as any tired career girl waiting for her husband to help with the dinner."

Conclusions

Sometimes when I spoke with Henriette Beaulieu, marveled at her impeccable house and impeccable children and at her great calm, the image of Madame, our village housekeeper, would float back, and it would seem that twelve years and an exuberant social change had left little mark at all on the women of France.

But that is not the case. The Henriettes and Madames today are fewer. Their worlds are challenged. Their convictions of the natural order of things are less common. There is growing intolerance of restrictive social codes, glorification of sexual inequities, and identity based on marriage and motherhood. More and more the old truces seem less compelling and logical. And there are perhaps better filters through which the average Frenchwoman can today assess her world and herself.

Stephanie struggles for what she is *almost* convinced could be a richer relationship, a freer way of life. But she is like a nervous runner who feels much better with one foot on base. She will not cut off her line of retreat to the old warm refuges. Michele, who was a revolutionary before she was a mother, knows what she wants—fulfillment as a person and as a woman, simultaneously, in a new image of liberty and equality. Free to choose: motherhood but not marriage; a home but not a fortress; love as a mutual confidence pact, not as a legal designation of bondage. But nobody is making it easy for her—not the state, not public opinion, not her mother—and even Philippe, who wants earnestly to be a part of that new equation, sometimes feels an anxious sense of challenge and loss. For Michele, too, emotional commitment to a new image of the self is more elusive than intellectual conviction. Her femininity finds almost joyful expression in some very conventional role dichotomies. Right now, like the majority of France's more liberated young women, she is trying to etch out a new synthesis for living that combines the best of both worlds.

Jacqueline is a kind of historian of the struggle, there to remind the Stephanies and Micheles that their problems are not new. She has her scars to prove it.

"Born woman," says Jacqueline, "that has never been easy. Anywhere. Anytime."

And, hands outstretched heavenward: "Born French to boot! Oop-la! It takes courage."

BIBLIOGRAPHY

Ardagh, John: *The New French Revolution*, Harper & Row, Publishers, Incorporated, New York, 1969.

Chombart de Lauwe, Marie-José, Paul-Henry et al.: *La femme dans la société*, Centre National de la Recherche Scientifique, Paris, 1967.

de Gramont, Sanche: *The French*, G. P. Putnam's Sons, New York, 1969.

Gregoire, Ménie: *Le métier de femme*, Librairie Plon, Paris, 1965.

Michel, Jacques: *Les nouveaux droits de la femme*, Dunod, Paris, 1970.

Sullerot, Évelyne: *La femme dans le monde moderne*, Hachette, Paris, 1970.

Guatemalan Women:
Life under Two Types
of Patriarchy

EILEEN MAYNARD

Introduction

The intent of this article is to explore the status and role of women living
in what are considered to be two strongly patriarchal societies and to discuss the effect of the two types of patriarchy on the women. Two distinct
cultures are represented in the village of Palín, Guatemala: the Ladino
(non-Indian) and the Indian cultures. By contrasting the role of women in
these two societies, we can perhaps learn something about what it means
to live in a patriarchy and how two types of patriarchy may have varying
effects on the women.

Before beginning our basic discussion, let us set the scene. Palín lies
southwest of Guatemala City in a semitropical region. The population of
approximately 4,000 is roughly 64 percent Indian and 36 percent Ladino.
If you should arrive on a weekday morning in Palín, you would see very
few men, as they are either working or at home. The main activity is centered at the market, held under the giant ceiba tree which dominates the
plaza. There you would be able to distinguish two groups of women. Most
of the merchants, sitting on the ground by their produce, are Indian
women. Their typical dress, braided hair wound around the head, and
bare feet would identify them as Indian. The type of dress worn by the

This chapter is based on 1½ years of fieldwork, carried out in 1960–61 under a Smith-
Mundt grant.

Indian women of Palín distinguishes them from all other women in Guatemala. They wear a blue pinstripe skirt, a wide red sash, and a white or colored loose blouse called a *huipil*.

Among the customers, you would see not only Indian women but also a scattering of Ladino women, dressed very much as lower-class or lower-middle-class women in the United States. A Ladino women would be wearing a cheap cotton dress or a skirt and blouse. She might also be wearing a cardigan sweater and perhaps an apron and be carrying a basket to hold her purchases. The dramatic backdrop to this colorful market scene is the majestic volcano called Agua, whose slopes provide valuable agricultural land for the Palinecos.

The Indians are descendants of the Pokomams, who were settled forcibly in Palín by the Spaniards in the seventeenth century. One might say that they are partially acculturated. Although the women have maintained their traditional dress, all but a few of the older men now wear Ladino-type clothing. Central Pokomam remains the primary language, but nearly all the Indians speak Spanish with varying degrees of proficiency. The Indian population depends mainly on agriculture for a livelihood; growing corn and beans for subsistence needs and—with excess land—such crops as coffee and pineapples. Some Indian men work as day laborers and in semiskilled jobs, but nearly all own or rent land. The typical Indian house consists of one or two rooms with walls of wattle and daub and a thatched roof. The kitchen, usually a separate building, is often made of cane walls with a thatched roof.

The Ladinos dominate the political and social life and consider themselves to be superior to the Indians. The social relations between the two groups result in a modified caste system. An Indian may become a Ladino if he so desires by taking on the Ladino culture. The transition from Indian to Ladino, however, is accomplished more rapidly by moving to another area where one's Indian origins are not known.

Most Ladinos are literate or semiliterate and live in adobe houses with tin or tile roofs. The Ladinos are divided into two social classes: the poor people and "the society." "The society" would be comparable to the middle class in Guatemala City. Most of the Ladinos depend directly or indirectly on agriculture to make a living. Some own medium-sized landholdings on which they grow coffee and sugar cane plus subsistence crops. Since manual labor is considered degrading, men of "the society" generally hire Indians or poor Ladinos to work their lands. Other Ladinos operate small businesses or work in the professions or in semiskilled or skilled occupations. A number of Ladinos combine occupations or may own land and have a small business or trade as well.

LADINO WOMEN, THE NOT-SO-SILENT MARTYRS

Attitudes toward Women

"The lowliest man is superior to the woman who is a queen." This phrase succinctly sums up the attitude of Ladino men in regard to women. Belief in the inferiority of women is necessary for the perpetuation of the hyper-masculinity or *machismo* concept. To be *macho,* a man must be able to boast of sexual conquests and of being the father of many children. A wealthy Ladino man proudly told me that his father had sired thirty-three children, all of whom he had managed to educate. Under *machismo,* a woman is a sex object or a mother. One may love a woman, but rarely does one respect her. Deep and lasting love is generally reserved for the mother. Love for one's wife in either a legal or consensual union is often of short duration, waning once the sexual conquest has been completed and the opportunity for a new conquest becomes available. Often a man is more tied to his family of orientation than to his family of procreation. This means that he feels greater responsibility to his parents and siblings than to his wife and children.

Since a woman is an inferior being, she can in good conscience be exploited. And this, in turn, leads to an exaggerated double standard. A decent woman would not take the initiative in sexual relations, even in marriage. Such action on the part of a woman would make her "no better than a whore." A married woman who seeks sexual satisfaction elsewhere can, under the law, be imprisoned for adultery. This law does not apply to adulterous males. Whenever a woman becomes involved in what are considered illicit relations, it is always the fault of the woman—the rationale being that a woman, by nature, is less in need of sexual satisfaction and therefore has more self-control than a man. A woman of "the society" who "takes a wrong step" will lose her social status; that is, she will be ostracized by members of her class. She may, however, recover her position through subsequent good behavior. For example, a woman of Palín who had left her husband for another man regained her social standing after many years of faithfulness to her second husband.

In contrast, a man may outdo the actions of a Don Juan Tenorio without any effect on his status. The fact is that such behavior may indeed enhance his social position. However, occasionally a man's amorous exploits may go beyond accepted limits—and this may affect his reputation but not his status. An instance of this was a Ladino man who after many years of marriage and nine children abandoned his family for a woman of dubious repute. He and the woman remained in the village, and among their various business enterprises was the running of a house of assignation. Because his first wife was highly thought of in Palín and because of the nature of his present life-style, this man is subject to criticism. In asking about his present standing, a man of "the society" said, "He is still of our class, but we no longer treat him with the same confidence as formerly."

Childhood and Adolescence

The birth of a boy calls for much greater rejoicing than the birth of a girl. In fact, the birth of a girl may even be considered somewhat of a tragedy. On visiting a Ladino home where a girl had just been born, I congratulated the grandmother on the new arrival. She looked at me with sad eyes and replied, "I'm sorry that the infant is a girl because the life of the girl is such a hard one." Shortly afterward, the same sentiment was expressed by a young Ladino mother of two sons. We were watching a group of little girls playing in the street. The woman said, "It would be nice to have a girl to dress up in pretty clothes, but I'm glad I have only sons because to be born a girl in this society is to live a difficult life." It is interesting that I never heard a woman say that she preferred having sons because males are superior. The theme of the preference was always "the hard life of the woman."

The infant girl is, however, treated with as much affection and care as the infant boy, and early childhood is a period of relative permissiveness. It is only when she becomes old enough to be useful around the house that the girl is treated differently than her brother. Like her brother she attends school, but after school she has tasks to perform. The Ladino girl must help with the household chores, baby-sit with younger siblings, and run errands. It is only among the wealthier Ladinos, who have servants, that a girl has a great deal of time to play with her peers. The girl also learns at an early age to wait on her brothers and on adult males in the household. The Ladino girl learns responsibility and her position vis-à-vis males early in life.

The boy, on the other hand, is allowed to run in gangs after school and after supper. He rarely has any responsibilities in the household. At home he is pampered and waited on even in the poorer families. It is interesting that the women complain vehemently about the irresponsibility of the men and yet help to perpetuate the system in the socialization of their sons by not teaching them responsibility or respect for women. I know of one woman who tried to alter the pattern. Her husband had left her and she was determined that her sons were not going to grow up to be "like their father." She assigned various chores to the boys such as sweeping out the patio, going after the milk, etc. Her attempts, however, failed because of the pressures of the peer group. It was a case of "Why do I have to do it? None of the other boys do."

At adolescence, the Ladino girl is pretty well trained in household duties and may become an economic asset as well by helping out in the family store or working as a domestic. It is only among "the society" that the girls are sent away to secondary school. From economic necessity, the boys of the poorer families also leave school to work in low-paying occupations or to learn a trade.

Adolescence is, of course, the time for courtship. Girls in the poorer class are generally granted some freedom, but girls of "the society" are watched quite carefully. Ideally they must be chaperoned at social events or during a home visit of a boyfriend. Ladino philosophy holds that a boy and girl cannot be alone for any longer than fifteen minutes without something happening. A young Ladino woman told me of the humiliation she experienced when she went to a movie with a boy and did not come home until shortly after dark. The mother accused the boy of taking advantage of her and dragged the girl off to a midwife for an examination to determine if she was still a virgin. Also, it is assumed that nonrelatives of the opposite sex who live in the same household are likely to have sexual relations. This would apply especially to servants and males of the household and to a girl and her stepfather. One simply does not have a cross-sex friendship between nonrelatives. This is an inconceivable relationship. When a girl pals around with a boy, he is either a relative or a boyfriend.

In spite of the restrictions placed on courtship, a girl will always manage somehow to meet a boyfriend. The ideal courtship pattern is for the boy to visit the girl in her home, where they will be under the surveillance of the family, and for these visits to end in a formal engagement. This often does not occur because in numerous cases the girl's parents do not approve of the boy and forbid her to see him. It is agreed by all that this is a foolish prohibition because the couple will meet in secret and eventually may run away together without the benefit of a legal union.

Marriage and the Family

A poor Ladino girl has few alternatives as regards her future family life. She may marry or enter into a consensual union with a high probability of being abandoned. Upon losing her man she can seek another mate or take the full responsibility of providing for her children. Or the poor Ladino girl who is attractive to men may become the mistress of a wealthy man and so forfeit her reputation.

Often Ladino girls are filled with romantic fantasies and are said to be lightheaded until they settle down with a man. Most girls are thus not very realistic in considering their future, but a few of the more socially aware

are quite cognizant of their prospects; one might say that they are caught between the dream and the reality. This is exemplified in the case of Luisa, an intelligent and vivacious girl from a poor family. Luisa's father abandoned her mother before she was born. Since that time, the mother has had temporary unions with other men, all of whom have left her. Luisa has determined that this will not happen to her. She attended business school and is working as a secretary. With the money she earns, Luisa helps to support her mother and younger sister. Although she shares the romantic notions of other girls her age, she has few illusions about her chances for fulfillment:

> I want to marry someday and have children. Every woman who is really a woman wants children. But I want a good man and this is difficult. I don't want to marry until I am twenty-four because when I marry I will lose my freedom and have to stay in the house. Perhaps my husband will abandon me. In Guatemala, the woman loves too much. That is her trouble. She shows her feelings and is rewarded by losing the man or by bad treatment. What she should do is not to treat him too well and keep him in doubt.

For the Ladino girl of "the society," the future is a shade brighter. She is very likely to marry legally a man in her own class, but this does not guarantee that she will not be abandoned or maltreated. This Ladino woman, however, may have a better education than the poor Ladino woman and so perhaps be better prepared to earn a living for herself and her children should she be deserted. Even if her husband does not abandon her, he is very likely to have extramarital affairs that affect her emotionally and drain family income. Also, the fact that, despite her high aspirations, what she can achieve on her own is limited—she will very likely suffer frustration.

The ideal pattern among the Ladinos is the establishment of a nuclear family through a legal and a church marriage and neolocal residence. This, however, is much more ideal than real. Over half of the Ladino unions in Palín are of the consensual type and extremely unstable. Economic circumstances rarely permit a couple to set up a separate household, especially in the first years of marriage. Even when they are able to do so, other relatives often live with them. A newly married couple may live with either set of parents. It depends on who has the most room and is the most willing to shelter the couple. The type of residence does not affect greatly one's ties with the family of orientation. Both wife and husband retain close relations with their parents and siblings even though they may live outside of Palín.

There are several marriage patterns among the Ladinos. The concept of *machismo* plus limited economic resources may lead to serial monogamy. Since a man desires to make sexual conquests but can rarely afford to support more than one family at a time, he will live for a while legally or consensually with one woman and, after the birth of one or more children, will desert her and establish another nuclear family elsewhere. He may or may not retain contact with his abandoned family or contribute economically. This depends on his character, his economic circumstances, and geographical proximity.

This pattern leaves the woman in a precarious position emotionally and economically. If she is still fairly young and attractive, she may soon be able to replace the man who abandoned her. In the meantime, she usually has to assume the total burden for her children's support. It is not uncommon for a woman, especially from the poor class, to have had children by two or three men. In this case, she may eventually be left with the full or partial responsibility of supporting all her children.

I had two neighbors in this position. Marta is now a woman in her forties who has had children from three consensual unions. At the present time, she has no husband to help support her and has little hope of finding one. Her oldest son and his wife live with her and give her some financial help. Marta also supports an aged mother who lives with her in a tiny two-room house. Marta is not despondent about her situation. She manages to eke out a living by raising pigs and selling cooked food in the plaza and baked goods from door to door. Marta is a generous woman despite her poverty and is always willing to help out those even more unfortunate than herself.

Another neighbor, Maria Teresa, was abandoned by her first husband, by whom she had two children. Being pretty and still young, she found a truck driver who lived with her for a year. After the birth of their first child, he left her for a woman in the nearby city of Escuintla. For several days, much to the cruel amusement of the neighbors, Maria Teresa stood long hours by the side of the highway, hoping to flag down the truck driver and get some money for their child. Maria Teresa has had a hard time subsisting. Lately she has been making tortillas to sell to some of "the society" families.

Another, not so common pattern is for the man who has established several nuclear families to return to his first wife when middle age approaches or "when no other woman wants him." This happened to another of my neighbors, doña Clara. Doña Clara had not sought a replacement for her husband after he left her with four small children. She supported her children by operating a small store for fifteen years. Two years ago, her husband returned, bringing with him a daughter from his last consensual union. Unlike Marta and quite atypical of Palín women, doña Clara appears beaten down by life. She has a haggard countenance and speaks in a plaintive voice.

A third pattern is for the man to have a fling with one or more women and then to marry and settle down to raise a family as a worthy member of "the society." In several cases of this kind in the village, upon marriage the man brought with him a child or children from his former liaisons for his wife to raise.

Another pattern, more common in "the society," is for the man to marry and remain with his legally constituted family for the sake of inheritance and family continuity. He will, however, establish what the people call "a branch office" either in Palín or, preferably, in a nearby town. This, from the man's point of view, is an ideal pattern, but not many can afford it.

Effect of the Patriarchy on the Women

Given the irresponsibility of the men to their families of procreation and the lack of vocational opportunities for women, it is little wonder that the Ladino woman considers the life of the woman to be a hard one. The Ladino woman often loves deeply but finds that she cannot depend on her mate emotionally or economically. Her ideal is to form a stable union and be mainly a housewife and mother, but male character and economic conditions seldom allow her to achieve this ideal. One might say that nearly every Ladino woman is, has been, or will be a career woman, and yet few women are trained for such a role. Even with a working husband, she may have to contribute to the economy of the household because of a low income and high aspirations for her children. Unfortunately, due to lack of training, she often has to accept the more menial and low-paying jobs or run a small business. The Ladino woman, however, is generally highly resourceful and can be hardheaded when it comes to commercial enterprises. Most of the stores of Palín are operated by women.

The resourcefulness of the women becomes apparent when one looks into how they manage to make a living for themselves and their children. Doña Jesus, for example, is a quick-witted and high-spirited woman who has dreams of a better life for her children. She owns and operates a small pharmacy, is the leading midwife, and is also a dressmaker. Doña Francisca supports her children by serving meals to transients and by acting as a midwife. I have rarely seen doña Francisca sit down for longer than two minutes at a time. She finds great satisfaction in her children. Her oldest son is a graduate engineer and her oldest daughter is in nurse's training.

One might hypothesize that the Ladino woman would find solace from knowing that other women also suffer from an irresponsible patriarchy. She might, in fact, become resigned. Such is not the case. Mutual grievances form the basis of "woman talk." At these talk sessions, the women give vent to their feelings about men. The Ladino woman is often high-spirited and not prone to suffer a silent martyrdom. No doubt her volubility in regard to her grievances helps to maintain mental health. Due to the insecurity of the woman's position, however, one finds some signs of psychological disorders. These often take the form of psychophysiologic disorders such as rashes.

Among the mitigating circumstances for the Ladino woman is not only the spiritedness that she is, within limits, allowed to express, but also the security she finds within the extended family system. The ties with her parents, siblings, and other relatives are not greatly weakened by marriage. She has a number of relatives who may help her out in a crisis. Her brothers are often the only men she can count on when male help is needed. I have heard it said that it is a tragedy for a girl not to have brothers. This means she is without defenses and can more easily be taken advantage of by men. A man may maltreat his own wife but be highly indignant if his brother-in-law mistreats his sister and may interfere on her behalf.

The major compensation for the woman is her close, affective relations with her children. It is generally the mother, not the father, whom the children love and depend on for emotional support. Through her children's accomplishments, especially her sons', and their reliance on her, she gains a sense of achievement and fulfillment. This is probably one of the reasons she perpetuates the pattern of male dominance. Through spoiling her sons and flattering their egos, she keeps them emotionally dependent on her. Sons may also be sources of economic aid and, by raising their social status through education and vocational achievement, they may also raise the social status of the mother.

A point which has not been touched on in regard to the woman's position is that she is often the dominant person within the nuclear family. The lack of responsibility of the Ladino man to his family of procreation can easily result in the formation of matri-centered families. By default, the Ladino man weakens his position within the family. A man who appears sporadically or abandons his family cannot exert a great deal of influence on his children. While the man is present, the family may be said to be patriarchal, but even this depends on the relative forcefulness of the personalities involved. In some cases, the situation is that of a token patriarchal family. Thus although the society remains patriarchal, the family, in numerous instances, may actually be matriarchal. In fact, one might argue that the survival of Ladino society depends on the women, since it is often they who have the major responsibility for maintaining the family through the socialization and support of their children.

The patriarchy of Palín has produced resourceful women. It has also produced women gifted in the art of deceit. A spirited, ambitious woman caught in the web of restrictive rules must find some means of achieving her aims. She can do this by charm or deceptive tactics or both. A girl with imagination can always conjure up a vital errand so that she can meet a boyfriend, and the same is true for the married woman who wants to get out of the house to visit friends or for some other reason. The art of deception is a necessary tool of the oppressed.

In summary, the adult Ladino woman is often in a precarious position both emotionally and economically. This has resulted in feelings of martyrdom which are expressed in statements about the hardships of being a woman and the irresponsibility of males. In spite of this, most Ladino women are spirited and cheerful. From expediency, the women have become adept in eking out a living and attaining some of their goals despite restrictions based on male dominance and, in numerous cases, they are the lifeblood and soul of the family.

INDIAN WOMEN, THE ECONOMIC PARTNERS

Attitudes toward Women

As in Ladino society, Indian women live in a patriarchy; but as we shall see, it is quite a different type of patriarchy. There are, however, some similarities between the two societies in regard to the status of women and in the existence of a double standard.

The Indian male is ideally the authority figure within the household. As a male, he is entitled to the respect and obedience of his wife and children. The woman is the early riser, the one who gets up to light the fire and prepare breakfast for the workingmen of the household. She is there to wait on the males when they return from work. The symbols of women's subordination can be clearly seen in the overt behavior patterns. When the men have male visitors, the women fade silently into the background. On the few occasions when a man and wife go out together, the woman does not walk beside the man but a few paces behind him.

The concept of masculinity also includes having sexual exploits and many children. But a prime ingredient of Indian masculinity is that of responsibility to one's family and to one's community. Concomitant with responsibility is the high value placed on hard work. The ideal Indian man is one who works hard to support his wife and children and to serve his community in religious, political, and advisory roles. The Indian man may have extramarital affairs, but ideally not to the point of abandonment or economic neglect of his family of procreation. The male viewpoint is reflected in this statement of an Indian leader: "To take a woman by force is a terrible sin, but if a woman is willing, why not? But to leave my wife for another woman? Never."

On the other hand, a woman is expected to remain a virgin until marriage and then to be faithful to her husband. A breach of the moral code may mean not only a loss of reputation but a loss of her children to their paternal relatives. A "good" woman does not leave the house except for required errands or to visit family members, and she does not talk unnecessarily to men who are not her consanguine relatives.

The Indian woman's social position, however, is not really so much one of inferiority as one of separate status from that of the male. By the very nature of the allocation of duties according to sex, each sex needs the other to survive. The men are the agriculturists, the stockmen, the housebuilders, and the keepers of the tools. The women are the housekeepers, the merchants who sell the excess agricultural produce, and the weavers who bring extra income into the family. One of the most respected patriarchs explained to me his doubts about the superiority of men: "Here they say that a man is worth more than a woman, but I don't know if this is true. A man can carry heavier burdens and can walk longer distances, but a man can't sleep with a man. He needs a woman. And he cannot have children. What do they say in your country?"

Childhood and Adolescence

The birth of a girl is usually a joyous event, especially for the mother. Indian men would prefer to have sons, but most Indian women like to have daughters because they will be companions to them and helpmates in their daily chores. Infants of both sexes are greatly indulged and become the center of family attention. Thus the first years of a girl's life are marked by the immediate gratification of needs and by a physical closeness to the mother. The Indian baby travels with the mother in snug Indian fashion—on the mother's back (*atuto*). At night she sleeps next to her mother. When set down to play, she is watched over by indulgent relatives who play with her and keep her from harm.

At about four years of age, this permissive treatment rather abruptly terminates for both sexes. Upon being able to understand verbal instructions, the child must begin to learn discipline and be weaned from too much maternal solicitude. Physical punishments may now be administered and the child is expected to stay with her peers rather than cling to the mother. Role play with other children now becomes the pattern. Little girls play the mother role by carrying *atuto* a doll or a puppy and grinding corn on a miniature *metate*. Boys and girls play "house" and "store" together.

At around six or seven years, sex differentiation in activities begins. Role playing gives way to real tasks. The girl helps out in simple household chores and runs errands. A very few may go to school, but usually for not more than two or three years. Some of the boys are sent to school long enough to learn to read and write, but the majority begin to accompany their fathers to the fields to learn agricultural tasks. Boys are generally pampered more than girls because "their work in the fields is so hard."

As the girls grow older, they learn more household duties, wait on their male relatives, baby-sit with younger siblings, and accompany their mother or other female kin to help sell produce in the market. Between ten and twelve years of age, the girl learns to weave simple items like napkins. In spite of her household tasks, the girl is allowed some time to play nearby with girls in her neighborhood. Skipping rope and playing jacks are favorite pastimes. The boy continues to help his father or may begin to earn minimal wages by working as a day laborer. When he returns from work, he is free to pal around with his male peers.

By the time of adolescence, both the girls and boys are pretty well prepared for their adult roles. Both are now economic assets. The girls may go with the adult women to sell produce or stay at home to weave and perform household chores. The boys are full-fledged agricultural workers and may be learning a trade as well.

Now is the happiest time for both sexes, the time for courtship. After work, the boys clean up and meet their friends on street corners where they stand around chatting and eyeing the girls. The girls are allowed more free time to gossip and giggle with their girlfriends.

Courtship is an exciting activity and takes an interesting aggression-resistance pattern in Palín. A traditional mode of courtship centers around the *paño,* a square, handwoven, and brightly colored cloth without which no Indian girl would venture into the street. She wears the *paño* over her head or around her shoulders, but very often she merely wears it folded over her arm. When a boy is interested in a girl, he waits until he can catch her walking alone in the street. He grabs one end of the *paño* while the girl hangs on tightly to the other end. What follows is a lively tug-of-war which looks all the world like a genuine fight to the uninformed observer. If the boy's feelings are reciprocated, the girl will allow the boy to hold one end of the *paño* quietly for a short time, and they will stand twirling it. The boy then lets go and the two walk along chatting merrily for awhile. If, however, a girl does not like the boy, she will continue to hang onto the *paño* until he gets the message and lets go. To make her point clearer, she may then throw a stone at him. Today, there are variations on the *paño* pattern, such as grabbing the girl's arm. Other aspects of courtship are the giving of gifts and the use of flattering statements. This is all a game which is greatly enjoyed by both participants and observers.

Once a boy and girl become serious, the parents are informed. They, of course, are no doubt fully aware of what has been going on. If the boy's parents have no objections to the match, they select a go-between, generally a highly respected older man who holds the leadership position of *tutat.* The *tutat* initiates a series of visits to the girl's parents to secure their permission for the marriage. He naturally does not secure permission on the first visit. That would be tantamount to admitting that one's daughter is not worthy of lengthy negotiations. After consent for the marriage is granted, the *tutat* and the boy's parents make a number of visits to the girl's home to make the marriage arrangements. These visits culminate in a formal engagement. Now the boy may visit the girl in her home. He comes bearing gifts to the girl and her parents and is served culinary delights cooked by his fiancé—under the careful tutelage of her mother.

Marriage and the Family

The marriage itself must wait until both families have accrued sufficient goods and money to hold a proper wedding fiesta. Although the groom's family absorbs a disproportionate share of the expenses, the bride's family also has obligations in the exchange of gifts between the families and in contributing food and music to the fiesta. Both a civil and a church marriage are considered necessary, and these ceremonies are followed by three days of celebration which include feasting and dancing to the music of the marimba. For the church wedding, the Indian bride must submit to the agony of having to dress in Ladino-style wedding attire—white dress and veil plus all the required accessories. It is no wonder she looks miserable, especially with her usually unshod feet squeezed into tight pumps.

Quite obviously all Indian couples cannot fulfill the requirements of an ideal marriage. Some will not have the patience to wait for the completion of the complicated premarital arrangements. Others cannot afford a lavish wedding and fiesta, and some will be hindered by parental disapproval. To meet such situations, there is an alternative pattern. It is called "stealing the girl," and it begins when the boy takes the girl to the outskirts of the village, where he has sexual intercourse with her. The boy then takes her to his house, and the girl's parents are quickly informed by a *tutat* of what has happened. Under these circumstances, the parents involved will usually arrange for the couple to be married as soon as possible, but with a simple wedding and fiesta. Sometimes even this cannot be arranged because of poverty or the opposition of one set of parents. Then the couple may wait years to be formally married, but married they will be. It is the Indian way.

This does not mean that consensual unions do not exist or that girls are not "stolen" and then abandoned. Such things do happen, but—by comparison to patterns among the Indians' Ladino neighbors—they happen rarely. The Indians feel that a church wedding is necessary for the institutionalization of a marriage, and they consider the marriage patterns of the Ladinos to be immoral. Since there is less disparity between the ideal and the actual marriage patterns in the Indian culture, the dream and the reality are more likely to coincide for the Indian girl.

The first months of marriage are said to be fraught with tension. The young couple may quarrel, or one or the other may fall ill. This is not ascribed specifically to the stresses involved in adjusting to married life but seems to conform with a general belief that periods following rites of passage are times of danger. However, difficulties connected with the nature of the residence pattern do arise, especially for the bride. Patrilocality is the ideal and the most common pattern, and this means that the woman must live with or near her husband's parents. Generally, the couple is provided with a separate house located within the family compound, but many household and economic activities are carried out cooperatively by those living within the compound.

Now the girl is under the watchful eye of her mother-in-law who, at least officially, is the one who assigns and oversees the household and economic tasks carried out by her daughters-in-law and unmarried daughters. The mother-in-law's role should be one of solicitous guidance and that of the daughter-in-law one of respectful submission. The problem is that the mother-in-law might take on the role of an officious and disparaging watchdog. On the other hand, the girl may resent being bossed and respond by being sullen or impertinent. Obviously, the hostility thus engendered threatens the tranquillity of the extended family household. In actuality, most mothers- and daughters-in-law manage eventually to settle into a pattern of mutual adjustment.

In the few cases of unresolved discord, the wife leaves or the couple moves elsewhere, either to set up a separate household or to live with the wife's parents. The situation of Lipa, a village beauty, and her mother-in-law is a case in point. Lipa simply cannot abide her mother-in-law who, although a proud and upright matron, is inclined to be overbearing. Lipa periodically quarrels with the good lady and then flees in tears to seek refuge with her godmother, who lives down the street. A reconciliation eventually takes place and Lipa returns—at least until the next fracas.

In reality, the move to a new household is not as traumatic for the bride as it may seem. The girl's parents live in the same village and often in the same neighborhood because of the preference for ward endogamy. In consequence, the girl retains the continued support of her family and has frequent contact with her parents and siblings. Also, many of the Indian girls are still adolescents when they marry and are not really prepared for motherhood. The good mother-in-law provides succor and instruction to the girl throughout pregnancy and childbirth. In fact, should the girl die in childbirth, the mother-in-law may be held accountable if it is felt that she did not take proper care of the girl.

Incidentally, not only the midwife, mother, and mother-in-law but also the husband, who is expected to assist, are present at childbirth. He facilitates the birth by holding his parturient wife from behind while she takes a squatting position. It is believed that by being present at the birth of his child, a man will become more aware of his responsibilities as a father. The young Indian mother often treats her firstborn as she would a doll, and she is allowed to thus enjoy her baby because the mother-in-law is there to oversee the care of the child.

Quarrels between wife and husband may arise when one or the other does not fulfill prescribed duties. They may also be touched off by the wife's overly spirited temperament or the husband's abusive behavior. It is culturally acceptable for a man to beat his wife for laziness or unfaithfulness, but maltreatment without sufficient reason may elicit the wrath of relatives. Ideally, if her husband has extramarital affairs but continues to live with her and support her, a woman has no recourse. But the Indian woman is not one to allow her husband to enjoy his amorous exploits, and recriminations result which shatter domestic peace. She is, however, fairly certain that he will not desert her completely. The Indian male is not only socialized to meet his responsibilities but is also emotionally attached to his family and the Indian community. If he transgresses the cultural norms, he is likely to suffer negative social sanctions. He will be pressed to return to the family hearth. Furthermore, since he will prefer to remain in the village, the laws governing child support can be more easily enforced.

The salient aspect of the Indian marriage is that it is strengthened by the couple's economic partnership, by the fact that the husband and wife need one another to provide the necessities of life. Men are the producers of food and women are the merchants who sell excess grains, vegetables, and fruits to bring in cash income. If there are no excess agricultural products, a woman may buy produce to sell. In this situation, she cannot compete with those merchants whose produce is grown by the males in her family. This usually necessitates having to sell outside of Palín, where she can hope to receive a higher price. This, in turn, entails having to pay bus fares, which further reduces her net gain.

The role of merchant involves having to carry heavy loads to the market, riding on second-class buses, and sitting long hours on the ground. Most women, however, enjoy the experience. They are able to see new sights and so broaden their perspective. Their role as merchant allows them to have greater contact with people outside of their cultural milieu than most men do. In Palín, the merchants who sell in the plaza can observe what is going on in the church and town hall and can pick up village gossip from their fellow townswomen. Palín women are not raucous or high-pressure saleswomen. They achieve success through pleasant personalities and being able to establish rapport with their customers. Some of the money earned may be turned over to the husband, but usually a woman keeps what she earns to meet household expenses. In fact, the Indian woman is often the family banker. It is she who holds the purse strings, although the allocation of cash income is a joint decision of man and wife.

The merchant role carries with it the danger of estrangement from

Palín culture and at times threatens the stability of the nuclear family. Occasionally, on her journeys, a woman will become acquainted with a man in a nearby town or in Guatemala City. This may lead her to leave Palín to marry or to form a consensual union with the man. A deterrent to the formation of such a union is to allow the woman to travel outside the village only in the company of relatives. Also, a woman would hesitate to take such a drastic step because it might mean losing the security of family support and having to adapt to an alien culture.

Another way to secure cash is by weaving napkins and such standard items of an Indian woman's dress as *paños,* sashes, and blouses. These are sold mainly to the Indian women of the village who do not weave because they are not adept at the craft or because they do not have the time to weave. Sometimes handwoven garments and napkins are sold to tourists and Ladinos. An Indian family of my acquaintance not only produces woven articles but also buys them from the more skillful weavers of the village, later reselling them to a store in Guatemala City that caters to the tourist trade.

Within the economic sphere, Indian women do have some limited choice of roles. Not all Indian women are gifted weavers or have the temperament for such a sedentary activity. Likewise, not all possess the extrovert qualities required of a successful merchant. In the extended household, such differences are taken into account in the assignment of economic tasks.

Other means of obtaining pin money are by raising chickens and pigs, acting as folk curers, washing clothes, and making tortillas for Ladino families. A few Indian women work as servants in Ladino households, but women of "the society" say that they prefer poor Ladinos as servants because Indians are inclined "to talk back." Ladinos like Indians to be humble (*humildes*), and the Indians of Palín are not noted for being *humildes.* On the other hand, most Indians except those in dire economic straits are reluctant to have their women work in Ladino homes unless they are certain of the "honorableness" of the family. There is also the fear that sustained contact with Ladinos will result in greater Ladinoization, which may mean the lowering of moral standards.

Thus all Indian women are career women, and career women without feelings of being exploited or of guilt because they are neglecting their children. Their economic activities are an accepted part of their role, and they know that their children will be cared for by women of the extended family while they are away.

In spite of being economically active and being assured of economic help from the husband, some Indian women suffer economic hardship. There are cases in which the household lacks land and other economic resources and where the husband is physically incapacitated. This is true in the case of Atafina, whose family owns no land and whose husband has a severe hernia. Being an astute woman, Atafina manages to help support the family by weaving and by curing sick infants for small fees. She also gathers firewood to sell. Her grown son works as a day laborer and earns extra money as a marimba musician. His young wife helps out by buying produce to sell in the market. The combined efforts of the household members just barely provide subsistence, but the spirit and enterprise of Atafina keep the family functioning.

The capability of Indian women is exemplified in María, a widow with small children. Instead of renting out her husband's land, María hired laborers to work it for her. She oversees the work and makes the decisions in regard to the proper utilization of the land. María is admired not only for her capabilities but also for the fact that she has not sought a replacement for her dead husband.

Effect of the Patriarchy on the Women

The Indian woman functions in a patriarchal society that subordinates women to the authority of males. All her life, as girl and woman, she must ideally submit not only to male authority but to female authority as well. When, as a bride, she leaves her parents, she comes under the domination of her husband and mother-in-law. It is often not until middle age that she can exercise authority in her own right, and then only if she becomes the manager of the women of an extended household.

Because of her sex, her freedom is restricted and she is subject to a moral code that grants considerable sexual license to males but says "Thou shalt not" to females. As an example of what can happen to a woman who defies this double standard, there is the case of Antonia. Antonia was married very young to a man she claims she did not want, but the marriage had been arranged by her parents. The man "was abusive" and physically maltreated her. Finally, she left her husband and went to live with José, his cousin. Having been unable to bring her back through the standard mechanisms of Indian culture, her husband had her tried for adultery. Antonia was sent to the women's penitentiary in Guatemala City, where she gave birth to a son. After her release, Antonia returned to José and the two have now lived together for a number of years, but the trauma of her experience has been only slightly eradicated by time.

Part of being born a female in Indian society is that one is subject to restrictions because of the power of female sexuality. This power emanates from the genitalia and is especially potent during menstruation and pregnancy. I learned of this belief quite by accident. One day, while in the Palín market, I was anxious to talk to some Ladino friends who were on the other side of the plaza. In a hurry to reach them, I jumped over some vegetables and fruits being sold by a Cakchiquel Indian woman from a nearby town. My action brought a quick shower of angry verbal abuse. I could not understand what was being said, but it was obvious that I had broken some taboo. I asked my Ladino friends what I had done, but all that they could tell me was that a woman never steps over the produce. It is a part of Indian market etiquette.

I then hurried to the home of an Indian friend and, after several hours of conversation, finally understood the significance of what had happened. A woman who steps over produce transfers some of her femaleness to the produce. If another woman buys some of the "polluted" produce and feeds it to her husband, the husband will lose his masculinity and become weak and lazy. It is even worse if a woman is menstruating or pregnant, because then her femaleness is even stronger than normally. It seems that a loss of femaleness to the produce may also be disastrous to a woman. If she is pregnant, she may miscarry. (It was not clear whether maleness could be transferred in the same way to females.) Because of the potency of their femaleness, women are dangerous to men and to crops. Perhaps the danger to crops is related to the fact that men are the cultivators. The menstruating woman is not segregated, but she is subject to a number of taboos. She should not walk in a cultivated field for fear of lessening the crop yield and should be careful, around the house, not to step over foods that are to be consumed by males. A man who has sexual intercourse with a menstruating woman will develop a fever and become "tame."

The choices open to a woman are highly restricted because of the inflexibility of the female role as defined by Indian culture and by her caste position in the larger society. She has no alternative but to become a wife and her economic roles are confined to those culturally assigned to women. She cannot aspire to such vocations as teacher or nurse. These roles, even if she could acquire a secondary education, are not considered attainable or suitable for Indian women. To achieve such roles would require her to become Ladinoized and thus alienated from Indian culture. It should be pointed out that Indian men are also limited in their vocational choices simply because they are Indian.

Within the Indian society there are no mechanisms by which a woman can raise her social status through individual action. A man, on the other hand, through good character and service to his community, may rise in the politico-religious hierarchy until he reaches the status of *tutat*. As a *tutat*, a position somewhat analogous to that of elder statesman, a man is entitled to deference and heedful respect of his counsel. To achieve this status, a man begins by serving in the religious brotherhoods or *cofradías*, which involves the sponsorship of religious fiestas. Later, he may be appointed or elected to political offices within the community. Since only literate women are eligible to vote in Guatemala, most Indian women are disenfranchised and so show little interest in politics. However, the wife of the *tutat* shares her husband's status and is also treated with respect. In fact, the word *tutat* literally means "mother-father," and in socioreligious activities, a man and his wife play the role as a couple. A man seeking leadership status needs the cooperation of his wife. It is said, for instance, that the wife of a *cofrade* has more responsibilities than her husband and can express her opinions freely at *cofradía* meetings. Clearly then, a man without a capable wife could not hope to achieve the position of *tutat*.

Because they live in a responsible patriarchy, most Indian women are not beset by the emotional and economic insecurity which results from the fear of being abandoned by their husbands. An Indian woman is fairly certain that her union will be duly institutionalized and protected by social sanctions. Her ties with her family of orientation remain strong and she can rely on the support of a wide range of relatives. Should all else fail, she has recourse to the use of sorcery, the very fear of which may keep a husband dutifully performing his expected role. Furthermore, her economic role assures a woman of a position of power within the family. Much of a family's economic status depends on her ability to manage household finances and to bring in needed cash income. One must also consider the strong personalities of Indian women, which make them a force to be reckoned with in the family and in the society. Within their own realm, they are supreme. A man would no more dare to interfere in household or economic activities that are culturally woman's work than a woman would dare to advise her husband on how to grow a better corn crop.

In general, Indian women do not feel exploited by men. This does not mean that they never grumble about their lot. One Indian woman told me with great vehemence that a woman was better off without a husband because "the life of the married woman is one of martyrdom." I must admit, however, that this type of remark is rare. Indian women are a cheerful group who like to tease and joke. Their work—except for the heavy burdens they have to carry—is not particularly debilitating. They usually have time to sit and chat among themselves or with visitors. Unlike Ladino women, they feel that the life of the man is harder than that of a woman because of the nature of his work. Most Indian men work long hours in the fields and their skin shows the ravages of sun and wind. Many also suffer from hernias.

Although restricted in activities, the Indian woman is not restricted from developing a strong personality. Shrewish women are definitely frowned upon, but the spirited woman is much admired as long as her spiritedness does not disrupt family harmony. In front of Ladinos, Indian women are not subservient, but neither are they outgoing. Among themselves, they are highly emotional—laughter and tears both come easily. The very nature of their personalities shows that they are not the victims of an oppressive patriarchy.

In summary, the Indian woman lives in a patriarchy which curtails her freedom of action and demands that she accept a double standard of behavior. Also, the norms of Indian culture and the fact of being Indian in a Ladino-dominated society lead to a rigidity of role activities which limit the range of choices. Yet within the social fabric the Indian woman enjoys a large measure of emotional and economic security, because the patriarchy is a responsible one. Although prevented from achieving higher social status through her own efforts, the woman shares any honors accorded to her husband and can find satisfaction in the knowledge that she was instrumental in his success. Indeed, being the wife of a *tutat* confers on her an aura of dignity and respect. In the home, a woman is supposedly subordinate to her husband, but in actuality she is his equal not only because she is an economic partner but also because of her temperament—a temperament which defies any pressures to be submissive.

THE RESPONSIBLE VERSUS THE IRRESPONSIBLE PATRIARCHY

Indian and Ladino women share much in common. Both live in patriarchies and both combine housewifely duties with economic pursuits. In both groups, there is considerable continuity of role activities in the various stages of life and a measure of security from living in an extended family system. There are, however, some important differences which greatly affect emotional and economic security and opportunities for individual achievement.

For Ladino women, living in a patriarchy has resulted in unsatisfactory relations between the sexes because of the *machismo* concept, which glorifies the exploitation of women. Women and men have varying expectations in regard to sex roles and family life. This results in frustration, emotional upheavals, and feelings of martyrdom on the part of the women. The dreams of the dewy-eyed adolescent girl "in love with love" fade only too soon into the realities of abandonment or infidelity and the necessity of supporting her children. The Ladino patriarchy dooms the woman to disillusionment, compromises her honor, and robs her of satisfying sexual relations.

The patriarchy places the Indian as well as the Ladino woman in a lower societal position, limits her freedom, and subjects her to the frustrations of male infidelity. Since, however, the concept of Indian masculinity includes responsibility to the family of procreation, the Indian woman is much more secure both emotionally and economically. Marriage for the Indian woman means more of a partnership—a partnership marked not so much by a battle of the sexes as by mutual help.

Also important in assessing the role of women is the degree of difference between the ideal and actual patterns. The Indian patriarchy rewards male responsibility through its leadership patterns and provides mechanisms of social control to enforce norms concerned with marital responsibilities. In consequence, there is considerable congruence between ideal and actual patterns. The Indian girl caught up in the excitement of courtship is fairly certain that it will end in the formation of an honorable union. In marriage, her rights are protected by Indian custom, which demands that a man remain tied to his family of procreation to help in the socialization of his children and to provide economic support. The woman who is a conscientious and faithful wife has the right to expect support, good treatment, and copartnership with her husband in his religious offices.

The Ladino girl enjoying the courtship period envisions herself dressed in the traditional bridal gown, standing at the altar. Her ideal is to settle down with her beloved to be cherished and cared for forever. The reality is more often being "married behind the church"—which means that she will form a consensual union, a union which compromises her honor and may end in the desertion of her mate. The rights of women in Ladino society are more chimera than reality because of a lack of means to enforce them.

Among the Ladino women of Palín, expectations of the role of wife include being a housewife and mother, not a career woman as well. However, irresponsibility of the man and high aspirations force 90 percent into combining economic activities with housewifely duties. To be sure, some Ladino women enjoy their economic roles, since these are the means to achievement and the keys to greater freedom of action. But many feel ill-prepared and hence martyred by their economic tasks. Also, if a woman allocates too much of her time and energy to economic pursuits, she may be accused of being too ambitious and of neglecting her family.

The Indian woman suffers from none of these conflicts. Economic tasks are a part of the expected role of women. If she did not engage in them, she would be considered an unworthy wife. The woman who is a merchant, for example, will not be reproached for being away from home. It is expected that her in-laws and older daughters will perform her household tasks and take care of younger children while she is at the market.

So far, it seems that Indian women fare better than their Ladino neighbors. This is so when one considers such factors as security and congruence of ideal and actual roles. However, Ladino women have an advantage with regard to choice of economic roles and opportunities for individual achievement. The rigidity of the female role in Indian culture and the caste position of Indians confine Indian women to limited roles. An Indian woman has little choice in her economic roles—the main ones being merchant and weaver. She cannot aspire through her own endeavors to roles which confer high social status. Only through her husband can she improve her status. For the intelligent and ambitious woman with an ineffectual husband, this can be a source of frustration leading to feelings of envy and failure.

The Ladino woman, on the other hand, may, through intelligence and hard work, raise her social status somewhat—or at least that of her children. She may, by her business acumen, make a success of a commercial enterprise, or, by acquiring some education, become a secretary, teacher, or nurse. Granted that the Ladino woman is also limited in her choice of vocational roles, much more so than the American woman. The patriarchy considers women intrinsically incapable of assuming the higher-status professional and administrative roles and holds that a woman's proper role is to raise children and reinforce male egos. The truth of the matter is that both Indian and Ladino societies deny their women full opportunity to utilize their talents and capabilities. Of course, no patriarchy allows women to function fully as human beings. It is just that some are less oppressive to women than others.

When one looks at women vis-à-vis the family in the two societies, one is less inclined to talk about a patriarchal system. It would be safe to say that most of the Indian and Ladino families are only mythically patriarchal. The woman's position of power within the Ladino family is due to the man's abdication of duties. This not only makes her the actual head but the *élan vital* of the family as well, and this, in turn, keeps the society functioning. Within the Indian society, the source of a woman's power in the family lies in the cultural definition of her role, a definition that recognizes her importance as wife, mother, and economic partner. All these roles are complementary to the man's role.

One cannot dismiss the character of the women in determining their position and power. It is noteworthy that the patriarchy in neither society has produced women prone to submissiveness. High-spirited and resourceful women are in the majority. In Ladino society, to survive the exigencies of life, the woman must develop strength of character or she and her children may perish. In Indian society, the woman's strength of character is derived not only from the struggle to survive but also from a cultural comprehension of the importance of the woman to the welfare of the family. In conclusion, one cannot know the women of Palín without a feeling of great admiration—admiration for their strength and cheerfulness in the face of considerable adversity.

The Women of North and Central India: Goddesses and Wives

DORANNE JACOBSON

Her red sari bespangled with tiny mirrors, a statuesque village woman balances gleaming brass pots brimming with water atop her head as she returns to her whitewashed home from the well. In a suburb of New Delhi, a well-to-do housewife draws water for her bath in a pink bathtub. With only her hands and feet protruding from an all-enveloping black cloak, a Muslim woman rides in a curtained, horse-drawn carriage to a city bus station. A bareheaded young lecturer in English drives her family's car to a college in a large town. Outside a village, a woman carries a head load of gravel in an iron pan for a road construction project as her tiny child sleeps in a cloth hammock hung from a nearby tree. A slight, gray-haired woman brings to order the Parliament of the world's largest democracy. With an emaciated child astride her hip, a gaunt woman in a tattered sari stretches out her hand to beg for coins from a plump civil servant's wife in a busy railway station. Completely covered by a white cloth over her silken sari, a young village bride huddles apprehensively in a corner, awaiting her first encounter with the youthful husband she has never seen. A bare-breasted girl of the Muria tribe walks arm-in-arm with her lover in the moonlight at a country fair. A Christian woman of old Delhi sweeps her small apartment in a crowded tenement. High atop a heavily loaded bullock cart, a

At the rock temples of Ellora, sculptures 1500 years old depict idealized feminine beauty.

nomadic blacksmith woman rides to a new roadside camp. In a small village, a woman prostrates herself before a mud shrine and beseeches Goddess Durga to save the life of her sick child. A Calcutta woman physician hurries to the home of a patient stricken with typhoid. Social workers, road sweepers, college students, field laborers, matriarchs, and quiet brides; these are all women of India.

Ornamented with finery, revered as mother and goddess, concealed behind a veil, or despised as a widow, the Indian woman has long been an object of interest and fascination to Westerners and to her own countrymen. The subject of countless works of art and literature through the ages, from the ancient epics and the cave paintings and voluptuous statuary of Ajanta and Ellora to the cinema, novels, and greeting cards of today, the

Indian woman has been depicted as graceful and loving, a gentle creature in need of protection and guidance, yet hard-working and strong enough to withstand with dignity cruel blows dealt her by fate.

Those who have attempted to know the women of India have never been successful in finding a stereotype, because there is no single Indian woman. In fact, the diversity of women in India defies imagination. Geographic, occupational, economic, religious, and caste differences are vast.

Each region is unique in many respects—verdant Bengal, the hot Gangetic plain, the mountainous Kashmiri and Himalayan areas, the productive Punjab, desert Rajasthan, fertile and forested Central India, and the humid rice lands and airy uplands of South India. Within each region the crowded urban centers and busy market towns contrast with the rural villages, where four-fifths of India's population lives. The cities are peopled with clerks, merchants, laborers, officials, factory workers, teachers, and other workers engaged in thousands of different tasks. The villages are inhabited mostly by farmers and craftsmen and people who perform services for them. In the cities, elegance and wealth, squalor and poverty are found in close proximity. Even in the villages, a few landlords drive cars while many villagers are too poor to own bullock carts. Hindus, Muslims, Sikhs, Parsis, Christians, Jains, and Jews all bargain in the bazaars and markets, but in most parts of the country the majority of the people are Hindus.

Almost all of India's nearly 575 million people are born into and marry within one of thousands of caste and castelike groups. Each such group is ritually ranked in relation to other groups, and most castes are traditionally associated with an occupation, from high-ranking Brahmans (priestly castes) and middle-ranking farmer and artisan groups, such as potters, barbers, and carpenters, to "untouchable" latrine cleaners, washermen, and butchers. The greatest number of castes are found among the Hindus, but even Muslims and Christians recognize caste differences among themselves. Additionally, there are many groups, usually referred to as tribes, whose members often live in forest areas and are considered to be somewhat outside the caste system. Even a small village of a few hundred people may count among its citizens representatives of a score of different castes, several economic groups, and two or three religious groups.

An essay such as this can barely touch upon the great variety of lifestyles to be found among the women of even half of India—those of the regions lying north of the Narbada River, which almost bisects the country. Broadly, these areas are known as North and Central India and are characterized by a general similarity of environment and culture, the basic patterns of which are overlaid with diversities large and small. This paper does not discuss the women of South India, who have much in common with women of the North but whose lifeways differ significantly in some respects. The women of India's many and diverse tribes are only mentioned.

Although urban women are also discussed, this chapter focuses on the rural women of North and Central India, women who are often depicted in idyllic scenes by India's modern artists wearing colorful traditional clothing, peacefully grinding wheat in hand mills or carrying pots of water. Mostly illiterate and unable to write about themselves, village women, who constitute 80 percent of India's female population, are often slighted in treatises and official writings that purport to analyze "the status of women" in India. Three important threads wind throug the lives of these women: separation of the sexes, concern with hierarchy, and restraint.

As an anthropologist, I lived and did research in a small village in the Central Indian state of Madhya Pradesh, and many of the women I discuss are those I met in Nīmkherā village and adjacent areas near the city of Bhopal. I also draw upon other studies of rural and urban Indian women carried out in recent years by other researchers.[1]

NORTH AND CENTRAL INDIA

North and Central India include many different kinds of terrain, from mountains in the north to desert in the far west and lush greenery in the east. But most of North India is occupied by the great plain of India's most sacred river, the Ganges. Upon this densely populated, open, flat land lie wheat fields thickly dotted by clusters of windowless, mud-walled houses. Much of Central India consists of the black-soiled Malwa Plateau, a rich wheatland bordered by forested hills sheltering deer, antelope, tigers, leopards, and wild boar. Here mud-plastered stone houses roofed with handmade tiles are grouped a few miles apart, separarted by fields and forest. Throughout most of India north of the Narbada, wheat is the staple crop, and herds of humped cattle are omnipresent. Rice, lentils, and millet are other important food crops. Water buffaloes, valued almost everywhere as milk producers, are used in some areas as draft animals.

Most of these parts of India have a monsoon climate, with three distinct seasons. From late March through June the land is parched by hot winds and soaring temperatures. Fields lie dry and empty of all but stubble, while the people busy themselves with weddings and visits to kinsmen. In cities, offices are often empty as their occupants take long tea breaks and vacations. In late June the skies darken and the desiccated land is rejuvenated by torrents of rain pouring down unceasingly for days at a time. Greenery appears everywhere, and children wear fragrant blossoms in their hair. Bullocks pull plows through the sodden wheat fields, and rice plots are sown by hand. At night, villages reverberate with sounds of exuberant singing.

Days gradually become drier and cooler throughout the green season until November, when the rain stops and the nights are clear and cold. The wheat has been sown and grows tall, even as rice is harvested. Many religious festivals and holidays are observed during the cool months, and villagers and city dwellers alike make pilgrimages to the holy sites of Hinduism. Suddenly it is March again, and the wheat is harvested just as the days become unbearably hot.

Even city dwellers are attuned to the agricultural cycle, the timeliness and sufficiency of the rains, and the abundance of the harvest, for any aberration in the cycle means food shortages for all but the most prosperous. The phases of the moon are closely watched by both urban and country dwellers, since calendrical religious activities are timed in accordance with the lunar phases. Thus virtually all Indians are constantly aware of the physical world and cosmos around them.

In North and Central India, ancient civilizations were born. Kingdoms rose and fell, and invaders from the northwest—Aryans, Greeks, Persians, and Afghans—added their biological and cultural heritages to the Indian melange. Hindu emperors were superseded by Muslim sultans, and graceful Muslim monuments like the Taj Mahal challenged the architectural preeminence of the intricately wrought, carved Hindu caves and temples like Ellora and Khajuraho.

Today, although most of the inhabitants of the northern half of India speak varieties of Hindi, more than a dozen other languages and dialects—almost all classed within the far-reaching Indo-European language family—are also spoken.

APPEARANCE AND DRESS

Physically, most North and Central Indians are taller and fairer than most South Indians, but the range of physical types is great, even within a single village or a single caste. Skin tones range from light olive to dark brown, and hair varies from dark brown to jet black. Most women are slender and small-boned.

Generally, fairness of skin and a slight plumpness are considered essential to beauty. A girl who has been ill may be told, "Oh, you poor thing. You've become very black and skinny." Movie stars are typically rather fleshy, with skin the color of wheat paste.

Most Indian women wear saris, garments consisting of several yards of cloth that may be draped about the body in different ways. Urban women usually wear the sari draped into an ankle-length skirt and then pulled across the bosom and over the left shoulder. Under the sari are worn a tight-fitting open-midriff blouse and a long petticoat. City saris are made of colorful printed cottons and silks, almost always immaculately clean and neatly ironed (village women tend to be less fastidious). Muslim women wear a head scarf, long gathered pants, and a tunic. This costume, freshly starched, is also a favorite of high school and college students. In cheaper cottons and synthetics, it is worn by many Muslim village women as well.

In the cities, much of the jewelry women wear is of gold, including dangly earrings, bangles, necklaces, and tiny nose ornaments worn through a small hole in the nostril. Essential to the costume of the nubile girl and married woman are colorful glass bangles that cover the wrists and a cosmetic mark on the forehead—for Hindus a dot of vermilion or a gilt spangle and for Muslims a small black line. Married Hindu women also put vermilion in the part of the hair. Virtually all city women have long dark hair, oiled and braided into one or two long plaits or wound into a bun. Unlike villagers, most urban women keep their hair uncovered.

Throughout North and Central India, city women dress very much alike, with only a few regional differences in the manner of draping the sari. It is among the Hindu villagers that regional variations in styles of dress are pronounced. In the Delhi area, village women wear a head scarf and a long-tailed shirt over a full skirt. Punjabi Hindus and Muslims don tunics and pantaloons, and in Rajasthan, tie-dyed saris are worn over colorful cutwork blouses and full, hand-printed skirts. There, clothes and lacquer jewelry may be studded with tiny mirrors, and some women bind their hair into a conelike shape atop the head. Arms, ankles, and heads are bedecked with heavy silver and ivory jewelry.

In Madhya Pradesh, villagers wear long, full skirts, puffed-sleeved blouses, and colorful cotton saris. Their jingling silver and gold jewelry includes a head peak, earrings in upper ear and lobe, nose plug, necklaces, three or four heavy bracelets and half a dozen glass bangles on each wrist, rings, thick chain belt, and clunky ankle and toe ornaments. Here, an undecorated wrist or ankle is considered naked. Hair is arranged in several small braids and pulled back into a large one, tightly bound with string.

Eastward and closer to the Ganges, in eastern Uttar Pradesh and Bihar, village women wear drabber costumes—little jewelry, often no blouse or petticoat, and a thin-bordered white or maroon sari pulled around the body and over the head to cover a single plait of hair. Bengali villagers wear blue-bordered white and colored saris without much jewelry, although festival days are enlivened by the appearance of young women in brilliant colors. The tribal women of Bengal, Bihar, and Madhya Pradesh seldom wear blouses with their mostly white, knee-length minisaris and heavy jewelry. Nomadic blacksmith and gypsy women are conspicuous in multicolored mirror-work clothing and ivory bangles from wrist to shoulder. Village women usually go barefoot, but in public almost all city women wear sandals.

For all Indian women, clothing and decoration of the body are very important. The soft draping of fabric—sari or long head scarf—about the

A group of Lambadi women wear mirror studded clothing. Originally from Rajasthan, these former gypsies now live in Poona where they work as day laborers.

face and shoulders and the frequent manipulation of the cloth are the essence of femininity. To feel pretty, the woman must also have long, braided hair, musical and glittering jewelry, and eyes outlined with lampblack. Hands and feet are objects of great aesthetic concern and are often decorated with intricate designs in scarlet paint or russet-colored henna. Tattoos ornament the limbs of many village women. Much of the artistry of India is devoted to personal adornment of the feminine figure. Hindu goddesses are depicted wearing not the drab drapery of the Virgin Mary but gold-bordered red saris, dazzling jewelry, and luscious garlands of flowers.

For the Indian woman, sumptuous personal decoration symbolizes material and social well-being. Jewelry is an important form of wealth and is usually a woman's most important material asset. In most parts of India, it is only the destitute woman who displays no jewelry and the unfortunate widow who breaks her bangles, shaves her head, and wears only white.

In contrast to their womenfolk, Indian men often look quite drab. City streets teem with men in pure white shirts and pants, their oiled black hair glistening in the sun. Villagers and a few city men wear white caps or turbans, but only in the desert areas of western India is it usual to see yellow and red turbans and intricately embroidered flared shirts. Most village men wear a long piece of white cloth wound around and between the legs and heavy leather shoes or sandals. The contrast between men and women's dress is sometimes striking. Among well-to-do Sikhs, it is customary for a bride to wear fine silks and jewelry for thirty days after her wedding. One evening on the streets of Bhopal, I met a recently married Sikh friend Harlal Singh, who introduced me to his new bride. Mrs. Singh wore an elegant purple brocaded sari and heavy earrings and necklace studded with small pearls and rubies. Her arms were encased in dozens of pure gold bangles. Harlal wore a pair of grey cotton trousers and a brown plaid sport shirt.

GROWING UP IN NORTH
AND CENTRAL INDIA

Rambai, a middle-aged Hindu woman of the high-ranking Bagheli Thakur caste, first came as a girl of fifteen to live with her young husband and his family in Nimkhera, a village of about 550 people in Central India. The joint family household of which she became a part consisted of her huband's parents, his two older brothers, their wives and children, and her husband's younger sister and brother, all sharing a home and the produce of the family fields. Their house, of whitewashed mud-plastered stone, was roofed with country tiles and decorated with well-worn wooden carvings of horses' heads set into the door frame. Like the house in which she had grown up in a not too distant village, her new home was furnished with large, built-in grain bins, rope-strung cots, metal trunks, quilts, and a variety of shining brass water pots, cooking utensils, and earthenware storage jugs.

In most of North and Central India, a bride usually leaves the village of her birth to reside with her husband and his family in another village. After her marriage, she is considered a member of her husband's kin group, a lineage including patrilineally related males, their wives, and their unmarried daughters.

When Rambai first realized she was pregnant, she was about eighteen, and she was delighted at the prospect of having a baby. Some of the neighbor women had begun to whisper that it was taking Rambai a long time to conceive, but at last her own baby was to be born! Rambai hoped it would be a boy; after all, it was best to have a boy first. She wanted to have several children, including girls, but it was important to have a boy. Rambai's mother-in-law, Hirabai, suspected the girl might be pregnant when she continued to cook every night for three months straight. When a woman menstruates, she does not cook or enter the kitchen or touch others, since she is considered ritually unclean for five days. But Rambai had failed to ask anyone to take over her cooking tasks for three months, and finally the older woman asked her, "Is something there?"

Shyly dropping her eyes, Rambai mumbled, "Who knows?" Suddenly engulfed in a warm glow, Hirabai admonished, "Then don't go anywhere, and don't drink too much tea." Rambai knew that her mother-in-law was advising her to keep away from places where evil spirits might lurk to harm her or her baby and to refrain from eating foods said to be inherently "hot"—such as tea, meat, eggs, and onions—because they would cause too much heat to build up in the womb. Rambai knew that during her pregnancy she would be regarded as a very special and auspicious person.

Rambai's husband Tej Singh also began to suspect something when his wife did not sleep apart from him for three months. And one day his older sister-in-law laughed and said, "You should keep away from your precious one, you know! But I suppose you won't be able to do that!" Rambai had been too shy to tell him and he too shy to ask.

It was not too long before her mother-in-law had hinted to the neighbors of Rambai's condition, and Rambai noticed that visitors to the house smiled at her and sat at a little distance from her. She knew they did not want to be accused of unwittingly carrying a spirit or ghost into contact with her, since, after all, no one knew if the baby would be born properly and live. One visitor, old Mograwali, told Rambai and her mother-in-law about her own unfortunate experience with a woman possessed by a ghost.

> Once, not long after I had a baby, I went to the well to get water. A strange woman was there at the well. She came rushing up to me and put her wet hands flat against my chest. I was young then and didn't know what she was doing, and I didn't think anything of it. But when I got home, I began to have a burning sensation in my chest, and my milk dried up. My baby got very weak and died. I found out later that woman was possessed by a ghost, and the ghost made her do that to me so it could attack me and my baby.

"Yes, bride, you see me now with only three daughters, but sitting before you is the mother of twelve children." Mograwali's eyes filled with tears as she remembered her nine dead babies. She held up her hand, fingers outstretched. "Five, five were boys."

Rambai knew it was a special tragedy of Mograwali's life that she had been deprived of sons. Fortunately, her husband was still alive, but if he died, who would support the old woman? Her daughters were married and living in other villages with their husbands and their families, and Mograwali was too old to work. Perhaps she would be able to visit her daughters for long visits, but after all, she would not want to be considered a beggar, dependent upon her daughters. Maybe that was why Mograwali was such a miser; perhaps she was saving money for her possible widowhood. How much luckier her own mother-in-law was. With sons and daughters-in-law in her house, her mother-in-law would never be without someone to look after her.

For the next several months, Rambai refrained from strenuous work. There were others in her large household who fetched water and cleaned the cow dung out of the cow sheds. But as the youngest daughter-in-law, Rambai continued doing most of the cooking, squatting beside the small earthen oven to prepare rotis—flat, tortillalike wheat cakes—and to stir pots of vegetables and lentil sauce in the dark kitchen, over a fire of cow dung and wood. She was glad she did not have to work in the fields, the way poor pregnant women do, or to continue with all the household work, as do women who have no sisters-in-law to help them.

Rambai went for a visit to her parents' village, where she rested and enjoyed herself for about a month. She would have loved to stay there with her mother and her dear family members to have her baby, but it was forbidden. A girl's first baby had to be born in its father's house, or something terrible would happen. So, as the imminence of her motherhood became obvious, Rambai returned to her husband's home. (In some other parts of India, a baby is born in its mother's parents' home.)[2]

One evening a few weeks later Rambai felt labor pains. She did not know what to do, how to tell her mother-in-law; it was so embarrassing. Sitting quietly next to her husband's little sister, she felt afraid. "Lalta, go ask your mother if I could have a little nim tea, I have a stomachache." The leaves of the nim[3] tree are good for soothing many pains. Soon her mother-in-law was beside Rambai, feeling her stomach and then whispering to Rambai's brother-in-law to go and call the midwife. The time had come.

Rambai lay on an old sari on the earthen floor of a tiny room used by five or six generations of parturient women before her. With her were her mother-in-law and the midwife, a member of an untouchable caste who was allowed in the house only to assist in childbirth. As the pains grew worse, Rambai felt like screaming, and she moaned loudly. "Sssh, bride. What will the men think? They can all hear you," her mother-in-law admonished. Rambai thought of her father-in-law and his overnight guests sleeping just a few feet away on the other side of the wall and grit her teeth silently. The midwife urged her to squat. "If you lie down, the baby will never come out." With every contraction, the woman pressed hard on Rambai's belly, trying to force the baby down and out.

Finally, at dawn, when Rambai thought she could stand it no longer, it was all over. "Eh. It's a little girl," the midwife announced. Rambai's heart sank. A girl. Was it worth all the pain? Her mother-in-law was consoling. "Never mind, all babies are made by God. You'll have a boy next time." After the afterbirth had been delivered and the cord cut with a sickle, the midwife wrapped the baby in a bit of old cloth. Rambai took her squalling infant in her arms. She was beautiful.

There were a number of rituals to be taken care of. Lalta was asked to fetch a flat basket of wheat, a bit of salt, a few red chilis, and a betel-nut cutter. The baby was laid in the basket alongside these items. "This will make sure she's clever," Hirabai murmured. The baby was given a sponge bath and rubbed with a ball of dough, "to make sure she isn't hairy." The placenta and umbilical cord were buried in a small hole under the cot that was now brought in for Rambai to lie on, and a smoldering chunk of cow dung was placed atop the filled-in hole. No one said so, but Rambai knew this was done to prevent spirits or evil persons from harming the baby through magic performed on the discarded matter so intimately associated with her. Rambai's husband's young brother was called and informed of the birth. Through him the menfolk would learn the news and note the time, necessary for drawing up a horoscope. The Potter woman was sent for and soon appeared with a special earthenware water pot dabbed with cow dung. In this pot Hirabai prepared a special brew of medicinal herbs, a strength-giving tea for the new mother to drink during the coming days of recovery. The midwife was paid a rupee and a few pounds of wheat; she would have received more if the baby had been a boy.

That evening, as Rambai and her baby lay on the cot in the birth room with the door shut, a score of women and girls gathered in the courtyard to celebrate the birth. The pleasant strains of childbirth songs lulled the new mother to sleep.

> The new mother has appeared with a tiny baby in her arms,
> She is standing in the courtyard.
> Her mother-in-law has come, prepared the herb tea,
> And is asking for a gift.
> Instead of giving, the new mother says,
> "My husband has gone with the key. . ."
> Sister-in-law has come, bringing a sweet,
> And is asking for a gift. . . .
>
> Listen, oh my Raja, your mother is sleeping upstairs, go call her to help me.
> Listen, oh mother, your daughter-in-law's waist is tiny, come share her pain.
> Listen, son, hearing the words of that woman pierces my heart.
> Listen, mother, she's an outsider, do this not for her but for me. . . .

For three days Rambai and her baby were in a state of ritual pollution and no one came too close to them. Her mother-in-law asked the Brahman next door to determine the most auspicious moment for the new mother to begin suckling her child and came to the door of the room to let her know. No one except the closest family members were allowed to see the the baby, whose forehead and the bottom of one foot were dabbed with spots of lampblack to protect her from the evil eye. When the Barber woman came to give Rambai her cleansing bath and massage after three days, Rambai casually draped a bit of cloth over the baby so she could not be seen. After the bath, mother and baby moved into the main room of the house.

For the next week Rambai did nothing but rest and tend to her baby daughter, whom she called simply Munni ("little girl"), a common nickname. The baby was later named Radhabai, but everyone continued to call her Munni.

Then a special blessing ceremony, the *Chauk,* was held. At dusk, dressed in her finest clothing and jewelry and draped with a white coverall sari, Rambai was made to sit with her baby in her lap on a tiny wooden platform over a pile of grain and a design drawn in flour, inside the house. Munni's father's sister blessed the mother and child by waving a small lighted oil lamp around them seven times and dabbing them with a bit of turmeric paste. With wet, bejeweled hands, Rambai touched the water pots as if to imbue the sources of the household's food and water with her own fertility. The Barber woman, who directed Rambai in the ceremony, told her to throw some small bits of fried pastry toward the sun. "If you want another baby soon, don't throw them very far." Rambai barely moved the pastry bits; maybe she would soon have a son. Next, she worshiped a design her sister-in-law had made of cow dung on the wall near the front door and went into the house. Her mother-in-law paid the Barber woman some coins and grain. Later, after supper, a large group of women assembled to sing more childbirth songs. Again, Rambai and her baby remained unseen throughout the evening, although they could hear the songs. Hirabai distributed large chunks of brown sugar to the women to celebrate the successful completion of ten days of life by her son's first child.

Forty days after Munni's birth, the last vestiges of ritual birth pollution were removed in a special bath, and Rambai again began cooking and sitting with other members of the family, her tiny baby on her lap.

About a month later, Rambai's father and brother came to visit her and her baby. They brought with them a special collection of gifts traditionally given to a daughter's first baby—a colorfully painted cot, a pair of silver ankle ornaments, a patchwork cap, and a bright little dress. They also brought new clothing for Rambai and all the adult members of her husband's family. When they went home, they took Rambai and Munni with them for a long visit.

A young Thakur woman takes pride in her daughter.

Four months later, when Rambai and the baby returned, Munni's head was ceremonially shaved and her birth hair offered to the gods to ask them to protect her.

Little Munni was a treasured child, beloved of her parents and her grandparents on both sides. She spent her childhood amid the large joint family all living under one roof, and she and her mother visited for long weeks with her mother's family. Her mother's brother and his wife were as dear to her as those in whose house she was born. Like other children, she was reared to perceive herself as a member of a circle of kinsmen rather than as a unique individual.

Munni helped her mother with household tasks and caring for her little brothers and sister, who were born before she was ten. As a child she was never particularly aware of any special treatment being given to her brothers; in fact, it was she who often felt superior. Whenever Munni visited her maternal grandparents, her grandmother always touched her feet and gave her a few pennies for her very own. "Little girls are like goddesses; it's good to touch their feet," she heard people say. Boys never had their feet touched. And when she was six, she was one of nine little girls selected to take part in the annual village worship of Matabai, the Mother Goddess who protects the village. She felt very honored as she and the other girls sat on the festival platform where all the important men of the village were helping the Brahmans in the worship service. In front of several hundred people, the village headman and two Brahman men touched the girls' feet, draped their shoulders with new saris, and served them a fine dinner, which they ate on the spot. She was a *kanyā*, a pure little girl.

Had Munni been born in another time or place, she might not have been so fortunate. Among the warrior-caste Rajputs and Thakurs of Rajasthan and parts of the Ganges area, female infanticide was often practiced until about fifty years ago, and even today girls are not treated as well as boys in many places. In Senapur, a village near Varanasi (formerly called Banaras), on the Gangetic plain, women do not sing to welcome a baby girl, although the arrival of a boy is celebrated with drumming and singing. In fact, the birth of a girl may be cause for dejection and recrimination. Upon the arrival of her son's first child, a village Brahman woman of Kashmir exclaimed, "Natha, my firstborn, did not deserve a daughter. My daughter-in-law is unlucky and has brought bad luck into the family" (Madan, 1965, p. 78).

In northern India, male offspring are valued not only because of the economic security they represent to their parents but also because they assure the continuation of the family line. Further, in much of North India, a girl is a considerable liability, since her parents must sponsor a costly wedding for her, provide her with a large dowry, and, after every visit to them, send her to her husband's home with a trunkload of gifts for her in-laws. In the Gangetic area, a Thakur girl must be wed to a boy of a family of higher status than her own, and this often presents problems to the girl's parents. Mildred Luschinsky, who lived in Senapur village and has written about its women, overheard a high-caste woman say to her baby granddaughter as she held her up in the air, "Now she should die. I tell her she should die. She is growing bigger and soon there will be the problem of finding a husband for her. . . . It's a great worry." Still, she treated the baby with love and affection (Luschinsky, 1962, p. 82). In Khalapur, a large village north of Delhi, girls are similarly considered a financial liability to their parents. Although they are loved, girls do not receive the medical care boys do, and twice as many girls as boys die before reaching maturity (Minturn and Hitchcock, 1966, p. 97). In Central India, where Munni was born, a girl is much less of an expense to her parents and her husband is usually from a family whose status is similar to that of her own family.

In most parts of North and Central India, there are fewer females than males. In Uttar Pradesh, the state in which Khalapur is located, there are 909 females per 1,000 males. In Madhya Pradesh State, where Nimkhera is situated, there are 953, in Rajasthan 908, and in West Bengal 878 females to 1,000 males. These figures probably reflect the fact that in some rural areas, better medical care is made available to males not only in infancy but also in adulthood. Women are prey to all the contagious diseases that afflict men and suffer the additional hazards of pregnancy and childbirth (usually at home, at the hands of midwives who are uneducated and unfamiliar with the germ theory of disease). They are also in frequent proximity to dangerous cooking fires which all too often set clothing ablaze. Most villages have no medical facilities, and travel to towns and cities—even to see a doctor—is generally disapproved for women. In any case, villagers often distrust urban medical facilities and prefer to try their own remedies. Rambai's mother-in-law is proud of the fact that not once in her life has she ever seen a doctor.

In cities, although boys are still highly desired, the birth of a girl is not considered a disgrace or a calamity; a few modern, Westernized families seem not to prefer boys over girls.

Yet even in Khalapur, where baby girls were sometimes killed in the last century, some mothers admit to actually liking their daughters better than their sons. Throughout much of North and Central India, girls are viewed sentimentally, treasured as creatures who stay with their parents but a short time and then are sent away to live with their husband's families. Mother and daughter are often very close, since they spend most of their waking hours together, and the mother sees in her child a diminutive of herself, a girl now happy in the security of her home but destined to be exiled among strangers after her marriage.

As soon as she is able, perhaps at the age of six, a girl is encouraged to help care for her younger siblings. Little girls playing together often carry babies with them on their hips. In a village, dolls are scarce, but there are babies in abundance. Whenever a baby cries, his big sister carries it to its mother to be nursed. Thus, from a very young age, a girl is trained to care for babies, and she considers child care an essential and important part of her life. Adolescent girls seem to love being with babies and seek opportunities to carry them about.

Small girls enjoy imitating their mothers in daily work. They practice balancing water pots on their heads, try to push the heavy grinding stone in its circular path, and crouch beside the stove while dinner is being prepared. Seldom overtly praised, children learn primarily through observation and participation rather than direct instruction. Although some North Indian mothers consider their daughters to be guests in their homes and expect little work of them, in Senapur a mother may admonish her daughter to learn household tasks well, lest she embarrass her family when she goes to live with her husband.

In most parts of India, free schooling is available to all. Many village boys attend classes, but relatively few village girls do so. "What's the sense of teaching a girl to read and write? A woman's work is cooking and grinding" is a commonly expressed sentiment, reflected in the all-India rural literacy rate of 29 percent for males and 8.5 percent for females. Further, some villagers believe that an educated woman will be cursed by bad fortune—barrenness, widowhood, or, at the very least, dissatisfaction with traditional family life. Indeed, if eduction is to prepare a child for its role as an adult, it does seem logical to keep a girl at home beside the hearth where she can learn the skills she will use throughout her married life as a farmer's or artisan's wife. It is men who must be literate to deal sensibly with district officials, tax collectors, accountants, and moneylenders. Nevertheless, in some areas, an increasing number of village girls are being educated.

A higher percentage of city girls are in school. In urban India, literacy rates are 57 percent for males and 34 percent for females. Wearing shiny braids and neat white frocks, bright-eyed girls pore over their books at public and private schools. Like their country cousins, there girls too are preparing themselves for marriage, not to farmers but to clerks, bank tellers, merchants, government officials, and industrialists. A very few, perhaps unknowingly, are laying the groundwork for future careers as teachers, social workers, or doctors. After school, a girl is expected to go straight home, where she helps her mother in the kitchen or with younger siblings. Although she may have servants, the educated city girl is also expected to know the domestic arts when she marries.

Like her friends, Munni gradually learned the complex rules of purity and pollution pertaining to castes and foods. Before she was five, she was taught to avoid playing with or touching children of the "unclean" castes —Tanners, Washermen, Sweepers, and even Weavers. She learned that water and cooked foods become polluted by the touch of a lower-caste person, although sugar and raw foods do not. At women's gatherings, which she attended with her grandmother, she saw women of different castes sit in separate groups to receive helpings of boiled wheat from a high-ranking hostess, then hurry home before the food could be polluted. Whenever Munni came in from the village lanes where she might have come in contact with something impure, her mother sprinkled her with water before allowing her into the kitchen, which always had to be kept ritually pure. She learned that a person of her caste was allowed to eat small portions of mutton on occasion but would be terribly defiled by consuming beef, pork, fish, or even chicken. Sweepers, she learned, sometimes ate pork, which she considered most disgusting.[4]

As a little girl in Nimkhera, Munni spent most of her time with her mother, but her uncle sometimes carried her about on his shoulders. When he sat in groups with other men of the village, Munni—still a mere toddler —sat in his lap and listened to the conversation. She jumped around and was treated nicely by all the men as long as she did not urinate on their sitting platform. But by the time she was five, she began to feel funny sitting with the men. She had already realized that girls and boys should not play together very much and that older girls and women never sat with men. In fact, some men and women never talked to each other at all, and many women veiled their faces whenever men came near. When her cousin's new bride came to live in the joint family, Munni observed that she hardly ever unveiled her face. Gradually, Munni learned the rules governing inter-action between men and women in her village.

Hindu girls and women who have been born in the village—that is, daughters of the village—never veil their faces in the village. They talk to all residents of the village, whom they consider their uncles, aunts, cousins, brothers, and sisters in accordance with the ties of fictive kinship that bind those who dwell in the same village. They are free to attend all women's social gatherings and festival observances in the village, fetch water from the well, and work in the fields if called upon to do so.

In contrast, a girl or woman married into the village is considered a daughter-in-law (bahū) of the village, and she cannot move about and in-teract with the same freedom. As a young bride, she must veil her face and refrain from talking to almost everyone in her husband's home, most espe-cially her father-in-law, her husband's older brothers, and all older men of the village. Whenever an older family member or villager enters the court-yard, he gives a warning cough and the bahu immediately pulls her sari down over her face. Only by accident or under rare circumstances does a man see the face of his son's or younger brother's bride. Motibai, an elderly high-caste woman, remembers such an event which occurred when she was very young. She tells the story proudly and with humor:

> Once on Jhanda Torna [a raucous holiday] I drank a lot of hemp drink. I wasn't in my senses; neither was my father-in-law; he was in the same condition. I went into the kitchen to cook, and I sat there with my head uncovered. I was plopping the rotis here and there, not even getting them on the fire. My father-in-law came in and saw me sitting like that. He said, "How are you cooking?" and then I realized and I covered up. He went and told my mother-in-law and said, "What a fine bahu we have; she's so fair!"

A young bahu should be circumspect in talking to her mother-in-law and not address older women of the village unless spoken to. In the presence of others, she should veil her face from her husband and refrain from talking or handing anything to him. (Munni rarely heard her parents exchange

Young Hindu wives keep their faces veiled when they go out to visit
the fields at dusk.

even a few words.) Further, she should not leave the house or go out in the
village without the permission of her husband's mother. She should not expect to attend village social functions unless there is a specific need for her
presence, such as at a ritual honoring the Mother Goddess (who blesses and
helps brides bear children) or a family wedding or other ceremony in
which she plays a role. However, a young woman who lives alone with her
husband and children or a woman of a poor family often finds it necessary
to go out to fetch water and do farm work. On the occasions when she does
leave the house, a young wife should keep her face covered and peer out
through the cloth. As she grows older, restrictions on her activities diminish.
Not until a woman is very mature and becomes the senior woman in her
household, however, is she free to visit neighbors, attend social functions,
and work outside according to her own wishes.

This veiling and seclusion of wives is called purdah. Muslims also observe purdah, but in a different way. Adolescent Muslim girls begin to veil
themselves and stay at home even before marriage. Once a girl reaches
puberty, she should wear a coverall garment called a *burkā* whenever she

A Muslim woman wearing a *burka* in public.

leaves her house. No matter how hot it is outside, a woman in a *burka* keeps her face covered and looks out only through tiny eyeholes in the veil. Unlike Hindus, Muslim women do not veil specifically from their husband's elder relatives and residents of their conjugal villages but from all strange men, men who are not their close blood relatives or close in-laws. Muslim girls are often too shy to have long conversations with their elder male in-laws, but they tend not to veil from them, as Hindus do. In villages, poor Muslims work in the fields without *burkas,* but in towns and cities, even the poor often wear the ghostlike garments. In general, it is considered un-seemly for a Muslim woman to go out unless she has specific work to do or is going to visit a relative. Both Hindus and Muslims consider shopping in the bazaar man's work.

In conservative circles adhering to the rules of purdah is a mark of high status and prestige. In conservative Bhopal, most Muslim students at a girls' college go unveiled inside the college compound but don *burkas* at the gate. One Pathan Muslim girl, studying to be a doctor, gave up the *burka* but was protectively escorted to and from college each day by a servant boy. In other cities, however, few highly educated Hindus or Muslims veil themselves today, and even in some villages, purdah has been relaxed over the past few decades. In Senapur, Mildred Luschinsky knew a young Thakur woman who refused to observe purdah at all, and her conduct was tolerated by the villagers, many of whom were lax in their own veiling behavior (Luschinsky, 1962, pp. 343–344).

Men and women are segregated under most conditions throughout much of North and Central India, but the segregation is especially pronounced in the Gangetic plain area. In many North Indian villages, there are separate houses for men and women, with husbands quietly visiting their wives at night in the women's quarters. In Khalapur, the narrow village lanes are used by men and village daughters, while wives travel from house to house via the flat rooftops of the women's houses (Minturn and Hitchcock, 1966, p. 23). In Central India there are no separate houses, but men gather on open-air porches and platforms while women remain inside courtyards. North and Central Indian village men often visit nearby towns and cities, but women rarely do so. When women travel on trains, they frequently ride in the separate women's compartments.

Rambai emphasized to her daughter that it was becoming more important for her to be modest in her demeanor and her dress. Her sari should be carefully wrapped and her skirt held in such a way that no one could see up her dress. This was important now that she was growing up, although when she was a child no one took notice of her bare bottom. She was told to keep away from boys and stay close to home unless she was sent on a specific errand, or her reputation would be in jeopardy. "Just look at that Sweeper girl, she roams here and there all day. Who knows what she does!" Rambai admonished.

During early adolescence, village and city girls alike learn that they must now segregate themselves from boys except those who are close relatives and that they must act like young ladies. Any village girls who are in school are usually taken out before puberty. One city girl from a well-educated, prominent family told me that when she reached the age of twelve her father informed her she could no longer swim in their club pool, even if she wore long slacks and a tunic for swimming as some girls did. "You're too big for that sort of thing now," her father said, and his decision was final.

In her autobiography, Ishvani, a member of a wealthy Bombay Khoja Muslim family, resentfully described the restrictions placed upon her behavior:

> Then we passed the Chappatti seashore. . . . [T]he promenade was thick with people taking the evening air. . . . The public consisted chiefly of men;

however there was a good sprinkling of Parsi and Hindu women in carriages;
they did not adhere to the purdah system so strictly as the Muslims. . . .
When I was a little girl my father used to bring me here on Sundays and
allow me to fly the biggest kite I could find. The sands were full of small
girls and boys, screaming with laughter . . . and the sky was dotted with
kites that looked like some gigantic birds of paradise. My greatest joy was
to get into a fight and bring down the biggest and highest kite belonging
to the other fellow, according to the rules of the game. It was a lot of fun.
Now at the age of fourteen such things were not to be thought of—I was
much too old. Even stopping the car for a few minutes on the promenade,
or taking a walk, was absolutely forbidden. There were thousands of girls like
me. Our faces were not covered with veils, but we were denied the most
important liberties. Visiting a relative in one's own car was permitted but
a hired taxi or vehicle would have given our parents heart failure. We were
escorted to weddings or religious ceremonies under a gimlet-like surveillance
[Ishvani, 1947, pp. 90–91].

As part of their training in feminine modesty, city girls learn to walk
gracefully, keeping their arms close to the body, not swinging like a boy's
(Cormack, 1953, p. 37).

Munni had heard older girls whispering about *"mahinā,"* something
that happened to a woman every month. She had an idea what it was, but
still she was not prepared for its happening to her. One day she found a
spot on her clothes. She knew it was something embarrassing and tried to
hide it, but her cousin's wife noticed it and took her aside. *Bhābhī* explained to Munni what *mahina* was and told her how to deal with it. She
told her to use cotton batting or even fine ash wrapped in bits of old saris
and other rags for padding and to dispose of the pads very carefully. "Put
them under a stone or a thick bush when you go out to eliminate. That
way no one can get ahold of them and do magic on them, and they won't
cause trouble to anyone else." *Bhabhi* told Munni a trick to ensure that
her period every month would be a short one. "Secretly put three dots of
blood on the cowshed wall, then draw a line through one of the dots. That
way your period will only be 2½ days long." *Bhabhi* also told Munni
never to touch a man or even a woman during her period. She should sit
apart from others and not go to religious or social events, because a menstruating woman is considered "dirty" until she takes a full bath five days
after the start of her period. After her bath, she can again enter the
kitchen, draw water, and resume normal interaction with others. Muslim
women do not follow all these restrictions, but they refrain from praying
or touching the holy Koran.

Munni never discussed menstruation with her mother, and no men of
the family learned of the event. But Munni's *bhabhi* quietly told Rambai,
"Your little girl has begun to bathe."

MARRIAGE

When she was young, Munni and her friends sometimes played "wedding." A small child posed as the bride and was draped in a white sari. Laughing children carried the "bride" to meet her "groom," a baby brother being cared for by one of the girls. But as Munni and her friends approached puberty, playing wedding was no longer fun. Their own weddings were not too far off, and the game became embarrassing.

It was very embarrassing to be married. First of all, even if a girl should want to be married, it would be shameless for her to admit it; her parents must arrange her marriage. Only a very brazen girl would ever ask questions about what it was like to have a husband. And a wife must never say her husband's name. Even to mention the name of his village is embarrassing. Sometimes girlhood friends whispered to each other about their husbands, but to discuss marriage with an older person would be shameless. Munni had heard older girls talking about sex, but she could never ask anyone about it. It is most embarrassing when a girl's husband comes to visit in her parents' village, where she does not veil her face. She must veil in front of her husband, but she should not cover her face in front of her parents. The only thing to do is run and hide. Munni knew a girl should never talk to her husband in front of anyone; it would be mortifying. Still, marriage would be very exciting, and Munni anticipated it with a mixture of eagerness and dread.

Unknown to Munni, her parents had already begun making inquiries about her marriage several years before she reached puberty, and they had hoped to have the wedding before the girl "began bathing." A generation ago, parents who had an unmarried pubescent girl in the house would have been severely criticized, but today villagers are more tolerant of marriages after puberty. Still, the average age of marriage for village girls in the Bhopal area is about eleven, and brides of seven or eight are not unknown in Central India. In 1955 the Government of India enacted a law providing legal penalties for those responsible for the marriage of a girl younger than fifteen or a boy younger than eighteen, but this law is widely ignored. Most villagers are ignorant of its existence, and since village marriages are not registered with any government authority, "child marriage" occurs with great regularity throughout the northern half of India. In Senapur village, near Varanasi, high-caste weddings usually unite couples older than the legal age, but low-caste children often marry before twelve. Despite early marriage, most village marriages are not consummated until after a second ceremony, the *gaunā*, which usually occurs after the bride has reached puberty or is fifteen or sixteen. City brides are usually older than seventeen, and college girls typically marry after graduation. In general, the age of marriage is rising throughout India.

Munni, like most Indian girls, considered marriage to be something that would happen to her without her having to do anything to make it happen. She never for a moment worried about the possibility of becoming an old maid—even the ugliest and most deformed girls were always married, even if not to the most desirable husbands. One old woman in Nimkhera, Lungibai, had been stricken with a crippling paralysis when she was about nine. Though she could only creep about in a crouching position, she was wed to an older man blind in one eye. Now widowed, she is the mother of four grown children and still runs her own household. Only once did Munni hear of an unmarried girl past fifteen—an idiot girl in a distant village. Somehow, every girl's parents found her a husband.

Munni would have been startled to learn that, in cities not too far from her village, there are scores of spinsters. Among the educated urban classes, there are nurses, teachers, social workers, and other women who for a variety of reasons have never wed. These women must walk a difficult path, for unmarried women attract attention even in cities. Forbidden by ultra-Victorian mores still in vogue in urban India to date men or to receive gentlemen callers who are not close relatives, the career woman must constantly guard her reputation and check her desires for pleasure. The network of communication in India is so efficient that a minor transgression would bring immediate disgrace to a woman and her family. In some coed colleges, teachers are quick to note a budding romance and report it to the girl's parents.

In rural India, too, chastity for the single girl and fidelity for the wife are considered ideal, but quietly committed sins are far from uncommon. In fact, old Mograwali sometimes whispered to Rambai's mother-in-law that they were about the only women in the village who were unsullied. This was an exaggeration, but it was true that barely a dozen of Nimkhera's 160 postpubescent females had never been the subject of innuendo or gossip. In fact, any grown girl or woman seen alone with an unrelated male is likely to be quietly criticized, but a public scandal rarely results unless a woman is extremely promiscuous or an illicit pregnancy occurs. In some areas, a woman is likened to an earthen pot which, once polluted, can never be cleansed, and a man is compared to a metal pot which is easily purified with water. Thus a promiscuous girl may find her reputation irreparably damaged, while an errant boy is forgiven. In North India, if a girl who goes to her husband pregnant is rejected by his family, she may even be killed by her own shamed father (Freed, 1971). High-ranking Muslims insist that a bride be a virgin, and the marital bed sheet may be inspected by the husband's female kin. Birjis Jahan, a Pathan Muslim, told me that a sullied bride would be returned to her family in disgrace, but she had never heard of such an incident. Hindus need pass no such test, and a village bride suspected of being nonvirgin is almost always accepted by her husband.

An unarranged "love marriage" is considered by most Indians to be a

Latif Khan and Birjis Jahan sit on their veranda, openly showing affection for each other.

daring and perhaps ill-fated alternative to an ordinary arranged marriage. Many urban youths who have studied and dated abroad return home to wed mates selected for them by their parents. Even a tribal girl who has lovers before marriage usually expects to marry a boy chosen by her parents (Elwin, 1968, p. 200). Intercaste marriages (seldom arranged) occur now with increasing frequency, particularly in cities, but they are still disapproved by the vast majority of Indians. Only in the most Westernized circles, among less than 1 percent of the population, do young couples date and freely choose their own mates.

In Nimkhera, one Pathan Muslim couple told me proudly of their arranged "love marriage." Muslims are often encouraged to marry cousins (although North and Central Indian Hindus forbid it), and young cousins who are potential mates normally know each other well. Seventeen-year-old Latif Khan and his sixteen-year-old cousin Birjis Jahan had a crush on each other and were secretly heartbroken when Birjis Jahan's parents engaged her to an older man. "Birjis Jahan's mother offered me some of the sweets Birjis's fiance had sent to her," Latif Khan remembered, "but I couldn't take any. I said I was sick and left quickly. I felt terrible." Each hesitantly confessed their true feelings to a relative, and their parents had a conference. Soon Latif and Birjis Jahan were happily wed, and even now, as the parents of twelve children, they say their love for each other is the most important thing in their lives.

By contrast, virtually all village Hindus are married to someone they have never met before or have perhaps only glimpsed. Although a Hindu girl should marry within her own caste, her groom cannot be someone to whom she is known to be related by blood. Most Hindus belong to a named patrilineal clan (*gotra*); a girl cannot be matched with a youth of her own or her mother's clan.[5] In some areas, members of other clans are also ineligible, as are members of lineages from which men of her own kin group have taken brides. From Rajasthan to Bihar, over much of northern India, a girl should not marry a boy of her own village. In the Delhi area, a boy of a neighboring village or even one in which the girl's own clan or another clan of her village is well represented must be avoided (Lewis, 1965, pp. 160–161). In Central India, although village exogamy is preferred, some marriages unite unrelated village "brothers" and "sisters."

Hindu men ask about available mates for their children among their in-laws and relatives in other villages, and they discuss the virtures of each candidate with their womenfolk. Munni's father and uncles spoke with many relatives and caste fellows and heard of several prospects. One youth seemed acceptable on all counts, but then Rambai learned from a cousin that his mother had been widowed before she married the boy's father. Although widow remarriage is acceptable among members of Munni's caste, children of remarried widows are considered to have a very slightly tainted ancestry. Munni's parents looked further and finally decided that the best candidate was a seventeen-year-old youth named Amar Singh, from Khetpur, a village 20 miles away. He was the eldest son of a well-to-do farmer hitherto unrelated to their family. Munni's father's brother was able to visit Khetpur on the pretext of talking to someone there about buying a bullock, and he made inquiries and even saw the youth. Amar Singh had no obvious disabilities, had attended school through the fifth grade, and his family had a good reputation. Thus, after all in the family agreed, they asked the Nimkhera barber to visit Khetpur and gently hint at a proposal to Amar Singh's family. His relatives sent their barber to similarly glimpse Munni as she carried water from the well and to learn what he could about her and her family. Before too long, the fathers of the two youngsters met and agreed that their children would be married. A Brahman examined the horoscopes and saw no obstacle to the match. Each man gave the other five rupees as a gift for his child. Later, larger gifts were exchanged in a formal engagement ceremony.

In Bengal, a prospective bride may have to pass a rigorous inspection by her prospective father-in-law. At one such public examination, a village girl was tested in knowledge of reading, writing, sewing and knitting, manner of laughing, and appearance of her teeth, hair, and legs from ankle to knee.

> Rishikumar . . . asked the girl to drop the skirt and walk a bit.
> The bride began to walk slowly.
> "Quick! More quick!" and silently the girl obeyed the order.
> "Now you see there is a brass jar underneath that pumpkin creeper in the yard. Go and fetch that pot on your waist, and then come here and sit down on your seat."
> The girl did as she was directed. As she was coming with the pot on her waist, Rishikumar watched her gait with a fixed gaze to find out whether the [toes] and soles of the feet were having their full press on the earth. Because, if it is not so, the girl does not possess good signs and therefore would be rejected.

The man read her palm, quizzed her on her knowledge of worship, demanded her horoscope, and asked that she prepare and serve tea. Even after he had found her acceptable and a dowry had been agreed upon, her bridegroom, eager to be modern, insisted upon seeing her—and could thus himself be seen by the girl and her people (Basu, 1962, pp. 97–102).

In cities, prospective marriage partners may exchange photographs and the youth and his parents may be invited to tea, which the girl quietly serves to the guests. Each group assesses the other's candidate quickly under these awkward circumstances. Frequently, a girl is rejected for having too dark a complexion, since fair skin is a highly prized virtue in both village and town.

For city dwellers, matrimonial advertisements in newspapers often provide leads to eligible spouses. These advertisements typically stress beauty and education in a prospective bride and education and earning capacity in a groom. Regional and caste affiliations are usually mentioned.

> REQUIRED FOR OUR DAUGHTER suitable match. She is highly educated, fair, lovely, intelligent, conversant with social graces, home management, belongs to respected Punjabi family of established social standing. Boy should be tall, well educated, definitely above average, around thirty years of age or below, established in own business or managerial cadre. Contact Box 44946 The Times of India.

> MATRIMONIAL CORRESPONDENCE INVITED from young, beautiful, educated, cultured, smart Gujarati girls for good looking, fair complexioned, graduate bachelor, well settled, Gujarati Vaishnav Vanik youth of 27 years, earning monthly Rs. 3000/-. Girl main consideration [i.e., large dowry not important]. Advertisement for wider choice only. Please apply Box 45380 The Times of India.

Sikh and Hindu college girls in Bhopal sing in celebration of a classmate's wedding to a man she met through a matrimonial advertisement.

Discussions of dowry are important in marriage negotiations in conservative Hindu circles in many parts of North India. The parents of a highly educated boy may demand a large dowry, while a well-educated girl's parents may not have to offer as large a dowry as the parents of a relatively unschooled girl. In Central India, dowries are not important, although expensive gifts are presented to a groom. In a few groups, the groom's family pays a bride price to the girl's kinsmen. Almost all weddings involve expensive feasts, and the number of guests to be fed is sometimes negotiated.

As her wedding approached, Munni heard her relatives discussing the preparations. She pretended not to hear but was secretly excited and frightened. No one spoke directly to her of the wedding, but nothing was deliberately kept from her.

For Munni as for other villagers, her wedding was the most important event in her life. For days she was the center of attention, although her own role was merely to accept passively what happened to her. She was rubbed with purifying turmeric, dressed in fine clothes, and taken in procession to worship the Mother Goddess. Her relatives came from far and near, and the house was full of laughter and good food. Then excited messengers

A Brahman bride is closely veiled as she receives gifts from her groom's kinsmen.

brought news of the arrival of her groom's all-male entourage from Khet-pur, and fireworks heralding their advent lit the night sky. Munni was covered with a white sari, so that only her hands and feet protruded, and amid a wild din of drumming, singing, and the blaring of a brass band, she was taken out to throw a handful of dust at her groom.

The next day was a rush of events, the most exciting of which was the ceremony in which she was presented with an array of silver jewelry and silken clothing by her father-in-law and his kinsmen. Under her layers of drapery, the bride could neither see nor be seen, but could hear the music and talking all around her. Many of the songs, sung by the Nimkhera women and female guests, hilariously insulted the groom and his relatives. Later, at night, in the darkest recesses of the house, her mother and *bhabhi* dressed Munni in her new finery. These valuable and glistening ornaments were hers, a wonderful treasure. Bright rings were put on her toes, a mark of her impending married state. Munni's little sister watched every ritual with wide eyes, realizing that one day she too would be a bride.

The wedding ceremony itself was conducted quietly at the astrologically auspicious hour of 4 A.M. by a Brahman priest, before whom the couple sat.

Amar Singh looked handsome in his turban and red wedding smock, but Munni was only a huddled white lump beside him. The priest chanted and offered sacrifices to the divine, and then, in a moving ritual, Rambai and Tej Singh symbolically gave Munni away to Amar Singh. As women sang softly, the garments of the couple were tied together, and the bridal pair were guided around a small sacrificial fire seven times. With these acts, Munni and Amar Singh were wed and Munni officially became a *bahu*, a daughter-in-law and member of her husband's lineage.

As a *bahu*, she became a symbol of fertility, of promise for the continuation of her husband's family line. She also became an auspicious *suhāgan*, a woman with a living husband. In the word *suhagan* is emphasized the concept that neither man nor woman is complete as an individual but only in their union. Traditionally, no woman except a prostitute remained unmarried, and villagers believe that men who die single become ghosts who haunt the descendants of their more fortunate brothers. For some devout individuals, asceticism may be a stage of life, but except for a few holy men, all people are expected to marry.

The next day was another round of feasting, fun fests, ceremonies, and gift giving. As a sendoff for the groom's party, Munni's kinswomen playfully dashed red dye into their faces. The relatives departed, and the house was quiet. Only tattered colored paper decorations and her new jewelry served to remind Munni of her change in status. Life continued as before.

The bride's veiled kinswomen mock the groom's relations with insulting songs and dash red dye into their faces.

But Munni and Amar Singh, though strangers to each other, were now links between two kin groups, and their male relatives began to meet each other and become friendly. Munni's relatives were always properly deferential to Amar Singh's, as befitted the kinsmen of a bride in relationship to those of her groom. It would have been improper, too, for Munni's mother to meet Amar Singh or his mother or to speak to any of his male relatives. Having given a bride to Amar Singh's family, it now would be shameful for Munni's family ever to accept their gifts or hospitality.

Among Thakurs in North India, a girl is given in marriage to a boy who belongs to a group of higher rank than her own. Thus the bride's kinsmen are not merely deferential but are considered actually inferior to the groom's kin. This lower status of the bride's family adds to the relatively low status all North Indian brides have in their new homes. Among most Muslims, however, the kin of both bride and groom consider themselves equals, particularly since they often are close blood relatives (for example, the children of two siblings may marry).

The Muslim wedding consists of a series of rituals, gift exchanges, and feasts. The couple are legally united in a simple ceremony during which both bride and groom indicate their assent to the marriage by signing a formal wedding contract in the presence of witnesses. The groom and his family pledge to the bride a sum of money, known as *mehr,* to be paid to her upon her demand. (Most wives do not claim their *mehr* unless their husbands divorce them.) During the wedding the bride and groom sit in separate rooms and do not see each other. Latif Khan's mother was married by mail to her first cousin, living hundreds of miles away, and did not see her husband for over a year.

Munni expected to spend the rest of her married life as Amar Singh's wife, but she knew she could remarry if he died. In her caste, as among most high-ranking groups, divorce is always a possibility, but it involves shame. For a Brahman girl, her first marriage would definitely have been her last until recently. Although most Brahman widows are expected to remain celibate for life, some Brahman groups now allow young widows to remarry without suffering ostracism. Among high-ranking Muslims, divorce is relatively rare but it does occur, and remarriage is usually easy. In educated urban Hindu circles, divorce is almost unthinkable; but among tribals and low-status Hindus and Muslims, it is not uncommon, and scandalous elopements occasionally take place. In any case, a second marriage for a woman never involves the elaborate ceremonies of the first wedding but may simply entail setting up house with a new man.

During past centuries, very high castes prohibited widow remarriage, and a widow was sometimes expected to immolate herself on her husband's funeral pyre. This practice, known as *sati,* occurred in only a very small percentage of families and was legally abolished over a century ago. Rajputs remember with pride the *johār,* the rite in which the widows of warriors slain in battle died in a communal funeral pyre (Carstairs, 1967, p. 111). Today, reports of *satis* appear in North Indian newspapers once or twice a year.

In the past, a widow was sometimes treated harshly, since the death of her husband was thought to be punishment for her misdeeds in a previous life. However, widows of lower-ranking castes have always been allowed to remarry.

Under Indian law today, any woman may divorce her husband for certain causes and any widow can remarry, but considerations of property and social acceptability rather than legality usually determine whether or not a woman seeks a divorce or remarriage. Among Hindu villagers, a widow who remarries customarily loses her rights in her husband's land. If she has young sons, a widow usually remains unmarried in order to protect her children's rights to their patrimony.[6]

In North and Central India, monogamy is generally practiced. Hindus may legally have only one wife, but Muslims are allowed four wives under both Indian and Muslim law. Village Hindus, whose marriages are seldom registered with legal authorities, occasionally take two or three wives, and the women of some Himalayan groups have several husbands.[7] Wealthy Muslim men occasionally avail themselves of their legal limit, but most cannot afford to do so. When Yusuf Miya, a Bhopal man, wanted to marry a second time, his wife spoke of suicide and the matter was dropped. Some women, particularly those who have borne no children, do not openly object to having a co-wife. In Nimkhera, one untouchable Sweeper man has four wives, all of whom contribute to his support.

Munni spent three more years in the bosom of her family, happily taking part in household and agricultural work and enjoying the frequent festivals observed in the village. Not long after her wedding, she went with her brothers and father to a fair in the district market center, where they watched the Ram Lila, a religious drama, and bought trinkets in the bazaar.

The next winter, her grandfather was stricken by pneumonia and died. This tragic event deprived the family of its patriarch and Hirabai of her husband. As she wept beside her husband's bier, her glass bangles were broken, never to be replaced. After the cremation, relatives arrived to pay their condolences and to take part in ritual gift exchanges and a large death feast. Munni joined the visiting women in weeping and singing sad songs.

The following year she went with her parents, uncle, and a large group of villagers by train on a pilgrimage to Varanasi and Allahabad, where they bathed in the sacred river Ganges. Her father's older brother carried with him a small packet of his father's charred bones, which he threw into the river. The trip was exciting and eye-opening. Although it was expensive, the journey allowed the pilgrims to carry out important religious and family obligations and was therefore considered more a necessity than a luxury. Munni knew that her idyll among her natal kin would not last much longer. Many of her friends had already been sent to their husbands' homes, and Munni too would soon go. Her *gauna* (consummation ceremony) was set for March.

The night before her *gauna*, Munni's *bhabhi* (her cousin's wife) took her aside and told her about sex and what to expect from her husband. Munni had heard some stories from her friends but was shocked to hear the details. (Parents and children never discuss sex.) Her mother reminded her that she was going among critical strangers and that she should do whatever work was asked of her without complaint.

Beating drums and blaring trumpets soon announced the arrival of Amar Singh and a group of his male kinsmen. Munni sat passively as her mother and the Barber woman dressed her in finery and ornamented her with silver. She was truly agitated: now she would meet her husband and her in-laws and see Khetpur, the village in which she would spend her adulthood. Her life would be forever changed.

Her departure from her parents, grandmother, brothers, sisters, uncles, aunts, and cousins was heartrending. Clinging to each in turn, she sobbed piteously and pleaded not to be sent away. They too cried as they put her into a small covered palanquin and saw her borne away by her in-laws. With her went baskets of food and clothes and a little cousin to act as intermediary.

Heavily veiled, she was transferred to a bus and sat miserable and silent for the entire journey. At Khetpur she was put into a palanquin again and carried to her new home. Women's voices all around were talking about her, referring to her as *dulhan* (bride), *bahu* (daughter-in-law), and *Nīmkherāwālī* (the woman from Nimkhera). Here in her husband's home she would never be known as Munni.

There were some "games" she had to play with her husband before a group of village women who had gathered to sing and welcome her. Almost overcome with shyness and apprehension, she was made to sit near her husband and compete with him in finding some silver rings in a platter of turmeric water. Whichever partner won this game was said to be likely to dominate in the marriage. It is rare for a veiled and shy bride to win, and Munni, too, lost the competition. Then the couple were taken inside the house and told to feed each other some rice pudding. Embarrassed and awkward attempts ended when Amar Singh ran out of the house. Finally, Munni's mother-in-law escorted her to a decorated cot, left, and locked her in the room. Clutching her veil, Munni apprehensively awaited her husband. He came in quietly, after the house was silent, and put out the lamp.

Modesty required that she try to fend him off and succumb only after great protestation (even an experienced girl must feign modesty), but Munni was sixteen at her *gauna* ceremony and her introduction to her husband was not traumatic. Some younger girls have been genuinely terrified of their husbands, and their *gauna* nights have involved virtual rape. One Brahman girl, Kamladevi, who met her husband when she was just thirteen, described her *gauna* as follows:

> I had my *gauna* when I was still little; I hadn't started bathing yet. My *bhabhi* told me about sex and what to expect; I was really frightened. I came to Nimkhera and stayed for three days. The first night I slept with Amma [her husband's grandmother]. The second night Jiji [her husband's cousin's wife] took me into the house and told me to sleep there. She said she'd be coming in shortly. She spread the blankets on the bed, and then she went out and locked the door from outside. I was really scared; I cowered near the door. I didn't know it, but he [her husband] had gone in before and hidden in the dark near the hearth. He came out then and grabbed. hold of me. I let him do whatever he wanted to do; I just clenched my sari between my teeth so I wouldn't cry out. But I cried a lot anyway, and there was lots of blood. In the morning I changed my sari before I came out of the room, and bundled the dirty sari up and hid it from everyone. I had a fever, and I was so sick that some people criticized him for sleeping with such a young and weak girl. My brother came to get me on the third day and took me home.

Munni stayed in her husband's home for a week before her father and a group of male relatives came to fetch her. During the week she became acquainted with her husband and was viewed by all his female relatives and friends. Each woman paid her a small sum for the privilege of looking under her veil at her shy face with downcast eyes. All commented on her complexion (they said she was fair) and on the clothing she had brought. She spoke almost nothing to anyone but her own little cousin and Amar Singh's little sister, to whom she was *bhabhi*. Several songfests were held by the women, most of whom had themselves been brought to Khetpur as brides.

At home again, Munni unveiled, relaxed, and enjoyed her normal life for several months until her husband's father came to escort her to Khetpur again. On her second visit, she was no longer a guest but was treated more like a member of the household. She began cooking, sweeping, and grinding. Her mother-in-law was polite, and Munni docilely performed the tasks expected of her. After three weeks she again went home for several months.

Munni is now a young woman of about twenty-one, the mother of a baby daughter. She continues to spend a few months of each year in her parents' home.

Not all girls have a *gauna* ceremony. Most Muslim girls and educated urban girls marry after puberty and go immediately to their husbands' homes. Nor do all girls have such an easy transition between their natal and conjugal homes as did Munni.

In much of North India, a girl is sent on her *gauna* and remains in her husband's home for a year or more, sometimes until she has produced a child, before she is allowed to visit her parents. Such an abrupt transition is a difficult one for a young girl. In Senapur, among a sample of sixteen Thakur women, five had remained with their in-laws between seven and eleven years on the first or second visits there. Four had never returned to their parents' villages because their parents had died (Luschinsky, 1962, pp. 350–351).

In Central India, older wives go home at least once or twice a year for visits and festival observances, but in parts of North India several years may elapse between visits. This is partly because of the expectation that the parents of a visiting daughter will send expensive gifts to her in-laws when she returns to them—so that few parents can afford frequent visits from their daughters. In Central India, however, a visiting daughter receives relatively modest gifts and may provide vital services in her natal home (for example, helping with the harvest or doing housework for a sick mother). Consequently, whereas a North Indian bride is clearly shifted from one household to another at her *gauna,* the Central Indian bride may become an important participant in the activities of two households. However, as expressed in the childbirth song (p. 109), the young mother may feel herself to be and may be considered to be an outsider in her marital home for some time.

Given the fact that a wife is expected to live with her husband's family, usually in a village other than that of her birth, teenage marriage makes sense. A young girl easily falls under the tutelage of her mother-in-law and can be socialized to life in her husband's family. The new bride, although the center of attention for a while, has the lowest status of any adult in her new residence. Young and alone among strangers, effaced by her veil, the bride can be happy in her new surroundings only by adjusting her behavior to satisfy her in-laws. If she quarrels with her mother-in-law, her husband cannot take her side without shaming himself before his elders. Thus she quickly learns the behavior appropriate to her role as a young *bahu* in a strange household.

Virtually every new bride longs to return to the security of her natal home. Even though she may be secretly thrilled by her relationship with her husband, a bride rarely enjoys being sequestered and ruled by her mother-in-law. Songs stress the unhappiness of the young wife in her new residence, and young girls eagerly seize any opportunity to return home. Sometimes a young wife is so unhappy she commits suicide, typically by jumping in a well. Few girls can go home when they wish; a young wife must be formally called for, with the permission of her in-laws, and escorted by a responsible male from her natal household.

For the village bride, marriage does not mark attainment of independent adulthood but signals the acquisition of a new set of relatives to whom she is subordinate. Her actions had previously been guided by sometimes indulgent parents; with marriage and *gauna,* they fall under the control of adults who are far less likely to consider her wishes. She herself can attain a position of authority only by growing older, becoming the mother of children, and outliving her mother-in-law. Until she is at least middle-aged, a woman is usually subordinate to and protected by others.

WOMEN'S STATUS

According to ancient Hindu texts and tradition, until about 500 B.C. women in India enjoyed considerable freedom in choosing their mates and taking part in public functions. Equal to men in religious matters, upper-class women were well-educated and married late. Divorce and widow remarriage were acceptable. But during the next thousand years, women's position gradually deteriorated: educational and religious parity was denied them and widow remarriage was forbidden to those of high-status families.[8] Still quoted on the proper role of a woman are the laws of Manu, written during this period:

> She should do nothing independently, even in her own house.
> In childhood subject to her father, in youth to her husband,
> And when her husband is dead, to her sons, she should never
>   enjoy independence. . . .
> Though he be uncouth and prone to pleasure,
> though he have no good points at all,
> the virtuous wife should ever
> worship her lord as a god. [Basham, 1959, pp. 180–181].

In this treatise and in more recent Indian writings is embedded the notion that a woman must always be subordinate to men. In fact, virtually everywhere in India today, women's status relative to that of men appears to be low. As one Nimkhera woman said, "Men are high and women low; this is the rule of the world. Men are the breadwinners. In the wedding ceremony, the woman is given to the man, and she belongs to him." In villages, a woman walks behind her husband, and a *bahu* sits on the ground in the presence of her father-in-law. A woman asks permission from her father or husband before traveling far from home.[9] A woman is considered polluted monthly and is segregated from others. She should eat after her husband does and may consume his leavings; her leavings would defile him. Even if she is a Brahman, she cannot become a priest and conduct ceremonies as men do. A Muslim woman does not pray in a mosque as men do. If she is of high status, she marries only once, but any widowed or divorced man may marry again if he can find a bride.

Very importantly, by traditional Hindu custom, a woman does not inherit land or house from either parents or husband; such property is inherited patrilineally only by sons and can only be used by a widow during her lifetime. A widow cannot sell her husband's land or give it to her natal relatives, and if she has no sons, the land is claimed by her husband's closest male patrilineal relatives upon her death or remarriage. In fact, the only property over which a village Hindu woman has full rights of ownership is her jewelry, particularly that given to her by her own relatives (jewelry received from her in-laws may be borrowed or pawned by them and would not be hers to keep in case of divorce). Only occasionally does a Hindu man with no sons formally will his property to his daughter. Modern Indian law assure widows, daughters, and mothers the right to inherit and absolutely own property, but few village women would risk alienating their kinsmen by challenging tradition.

Some observers feel that the veiling and seclusion of women indicates low female status and that men prevent women from taking part in community politics and commerce and restrict them to home activities.

Although it is true that, in general, women's status is lower than men's, it is not as low as these outward signs might indicate. In any case, men did not consciously organize a system to dominate women. Both men and women are actors in a complex social and ecological system which functions reasonably smoothly and provides benefits to both sexes. Men do dominate activities outside the home—they take positions of leadership in their communities, make important decisions pertaining to agriculture, and make most purchases. Nevertheless, women affect men's actions and have important spheres of influence of their own. It is really a mistake to see women as competing with and being restricted by men; rather, male and female roles are clearly distinguished, and the sexes are seen as complementary to each other. As one educated Muslim girl explained, "We don't feel inferior or superior to boys. We each have our separate roles" (Cormack, 1953, p. 36).

A number of cultural symbols stress the value of women. Another ancient text, the *Mahabharata,* says:

> Even a man in the grip of rage will not be harsh to a woman, remembering that on her depend the joys of love, happiness, and virtue. For woman is the everlasting field, in which the Self is born. [Basham, 1959, p. 182].

Goddesses are worshiped throughout India, and in the village Hindu wedding ceremony, the bride is likened to Lakshmi, the goddess of wealth. And in a Central Indian ceremony (p. 112), nine young girls are worshiped and offered gifts by priests and important men.

Nevertheless, men's view of women—and women's view of themselves—is ambivalent. Throughout India, the concept of motherhood is revered. The words *Mātā* and *Mā* ("mother") connote warmth, protection, and life-giving power. Ideally, a child should always honor his mother. The cow, sacred to Hindus because of her usefulness as a producer of milk, dung, and bullocks, is called *Gao-Mātā* ("mother cow"). The most powerful local goddesses, responsible for the care and protection of whole villages and regions, are known as *Mata*. Yet it is Sītalā Mātā who brings smallpox and may injure those who displease her.

Normally, sexuality must be assumed as a prelude to motherhood, yet it is as a sexual being that woman is feared and despised. Brahmanical tradition views women as shameless temptresses lacking in self-control and likely to go astray unless controlled by their menfolk. A woman can bring devastating shame to her family by engaging in sexual activity with a man of lower caste. Further, a menstruating woman may use her pollution to harm others—for instance, if she goes near a smallpox patient, the patient will die, because the smallpox goddess is thus offended.

A goddess gains power by controlling her sexuality; a mother goddess is not a mother in the normal sense. Shiv Prasad, a learned Nimkhera Brahman, explained the position of Matabai, the goddess most worshiped by the villagers: "Matabai is not married. She is the mother of us all, the mother of the world. She creates everyone and also destroys them. She is a form of the goddess Durga." The ceremony at which the young girls (*kanyas*) are worshiped takes place at the Matabai shrine. "The *kanyas* are like the goddess Durga, like nine Durgas," he explained. Thus chaste womanhood is powerful and worthy of adulation.[10]

Most Hindus, however, are not consciously aware of this association. On a day-to-day basis, women are neither idealized nor despised but treated as ordinary mortals with normal human strengths and weaknesses.

Some men believe that women have a stronger sex drive than men do, but others realize that it is men who usually initiate lovemaking and who secretly visit prostitutes. Some men regard women as weak and flighty and in need of male guidance, while others recognize feminine expertise and strength in particular areas of life. Nearly every man feels that having a wife is essential to his happiness and to the smooth running of the home. A few men perhaps suspect that it is difficult for a woman to always behave properly. A Weaver man of Nimkhera who is very devoted to his wife contrasted masculine and feminine behavior:

For instance, at a religious drama, a man can laugh loudly, but a woman has to laugh quietly. She shouldn't raise her voice, and she should obey her husband. She can't roam around at night. But a man can do all he likes, except drink, steal, or go to prostitutes.

Women are usually dominant in home activities—in matters relating to birth, child care, housework, and food preparation. Further, even though men are usually in charge of work outside the house and bringing home food and money, women are responsible for storing and allocating these resources. When a farmer wants to buy a bullock, he usually discusses it with his wife, and it is from her that he gets the money. She usually tells him when to buy new clothing for the family and which foodstuffs are needed from the bazaar. However, many urban wives do their own shopping, and a high percentage of merchants and customers in tribal bazaars are women. In any case, both men and women must make their purchasing decisions within the limits imposed by each family's financial situation.

In ritual matters, too, women perform essential roles. They vigilantly ensure ritual purity of household food and water, although their husbands may transgress caste food rules at urban restaurants. Through prayers, fasting, and ceremonial observances, women enlist divine succor for their families. In the Varanasi area particularly, women are almost wholly responsible for seeking divine aid to ensure the health and well-being of their menfolk and children.

Women also help make important decisions in other family matters, especially in the selection of mates for their children. Men do some of the scouting, but, through their networks of ties with women in other towns and villages, women frequently have access to information vital for evaluating prospects. Muslim women particularly play essential roles in the selection of wives for sons and nephews, since most marriageable Muslim girls are in purdah and can be seen only by other women and a few male relatives. And women control other women—mothers and mothers-in-law control their daughters and *bahus*. In Khalapur, reflecting the social and residential cleavage between men and women, the Rajput woman who heads a woman's house has considerable authority over others (Minturn and Hitchcock, 1966, p. 46).

The fact that women are secluded and veiled does in some ways contribute to male domination, but in other respects purdah is a mark of high status. In ancient times noble women veiled their faces and traveled in curtained litters to protect themselves from the profane gaze of commoners. Today, the association of seclusion and prestige remains. Poor Muslim women strive to remain housebound as much as possible, in emulation of the strict seclusion only wealthier Muslims can afford. One upward-mobile Muslim woman in Nimkhera told me, "I never go out in the village without my *burka*. One of those Farmers or even a Sweeper might see me."

Her tone·implied that such an occurrence would degrade her. Well-to-do village Hindu men take pride in their ability to afford farmhands and water bearers, thus freeing their wives from the need to leave the courtyard to visit the fields or wells. The women value their status as well-cared-for ladies of relative leisure.

In addition to its association with economic well-being and high rank, purdah has other meanings. Traditional town women appreciate the protection the veil affords them from the stares of lecherous men. For Hindus, veiling is an expression of distance between a woman and her husband's relatives. Noting that a young high-caste woman of Khalapur village covers her face even in front of older low-caste servingmen, Hitchcock states that this is a sign of respect for the man's status as a man (Minturn and Hitchcock, 1966, p. 34). But this is not really so: the woman veils from the servant because of his position as village "older brother" of her husband, a relative in whose presence she feels shy and to whom she should show respect. She also veils from older women in her husband's village, but in her parental village she never covers her face, whether in the presence of men or not. For Hindus, veiling also contributes to harmonious family living.

Nevertheless, purdah restrictions on the mobility of traditional women do contribute to their subservience to males. A village woman of good reputation should not travel to another village or town except for an approved purpose. It is significant that in a country where travel has traditionally been by bullock cart, women never drive bullock carts. Even among the wealthy urban classes one seldom sees a woman driving a car. Thus unless she has access to a bus line, a woman cannot journey far without a male accompanying her. Attendance at a school or nonreligious public meeting would usually be disapproved by family elders. As a result, sequestered women are often poorly educated and ignorant of events outside their own villages. Even within her conjugal village, the young wife is isolated by restrictions on her movement. She is unable to visit freely with neighbors and consequently forms few bonds of friendship within her husband's village.

It is not surprising, then, that the vast majority of women do not obviously play any part in extrafamilial politics. In villages it is rare to find a leader among women. Every village now elects representatives to a government-sponsored village council, and traditional caste and village councils also meet to consider disputes. Almost never is a woman a member of a traditional council, but in some villages a seat on the government-sponsored council is reserved for a woman (Mayer, 1960, p. 114). Indian women have had full suffrage since 1949, yet many either fail to vote or cast their ballots for the candidates of their husbands' choice. The Prime Minister of India is a woman, and women have been chosen to serve as cabinet ministers, governors of states, ambassadors, United Nations officials, and members of state legislatures and the national parliament. But India's politically em-

The Queen Mother of Jaipur, Rajasthan, leaves the Jaipur polo grounds after viewing a match.

inent women are hardly representative of the populace; they are of the highest urban educated classes and include former Prime Minister Nehru's daughter and sister as well as the Queen Mothers of Gwalior and Jaipur. These are women who were part of a select elite before they entered politics.

The relationship of a woman to her husband is not simple to characterize despite the formal trappings of female subservience. At first, husband and wife are usually strangers shyly meeting each other at night. Their first encounters may be cold enactments of the sex act, but later meetings may become romantic. Embarrassment gives way to warmth and pleasure. The traditional bride shyly veils her face from her husband, but he gradually encourages her to talk. Publicly, the young Hindu couple pretend indifference to each other, and the wife veils her face from her husband. Neither utters the other's personal name. They cannot be daytime companions, and not until middle age do they exchange words in the presence of other adults. Among the Brahmans of Kashmir, a wife is called "the parrot of the pillow," in reference to the fact that she is free to talk with her husband only when they are in bed (Madan, 1965, p. 136). Even very Westernized couples usually refrain from public displays of affection. A well-educated young woman from a large city told me that in her entire life she had never seen a couple embrace or kiss.

In cramped quarters, lack of privacy in the joint family may stifle development of understanding between husband and wife. A Bania (merchant caste) youth of Jaipur City wrote in his autobiography:

> Wife wants to learn alphabet—but because there is no separate room I cannot coach her. She may like to go with me to the garden or cinema or exhibition, but the fear of family members, which is quite genuine, closes her mouth. All her intentions have been killed—she has never asked me for anything. It proves sufficiently that it is my family circumstances which have killed all her enthusiasm. . . . If I can have one year living [alone] with my wife, I can get to know her and teach her things. [Carstairs, 1957, pp. 296, 306].

A husband may attempt to exert dominance over his wife. One young Brahman groom in Nimkhera threatened his bride that he would beat her if she fought with his mother and grandmother, although he will probably never carry out his threat. Women also speak of male dominance as a given: asked what would happen to her if her husband caught her in an affair with another man, a young woman replied, "He would beat me till I had no skin left." If he were caught cheating, she said, she would merely stop talking to him for a while or go home for a long time.

In fact, some spouses are indifferent to each other and some husbands do beat their wives, but many couples become quite devoted and, particularly in nuclear families, enjoy equal partnerships, making decisions jointly and showing consideration for one another. Most older couples treat each other as equals.

Yusuf Miya and his wife are an example of a couple who really care for each other. Yet Yusuf has made his wife unhappy by becoming involved with other women, and her only defense is to withdraw affection and weep. Still, after they make up, they make love and are friends again.

Among the Bhils of Rajasthan and other tribal peoples, genuinely affectionate marriages are common, since either partner can abscond with a lover if he or she is dissatisfied with his or her current spouse (Carstairs, 1957, p. 132).

Old Motibai and her husband, the Nimkhera temple priest, have an easy going relationship in which she takes the lead. He unimaginatively carries out his temple duties, but she has exercised skillful entrepreneurship in starting and running a small shop. In spite of her obviously dominant role, when asked who was the strong one in their marriage, Motibai replied, "Oh he is, definitely." Such an answer actually bolsters her own prestige, since henpecked husbands are ridiculed and dutiful wives admired. In India as in the West, a woman cannot expect to improve her status in the community by openly belittling her husband. Motibai considers herself a perfect wife:

Motibai, a self-assured high caste village woman.

A perfect wife will do what her husband asks her to do and won't answer him back or fight with him. She will have sexual relations only with her husband and with no other man. She should also become a *satī* after his death, although nobody does that nowadays. That's not so necessary now.

Widely admired as the epitome of wifely perfection, the goddess Sita remained patiently chaste and obedient to her husband Ram despite the fact that she suffered hardship and was banished by her suspicious mate. It would be most difficult for an ordinary mortal to be so devoted.

No Nimkhera woman actually treats her husband as a god, and some young women consider themselves sufficiently separate from their husbands to criticize them without fearing that the criticism will reflect on themselves. Sunalini Nayudu, my assistant, asked some women, "Should a woman think of her husband as a god? Should a wife obey her husband all the time? Do you actually obey your husband?" Motibai replied, expressing the ideal:

Yes, a husband is a god. We touch his feet, and after he comes home from a pilgrimage, we wash his toes and drink the water. A wife should obey, but not if she is told to do a bad thing, like going to another man. I always obey my husband; I have to.

Then she added candidly, "But if he gets mad at me, I get just as mad at him." The middle-aged Barber woman replied, "I don't know. I usually obey, but when he isn't here, I do what I think is best. He also listens to me. We're equal." Kamladevi, a young Brahman wife who on other occasions had indicated a disdain for her husband, said, "Oh, no one's a god. Why should a woman obey her husband all the time? I do what I want to most of the time." Her sister-in-law agreed, "Oh, everyone says a husband is a god, but no one's a god."

Sundarbai, a high-caste mother of four, has a poor relationship with her husband. He is cold and seldom talks to her, and his mother and other members of the joint household accuse her of not doing her share of the work. Sundarbai retaliates by spending about six months of each year in her parents' home and sometimes threatening never to return. A young Thakur woman who was dissatisfied with the amount of jewelry she received for her wedding refused to return from her parents' home until she was given Rs. 3,000 worth of jewelry. She held out for two years and finally received several expensive ornaments.

Some village and urban women turn to deep involvement in religion when they cannot find satisfaction in their marriages. In North India, where a woman cannot so easily return to her parents' home, a pilgrimage may provide a needed respite from her husband and his relatives. Other women devote many hours to prayer or depend on their children for affection.

FAMILY LIVING

In North and Central India a bride almost always goes to live with her husband and his parents and siblings in a joint family unit. She may live in a joint family all her life, or the group may lose members through death or division and she may find herself in a nuclear family, that is, with only her husband and unmarried children. Nuclear family living is particularly characteristic of people who do not own large amounts of land or property or who find it advantageous to move away from their homes in search of employment or both. For example, government servants who are frequently transferred are given small living quarters and usually live in nuclear families. So do landless laborers, artisans who live in areas unable to support more than one of their kind, and Westernized professionals. Some landed farmers live in nuclear families, but usually not for long. For a farmer, joint family living is usually economically advantageous, since it involves a group of kinsmen living and working together on their cooperatively farmed land. Except in some urban circles, the joint family is the ideal, and some of India's wealthiest industrialists live in large joint families. In spite of the ideal, however, brothers often quarrel and divide their property after the death of their parents.

Joint family living is frequently found among the village kinsmen of urban migrants. When a village man migrates to the city to work in a factory or as a laborer, he usually leaves his wife and children behind with his family. He lives alone or with fellow male workers in the city and may visit his family only once or twice a year.

The nature of a woman's relationships with her in-laws depends to a great extent on whether she is living with them in the same household. The wife of a government servant living away from his parents may meet her parents-in-law only occasionally, and she and her husband consequently have as much autonomy as his job allows. But a village farmer and his wife living with the husband's family must daily modify their actions to satisfy his relatives. Restraint and concern with hierarchy permeate joint family life.

For the village Hindu woman, purdah observances are important. Her respectful veiling and avoidance of her father-in-law and husband's elder brothers are ideally lifelong, but in some families a middle-aged *bahu* may exchange a few words with an aged father-in-law. The bride also veils from her mother-in-law for a short period of time and from her husband when others are present. Such veiling is an aid to harmony within the joint family, since it emphasizes the subordinate relationship of the woman to those in authority in the family and deemphasizes her tie to her husband. Veiling and seclusion in her conjugal home constantly remind a woman of her position as a *bahu* who must quietly subjugate her individual wishes to those of the group.

The fact that a woman veils from her husband in the presence of others also provides a small amount of privacy for each couple, since husband and wife converse only when they are alone and what they say to each other is not known to anyone but themselves. A young wife also finds that the veil shields her somewhat from the constant scrutiny of others in her new home.

In most Muslim families, purdah is observed not from related males but rather from strangers. A bride may be shy in the presence of her father-in-law and husband's elder brother, but if she has married a cousin, these men are her close relatives and she may be at ease with them. Muslim purdah serves to define the kindred group vis-à-vis outsiders and thus heightens the family's sense of unity. The seclusion of marriageable women from strangers also helps to ensure that a girl will marry only a man acceptable to her family. This is particularly important for Muslims of property, since Muslim women inherit and control land and other valuables.

A woman should ideally be subordinate to her mother-in-law and do as she says. In North India a bride may be expected to perform small personal services for her mother-in-law, such as massaging her arms and legs. Many *bahus*, however, resent taking orders from the mother-in-law and talk back or even quarrel openly. Gradually, a *bahu* feels more and more confident in her new home, and as the years pass, she may come to dominate her aged mother-in-law completely. Occasionally a woman and her *bahu* have a warm, loving relationship, but this is not the rule. It has been reported that a woman may even meddle in the sex life of her son, restricting his access to his wife to only once a week. But most women are eager to have grandchildren and would encourage rather than discourage sexual activity. (In a joint family household, each couple of childbearing years normally has a private room in which to sleep, although the rooms may be used by others during the day. In some regions, men visit their wives discreetly only after dark. Older couples usually sleep apart.)

Although she avoids her husband's elder brother, a woman has a warm, joking relationship with her husband's younger brother, her *devar,* to whom she is *bhabhi.* A *bhabhi* and her *devar* tease and jest openly about sex and may be confidantes. In some parts of North India it is permissible for the two to have sexual relations, but in other areas such activity would be condemned.

To a woman, her husband's elder sister may be a critical and annoying person who visits all too frequently. But her husband's younger sister may be like her own little sister, pleasant and loving, shyly confiding her own fears of marriage or her difficulties with her husband.

Other important people in a woman's marital home are her husband's brothers' wives, women brought there, like herself, as brides. Sisters-in-law call each other "sister" and may be good friends, but they often quarrel over the division of household work and supplies. Men frequently blame quarreling sisters-in-law for causing the division of the joint family. A young woman's first trysts with her husband may be arranged by her older sister-in-law (Luschinsky, 1962, p. 335).

The oldest woman in a joint household is usually able to communicate more easily with all members of the family than can anyone else. Her children should not discuss certain matters or openly disagree with their elder brothers and father, and her *bahus* remain silent before their male elders. Thus an aged husband may rely upon his wife for communication with the younger members of his family (for example, see Madan, 1965, p. 137).

In many families, a father is expected to be authoritarian while the mother may be indulgent. Children often feel constrained in their father's presence but at ease with their mother. The closeness of a woman and her son may diminish after the arrival of the son's bride; but most sons and daughters always feel a special affection for their mothers.

A woman's love for her mother continues long after her marriage. From the loneliness of her husband's village, a girl may even idealize her mother and natal home as the epitome of love and warmth. Her father, too, takes on the aura of a savior when he comes to escort her home on a visit.

A woman's relationship with her brother should be a special one of mutual love and concern. An older sister has cared for her brother during childhood and an older brother has helped care for a little sister. After a sister marries, her brother is expected to visit her, bring her home for visits, and bring gifts to her, her children, and her in-laws. The word "brother" is used even outside the sibling tie to denote affection. One Hindu festival, Raksha Bandhan, celebrates the brother-sister bond; a sister ties a sacred protective thread around her brother's wrist, and he reciprocates with a gift. A woman's love for her brother is communicated to her children, who accompany her on visits to her childhood home and are indulged by their mother's brother. Sisters, too, may be close, but no mutual obligations exist to ensure a lifelong bond. In North India, sisters are usually married into distant villages and may not see each other for years. First cousins who have grown up in the same household normally treat each other like true siblings, and all cousins address each other as "brother" and "sister." There is a notable lack of sibling rivalry between both true siblings and cousins (see Minturn and Hitchcock, 1966, p. 137).

Within each village, children of the same generation consider themselves "village siblings." Young people who ceremonially "hear Ram's name" together from a guru become ritual siblings. In Khalapur, women who are good friends may become ritual sisters.

The affinal relatives most important to a young Hindu woman, her husband and his mother, normally never meet her own mother. Purdah restrictions prevent these affines from interacting freely, and consequently they know each other only through what the young woman tells them about each other. The fathers-in-law may meet, but they too feel constraint in each other's presence. The formality of these relationships reflects the fact that the natal and conjugal kinsmen of a Hindu woman belong to different patrilineages and to some extent are rivals for the allegiance and services of the woman who unites them. Villagers say that an important reason for marrying their daughters to men of other villages is to insulate a woman's parents from her parents-in-law.

In Central India, a woman's happy visits to her parents' home are ended when her in-laws come to fetch her back. Since women are in short supply in this area, both groups benefit from the services of a woman and both seek her presence. A woman often feels unhappy and overworked in her husband's home, and she may hate to return.

After a visit with her parents, Halkibai (center) cries bitterly
as she leaves for her husband's home. Her mother and a
neighbor also weep.

The departure of a daughter for her husband's village after a visit is
usually sad for both the girl and her parents. As she leaves her parents'
home, a young woman sobs, "Oh mama, oh papa, don't think I'm of
another house now. Oh mama, no one will come to get me now. I'm being
sent away forever." (A woman never cries when leaving her husband's
home.) The Nimkhera Barber woman once came to a women's gathering
with her eyes red from crying over her daughter Halki's departure for her
husband's village. Unlike other girls her age (about twenty), Halki is
allowed only short visits with her parents, and her mother-in-law is very
domineering. Other women tried to console the mother. "Your poor
daughter has to go to her in-laws after such short visits. Her crying is
heard all over the village, she cries so loudly. Whoever hears her feels his
chest burst with sorrow and pain," an elderly Brahman woman commented.

As the Barber woman began to cry again, the woman continued, "A mother gives birth to her girl after bearing her burden in her stomach for nine months; then she suffers the labor pains and brings the girl up with love and care. Then she has to torture herself and marry her off to some strange person. This is all so painful for a mother." Another woman added, "Yes, but if a daughter is happy in her husband's home, then parents find some consolation in the fact. But if it is her fate to suffer miseries in her new home, then the days of the poor parents turn into hell." On another occasion, when Halki's mother was crying after her daughter's departure, a neighbor consoled her by saying, "I too suffered thus in the hands of my mother-in-law, and that old woman died soon. So Halki's old mother-in-law and father-in-law will also die; don't worry about Halki. A mother's tears are never shed in vain; they always produce results." Thus, the mother-in-law's pleasure is the mother's grief, and vice versa, even in relationships less filled with tension than Halki's.

In the parts of North India where Rajput marriages link a woman with a man of a higher-ranked subcaste, the woman and her relatives are often made to feel inferior to their in-laws. Loving her children, who are members of their father's group, expected to assimilate to her husband's family and yet loyal to her parents, a woman may feel forever torn between the two sets of relatives.

Although the two groups of relatives are to some extent united by the marriage linking them, a tension always exists between them. The hilariously insulting songs a bride's womenfolk direct at her in-laws are one expression of this tension. (These songs, always expected, are never taken amiss.) Joking, respect, and avoidance relationships function to prevent the open expression of hostility, and apparently they are kept amicable in this way. The key principle here is that the individual's actions must be modified to enhance harmony within the family and among kindred. This principle is also exemplified in the public negation of a special relationship between husband and wife and even between parent and child (see below).

Virtually every Indian woman looks forward to having children. Village women usually say they want "as many as God gives me" and may hope to give birth to six or seven. Some urban women who have been influenced by government family planning campaigns wish to have just two or three children. In fact, although fertility is very high in India, infant mortality is also high, and the average number of living children per mother is between three and four. In Nimkhera, most middle-aged women have given birth to five or six children, of whom three or four have survived childhood. Four-fifths of Nimkhera mothers have lost at least one child, and one-third have lost four or more children. High infant mortality is an important factor in influencing women to have as many children as they possibly can, since, as in the case of old Mograwali, a woman left without a son at home is materially worse off than a woman with sons and *bahus* in her house. Further, every cultural value stresses the importance of children.

Having a child is essential to a woman's emotional health and to ensure her status in her family and village. In giving birth to a child, a woman knows she is contributing, as only she can do, to the well-being of her family. Cradling a tiny baby in her arms, she feels a deep sense of satisfaction and happiness. Further, having a son usually gives a young wife a boost in prestige. Childless couples are much pitied, and a barren woman is an inauspicious guest at a wedding or a *Chauk* (infant blessing) ceremony. A married woman with no children is considered incomplete, even as an unmarried adult woman would be incomplete. Fear of childlessness is sometimes so overwhelming that it seems to become a self-fulfilling prophecy: childless women go in droves to visit shamans who are believed to have the power to bless them with children, and a high percentage return with babes in arms to offer gifts of gratitude to these faith healers.

Some women feel that a woman's position in her husband's household and in his heart is dependent upon or at least bettered by her production of children. A man may seek another wife if his first wife has not given birth. One young and childless Thakur woman, ill with tuberculosis, got no sympathy or kind words from her husband. He refused to give her money for medicines or hospital expenses and seemed eager to be rid of her so he could marry a young widow with whom he was having an affair. A friend of the sick woman told me,

> Tulsibai's husband feels nothing for her. He told her, "If you're going to die tomorrow, you might as well die today and get it over with." You see, she doesn't have any children. Now, I have a son and little girls, and if anything happened to me, he [her husband] would worry about who would take care of his children.

Tulsibai later sold her jewelry to obtain funds and eventually married another man, by whom she bore a son, but she died shortly thereafter. But another childless woman, Jamnibai, of a low-ranking artisan caste, has lived quietly in Bhopal with her devoted husband for a dozen years. There have been no recriminations or threats of rejection, but there is an air of sadness about Jamnibai.

Contraceptives are used by a low percentage of villagers. Many villagers are ignorant of how to use such devices, and few ever visit a gynecologist who might instruct them. Lack of easy access to contraceptives and lack of privacy also militate against their use. Many villagers are suspicious of the government family planning campaigns, since they distrust government personnel in general.

In any case, many individuals perceive no value in limiting their families. One small village in the Delhi area was subjected to an intensive family planning campaign for six months, yet no one in the village adopted contraception as a result. There, as elsewhere, pregnant young women are given special care and attention, and some consider pregnancy an inherently desirable state. Twenty women were shown two pictures—silhouettes of a pregnant woman and an unpregnant woman. All saw the pregnant woman as happier, healthier, better fed, more secure, more influential, and more respected. Most of the villagers did not believe that individual use of contraceptives would slow population pressure on limited land resources. Some thought the growth of their village would lead to the opening of new shops, tea stalls, and other facilities which would provide job opportunities (Marshall, 1971).

Nevertheless, women who have borne several children without medical attention are often anemic or suffer from other illnesses and would like to prevent pregnancy. In Nimkhera, after having four children, Sundarbai resorted to avoiding her husband as much as possible, but she recently had her fifth child. After enduring the difficult birth of her seventh child, Phulbai, a poor Weaver woman, told me, "God has been good to us; he has given us enough children. Tell me how I can stop having children." Herbal medicines for contraception and abortion are said to be available but are seldom used.

In the Gangetic area, having children too close together is frowned upon; couples are expected to avoid intercourse during pregnancy and for two years after the birth of a surviving child. There, it is considered shameful for a woman to give birth after she has a grown daughter-in-law in the house. High-caste men in Rajasthan and elsewhere in North India attempt to limit their sexual activity, since they believe loss of semen is weakening (Carstairs, 1957).

Women's conversations frequently center around children and childbirth, and almost all women's gatherings include babies who are being cuddled and suckled. Young girls, who themselves are helping to care for younger siblings and cousins, watch and listen and grow up with the full expectation that they will become mothers. For villagers, there is virtually no alternative, but even city girls planning careers expect to have children. Girls hear of the pain of childbirth and learn in advance to accept it as part of being feminine. Still, a pregnant woman fears childbirth, not only for the pain but also because she knows she may die. Every woman has a relative or acquaintance who has died during late pregnancy or childbirth, and this knowledge perhaps increases her perception of pain. Maternal deaths are always very sad, involving as they do young women in the prime of life, many with young children. In about 1960 a Thakur woman in Nimkhera gave birth to a son, her sixth child. Her eldest daughter, about sixteen, had suddenly died the year before in her husband's village, and the family was desolate when the mother and her tiny son died four days after the baby was born. The father has never remarried but often calls his sister home to help, and the remaining four children are very responsible and cooperate in running the household. But the youngest daughter has been very troubled and often dreams about her dead mother and sister. She cries and sadly says, "My mother came to me again last night."

A child brings joy. Indians seem to truly love their children, not merely tolerate them. Family members all want to be near a baby, to look at it and to hold it. Children are included in every social event; there are virtually no separate childrens' functions except among the urban elite. Once two teenage village girls asked me to take their picture, and as I got out my camera, each grabbed a small child to hold. These were not their children; neither of them had any, so I asked why they were holding these children. "Because we like little children," they expained.

Every mother fears that her child will die, as she has seen so many babies do. The child is guarded from contact with people who might emanate evil influences and is kept away from sick children, whose mothers might magically take good health from another child to give to their own. Ever present is the fear of the evil eye, which even a loving parent can cause to fall on his child by admiring him too much. (No child is ever admired openly.) Smallpox, typhoid, cholera, eye infections, diphtheria, whooping cough, and myriad other diseases are constant threats. In cities and towns, children are often seen by doctors and "compounders" who administer injections and other medicines. But consistent with their distrust of government officials and in response to the haughty manner of some physicians, most villagers avoid hospitals and doctors as much as possible. Illnesses are frequently treated with herbal medicines, prayer, amulets, and wishful thinking. Although many children have been vaccinated against smallpox, villagers treat the disease by isolating the patient and appealing to Sitala Mata, the smallpox goddess. In general, the quality of medical care available to a child is commensurate with his family's wealth.

A mother's love and care are considered essential to the growth of a child, and no one is surprised when a motherless baby dies. Until a child is about ten years old, women are responsible for its daily care. A mother breast-feeds her baby—usually until he is two or three years old, washes him, changes his soiled clothes, and carries him about on her hip. Almost all babies are left with bare bottoms; when a child begins to urinate or defecate, his mother holds him to one side and later wipes up the mess. Some urban mothers put diapers on their babies or expect servants to clean up the messes on the floor, and a small percentage of urban women bottle-feed their children. As the child grows, his mother prepares solid food and feeds it to him by hand. She also supervises his play, bathing, and other activities. Although his mother is primarily responsible for him, a child's aunts and grandmother may also take an active role in caring for him. The child's father, uncles, and other male kinsmen may take an interest in him, but they rarely tend to his daily physical needs.

It is considered shameful for a young mother to flaunt her relationship with her baby before her elders, and it is even more shameful for a young father to do so. A new mother feels embarrassment in nursing her baby before elders in either her natal home or her husband's home, not because she is ashamed of exposing her breasts but because the child represents absolute proof of her sexuality. When she takes her new baby with her to visit in her parents' home, a young woman lets her mother or sister care for the child, the product of her relationship with her husband, as much as possible. The baby's father does not hold or kiss the child in the presence of his elder kinsmen or fellow villagers until the child is four or five years old. This sense of shame in dealing with one's child is in accord with two important themes in North and Central Indian culture: the deemphasis of the nuclear family unit in favor of the larger joint family unit and the separation of a woman's parental home from her husband's home. Young couples who live away from their parents and older and less traditional villagers openly dandle their children in public.

Children are never left alone; they are always with a parent, grandparent, older sibling, or other family member. Wealthy people sometimes engage a nursemaid to carry the child about, but most people do not allow a nonkinsman to care for a child.

TRADITIONAL TASKS

For almost all Indian women, work centers around child care, food processing, and care of the household. Some women perform other tasks both at home and outside the house, but they are still responsible for housework, which is considered woman's proper sphere.

In most of North and Central India, it is a man's job to bring home food for his family, having procured it either through sowing and reaping a crop or earning money and purchasing it. It is a woman's job to convert the raw foodstuffs—wheat, rice, millet, lentils, vegetables, tea, sugar, salt, fruits, meat, milk, and spices—into meals to serve to her family. Preprocessed or convenience foods are expensive, distrusted, and not widely available; consequently food preparation may occupy several hours of a woman's day.

The village woman must clean her grain of tiny stones and chaff by sifting, tossing in a winnowing fan, and picking through it. On sunny afternoons women gather in courtyards or on verandahs to clean grain and chat.

Wheat and lentils must then be ground, usually in a home mill. Young girls like to grind, two sitting opposite each other, turning the heavy round millstone to the rhythm of their singing. Wives also grind; turning the mill is good physical exercise for women in purdah. Grinding is time-consuming, however (it takes about twenty minutes for one woman to grind two pounds of wheat); in both cities and villages, those who can afford it have much of their grain ground at commercial mills. Rice is husked at home with a heavy wooden pestle, and salt and spices are ground by hand. Cow, goat, and buffalo milk is boiled to sterilize it and churned to obtain butter and buttermilk. Butter is clarified to produce India's favorite cooking oil, *ghī*, and mangoes and lemons are pickled.

Cooking may be extremely time-consuming, depending upon the elaborateness of the meals a woman's family expects. In most of the northern half of India wheat is the staple, made into flat *rotis* (unleavened bread) and served with lentil sauce or vegetables. *Rotis* are prepared fresh once or twice each day over the small horseshoe-shaped mud stove found in virtually every kitchen. Even city women who cook vegetables over small kerosene or gas burners usually make *rotis* on an earthen stove fueled with cowdung cakes or wood. Prosperous families may dine on a number of heavily spiced dishes at each meal, dishes that are almost always prepared in a relatively small kitchen by the women of the family. Some well-to-do families employ cooks, but traditional families allow kitchen servants to help only in cleaning grain, grinding, paring vegetables, and washing dishes. In village families, most kitchen duties fall to the sequestered *bahus*.

After each meal the earthen oven must be cleansed with a fresh layer of yellow clay and the brass platters and tumblers scoured with fine ash and water.

For village women, fetching water is an important task. Twice daily women and girls bear heavy brass and earthen pots filled with cool well water atop their heads. Young girls learn early to balance the pots, and Hindu girls are taught to avoid contact with ritually polluting lower-caste people between the well and home. Although the pots are heavy, women like to go for water, since it is only at the well that women of different households can meet daily to exchange news and gossip. Women in strict seclusion, wealthy Muslims and young *bahus* of high-status Hindu families, do not visit the well but depend upon their menfolk or male servants to bring water.

Men are in charge of major structural additions and repairs to a house, and women are responsible for maintaining the house's cleanliness and beauty. Every day a village woman sweeps her house and courtyard to keep the earthen floors clean, and, squatting, she cleans the cowshed of dung. She shapes the dung into round patties and plops them to dry in the sun. Patties prepared the previous day are added to a neat pile, the family's main fuel supply for cooking and warming fires in the winter. Every week

A young Brahman wife goes to fetch water.

she applies a fresh layer of cow dung paste to the floors to provide a clean, dustless surface.[11] Periodically, especially after the rainy season, house walls and courtyard floors must be patched and rebuilt with a mixture of mud and straw and then whitewashed.

Many village houses in Western and Central India are decorated with fine earthen bas reliefs around doorways and wall niches, sometimes beautifully colored with ochre, yellow, and malochite hues. The women of Rajasthan create incredibly intricate painted mud filigree cabinets and shelves studded with tiny mirrors inside their houses, and outside walls are painted with colorful warriors and elephants. Many women paint bright flowers and figures on their walls and draw curlicue designs in rice paste or whitewash on their doorsteps. Most urban women, on the other hand, take little interest in home decoration, devoting their artistic energies to decorating themselves.

Few women are responsible for the family laundry. Village adults usually rinse out their own clothing after bathing each day, and mothers wash their small children's clothing. Periodically, heavily soiled clothing is scrubbed by the village laundress and launderer, members of the Dhobi caste. City dwellers typically engage a Dhobi to wash and press all clothing. In many villages, tailors make almost all stitched clothing; but in some areas women sew baby clothes and some of their own garments. In Rajasthan and Gujarat, women spend months making cutwork and embroidered mirror-studded wall hangings, skirts, and saris. Rajasthani women also tie the knots for their colorful tie-dyed saris. Khalapur women gin and spin cotton to be made into cloth by weavers. Some middle-class urban women know how to make blouses and petticoats, but they usually depend on tailors to sew clothing for themselves and their families.

Many women work in their own fields or in the fields of others, but there is no agricultural task considered primarily women's work. The essential activity of plowing, which requires driving bullocks, is considered strictly man's province. Women are particularly active in rice cultivation in areas where the crop is grown, helping with planting and doing much of the arduous weeding, harvesting, and threshing. In some areas they also take an active part in sowing and harvesting wheat and other crops. Women who belong to poor families spend many hours in the fields each

A village daughter, home for a visit, plasters her porch with cowdung paste.

A low-caste daughter of the village harvests wheat.

year, but well-to-do women usually help only with the harvest and rely on hired men to help their menfolk with other tasks. In the Varanasi area, high-caste women do not work in the fields at all. Very poor women work as sharecroppers or hire themselves out as day laborers in the fields of others, thus contributing substantially to the family income.

In Nimkhera, women's assistance during the short but crucial wheat sowing and harvest periods is vital to most families, since these tasks must be completed quickly and short-handed families must hire outside labor. It is not surprising that a woman's parents and in-laws vie for her presence at these times.

Some village women help grow and sell vegetables and fruits; others help run shops. Some make rope for household use, and a few shape earthen roof tiles for sale. Poor women gather wild fruits, vegetables, rice, and *tendū* leaves, sold for use as country cigarette wrappers. Women work alongside their menfolk in cutting bales of hay for dry-season fodder and gathering firewood. A few very poor women herd goats, although animal herding is not considered safe for women, since animals graze in forest areas far from home.

Nimkhera women of all castes do at least some work in the fields, whereas high-caste women in the Varanasi area do none. This may contribute to the fact that the status of Nimkhera women in relation to men is somewhat higher than that of Varanasi women. Although virtually all women perform economically significant tasks, among peasant farmers it is feminine participation in agriculture which seems to be most closely related to female status.[12] Generally, however, Indian women who bring food and money from any source into the household enjoy greater independence than women who do not (Mandelbaum, 1970, pp. 48–50).

Very poor city women work as domestic servants for wealthy and middle-class families or labor on building and road construction projects, carrying head loads of earth and stone in the hot sun. Women of nomadic blacksmith groups work beside their husbands at the anvil. In a few areas, women work in mines and on tea plantations.

In many villages a special system of intercaste exchanges of goods and services exists. Under this system, which anthropologists call the *Jajmānī* system, service and artisan caste families have a hereditary right to provide certain services for the families of castes other than their own and in return receive traditional payments of grain, money, and other benefits. In some areas, *jajmani* ties between families have been in force for generations; in other areas, the system is breaking down. In any case, women of these castes perform traditional caste-associated tasks in addition to their normal housework, child care, and agricultural work.

In Bengal, women of the Santal tribe work as laborers on a construction crew.

A weaver woman weaves tapes for a cot.

Barber women do not cut hair as their husbands do, but in some areas they deliver babies, bathe mother and baby, cut women's toenails, dress brides, and direct *Chauk* (infant blessing) ceremonies. Barber couples deliver invitations to village functions and make leaf plates for feasts.

Tailor women sew and mend garments for their patrons; Washerwomen wash them. Potter women paint white peacocks and other designs on the earthen pots their menfolk shape and help deliver them to customers. Although many are now turning to other sources of income, some Weaver women still help prepare cotton and loom fabric and webbing for cots. In some areas, Tanner women help their menfolk process leather and make shoes. The "untouchable" Sweeper women of villages and cities perform the wretched and despised task of cleaning old-style latrines, and in some cases they deliver babies. In towns, very poor women of certain groups go out to beg.

For most Indian women the day begins before dawn. Village women rise early so they can work in the cool of the early morning, but even city women are up at 5:30 to prepare sweet milky tea for their families.

After rising, the village woman goes with her tiny pot of cleansing water to the field or roadside to eliminate; then she returns to wash her hands, face, and teeth. She has a snack, fetches water, folds and hangs the bedding from the rafters, sweeps, tends to the needs of the children, cleans the cow shed, and bathes. For Hindus, daily bathing is an essential prelude to the main activities of the day.[13] The village woman squats with her sari on and pours water over her head and body. The wet sari is adroitly removed and a dry sari put on without exposing the body; thus the village woman can bathe behind an upturned cot or in public at a pond or well. Some traditional urban women also bathe fully clothed, rubbing soap through the wet cloth, but private nude bathing is now common in cities (Cormack, 1953, pp. 25–26). After her bath, the woman can begin to prepare the main meal of the day, which she serves in the late morning. In Joint families, women eat after the men have finished. While a woman is cleaning the stove and dishes, her menfolk leave for the fields or office and children for play or school.

Afternoon activities vary greatly according to wealth and season. Prosperous high-caste village women at slack agricultural seasons sit around, some cleaning grain, some napping or talking. Poor women of low status go out to work in the fields, at the threshing floors, or at other income-earning tasks during busy periods of the year. Wealthy city women nap, read, or visit friends.

In the evening, village women and girls fetch water and tie the cattle returned from a day of grazing in their sheds. City women sometimes go with family members to shop at this hour in colorful, crowded bazaars. After again going to eliminate, village women light the lamps and prepare supper while men smoke and talk.

Villagers usually retire after supper, but on special nights men and women gather separately to sing until midnight or later.

It is clear that women perform a wide variety of tasks and that their services are essential to the well-being of their families and the nation. Because of the relative scarcity of females throughout much of North and Central India, there are many men who live as bachelors. These men, and those whose wives spend long periods visiting in their natal homes, compain bitterly of the difficulties of living without a wife to help with household and agricultural work. They fetch their own water, cook simple meals, and either hire women or impose on female relatives to grind wheat and make cow dung cakes. No single woman who desires a husband is long without one except in cities. Nevertheless, there are cultural limitations to women's activities, and women usually perceive their jobs as being less important than those of their menfolk. In fact, women consider themselves beholden to and dependent upon their fathers, brothers, and husbands. I once asked Sukkibai, a wizened and overworked Sweeper woman about her relationship with her alcoholic husband. The man had married Sukkibai when she was a girl and then brought three other women to be his wives.

These women all sweep latrines and weave baskets and turn their earnings over to their idle husband, who uses a good part of the funds to buy liquor. Sukkibai said her husband would beat her if she were to buy even a set of cheap glass bangles without his permission. "Why do you stay with him?" I asked. "Oh, then where would I go?" she replied with a sigh. Women of higher caste echoed this sentiment. A Barber woman very active in agricultural and traditional caste work said, "I have to listen to whatever my husband tells me. Otherwise where would I go? He's the breadwinner." A hard-working Thakur woman once said, to the agreement of the Barber woman, "Why do you think men marry? It's only for sex."

The fact is that under the traditional Hindu inheritance and residence system still in force in villages, women are beholden to men; without dependence on a man who controls land, the ultimate source of food and the location of their home, a woman's position is most difficult. A woman alone in the world indeed lacks security.

A Hindu widow has rights to the fruits of her dead husband's land, but without sons she finds managing the land difficult. Even landowning Muslim women need men to help administer their land. A woman cannot plow herself, so must hire men to drive the bullocks. She must be vigilant to prevent cheating and stealing of her crop. With no male to take her part in court or to bribe officials, she may find even her land stolen by unscrupulous relatives.

Purdah restrictions on women's movements outside their homes add to their dependence on men in the realms of marketing and money, but women have some autonomy in these areas. Although men make almost all bazaar purchases, women buy from small village shops, from itinerant vendors, and from stalls set up at fairs. Glittering glass bangles, vegetables and fruits, sweets, combs, blouses, sweaters, and even saris are sold door-to-door in many villages. Women pay with the family cash left in their care, or—more usually—with grain, to which they have free access. Some women, in fact, residents of joint families, secretly sell grain to traders to add to their own personal hoard of money and jewelry. Some well-to-do women lend money clandestinely or openly and collect high rates of interest.

Many women feel they should consult their husbands before buying expensive items, but some women who are earning members of the household say they are entitled to spend money as they please. Generally, poor, lower-caste, and tribal women buy a higher proportion of things on their own than do wealthier and high-status women. But Birjis Jahan, Latif Khan's wife, who is in charge of the family's treasury, sends servants to make purchases for her. She once went out in a relative's jeep, veiled in her *burka,* to buy living room furniture from a private seller. Her husband was angry with her but pleased with the furniture. Birjis Jahan is also in charge of marketing vegetables grown on family land; she lets a male servant sell the produce and bring her the proceeds.

A Muslim woman has the legal right to demand her *mehr* money, pledged by her husband at her wedding, at any time. "A man has no right to complain about what his wife does with the money," Latif Khan explained to me. But normally a woman does not demand *mehr* unless her husband is squandering the family funds or divorcing her. Traditional Muslim and modern Indian courts uphold a woman's right to her *mehr*.

A woman's knowledge, cleverness, and confidence in herself greatly influence the decisions she makes. A clever woman can create her own nest egg and persuade other family members to take her point of view without arousing their antagonism. But purdah observances and restrictions on her education and activities may render her ignorant of agricultural matters, prices, bargaining, and many other things. In these areas, many women are glad to accept the advice of informed men.

NEW OCCUPATIONS

Traditionally, an Indian woman worked outside her home only if she had to. The woman who earned money was pitied for her poverty and for her husband's inability to provide for his family. In both villages and towns, women of the lower classes have always worked in the fields of others, as domestic servants, and carried out traditional tasks while their wealthier neighbors performed domestic chores in the privacy of their homes and worked only occasionally in their own fields. The association of female money-earning and low status in society continues in villages and in traditional urban circles, but today more and more women of the middle and upper urban classes are working outside their homes. Using the education they have obtained in high schools and colleges, these women are taking an active part in the modernization of their country.

Mahatma Gandhi, the great Indian nationalist, was partially responsible for making it socially acceptable for these urban women to come out of their homes. A man who cultivated traditional personal habits in himself and who found favor with Indians of all walks of life, he advocated women's rights and insisted that it was women's duty to come forth and work for the independence of the country and the uplift of the poor and unfortunate. Women by the hundreds demonstrated, marched, and were jailed for their anti-British activity. After independence was won, some of these women, particularly Hindus, Parsis, and Christians, continued to work outside of their homes.

More important forces bringing women into the salaried work force have been the urbanization, industrialization, and modernization of the country. Village women can still carry out economically useful tasks within the family and the small community, but if city women wish similarly to contribute to the family economy, they must seek paid employment. Fur-

A young woman of Indore City, a college lecturer.

ther, participation in certain occupations may bring prestige to a family living in a world affected by Western values.

Most of the occupations in which Indian women have achieved prominence are clearly related to their traditional nurturing and domestic roles. Women work as teachers at all educational levels but particularly in girls' schools and colleges. Before independence, some women actively crusaded in the cause of women's rights, determinedly working against purdah, child marriage, and for better treatment for widows. For example, Pandita Ramabai, one famous widow, founded a home and school for high-caste child widows in Poona, and Sister Subbalakshmi, a child widow herself but educated by a determined father, founded similar institutions in Madras. Today women staff schools of social work and institutions such as orphanages and child welfare centers throughout the country. As village-level workers in the national Community Development Programme, they teach village women about hygiene, family planning, smokeless ovens, and kitchen gardens. Many women have become nurses (particularly Christians) and doctors. The term *lady doctor* is synonymous with *obstetrician-gynecologist*, since most female doctors specialize in that field and Indian women are most reluctant to visit a male gynecologist.

Women are active in business enterprises, journalism, writing, the theater, cinema, art, and even law. A few women also work as clerks in handicraft shops and boutiques and a very few as stewardesses, but virtually none are bank tellers or waitresses. Although some women work as office clerks, the vast majority of India's office workers, including secretaries, are men. Government tourist information centers are staffed by women, and the All-India Handicraft Board has been directed by a woman.[14]

The life of the middle-class working woman may be difficult. In conservative towns, a woman alone on the street or on a bus may be molested and annoyed by men. Discrimination against women in some fields is very great, and in virtually no field are they in the majority. Most working women could never aspire to an executive position, and, as women seek equality in pay and opportunity, they find employers refusing to hire them. Further, on a day-to-day basis, a working woman may encounter substantial opposition from her own family. In the realistic film *Mahanagar,* Satyajit Ray dramatized the conflicts in the life of a Calcutta woman of modest means and demeanor who agrees to sell knitting machines door-to-door. Although the family's finances are enhanced by her earnings, her husband's parents, with whom she lives, feel like beggars in accepting money from their own daughter-in-law. Her husband feels emasculated by her ability to earn money, especially when he loses his job and she becomes the family's sole support. He is almost crazed with jealousy when he sees her wearing sunglasses and having tea with a male associate, and their whole relationship is threatened by her venture beyond the traditional domestic sphere. In the film the couple's love for each other overcomes their difficulties, but in real life such conflicts often lead to a woman's giving up her career plans at the whim of her husband or other family members. Many working girls quit their jobs when they marry. But for upper- and middle-class women who continue to work after marriage, care of children and home is greatly eased by the ready availability of domestic servants and the presence of a grandmother in the home.[15]

However, life may be extremely difficult for the domestic servants, factory workers, and other poor working women of the cities, many of whom are recent immigrants from villages. In a single crowded tenement room or shack, a woman cooks at a small stove in one corner as her children dodge clothes hanging from a line stretching across the room and her husband reclines against a pile of bedding and trunks in another corner. In the worst of the urban dwellings, the hutments, monsoon rains pour through the patchwork roofs to drench the occupants and their meager possessions and make of lanes a mire that assails the nostrils. From this environment the poor working woman must emerge fresh each morning to travel to her job, where she earns about 30 or 40 cents a day.

RELIGION

Religion is an important part of daily life for almost every Indian. Whether Hindu, Muslim, Sikh, Christian, Jain, or Parsi, an Indian considers his religion an important part of his identity. Others relate to him as a member of a particular religious group—so much so, in fact, that conversion to another religion is legal grounds for divorce and loss of inheritance.

Hindus worship a great many gods, goddesses, and spirits which sophisticated Hindus consider manifestations of one divine entity. Virtually all believe that souls pass through a number of existences. Although an individual's fate is "written on his forehead by God" at birth, a person is held accountable for his actions. Sinners may be reborn as subhuman creatures or untouchables, while those who fulfill the duties appropriate to their statuses in this life will be rewarded with a higher birth in the next. In the orthodox view, the ultimate reward is release from the cycle of reincarnation and union with God, but a Khalapur girl felt that the highest reward would be rebirth into one's own household (Minturn and Hitchcock, 1966, p. 70). Nimkhera women believe a woman could never be reborn as a man.

Although women are excluded from the Hindu priesthood, they participate in most important ceremonies and observances in the home and temple. In some areas, men carry out most daily temple and home rituals, while elsewhere women are responsible for daily · worship. Throughout India both men and women maintain religious fasts, but more women than men fast. Women's most important contribution to religious life is performing rituals connected with the life cycle and calendrical festivals, rituals considered vital to the well-being of the individual, the family, and the community. In Khalapur and Senapur, women are much more conservative in religious matters than are men, and women are therefore the main participants in these rites (Luschinsky, 1962, p. 644 ff.; Minturn and Hitchcock, 1966, p. 65 ff.).

The number and diversity of Hindu rituals performed throughout India are astounding; an encyclopedia could hardly catalog them all. Rituals range from simple devotional prayers and offerings to elaborate processions. In a town near Delhi, a woman daily lights an incense stick, places it before a colorful picture of Lord Krishna, and silently mouths a prayer for her son away at college. An Indore woman visits her special prayer room every day to place marigold blossoms, incense, and a small oil lamp before the family collection of brass images of deities. Respectfully, she garlands a framed photograph of her deceased husband. In Senapur, women gather at the shrine of Sitala Mata, the smallpox goddess, to offer food and flowers to her in exchange for her protection. In Calcutta, masses of people, including brilliantly dressed girls and women, gather to watch the annual procession honoring Durga. Elaborate images of the goddess are worshiped and, amidst a deafening din of fireworks and band music, are borne through the streets to be dumped into the river. Near Karauli, a small Rajasthani town, pilgrims congregate at a hilltop temple for the annual festival honoring Kela Devi. Far into the night women seeking to please the goddess with their devotion dance before the temple, their skirts swirling and veils covering their faces. In the morning they gather to watch the Maharaja of Karauli preside over the sword-swift sacrifice of a large goat to the goddess.

Observances like these occur every day throughout India. Even in a small village like Nimkhera, in a single year there was daily worship in the village temple and many homes, 112 festival days, and 104 days on which life cycle rites were performed.

One festival, Divali, the festival of lights, is observed throughout much of India. In Nimkhera as elsewhere, this fall festival centers around the worship of Lakshmi, the goddess of wealth, and wealth in all its forms. The women of each household shape a large heap of cow dung into a recumbent man on their doorstep; this embodiment of the usefulness of cow dung is later worshiped. Men and boys bathe the village cattle in the pond, and women prepare fine festival foods. In the evening, small earthen oil lamps are lit outside each house, and several lamps are lit before a pottery figurine of goddess Lakshmi. The women of each household contribute their jewelry to a glittering pile of money and cattle ornaments before the goddess, as if to ask her to increase their wealth. In every cow shed men offer wheatcakes to the cattle, and the sound of firecrackers resounds through the village. The next morning, the cattle are decorated with bright ornaments and paints and driven out to graze. Men and women gather to sing hymns and other songs. The next day, women prepare two more cow dung sculptures, and girls ritually bless their brothers.

The spring harvest festival of Holi is celebrated over most of the northern half of India. Holi is certainly India's most colorful holiday: merrymakers throw bucketfuls of purple and red dye on each other. In many villages, Holi is the occasion for battles between men and women; women pelt men with cow dung and beat them with sticks and men fight back with hilarious verbal abuse. The opposition expressed is not between men and women in general, but between affines: only village *bahus,* never daughters, join the fray. In Nimkhera, on Holi, women stage a private session of skits,

During the Jhanda Torna festival, low-caste wives wage a raucous battle against the village men.

including hilariously sexy parodies and absurd situation comedies. But the festival ends on a note of utmost seriousness as all the villagers, dressed in their finery, proceed to the Mother Goddess shrine to witness the offering of coconuts and the sacrifice of a goat. Later, sounds of groups of men and women singing echo through the moonlit village lanes.

In Nimkhera, the spirit of Holi is carried over into Jhanda Torna, a semireligious holiday celebrated at night about two weeks later. To encourage a mood of abandon, marijuana tea is served to men and women as they gather around a tall wooden pole topped with a bag of brown sugar. With flailing sticks, a group of low-caste wives vigorously defend the pole from the attack of a large number of men of all castes. The men protect themselves with T-shaped shields as they advance and retreat to the sound of rhythmic drumming. High-caste women and Muslims are fascinated spectators. The uproarious battle eventually terminates with the men's victorious uprooting of the pole and seizure of the sugar, but not before several have suffered painful blows. Later, a professional dancing girl performs.

Participation in ritual activities brings happiness and a sense of importance to most Hindu women. Although belief in the divine is strong throughout India, women perhaps even more than men are devout believers in the supernatural. Only through proper performance of rituals can deities and spirits be placated and persuaded to bring benefits of good health and wealth to a woman and her family. In carrying out these rituals, a woman feels she is doing something important to benefit her family. In Nimkhera, the young Brahman woman Kamladevi had lost three babies. Even before she became pregnant again, she began to diligently worship a goddess said to help women have healthy babies. Kamladevi is now the mother of a healthy little boy, named after the goddess.

Further, Hinduism provides opportunities for recreation and emotional release. The many worship services, rituals, ceremonies, and pilgrimages that are part of the religion are not only occasions to worship God but also entertaining and fun. Participation in religious activities is a socially and morally acceptable reason for a sequestered woman to leave her house to interact with other women or for a hard-working family to enjoy a trip to the Ganges or other holy place. In fact, failure to perform prescribed rituals outside the home could bring divine retribution.

The proportion of religious activity carried out by Hindu women seems to be correlated with their status vis-à-vis men. In Central India, where women are not always subordinate to men, both sexes participate actively in rituals and festivals. In contrast, the women of Senapur, who seem to be of significantly lower status than their menfolk, are responsible for nearly all religious ceremonies. There, men can easily satisfy their needs for recreation, sociability, and emotional catharsis outside religion. Further, "men make many decisions which affect women, and women sometimes have very little, if any, voice in the decisions. Aside from household work, religious activities provide the only opportunity for women to take initiative in major endeavors" (Luschinsky, 1962, p. 718).

For those who do not find complete satisfaction in their family life, religion provides an acceptable outlet in the form of lengthy prayer, worship, pilgrimage, and even spirit possession. In the village of Shanti Nagar near Delhi, Daya, a bride of the Tanner caste, became ill through spirit possession. In interviews with Ruth Freed, Daya revealed that she was having difficulty adjusting to her new role as a wife and veiled *bahu*. Her spirit-induced illness allowed her to draw attention to herself, express hostile feelings, and to otherwise act in ways that would not normally be socially acceptable. In Senapur, veiled *bahus* who visit spirit-possessed male shamans sometimes themselves become possessed and writhe and shake so much that their clothes fall from their shoulders (Freed and Freed, 1964; Luschinsky, 1962, pp. 694–709). Such performances provide important emotional outlets for these girls. Among some tribal peoples, women act as shamans (Elwin, 1958, pp. 210–211). Through religion, family conflicts can often be skirted or resolved without hostility or confrontation.

Religious activity is not only psychologically beneficial but may also help cure physical disability. Many sick worshipers report cures following pleas to the divine.

Starkly monotheistic in doctrine, Islam provides fewer religious activities for women. Religious Muslim women may fast during the month of Ramzan and pray five time each day to Allah (at home rather than in a mosque as their husbands do), but most women do not pray that often. Muslim festivals are few and unelaborate, but women participate in all of them. The most important holiday is Mithi Id, celebrating the end of Ramzan. After prayers, dressed in bright new clothing, separate groups of men and women visit neighbors and relatives to exchange Id greetings. Holiday food is prepared and eaten. On other occasions women visit famous Muslim saints' tombs to seek boons. Shi'ite Muslims, in the minority in India, observe Muhurram, commemorating the martyrdom of the Prophet's grandson. Women gather to hear a priest read a traditional text telling of Hussein's demise; an occasion that has been described as follows:

> A few hundred women arrived, dressed in deep mourning, sat on the rush mats with tears coursing down their cheeks and listened to the priest. While they beat their breasts in delicate anguish, they gazed slyly at the marriageable girls of the community out of the corners of their eyes [to find matches for their sons and nephews]. The older women, however, were more sincere. They thumped their chests so violently and wept so copiously that they sometimes fainted.
>
> . . . [The women next to me] were behaving strangly. . . . Tears rolled down their red, agonized faces; the knuckles of their fists beat a violent tattoo on the floor. They writhed uncontrollably and from time to time their heads fell back against the wall on which we leaned with a resounding whack. [Ishvani, 1947, pp. 99 and 102].

Ideally, every Muslim should read the Koran in Arabic at least once. Even otherwise illiterate girls are guided through the sacred book by a teacher. Thus religion may provide an uneducated girl with her only contact with reading and add to her sense of dignity.

AMUSEMENTS

In recreation as in so many other aspects of Indian women's life, restraint is a key principle. Women find most of their pleasures and relaxation in the course of their daily lives in their homes and local communities in the company of other women. For most, life is far from hedonistic, and young wives confined to their courtyards often complain of boredom.

One small pleasure can be enjoyed daily by most women: chewing the mildly intoxicant betel nut and leaf, mixed with a pinch of tobacco or a pungent cardamom seed. In some parts of North India, village women also smoke the hookah (water pipe) or an occasional cigarette. On Holi, some

Halkibai shapes a papier-mâché bowl.

village women drink a marijuana tea that makes them feel giddy. But even in castes which permit the drinking of alcohol, women rarely do so.

Some women enjoy handicrafts. Nimkhera women decorate their house-fronts with mud bas reliefs, and some also create elaborate earthen grille-works around the shelf on which water jars are kept and around the sacred basil plant which stands before most homes. Girls visiting their parents make prettily shaped papier-mâché bowls, and some weave small baskets and make beadwork chokers and patchwork fans. It is to women that al-most all of India's traditional nonprofessional art work is attributable (Un-tracht, 1968, p. 149). In cities, educated women knit sweaters, paint pic-tures, read books and fashion magazines, and write letters. They may also find amusement in visiting sari and bangle shops.

Among traditional villagers, women almost never gather merely to en-joy each other's company, and they have no formal associations. Neighbors chat and occasionally tell stories about village events as they clean grain or make rope, huddling around a warm fire on a winter night. Larger parties are held to sing in celebration of a religious holiday, a wedding, or a birth. These events are so frequent that village women gather to sing scores of times each year. Clustered together on a dimly lit verandah, women and

To welcome the gods to her home, Motibai draws
auspicious designs on her porch.

girls of all ages talk and sing traditional songs appropriate to the occasion.
The nighttime songfest goes on for hours, ending only when the hostess
passes out sweets or boiled grain. Clutching their little bundles of refresh-
ments, their bracelets and ankle ornaments softly jingling, the sari-draped
figures walk through dark and quiet lanes to their homes. City women, too,
enjoy singing at weddings and at special gatherings devoted to singing
hymns.

Middle- and upper-class urban couples sometimes go together to Western-style dinner and tea parties, but even there women tend to gather in
one room and men in another.

City women also attend movies—escorted by a brother, father, husband,
or son. They enjoy the lengthly dramas featuring religious themes, famous
heroes of the epics, never-ending singing and dancing, and involved romance. D. P. Mukerji has written, "Indian films are, in fact, one long

exercise in wish fulfillment and offer tempting avenues of escape from the drudgery of family life and disappointments in the love that-might-have-been" (1951, p. 797). The lilting film songs are very popular throughout India.

Throughout most of North and Central India, women who value their reputations do not dance except under certain limited circumstances. Typically, the "dancing girl" is also a prostitute; to traditional villagers, the image of the completely debased and public woman of no morals is best conjured up by the phrase "dancing naked in public." Even prostitutes are well dressed when they perform their public dances. Film stars who dance in scanty clothing in movies may amuse urban viewers, but they scandalize most villagers. Village women who allowed me to photograph them extracted a promise that I would not sell their pictures to Bombay cinema producers who would "make the photo dance in a movie." In Nimkhera, women and girls celebrate Holi by performing slow-moving walk-through reel dances and some women perform brief but energetic dances to bless a groom at a wedding or *gauna* ceremony, but no men other than the groom may watch these hurried performances. In contrast, men publicly join in a vigorous stick dance many times during the rainy season. Once or twice a year prostitutes or female impersonators visit the village; women and girls stand in the dark shadows behind the enthusiastic male viewers to watch the dancing performances.

In some educated urban circles, girls are taught classical dancing by a dance master. Young schoolgirls give singing and dancing programs, but after puberty they usually perform only within the family circle if at all. In her autobiography, Ishvani wrote of secretly indulging a passion for dancing, all the while fearful that her stepmother would catch her at this "shameless" pastime (1947, p. 67). But the women of Mathura, Lord Krishna's birthplace, are famous for their devotional dancing, and at not-too-distant Karauli women dance before the goddess. Gypsy women sometimes join in a circle dance. Only among tribal peoples do men and women openly dance together. On moonlit nights unmarried young people gather together to drink toddy and dance with their arms around each other in long lines to the sound of drumming and beautifully haunting singing. Among the Muria of Bastar District, young couples then retire to the dormitory where all teenagers sleep.

Neighbor women sometimes play pachisi, but village females do not normally play vigorous sports or games. Their most energetic play is during the rainy month of Savan, when girls don bright clothes and go on porch swings to celebrate the promise of fertility of the land—and themselves. City schoolgirls play volleyball and table tennis, and a few years ago a team of young Indian women attempted to scale Mount Everest. In some cities a few women ride bicycles. Well-to-do women of the larger cities also belong to sports clubs where they can meet to swim, play tennis, and have soft drinks or tea. Anglo-Indians have been particularly active in organized sports.

Itinerant entertainers visit many villages to amuse and amaze spectators with trained monkeys and bears, magic shows, sword-swallowing acts, devotional songs, and hand-cranked peep shows.

Dating is severely disapproved in most circles, and even a married woman should never publicly admit that she enjoys sex. However, making love is an extremely common amusement. In some villages it is assumed that any healthy young woman not living with a vigorous husband will find a lover, and this has certainly happened in many cases. It is for this reason that the parents of a Nimkhera Brahman man who died tragically in his early twenties did not object when his young widow remarried. "She was very young; it would have been hard for her to bear it," her former father-in-law explained to me. If she had become promiscuous, the entire family would have been shamed.

In the Himalayan village studied by Gerald Berreman, it is assumed that any man and woman who have ever met alone in the jungle have had sexual relations (1963, p. 173).

Although most women say a man's sexual desires are always stronger than a woman's, Tejibai, a young Thakur mother, once told me jokingly that she was looking forward to her husband's return from a pilgrimage, "so we can do it day and night." One Nimkhera man and his wife happily admit to having sexual relations twenty-five nights of every month.

Few women travel just for pleasure: outings and journeys are undertaken only for specific, approved purposes. Males have much more freedom to gallivant, although they ideally combine errands with pleasure.

Women often visit relatives, either for long stays with their parents or cousins or, in cities, for just an afternoon. Groups of village women sometimes walk to neighboring villages to pay ceremonial calls or gather for religious picnics near a shrine. Virtually the only events village Hindu women admit to attending "just for fun" are the country fairs; yet these fairs, too, are centered around religious dramas. Groups of men and women go on pilgrimages to distant holy cities, but it would be almost unthinkable for a group of village women to go to a nearby town just to see a movie.

For most Indian women, visiting holy sites remains the most delightful recreation. Sunalini Nayudu, my former assistant, now in charge of training women to work in villages as social workers, recently wrote of an educational tour on which she led her students to visit social welfare institutions in North India:

> Practically all our trainees are married women; some are even grandmothers, having been married at the age of 10, 12, 13—by the time they reach the

age of 30 to 35 they have become grandmothers. Except for three Christian girls, all are Hindus. Taking all these mothers and grandmothers to Allahabad and Varanasi [holy cities on the sacred Ganges River] on an educational tour was really difficult. We visited more temples than social institutions. It was more like a pilgrims' trip, with everyone consulting the holy men and having huge *tikas* [auspicious red marks] put on their foreheads. Forty-three such charges were on our hands, and having just three days in each place to visit many social institutions at the appointed time was really too much for us four teachers. All these trainees are village girls who have lived all their lives in an orthodox atmosphere, fearing God and the devil to a great extent. They were singing religious songs the whole time. We vowed never to choose a holy place for an educational tour again [1971, personal communication].

Latif Khan and Birjis Jahan occasionally travel with their children to visit relatives in Bombay. There, far from conservative Bhopal, Birjis Jahan doffs her *burka* (cloak) and, in the company of a sophisticated cousin or her husband, visits shops and cinemas. Many middle- and upper-class urban families travel together on trains and buses to visit relatives in distant areas and even to vacation in beautiful Kashmir or the foothills of the Himalayas. The very wealthy even travel abroad. But for many the enjoyment of such a trip is enhanced if it can be combined with visits to holy pilgrimage sites.

THE OLDER WOMAN

Rambai's mother-in-law, Hirabai, is now over sixty years old. Her beauty has long since faded, and she wears little of the jingling jewelry that once signaled her presence—her silver and gold are now worn by her granddaughters-in-law. She considers it a great misfortune that she is a widow, since every woman hopes to die before her husband. The very word *widow* (*rānd*) connotes inauspiciousness and sorrow. But she does not regret being old; she takes pride in her position as the senior member of a large and reasonably prosperous joint family. She has enjoyed years as a mother and a grandmother, with her sons, *bahus,* and grandchildren living with her. Sometimes she remembers with sorrow the deaths of two baby sons and a daughter decades ago, but more often she proudly contemplates the joy her living descendants have brought her. She has been fortunate enough to welcome great-grandchildren to her family. Now older than most men in the village, she rarely needs to veil her face. She is free to attend all the festive and social events denied her as a young *bahu,* long ago. Now she seldom cooks, leaving kitchen work mostly to her *bahus,* but she continues to help care for the small children and perform other household tasks. Further, she is in charge of keeping the family funds safe and telling her sons what to bring from the bazaar each week. She is a useful and needed member of the family.

Not so prosperous is Santibai, an old woman of the Daroi Gond tribe, who lives but a few lanes from Hirabai. Santibai is a wizened widow, living with her son and his wife and child. Laborers on Latif Khan's land, Santibai and her family work long hours in the fields—planting, weeding, and havesting—while the baby plays beside them. In the evening they return to their small house of sticks and mud to cook a simple meal. Santibai keeps the family treasury, but there is usually very little in it. Years ago she lost four little sons and a daughter, and her young *bahu* has already lost three babies. But the old woman is blessed with a son and *bahu* who respect and love her. Her daughter, married in a nearby village, visits five or six time a year.

Srimati Parvati Misra lives comfortably in a town near Delhi with her husband, a school principal, and her youngest son and his wife and children. She enjoys her quiet domestic life and spends much time in the kitchen preparing foods she knows her husband and son will enjoy. Most of the rest of the housework is taken care of by her *bahu* and a servant girl. Srimati Misra looks forward to receiving letters from her eldest son, a lecturer at a college in England. A few years ago when he and his wife had a new baby, they invited her to stay with them for a year. She went, but after only a few months she returned home because her husband and younger son wrote of how much they missed her in the household.

All these women have in common the fact that they have never seen a retirement village or an old people's home. In the final years of their lives they are surrounded by their families and are busily performing tasks useful to themselves and to others, never doubting their roles as loved and needed women.

Throughout her life the Indian woman may encounter unhappiness and frustration: poverty, illness, painful separation from her parents and her daughters, the death of a child, a dictatorial husband or a domineering mother-in-law. But with rare exception, she has a clear sense of what she is and what she should be doing. When, as a child, she grinds a bowl of grain into soft flour; as a *bahu,* she shyly presents her newborn son to her husband; or, as an adult woman, she sees her demure daughter properly married to a boy of a respectable family, she receives no overt expression of praise or gratitude. But she knows that she is doing what is expected of her and feels a deep sense of achievement. Except for the most unfortunate —the very ill, homeless beggars, or women deprived of near kinsmen— Indian women are reasonably happy and fulfilled. Every woman complains, for to pride oneself on one's good fortune would be to tempt the fates, but few women would trade places with anyone else.

NOTES

1. I wish to express my gratitude to the National Institute of Mental Health for supporting my research in India from 1965 to 1967 and to the American Council of Learned Societies for a postdoctoral grant. I also wish to express my appreciation to Kumari Sunalini Nayudu, my assistant in the field, and to the people of "Nimkhera."

I am indebted to Suzanne Hanchett, Jerome Jacobson, Mildred Luschinsky, Sunalini Nayudu, Mirian Sharma, and W. G. Sheorey for their helpful comments on an earlier draft of this chapter.

All personal and village names in this paper are pseudonyms. In this chapter, diacritics are used only at the first appearance of each Hindi word.

2. Helen Gideon has written a warm and intimate account of the birth of a Sikh baby at his mother's home in the Punjab (Gideon, 1962).

3. *Melia azadirachta.*

4. Dietary restrictions vary greatly from caste to caste and are an essential element of caste identity. Generally, vegetarian castes rank higher than meat eaters, although the high-ranking former warrior castes (Rajputs and Thakurs) are nonvegetarian. Many Indians find the thought of eating meat, especially beef or pork, disgusting. In Khalapur, Rajput woman are vegetarian; when their menfolk want meat, they cook it themselves, away from the kitchen (Minturn and Hitchcock, 1966, p. 44).

5. There are a few low castes in Western and Northern India which lack clans, and in a few areas and among certain low-caste peoples of North India, marriages within the clan are acceptable (Mandelbaum, 1970, pp. 144–148; Miriam Sharma, personal communication).

6. For further information concerning legislation affecting Indian women, see Luschinsky, 1963.

7. In the Dehra Dun area of the Himalayas, brothers share their wife or wives and divorce and remarriage are frequent. A woman works hard in her husband's village but is allowed much freedom in her parental home. In the Jaunsar-Bawar sector, she is free to have love affairs and even become pregnant in her natal village (Majumdar, 1960, pp. 124–132; Berreman, 1963, pp. 171–173).

8. For detailed information on women in ancient and medieval India, see Altekar, 1962, and Thomas, 1964.

9. In Nimkhera, a young divorcée of tribal descent became promiscuous. The village elders warned her father to control her behavior, but when the girl continued her sexual activities, a group of irate men attacked and beat her father. Clearly, the villagers faulted the father for not exercising his paternal authority.

10. In a paper about an alternately benevolent and malevolent goddess of South India, Brenda Beck has shown that the goddess's vacillation is due to her ambivalent position as unmarried and chaste yet attended by a would-be lover. Only the married goddess (for example, Parvati, the wife of Shiva), whose power is transferred to her husband, is completely benevolent (Beck, 1971).

11. Village women of all castes handle cow dung as a matter of course. Cow dung is considered a purifying and cleansing agent, although adult human fecal material is regarded as filthy and polluting. Cow dung is in fact a very valuable substance, providing India's major source of fuel and fertilizer. Westerners sometimes wonder why Indians tolerate so many aged and skinny cattle in their villages and cities, but until they die these cattle are capable of converting otherwise useless scrub grass and vegetable garbage into useful cow dung (see Harris, 1966).

12. In a survey of forty-six peasant communities around the world, Michaelson and Goldschmidt found that of six societies in which women did much of the agricultural labor, male dominance was inconsistent or absent in five. Of thirty-seven peasant com-

munities in which the female contribution to agriculture was relatively small, male dominance was strong in thirty-four. Feminine control of other significant economic activities such as sericulture, marketing, or the collection and sale of shellfish did not appear to diminish male dominance (Michaelson and Goldschmidt, 1971, p. 333).

13. Indians who are aware of the fact that Westerners do not always bathe daily and use toilet paper to cleanse themselves are disgusted by these habits. Traditional Hindu parents who send their children to missionary schools where they come in contact with "dirty Christians" insist that the children bathe when they come home from school.

14. For a history of the women's movement and a survey of modern women's activities in India, see Baig, 1958. For all their hard work, relatively few women have achieved eminence. In "Who's Who In India," published in the *Times of India Yearbook* for 1971, only 18 of some 600 entries are women—or 3 percent. (This roster was presumably compiled by men.)

15. Several factors in Indian society supportive of the educated working woman have been outlined in a paper by Karen Leonard. Some of these actors are:

1) Adolescent Indian girls of educated families are encouraged to concentrate both on schoolwork and on household and religious duties rather than to establish relationships with boys, as American girls do. Anticipating an arranged marriage, the Indian girl does not need to divide her attention between her education and attempts to find a husband for herself, and she avoids the "sex object" aspects of western female adolescence which often prove dysfunctional for a career woman.

2) The earning power of an educated and employed bride may be an important asset in arranging her marriage.

3) The separation of sex and family life from the white collar working world seems to mitigate sexual competition and conflicts in the Indian occupational context.

4) Separation of the sexes in educational facilities is largely responsible for the high number of women academics of all ranks in India today, just as feminine modesty and sex segregation have encouraged the training of large numbers of women doctors (Leonard 1973).

BIBLIOGRAPHY

Altekar, A. S.: *The Position of Women in Hindu Civilization*, Motilal Banarsidass, Delhi, 1962.

Baig, Tara Ali (ed.): *Women of India*, The Publications Division, Government of India, Delhi, 1958.

Basham, A. L.: *The Wonder That Was India*, Grove Press, New York, 1959.

Basu, Tara Krishna: *The Bengal Peasant from Time to Time*, Asia Publishing House, Bombay, 1962.

Beck, Brenda E. F.: "Mariyamman: The Vacillating Goddess," unpublished ms., 1971.

Berreman, Gerald D.: *Hindus of the Himalayas*, Oxford University Press, Bombay, 1963.

Carstairs, G. Morris: *The Twice Born: A Study of a Community of High-Caste Hindus*, The Hogarth Press, London, 1957. [1967 ed., Indiana University Press, Bloomington, Ind., and London.]

Cormack, Margaret: *The Hindu Woman*, Teachers College, Columbia University, New York, 1953.

Elwin, Verrier: "Tribal Women," in Tara Ali Baig (ed.), *Women of India*, The Publications Division, Government of India, Delhi, 1958.
————: *The Kingdom of the Young*, Oxford University Press, London and Bombay, 1968. (Abridged from *The Muria and Their Ghotul*, 1947.)

Freed, Ruth S.: "The Legal Process in a Village in North India: The Case of Maya," *Transactions of the New York Academy of Sciences*, series II, vol. 33, no. 4, pp. 423–435, 1971.

Freed, Stanley A., and Ruth S. Freed: "Spirit Possession as Illness in a North Indian Village," *Ethnology*, vol. 3, no. 2, pp. 152–171, 1964.

Gideon, Helen: "A Baby is Born in the Punjab," *American Anthropologist*, vol. 64, pp. 1220–1234, 1962.

Harris, Marvin: "The Cultural Ecology of India's Sacred Cattle," *Current Anthropology*, vol. 7, pp. 51–66, 1966.

Ishvani: *Girl in Bombay*, The Pilot Press, Ltd., London, 1947.

Leonard, Karen: "Educated Women at Work: Supportive Factors in Indian Society." Paper presented at the Annual Meeting of the Association for Asian Studies, Chicago, 1973.

Lewis, Oscar: *Village Life in Northern India*, Vintage Books, Random House, Inc., New York, 1965.

Luschinsky, Mildred Stroop: *The Life of Women in a Village of North India*, Ph.D. dissertation, Cornell University, Ithaca, N.Y., 1962.

———: "The Impact of Some Recent Indian Government Legislation on the Women of an Indian Village," *Asian Survey*, vol. 3, no. 12, pp. 573–583, 1963.

Madan, T. N.: *Family and Kinship: A Study of the Pandits of Rural Kashmir*, Asia Publishing House, Bombay, 1965.

Majumdar, D. N.: *Himalayan Polyandry*, Asia Publishing House, Bombay, 1960.

Marshall, John F.: "What Does Family Planning Mean to an Indian Villager?" Paper presented at the Annual Meeting of the American Anthropological Association, New York, 1971.

Mayer, Adrian C.: *Caste and Kinship in Central India*, Routledge and Kegan Paul, Ltd., London, 1960.

Michaelson, Evalyn Jacobson, and Walter Goldschmidt: "Female Roles and Male Dominance among Peasants," *Southwestern Journal of Anthropology*, vol. 27, no. 4, pp. 330–352, 1971.

Minturn, Leigh, and John T. Hitchcock: *The Rājpūts of Khalapur, India*, Six Cultures Series, vol. 3, John Wiley and Sons, Inc., New York, 1966.

Mukerji, D. P.: "The Status of Indian Women," *International Social Science Bulletin*, vol. 3, no. 4, pp. 793–801.

Thomas, Paul: *Indian Women through the Ages*, Asia Publishing House, Bombay, 1964.

Untracht, Oppi: "Ritual Wall and Floor Decoration in India," *Graphis;* vol. 24, no. 136, pp. 148–178, 1968.

Lau, Malaita:
"A Woman Is an Alien Spirit"

ELLI KÖNGÄS MARANDA.

Introduction

This article is a description and a discussion of the position of women in a traditional society, the Melanesian Lau of the Solomon Islands. I lived among the Lau for nearly two years and collected all my material on women in the Lau language. Some data used here are verbatim testimonies given by the people; these will be presented as quotations. Most of the data, however, come from direct observation, even participation; to the Lau, I was a woman first and an anthropologist second. I was not permitted to break any of the taboos that regulate Lau life.

It would be totally futile to maintain that Lau women are not inferior to Lau men. The men think they are, the women themselves think they are, and everyday life reflects this tenet. When the Malaita Council, urged by the British colonial administration, held an election during our stay, I sat on the village plaza all day to see in what order people voted. The chiefs and priests and other dignitaries voted first, then men of lesser stature; only after the last man had cast his vote was the woman of the highest status allowed to approach the ballot box. British law dictated one person, one vote; but the traditional hierarchy would not give way. Needless to say, nobody organized the order of voting; people found their turns spontaneously.

Saying that women's inferiority is taken for granted in a society charac-

177

terizes but does not fully describe the situation. How this principle is expressed varies from society to society. In each society women have their particular rights and obligations; they have a career of a kind to pursue. Much of Lau women's inferiority may rest on their virilocal residence: women cannot have power because they cannot live on their natal islands. It struck me during my stay that whenever a woman was on her home island, she acted with more authority than she would among her husband's people. I shall return to this point later, when I describe spirit possessions.

Culture can be viewed as man's one-upmanship over nature. Consider facts such as that Trobriand Islanders, to separate men from nature, deny that men sire children. Animals have intercourse and become pregnant; people have intercourse and open channels for spirits to enter the womb.

Lau, too, deem it necessary to make a point about nature and culture. Women, through their individual biological cycles of menstruation, pregnancy, and childbirth, are capable of producing more members of the community of the living. To balance this out, men have instituted their own collective ceremonial cycles through which they produce members of the community of the dead—spirits *agalo* to be worshiped. Women give birth to people, but men give birth to gods.

I am thus postulating a kind of sex rivalry as a key to Lau culture and society. The hypothesis is that the complex ceremonial life of the Lau can ultimately be viewed as a compensatory mechanism for men.[1] If the mechanism exists, we still have to find how it works.

Lau society consists of face-to-face communities. In such a setting, norms and reality are far closer together than in ours. As will be seen, the system of prohibitions, even if complex, is followed scrupulously by all, even by those who have officially renounced the traditional ("pagan") religion. The taboo system is based on a few principles only: male is equated with the high, with the before, and with the sacred; female is equated with the low, with the after, and with the polluted. Where such close mapping takes place, neutralizing agents will also have to be found, otherwise conflicting forces would clash. One neutralizing agent is water: water washes off both sacredness and pollution. In the charged relations between men and women, there is only one very relaxed one: that between a husband and wife.

In this essay, I shall first give a brief ethnographic background showing how the status of women is manifested in various aspects of Lau culture and society. I shall then delineate women's roles during their life cycles. Finally, I shall discuss authority and the ways in which women can defy male domination or otherwise influence decisions.

SETTING

Data used in this exposition were collected in Lau Lagoon, Malaita, British Solomon Islands, during twenty-two months of fieldwork between 1966 and

1968.[2] Unless otherwise indicated, the discussion pertains to contemporary circumstances. We lived on Fou'eda, the ancestral island of the Rere clan, whose membership is about seven hundred persons. Fou'eda is in the middle of the 27-mile-long lagoon in Makwanu passage. Most people in the Makwanu region are pagan.

The self-definition of the Lau is *toa 'i asi,* sea people (as opposed to the neighboring *toa 'i tolo,* inland dwellers). In 1967 they numbered 5,265 persons living on "artificial," that is, man-made, islands in the lagoon or directly in coastal villages on the natural islands of Malaita, Basakana, and Maana'oba, the last in the lagoon itself. In 1966, there were fifty-nine artificial islands; in 1968, sixty-two.[3] Additionally, there are twenty-six coastal villages.

The Sea People live at the water's edge and draw their living from fishing (done only by men), shell-gathering (done only by women), and growing yams and potatoes (done by both sexes. Pigs, eaten only by men in ceremonies, are raised in sties built on piles above the water.

Since the cultivation zone on Malaita Island to which the Lau have claim is seriously restricted, trading with the inland dwellers is of some importance. Trading takes place in the native markets, which meet regularly at customary marketplaces. Surplus fish, taken there by women, is exchanged for taro, bananas, an occasional watermelon, and such items as needles made of the bone of the flying fox, needed for sewing pandanus rain mats. Also in the markets men do extensive trading in fish and vegetables for ceremonies. In addition, markets provide an occasion for socializing, and women often go there just to chat. Communication at the market takes place between sea women from different communities rather than between sea women and hill women except in cases—now rare because of the decline in marriages between Lau men and hill women—where a woman meets her hill relatives.

Lau society is in a state of perceptible change but not of crisis. On pagan islands, pagan religion rules. Christians can visit pagan islands, even live on them, provided they break no taboos. The Melanesian Mission gained a foothold in certain important Lau communities (for example, Sulufou Island) early, over forty years ago.[4] Its position is at present frozen, and no proselytizing is visible. The northern tip of the lagoon has been under the influence of the Takwa Roman Catholic Mission, located on the shore, for thirty years. The missionary in charge in 1968 realized that the actual following was far smaller than records would indicate, and so the mission stopped the automatic baptism of children born in the health station and even of those who attend the mission school.

In midlagoon, the Seventh-Day Adventist Church has a membership of over one hundred persons. Funafou and Fou'eda, both ancestral islands, have Seventh-Day Adventist suburbs, Fakaloloma (or Fakaloma; or, from the English "new land," Niuleni), and Roba, respectively. These suburbs were founded to prevent Christianity from polluting the ancestral islands. In the native view, these Christian islands are fully comparable to the women's seclusion area, since births and menstruation are allowed there. No pagan man would step on a polluted island. Pagan women, however, can visit them, as they can visit the women's seclusion area. Fakaloma and Roba never had pagan altars and therefore differ radically from Sulufou, where altars have been profaned. I witnessed a long discussion between the women of Fou'eda in which they gave their reasons for not daring to visit Sulufou "where they have even built family houses on the site of the altars." Since *mamana* (mana) has its depository in the altars, the women were afraid of dying if they got in touch with the once sacred area. *Sua* (pollution) does not kill women, but direct exposure to *mamana* does.

It is generally agreed among the Lau that the restrictions apply only to traditionally defined social space, so that the tension between *mamana* and *sua* is only in operation where Lau people or people considered to be like Lau reside. Therefore all Malaita, including the government station in Auki, is under the regulation, as is the overseas Lau village Kokomu (kukum) on the outskirts of Honiara, Guadalcanal. Honiara hospital is outside the realm. Therefore, if a pagan Lau man became sick he resorted first to our hut (divided into the traditionally prescribed zones) and next to Honiara hospital. Mission stations and the Auki hospital are too close to Lau territory and polluted.

RELIGION AND KINSHIP

The Lau worship ancestors, *agalo*. Every man worships his own father. Men who were influential in life are influential when dead, but even a poor man will become a spirit and will demand sacrifices and impart *mamana*. Big memorial feasts are occasions held in honour of a recently deceased priest or important man or, formerly, *ramo* (war leader), but the whole clan commemorates the spirits of all its ancestors, "the spirit of the clan." It is a religion as Durkheim would define it.

Lau religion covers most aspects of the entire life, with a few secular areas left in between. Women do not take part in the cult as officiants, but they support religious life as active participants. When a clan is preparing for an important phase in the funeral cycle, its members abstain from eating forbidden food. Sometimes the abstention is experienced as a hardship. One day Sosoe, a priest's wife, brought me vegetable greens, saying sadly: "Here I have these vegetable greens, but Fou'eda has been declared sacred today, and I can't cook them. Why don't you have them?"

She could not consume the food, for in her way of cooking it she had to use coconut milk, and coconut must not be eaten when the clan is preparing for a feast. I said I'd cook them my way, by boiling them in salty water, and she was relieved. The food would not be wasted, and the taboo would not be broken.

Membership in a Lau clan is determined by birth, and a woman has lifelong membership in her father's clan. Clan blood is sacred, and therefore old people, children, and the helpless must be cared for. Clans are named either after places, as in Asi ni ngwane, (man's sea) or Taalitoo; or with an inexplicable proper name, as in Rere. Each clan has an origin myth. For instance, the Rere clan traces its origins to a quarrel between two brothers; the Sikwafunu clan believes that it was founded incestuously by a brother and a sister who were the only survivors of a great catastrophe. Clan myths are recited at memorial feasts by singers, invited from other clans, whose knowledge of the myths is checked before the singing.

Clan exogamy is preferred but not necessarily required; in fact, an endogamous marriage is called *folaabara,* a sunny marriage, and it is said that there will be no danger of curses in such a marriage. Although called brother and sister, the couple will actually be very distant biological relatives. In the case we had on Fou'eda, the two were tenth cousins.

SPACE

Lau Lagoon and the space surrounding it are divided into five conceptual zones. These are mapped in Diagram 1.

Tolo and *matakwa,* the two extreme zones, are thought to be dangerous because they are unknown and because they are inhabited by alien spirits (spirits of foreign clans and tribes in *tolo,* the spirit of the ocean in *matakwa*). No woman would venture into these areas alone, though men do engage in deep-sea fishing and in restricted travel in the hills.

The principal exploitation zones are *hara* and *asi.* Men and women (and grown children) garden in *hara;* men fish in *asi.* Fresh water is taken from rivers and brooks on which there is no habitation, the priests taking their water upstream and families taking theirs downstream. Menstruating women go to another river altogether for their water, traveling in the canoes of the women's seclusion area.

The middle zone, *asihara,* consists of *mai* (areas exposed at low tide), where the women gather shells, and *fera* (artificial island, community, village), where the people live. Lau communities are divided into three parts: the men's area, the women's area, and the neutral space for everyone. This tripartite division is repeated in the houses and in the canoes.

Although no island is exactly oval, Diagram 2—drawn after a drawing

tolo	'hills, forest, inland'
hara	'shore, gardening zone on the shore, gardens'
asihara	'lagoon'
asi	'sea, divided fishing grounds'
matakwa	'deep ocean'

Figure 6.1 *Zones of the Lau world.*

by Toata, a Lau man—represents the Lau conception of the shape of a village.

Maanabeu, the men's seclusion area, is sacred. It contains the altars, skull pits, and other very sacred relics of the clan with which only a priest can be in touch; men's clubhouses named after lineages; and men's lavatories, or "men's path." On some of the ancestral islands, several clans have their individual altars and men's houses; "men's path" is public to all men. Women's skulls are deposited in the skull pit, but no woman of any age may enter a sacred area at any time.

During our stay, two unintentional breaches of this taboo occurred. In one case, a young boy, perhaps ten years old, was baby-sitting and carrying his younger sibling on his shoulders when he decided to go to the "men's path." Thinking that the baby was his little brother, he went and set the baby down, only to find to his horror that it was his little sister. He rushed back to the village and the priest was alerted. A sacrifice was offered on the same day, and thus an imminent disaster was averted. Had there been no sacrifice, it was said, one of the family would have died.

A similar incident happened when two little children, a boy and a girl both about five years old, were paddling in the lagoon and unwittingly crossed a sacred spot, the octopus altar (the octopus is one of the ancestors of the Rere clan and hence has an altar in the lagoon). The little girl's mother noticed the event and started wailing at the landing place as if **her**

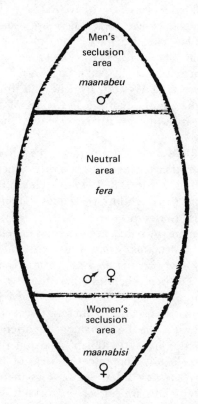

Figure 6.2 *Lau conception of a village.*

daughter were already dead. Again, word was sent to the girl's father, who happened to be on another island, and then to the priest. A sacrifice on the same day saved the little girl from certain death.

The women's seclusion area, *maanabisi,* is polluted. It contains the birth hut, and a clearly marked area around it, including the bare rocks on which delivery takes place. The area also includes a heap of stones in the lagoon where the woman buries the placenta and where aborted fetuses and children who die in the birth hut are buried. These places are *sua,* polluted in the extreme. In addition, the seclusion area contains several menstrual huts named after the sections of the village; a communal cookhouse; and the women's lavoratory area (women's path). No man may enter the women's area, but all men were born in the birth hut.

The religion demands that women stay in seclusion during menstruation and after each delivery. Far from viewing this as a hardship, the women welcome the seclusion as a monthly vacation. Since the seclusion area is polluted, it would make no sense to weave baskets that could not be brought back to the neutral village area. There are usually several women in seclusion together. They spend a lot of time cooking and eating. This done, they converse, and, above all, sleep. One time we took a Lau girl with us to the government station in Auki. She started to menstruate and was instructed in the secrets of Western hygiene, but during our brief stay she slept through all the nights and the best part of the days. She was conditioned to take it easy while menstruating. After the period was over, she woke up again.

In *fera* itself, the middle zone of the village (the whole community and all inhabited places are called *fera*) at the gate of the men's area, there is a village plaza, dance, and play field called *labata*. This is the arena of public activities: flute dancing (*'au*), children's games (*labala*), evening chats (*rebola*), and storytelling (*unu-unu*).

Family houses are set in rows that are oriented in relation to the taboo areas. Each house has a structure isomorphic with the whole village, as shown in Diagram 3. *Gouna ere*, the area of the fire, is as large as the bed and marked with a log. The bed is behind a partition.

Fire is masculine and *abu* (taboo) for women. Bed is feminine and *abu* for men except the woman's husband. If there are seats (low benches made of logs, tree stumps) inside the house, they are oriented so that men's seats are on the side of the fire and women's seats on the side of the bed. Visiting men or women do not step into the areas of fire or bed as such but sit down on their respective sides. Sitting logs in front of the house, if they are present there at all, are higher on the side for men and lower on the side for women. Houses are arranged so that the fire area in one

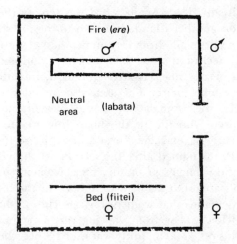

Figure 6.3 *Division of space in a Lau house.*

Men's seclusion area   *maanabeu*

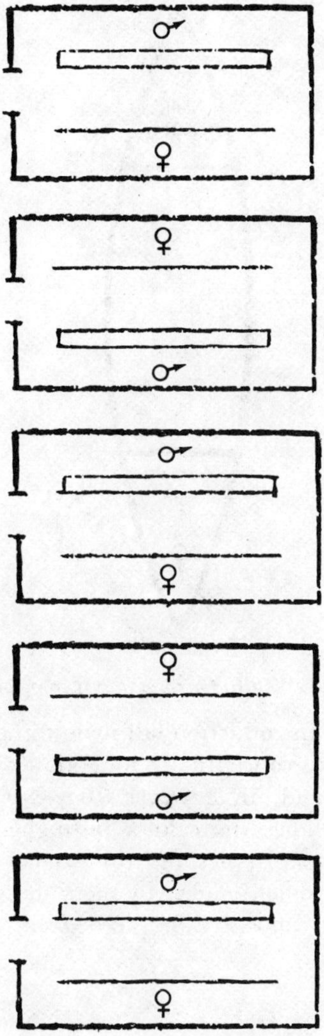

Women's seclusion area   *maanabisi*

Figure 6.4 *Arrangement of houses.*

house is adjacent to the fire area of the next. Likewise the bed area of one house is adjacent to the bed area of the next, as shown in Diagram 4.

The division of space into male-neutral-female found in the design of the village and of the family house is repeated in the family canoe, as shown in Diagram 5.

Figure 6.5 *Seating arrangement in a Lau canoe.*

As mentioned in the introduction, all male things are conceptually high and all female things are conceptually low. Man takes the lead: a woman walks behind her husband; if, however, they are walking downhill, the woman walks in front, since she cannot be higher than her husband. In a canoe, the man stands and poles and the woman sits and paddles. If the canoe of menstruating women is seen by men, the women press themselves low on the bottom of the canoe so as not to be seen.

TIME

Life on pagan islands is structured according to two determinants: the female biological rhythm and the male cultural rhythm. The former rhythm is individual and the latter communal, according to clan. Women are in seclusion during menstruation. That means that they may move only in the menstrual area. They are in double seclusion for thirty days after childbirth and cannot go outside the birth hut and the adjacent area—not even into the menstrual area. A woman's seclusion does not affect her husband's ritual or other activities in any way. Men are secluded themselves in the men's area for certain rituals and in double seclusion in their priestly houses after the death of a priest or during the preparation of a phase in a memorial feast.

Ritual time is structured in relation to elaborate memorial cycles which begin when the priest dies. His sons, real or classificatory, are in seclusion for "one hundred days" in the *maanabeu,* the men's seclusion area, right after his death and until the time when his skull is severed from his body. Altogether the cycle takes about thirty years, ritual phases are spaced at about two-year intervals, which allows time for pigs and vegetables to be accumulated.[5] During the memorial cycle, the whole clan oscillates between states of *abu* (restricted, marked) and *mola* (neutral, unmarked). Notably, women who are members of the celebrating clan must follow the taboo rhythm even when they reside as wives in the territory of another clan. Many of the taboos are periodic restrictions on the use of food, especially of coconuts, yams, and taro. Other restrictions apply; for instance, marriages may not be concluded when clan territory is taboo. Merrymaking, noisy play, and group singing are also forbidden when a village is *abu,* that is, when any clan in a village is celebrating.

RITUAL STATES

When a baby is born, it is *sua.* This is said to be so because the mother's blood is still in the baby. During the month of seclusion, the baby's blood changes gradually, until it is all new at the end of the month. In reflection of this diminution of the mother's blood, the *sua* of birth "lessens" as the seclusion progresses through three stages: *akwale dani ta'aa* (ten bad days), *akwale dani 'i lalo* (ten days in the middle), and *akwale dani ruu* (ten days of entering). On the thirtieth day, the mother and the baby have their hair shaved, and after that they move for the last night into the menstrual hut of the mother, to enter *(ruu)* the *fera* (village) the next morning, after their ritual bath.

In the village, all persons are *mola* (in an unmarked state), otherwise they would not be allowed in the village. All children are *mola.* A young girl starts alternating between the states of *mola* and *sua* (negatively *abu*) at the onset of her first menstruation, and a woman becomes "doubly *sua*" at delivery. A boy starts moving between *mola* and positive *abu* after he has been introduced to the spirits, but only men officiating in a ceremony are invested with *mamana.* There are thus five states possible, with male

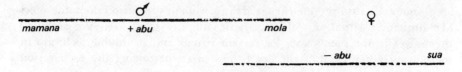

Figure 6.6 *Lau male and female ritual states.*

and female specializations and a common state, as depicted in Diagram 6. One must pass from one state to the next in a step-by-step order (as in the case of a woman at her *ruu:* birth hut to menstrual hut to village). At the border of each state-cum-space there is a rite of passage.

Emotional states derived from ritual states are symbolized in many ways, notably by the condition of the hair of the head. A man in mourning seclusion lets his hair and bead grow until the time of his neutralizing rite, when he cuts his hair and shaves his beard. A woman giving birth lets her hair grow until her rite of passage from birth seclusion, during which her hair and her baby's hair are shaved. A widow and her daughters have their hair shaved immediately after the death of the husband and then let is grow, not cutting it to normal length until after their months of mourning are over.

WOMEN'S ROLES

Childhood

From birth to puberty, a Lau girl is in the same position as her brother. Babies are sheltered, and although children are encouraged to develop the necessary skills, such as swimming, diving, and paddling, learning takes place in the group of youngsters, often supervised by young unmarried men. The lagoon is a playground as much as is the village plaza: children go swimming in the rain as well as when the sun shines. Both boys and girls are active, independent, boisterous. Taboos are learned very early, first, because everybody really follows them; second, because many of them are also physically marked: a stone wall separates the areas of the village, a log cuts the fire area from the rest of the house. Learning of active lore is constant and gradual: a boy follows his father, a girl her mother.

Lau children receive an education which is affectionate and permissive by any standards. Once a baby is born, it spends its first month of life in constant bodily contact with its mother. After its sociological birth (*ruu,* the entrance into the community), it is met on the village plaza by a priest who recites prayers for its welfare. The baby receives a name and a meal is arranged, sponsored by the father, who brings a big fish, and by the women, who bring taro-canarium nut puddings. The fish is said to be the male element and the pudding the female element in the meal; the complementing morsels are passed over each other to symbolize the union of male and female elements. The women admire the baby and call it *ngwela gia*, our child.

A baby does not have a separate sleeping place but sleeps on the mother's body. It is never put down for a nap. Until a child walks, it is always (and after it learns to walk, most of the time) carried on the hip, first for a number of months by its mother, then by elder sisters or brothers. The word for baby-sitting is *olingwela*, to carry a child on the hip. While baby-sitting, any activity is permitted if it does not wake the child from sleep. The baby-sitter even goes swimming with the baby on her hip.

A toddler is constantly watched. Toddlers are toilet trained rather early, first by being held over the edge of the water, then by being taken to the lavatory of their sex. The regulations of space are taught early, but otherwise few restrictions apply: young children spend their time playing and baby-sitting, roaming on the reef at low tide, swimming, diving, and paddling their toy canoes.[6] The are allowed a freedom of speech that no grown Lau possesses: they can and do utter curses which from the mouth of a married woman would be an invitation to divorce. If a child strikes another, compensation must be paid. A stranger never spanks a child, and its own parents rarely do.

A girl will start working occasionally with her mother when she is about twelve. Girls of any age may observe birth provided they do not step into the *sua* area, but in fact only little girls watch a delivery. At a birth in the maanabisi of Fou'eda on February 12, 1967, only the three-year-old daughter of the woman giving birth, a handful of girls from her age to eight years old, and myself constituted the audience. The older girls obviously knew the process.

Maidenhood

After her menarche, the girl is introduced to the village with a ceremony given in her honour.

A desirable young girl is fat and industrious. Girls are ordered about a great deal; they obey their elders and they work hard. Their tasks include work in the gardens, cutting and collecting firewood, fetching water from the rivers, collecting shells, plaiting women's mats, and cooking family meals. They work in groups and draw companionship from the crowd. Also, the work itself proves their achievements: "bundles of firewood, bundles of vegetables, and bundles of water bamboo" are public facts, clearly visible when the girls return to the islands in the afternoon. The following extracts from *'ainimae* (serious narratives) describe the qualities a beautiful girl (*haarii diana*) should have:

> Ngwaneia returned, arrived in Onefolo, arrived at Ngodona uo. He slept. The sun rose, and Ngwaneia thought: "I'll go further south." Ngwaneia arrived at Gouna arengo, arrived at Fou mae. And he was chewing betel in the men's area and looking at all the girls. He looked and saw Takerobo who had collected a big bundle of firewood and a bundle of water bamboo on top of it. She arrived and let her burden down in front of the house. Ngwaneia looked at her and asked Lalafi: "Whose daughter is that?". . . Ngwaneia asked: "Dear Buu, dear Taraia, dear Lalafi, I want to propose to your daughter Takerobo on behalf of my son Laakwai." And Buu said: "Very well, this is friendship, we two will be friends." ["The Myth of lirobakwa," told by Bobongi of Kwalo'ai, May 24, 1968].

Another narrative tells of Raunifelo and Buani ia, who are searching for a wife for Keraomea:

> Raunifelo went on, Buani ia went on, the two arrived in Abarafi, arrived and sat in the men's area and chewed. And Raunifelo watched the girls arriving. They had bundles of firewood, bundles of vegetables, bundles of water bamboo. Raunifelo saw Ngwane'oro, Modamae's daughter, Taalau's sister, Raunifelo saw her.
>
> And Raunifelo asked, asked Taalau, for he had seen that Ngwane'oro had brought bundles of firewood, and also bundles of vegetables, and beyond that bundles of water bamboo; she carried it all, arrived, and let down her burden in front of the house.
>
> Raunifelo watched and thought in his mind: "From where indeed is this girl? Her work in bundling is strong; she has bundles of firewood, bundles of taro, bundles of bamboo, bundles of swamp taro. She arrived and let her burden down; the front of the house is full." Raunifelo regarded that, and he thought: "Such a girl I will ask for, indeed, such a girl is worthy of Keraomea. . . ." ["The Myth of Keraomea," told by Bobongi of Kwalo'ai, June 7, 1968].

In this tale, Modo, Kunua 'i rake, and Maana 'au, on their father's orders, are looking for a wife for their younger brother Laenimota:

> They arrived in Takisangwaro . . . looked and saw a woman, Abariialasi. And Modo spoke, asked his set of brothers: "Did you see the beautiful woman who appeared? She came from the gardens, came here, and had bundles of firewood, further, bundles of vegetables, and further still, bundles of water bamboo. She is a strong woman to have carried these three things, the firewood bundle, the bamboo bundle, and the bundle of food." And

Modo spoke thus: "This woman we will reserve for Laenimota." ["The Myth of Laenimota," told by Ramoagalo of Fou'eda, January 7, 1967].

While girls are thus, normatively and actually, engaged in heavy work to heighten their marriageability, their brothers roam free; it is an honor for a man to have industrious daughters and idle sons. One might observe that since girls are married out and boys will reside patrilocally, there will be time to use the sons' services when the daughters are married and their duties directed toward their husbands' lineages.

Marriage

Woman's married state is a grave matter.

I will omit the details of the marriage arrangements; suffice it to say that the parents of the young man together agree on a bride for their son. The mother is involved because the future daughter-in-law's work services are to assist her. The father establishes a bond of special friendship with the father of the girl; a married couple's fathers are called *roongwairuana,* "a pair of friends" (cf. above, "we two will be friends").

A marriage is an economic affair of a certain magnitude. If a poor boy receives material help for the bride payments, he will be obliged to his helpers for the rest of his life. As if he were their adopted son, he will name his children after them and offer them his services. An adopted son is called *ngwela harea;* however, a young man helped to marry (but not "fed") is not called so.

The wedding, *dao 'uria geni* (arriving for the woman), is loaded with symbolism. The bridegroom does not participate; in fact, he hides on the shore. His brothers and sisters participate: the normal bride procession is ten canoes. Elder sisters of the groom hold the arms of the bride when she leaves her natal village, wailing aloud, decorated, anointed, and literally dressed in money—that is, in shell strings. The procession, forming an evenly advancing front, paddles in rhythm, accentuating the rhythm by slapping water high in the air. The bride is hidden under a pandanus wrap in the middle of the middle canoe.

The village awaits; young children have spent the day littering all the streets with branches and leaves fetched from the shore, adding whole anthills to the mess. The bride is received by the groom's mother, who holds two pandanus mats under her arm. These she sets down and moves so that the bride steps from the landing place to the boy's parents' hut without touching the ground. She enters but returns immediately to sweep the village; her first day in her new home is hard work, and there are many onlookers watching to judge her working ability. She is assisted by a work party from her own clan, who sweep with her and who remain for a month in the village to do all its work. When they leave, they receive individual payments.

As a wife, the young married woman (*geni fungao gia,* "the woman in an in-law relationship to us all") needs only to show her good will. Sexual relations are not expected to begin on the wedding night but some time during the first month, when songs are sung by night to celebrate the marriage and the youth of the two clans engage in general merrymaking. But before a new bride is pregnant, or could be pregnant, she is a stranger; she is undergoing a trial period, and she had better not prolong it. And with the rest of the husband's people she is also in a somewhat sensitive position. In the four or more years that have elapsed since her first menstruation—the marriage arrangements alone take a couple of years— she has been well trained in the work she is to perform after her marriage. Nevertheless, she is closely watched, and she is rated as a daughter-in-law. The husband's unmarried sisters are also interested in the bride; but if she does not show signs of being bewitched by a stranger (that is, if she does not act contrary to expectations), she has a good chance of being accepted. On the whole, the Lau remove blame from the deviant person and blame external agents when possible: a spirit possesses a person, love magic has been given to a person, spirits deceive a person.

In addition to working well, the young wife will, ideally, quickly become pregnant. She must have at least two children before she is allowed her first visit to her natal village. During pregnancy, she is not permitted to eat deep-sea fish, lest the child be victim to a "tidal fever" caused by the big fish "coming to eat" in the lagoon during high tides. Some women profess nausea during pregnancy resulting from seeing big fish or from tobacco smoke, even if, when not pregnant, they are smokers. In general, however, women claim painless pregnancies and uncomplicated births. Only a *maafaalu* (literally, "new door"; a primipara) is thought to be in danger, and she is advised not to eat too much in general lest the baby be too large for the still narrow passage. Even a *maafaalu* is required to deliver herself, but it is checked beforehand that she understands the situation.

Miscarriages occur; in the case of married women they are regretted, but unmarried girls are suspected of "drinking a plant," a concoction of herbs and water, to abort. One case had occurred just before our arrival, and one occurred in Funafou during our stay. In the former case, the boy's father, in the latter, the boy himself was accused of having prepared the drink. Both were formally charged in the native court, for abortion is forbidden by British law.

As a mother, the woman resides among strangers still, but her children are members of the clan. Lau women are generally proud of their children, and pregnancy and delivery are not considered hardships. A woman may relate that she fainted at birth, or was very sick, but she will stress that the birth was successful. It is perhaps for this reason that Lau women do not admit to stillbirths. I have dossiers of women who have reported to me that several of their children died after birth but that none was a still-birth. They say, "he dropped on the ground and died," but very seldom, even after insistent probing, do they admit, "he died in my belly." After the mother has delivered it, the baby is the responsibility of spirits, who take life or shelter life.

A woman has few property rights; "a woman cannot manage land, it must be a man." Yet her sons can have claim to her father's land in special cases; a father can grant land rights to his daughter. If the oral history of the Lau people is accurate—and in this respect it may well be—women have in the past been instrumental in the acquisition of the lands now held. In fact, it seems to me that the reason why Lau men no longer arrange marriages to hill women is that land has become scarce there too, and therefore marrying a woman from a group considered inferior is not worth it. The hill people have limited resources, whereas the sea people harvest where they have not planted and can actually accumulate property from the resources of the sea.

A woman's value is measured by the economic transactions conducted at her marriage: these can be quoted when the woman is long dead. A man is proud of having a wife as "valuable" as his mother was.

One can observe that girls are valued for their fathers and married women respected for their husbands. A married woman's title is 'afe (lady), but she will have to make her mark to become 'initei (a distinguished married woman). Her husband is 'initoo (a big man) if he was born to the position and did not prove himself incompetent. To be 'initei, a woman must be married to 'initoo, but she must have a dignity of her own—generosity, blameless conduct, industry, good children—and she must be advanced in age. She reflects her husband's status, but she has to have a reflecting surface.

A married woman owes loyalty in two directions: she has to follow the ceremonial rhythms of both her natal and her conjugal villages. It is difficult to measure marital harmony, but the general impression one gains is that Lau marriages are companionable and indeed happy. Marital quarrels occur but are never public. A man may beat his wife, for example, for not becoming pregnant or for not bearing sons; I have several accounts of this having happened, but I never witnessed it myself. Women quarrel, but always with other women. Sisters-in-law (wives of two brothers) especially are in competition, being key persons in two comparable alliances.

Strict decency is required of a married woman: she must under no condition let a man other than her husband even touch her body. I heard first-hand reports of the havoc created by a man when his wife Kaelonga's arm was touched by a young man approaching her for a betel leaf. The husband became enraged, chased the woman with an axe, and threatened to kill the young man. The woman, who belonged to the Rere clan, fled to our island, Fou'eda, to her nearest relatives. A formal compensation and settlement followed in time. Kaelonga was well into her middle age and nearly nine months pregnant. She stayed in Fou'eda, obviously longing to get back to her husband and children. On the day she was to return she waited impatiently on the landing place until a party of youngsters came for her.

A married woman cannot arouse even the slightest suspicion of infidelity. When she sits on the ground in front of the family house, a man may not cross over her legs. She may not be alone in the house with a strange man for the shortest while.[7] If a woman sleeps with another man, her husband divorces her without any possibility of reconciliation.

A husband, however, may be unfaithful; his adultery is usually discovered through the pregnancy of his mistress. If his wife permits it, he will take his mistress as a secondary wife. In one case, related to me with considerable glee and amusement by the wife in question, the wife went to the market and confronted her husband's mistress; upon returning home, she gave her husband a dressing down by preaching to him a full day and a full night. The man did not marry the mistress.

The wife's kinsmen always offer to take her back in such a situation and formally "arrive for her" with canoes. Although it is always her decision whether to stay on or to return, I do not in fact know of any case where the wife chose divorce, for the children would have to stay with the father's clan in their natal village in any case. The only exception would be a baby still nursing, but even he would have to be returned after weaning.

Widowhood

Death does not dissolve a marriage. If a widow so wishes, she can return to her natal village, but normally she stays on with her children. When her children grow up and marry, she is free to visit her natal village and does so, especially for *maea,* funeral wakes.

A widow may receive a proposal to marry; a widower may propose to marry. Both partners will have to acquire the permission of the clans of both the former and the prospective husbands. A ceremony is conducted which I see as a divorce from the dead spouse, and a compensation is paid to the clan on behalf of the children of the first marriage. The woman's children lose a mother, the man's children receive a stepmother, and neither situation is viewed as desirable. Once remarried, a widow severs all her relations with her previous children. They stay with their father's clan and resort to their "second father," the father's brother or his closest patrilateral parallel cousin. (The father, of course, has parallel cousins on both sides, but usually his matrilateral cousins do not live nearby.)

A remarried widow faces a dilemma: if she has bad relations with her husband, she is bad for him; if she has good relations with him, she is bad for his children, on the grounds that she draws the husband's attention from the children. Her bride price has been nominal; she has been "cheap" and cannot command respect.

Death

When, as normally happens, a wife or widow dies in her husband's village, her skull is later claimed by her own clan. Here too, "arriving for the woman" takes place: her kinsmen accompany her to reintegrate her into the community of her dead kin, just as they had accompanied her to integrate her into the community of her living allies.

If a woman's skull is for some reason not claimed, it is thrown aside in the men's seclusion area. As "an alien spirit," her skull cannot be placed among the skulls of her husband's clan.

Women who die in childbirth and who therefore cannot be handled will be buried on the shore. They become ghosts who chase pregnant women especially. They are heard on dark evenings wailing on the shore, sometimes passing in the lagoon, but far from villages and altars.

A baby whose mother died before he was born and who therefore never saw the light of day becomes *goosile,* a hostile spirit. He feeds on the mother's body juice, grows, and becomes a man-eating monster.

AUTHORITY

Decisions in Lau society are concerned with religion. Men decide in their seclusion area about communal fishing for feasts, ceremonial gardens, the construction of ceremonial canoes and temples, times of feasts, of putting the village under taboo, of opening the nut and the yam seasons, etc. It must be said in fairness that in these big decisions, men too are following schemes and schedules determined by tradition, and that it is difficult for even an influential and ambitious man to make innovations. Innovations are regularly suggested in the name of *agalo:* a priest's dead father appears to him in a dream or "in person" at dusk and reveals to him plans which he must follow. Revelations are then scrutinized in the council of elders, and the criticism is interesting: *agalo e suge gwa'ana,* "his spirit is cheating him." Lau society is a theocracy without gods.

But when the men, relying on tradition or on the examination of visions and dreams and having consulted diviners, reach a decision, the decision is announced in the village. The opinions of the women are not asked. Women are foreigners; as their current definition goes, they are *agalo 'ata fera,* "alien spirits." Since it is not relations with their own ancestral spirits that the cult deals with, decisions made by the cult concern them only indirectly. The women are concerned with the welfare of their families and the health of their children. The men know the cult; it is not for women to question the detail or the wisdom of cult decisions.

The *agalo* give *mamana,* the foundation and support of life, but they also withdraw their protection, often for reasons which cannot be fathomed. At such times, believers are apt to withdraw from their part of the relationship. Pierre Maranda has recorded an explanation of a pagan priest's conversion to Christianity: his ancestral spirit killed his son despite faithful worship. Disillusioned, the priest joined the church at hand.

The spirits concern themselves with the sacred, although the universe is defined so that realms such as health and welfare, which we might consider to be secular, fall into the domain of the sacred. Ultimate authority rests with the spirits, who reveal the truth (*mamana* also means truth) either in tradition or through revelation. In Lau Lagoon, there are fundamentalists with a thorough knowledge of tradition and a great suspicion for direct revelation. But whatever the channels of communication with the spirits—lore and custom or dreams and visions—men receive orders from the spirits and women receive orders from the men.

DEFYING AUTHORITY

Having laid down the rules of conduct for social groups in terms of sex, age, and social class, the Lau actively work to recognize the rights of individuals. Any person may demonstrate publicly if his rights have been slighted. Thus a child may cry loud and a woman may wail. Once a woman spent eight hours wailing because her sister-in-law had forgotten to get her an areca nut from the market. It was felt that she had the right to protest, although it was also remarked that she carried her protest too far, for "you should not wail for a nut as you wail for a dead person."

A women has at several stages of her career the right to veto. A girl's father may wish to *luia* her (declare her for celibacy).[8] She would then be raised in isolation in the darkness of her hut and spend her life unmarried. She, however, can refuse. We knew very well one case where this had happened and one where the girl consented to her father's wish.

When a boy's father brings a proposal of marriage, the girl can tell her parents she does not wish to marry that boy, and she need not present any reason other than her dislike for the suitor. This happens relatively often. In all the cases that came to my attention, the girl was the one who had exercised her veto right. Because the initiative comes from the man's side, the girl's opinion will be of necessity public, since marriage proposals are public affairs. Normally, a proposal does not come as a surprise. The boy, of course, may also object to the choice made by his parents, but his case may not become known, for he can say no before a public proposal has been made.

If an engagement has already been made, the girl can dissolve it by making deprecatory remarks in public about the boy. We witnessed one such case. Later, the girl will undoubtedly marry someone else.

If a woman is newly married, she can invite a divorce by cursing the *agalo* of her husband. The curse is *(feesia)basi maa 'oe* (defecate on) your father's sacred bow. Another curse with the same effect is *'ani tee 'oe* (have intercourse with your mother). The possibility of a curse is actively feared and often spoken about.

If a woman is desperate, she can curse herself. I know the living members of the following drama, related by Toata, a man of Roba Island:

> The husband can say what he pleases to his wife; the wife is afraid of saying anything. In quarrels between the woman and the mother-in-law, the husband often sides with his parents. Maela-asi always sides with Defe Daui [his father]. Afu Ramoga always sided with his mother; she is dead now. His first wife used to quarrel with his mother. I have seen them quarrel three times a weak. Not once did I see Afu Ramoga side with his wife. She used to cry very bitterly. She was sad all the time. When she became pregnant, she swore to Afu. "After this birth, I will give birth no more. Do not hope. Your mother may bear your children, but I will not." When she gave birth, she died. Afu Ramoga's sister nursed the boy for three years.

A women can at any time escape to the women's seclusion area, either to avoid being beaten or to stay there pretending she is menstruating until the time of the task she does not want to perform is passed. From January 19, 1967, to April 19, 1967, Ulufaka, a young bride brought to Fou'eda, pretended that she was menstruating for approximately half the time. This she did to avoid consummating her marriage. Frustrated, the husband, Aliki, tried to resort to the headman, who talked to the girl's parents; when it finally came out that the girl was calling another man's name in her sleep, it was decided that she had been given love magic and that she was beyond recovery. She was returned to her parents by night, and afterward the balance of the bride payment and connected reciprocal transactions were returned. After being severely reproached by her father, she fled into *masuu* (wilderness) and slept in trees. She was found on the third day. The flight had been an attempt at suicide, it was said.

A woman can show her greatest contempt by giving birth in the neutral, family part of the village. I recorded two histories of this having occurred in Fou'eda:

> Roko and her husband quarrelled, and her husband mistreated her. She was angry and prayed to the *agalo* of Kafo'ere, the *agalo* of Kwaena, the *agalo* of Funafou, to all the spirits of 'Ore'ore. And she fell ill. She was sick, and she lost her mind. And she stayed in her family house and gave birth to a child in the house. Her two children were asleep in the night, and their mother gave birth to a child in the house. And they said: "Oh, she is deranged. You have given birth in the village." And she said: "What?" They said: "There is a child on the floor." Their mother did not understand.
>
> And all the men of Fou'eda closed themselves in the men's seclusion area, for the village was now polluted. No married man came to the village. This went on for a long time. The child and the mother were taken in a canoe to sea. And those men waited and then performed purification ceremonies for this village. Fou'eda men sacrificed a pig and then they entered the village. And they went to Tafu on the shore, and they made a war party . . . they wanted to make Fou'eda sacred again. "We have killed a man, and we have made Fou'eda, where a child has been delivered, sacred again."
>
> Roko returned to the village and she died. People said: "The spirit of Fou'eda took revenge on Roko, so that she died." And the child born in the village died also. [Related by Kokosi, a woman of Fou'eda Island, January 14, 1967.]
>
> Kunua Small's wife Tanua, a woman of Funafou, when she married came to live on Fou'eda. The time of singing the wedding epics passed, the whole first month passed, and Tanua and her husband Kunua, those two lived in harmony. Then she got pregnant, they lived on. Kunua beat her and hit her with his hand. Kunua was jealous, for Tanua visited her natal village nearly every day [a five-minutes' paddling distance]. That's why he made a big thing of it and kept hitting her. But Tanua was furious and prayed to the spirit of Rere. . . . She waited and continued to pray, continued to be angry, and the day her child was due she fell ill. And the child shot forth in the house in the village. At sunrise they looked in and saw the child and the housefull of blood. The men of the men's area got frightened, took their canoes, and all fled to Maana-afe. They were afraid of dying because a child had been born in the village. Then they performed purification ceremonies. Then they performed *sulu agalo* for this child and its mother Tanua. Those two died. . . . Kunua took three pigs, three shell strings, and made Fou'eda sacred again. Then the men returned to Fou'eda. [Related by Aluta, a man of Fou'eda Island, January, 1967. Kunua is alive, a middle-aged man; he has remarried, and his second wife has had six daughters.]

A woman can also effectively check decisions about feasts. On December 12, 1966, the festivities of the severing of the skull of a dead priest, Bata, were under way in Fou'eda. Bata's daughter Kokoto, a widowed woman in her fifties, had come for the occasion from her husband's island. Bata's spirit possessed Kokoto, spoke through her mouth, and criticized the excessive spending. He said he was sorry for his people, for his children, and that they should not spend so many goods and so much food for his feast. I asked people what would be done. I was told the feast could still be held, in fact it had to be, but in a more modest manner.

On January 10, 1967, the following spirit possession took place: Kwaidorai, a man residing uxorilocally in Fou'eda, told his wife Kwalutafe that he was planning to arrange a sacrifice to his spirit (on the altar of the Kafoere clan, as he should). Upon hearing this, Kwalutafe was possessed by two spirits—her deceased son Saamani and an older spirit, Teo la tigi, who was accompanying him. Samaani said that when he died his father had made a solemn promise not to make sacrifices for three or four years. (Very nearly this long a time had passed, actually, since Saamani's death.) If the sacrifice were not canceled, "he would show him." Saamani's fury was based on the current theory of the cause of his death: he had fallen sick and died in a short time, and just before death he had seen the spirit of his father's father, Ratu. Thus it was Ratu who had wanted to kill him, and Ratu should not receive sacrifices.

Kwaidorai, assisted by other persons, talked to the two spirits. He negotiated with Saamani: "Allow this this time, and I will give you gifts." He also repeated several times, trying to soothe Saamani: "Anger is spent now." Since the sacrifice was to be directed for the welfare of Saamani's brothers, Kwaidorai also asked: "Do you want harm to come to your brothers?" Saamani answered: "Yes, I have brothers, but I am angry at you. . . . If you hadn't made a mistake in cult, your father would not have been angry at you and killed me."

Right after the possession, a man remarked to me that spirits can forbid the execution of any important plan. He added: "We were lucky that he spoke beforehand; if he hadn't, he could have killed children or done some such thing."

In connection with this possession, I asked if a person could pretend to be possessed by spirits. This never happens, I was told, but the spirit can lie. This is the case when the spirit talks about many things; when the spirit talks about one topic, and an important one, the possession is considered to be true, and the matter must be settled by either giving up the plan or striking a compromise.

Spirit possession can be interrupted if nothing constructive is expected of it. On June 8, 1967, Kwaidorai's and Kwalutafe's thirteen-year-old daughter Arasuu quarrelled with her brother Iinomae, a divorced man with a daughter living with him (the divorce was granted when his wife was caught *in flagrante delictu*). Arasuu was possessed by her dead brother Saamani's spirit and went into a hysterical fit. She was emitting inarticulate cries and tearing down the leaf wall of her brother's house. (Contrast this with her mother's spirit possession: Kwalutafe had spoken clearly and had not resorted to violence.)

When the scene started, I was working with Kokosi in her cookhouse, making notes on pregnancy, when Kokosi began acting very absent-minded. I also heard cries but thought they came from small children. Kokosi told me to follow her and walked to the scene, saw the raving girl, grabbed a woman's skirt which was drying in the sun, and passed it over the girl's head. The girl stopped instantly. A woman's skirt is *sua,* and *agalo* is its antipode; this *agalo,* true to form, made his exit. When the same *agalo* had spoken through his mother's mouth, he had bidden farewell ("now we two are parting"), and the same Kokosi had indeed made a polite reply; now, the mechanical act drove the spirit away without courtesies.

Not all women seem subject to spirit possession. In fact, I never saw a woman possessed anywhere but on her home territory, among her own clan. Possession is a mechanism through which a woman can have a say in decisions she wants to change. It is also a mechanism for the airing of grievances. A young girl, Faabongi, whose mother had died and whose father had remarried, was possessed by her dead mother Abu's spirit. The spirit spoke, typically, in the first person and accused "you two" (the father and the stepmother) of neglecting her children, of letting them starve, and of caring only for a baby born of the new marriage. I had not heard any comment or gossip in the village about the situation before the incident occurred; but while we were all standing in the darkness behind Faabongi's leaf wall (for about an hour) listening to the accusations, several people said to me: "Abu is right. It is a shame how those two treat Abu's children, this is all true." A young girl could never have presented her grievance directly, but when the spirit spoke through her mouth, she was listened to and her audience was convinced.

Conclusion

In this chapter I have, of course, spoken more of Lau women than of Lau men. In the society itself, the roles of the sexes are intertwined and complementary. All normal persons marry, all normal couples have children. Since the marriage of the parents—and for that matter, of many other people—is a situation observed daily in the extremely limited space of the artificial island, marriage holds no great surprises for the Lau. The norms and expectations, the rights and duties, are thoroughly known to the young people before they enter their married lives. They will step into line and stay in line, and all will go well.

Lau women are well aware that their life has its limitations. In the chats that they have in their leisure hours, they often talk about the woman's lot. One woman formulated it in this way: "My husband makes me pregnant, I give birth and nurse, he makes me pregnant, I give birth and nurse, he makes me pregnant . . ." Yet, not one woman answered yes to my question, posed in private interviews, if she wished to have no more children. All of them found the question meaningless. There are no means of regulating the number of births—and there is no particular reason to do so. The infant mortality rate is still high, for Western medicine has barely entered Lau Lagoon, and the doctor made occasional visits only when the anthropologists were in residence.

Then what do the women do? Being quite sensible, they make the best of what they have. As this chapter has shown, far from viewing the required periods of seclusion as a hardship, Lau women have turned them into monthly vacations. The woman's seclusion area is also used for other "selfish" purposes, for example, as a haven from a furious or—as in the case of Ulufaka—an unwanted husband. It is an area for women only, where they cannot be reached by everyday obligations.

When in the village, the women play a very active part in the life of the community. The feasts may yield no morsel of meat for the women, but the most spectacular dances are presented in the village plaza for them to enjoy. The last feast in the great funeral cycle is the women's feast. As daughters and wives and mothers, women hold key positions: the daughter will be the instrument with which an ambitious man finds a lifetime friend; the wife is a link between two clans; the mother bears and raises new members of the clan.

In Lau society, the most privileged carry the greatest burden. A rich man has many obligations; one is rich not for having but for giving. Regarding authority, a decisionmaker has the greatest of responsibilities. There are men who have refused to become priests after their fathers for fear of not being competent. Even those who have to make decisions decide in the name of their spirits, attributing the decisions to spirits and tradition. Since women do have mechanisms through which they can challenge authority should they need to, including spirit possession, is it any wonder that they are generally content to let their fathers and husbands make the decisions?

Although male dominance can perhaps be seen as universal, its basic interpretation must be in terms of order. Order in a general sense is the very basis of culture. It would be odd indeed if human societies had overlooked the most obvious ordering principle, that of sex. This is not to say that the most obvious principle is the most just.

However, a view of primitive women as "objects" is erroneous. Women are no more objects than are men; and, to a degree, both sexes are used by the collectivity toward its ends, whether religious, economic, or political.

NOTES

1. For previous reports and discussions of Lau society, see Elli Köngäs Maranda, "Les femmes Lau,—Malaita, iles Salomon—dans l'espace socialise: Notes de topographie sociale, *Journal de la Societe des Oceanistes*, vol. 26, June 1970, pp. 155–162; Pierre Maranda and Elli Köngäs Maranda, "Le Crane et l'uterus: Deux theoremes Nord-malaitains," in Jean Pouillon and Pierre Maranda (eds.), *Echanges et Communications: Melanges offerts a Claude Lévi-Strauss* (Mouton, the Hague, 1970), pp. 829–861.

2. I am grateful for the financial and moral support given by The Radcliffe Institute of Harvard University. The writing of this essay was facilitated by grants from the University of British Columbia and from the Canada Council. During the fieldwork as well as during the analysis of the data, I have enjoyed cooperating with Dr. Pierre Maranda; he studied Lau men's culture while I concentrated on Lau women's culture. My deepest gratitude is due to the people whose acceptance, hospitality, and patience made the work possible.

3. Island building was done during our stay; we have a series of photographs of the process. A man dives for coral rocks from the bottom of the lagoon and piles them on a raft. A group of children paddle the raft to the site. The builder constructs a firm stone wall 8 feet high to mark the boundaries and fills the interior by throwing in the rocks. Finishing the surface takes place later: sand and gravel are used to fill the cracks, clam shells are laid to form a surface which resembles a cobblestone street. Crushed antler coral is used to fill the uneven spots, and finally a layer of fine sand is laid down.

4. In *The Island Builders of the Pacific* (Seeley, Service & Co., Ltd., London, 1930), Walter G. Ivens gives a description of Sulufou ("Sulu Vou"), which, during his stay near the lagoon in 1927, was "still Heathen" (p. 9).

5. Since each clan has its own timetable, we were able to see all phases of the memorial cycle during our stay, some of them repeatedly.

6. In June and July 1968, we hosted a medical team sent by Harvard University to Lau Lagoon. Dr. Neville Henry, a pediatrician practicing in New Guinea, concluded that it would be impossible to imagine, in any circumstances, a healthier child population.

7. Once I asked a man to lift a heavy box into our hut. I was standing inside, and he answered: "As soon as you come out of your house, I'll be glad to do it." I stepped out, he carried the box in, came out again, and then I was free to reenter. Whenever my husband was absent from the island overnight, women would gather at our hut "to sympathize with you"—in fact, they were standing guard.

8. Cases of a man not marrying off his daughter are so rare that it is almost academic to ask why the institution should exist at all, even in theory. We did ask, and the stock answer was: "Because the father would like his daughter so much." Pierre Maranda has suggested to me, and I think his interpretation is correct, that if one of the important functions of marriage is economic—the establishment through the marriage alliance of a relationship of friendship and aid between clans—then the ultimate show of wealth is to *not* marry off a daughter. It is true that all men who have ordered a daughter into celibacy have been *'initoo* of the highest rank.

Complementary
Societies

Women of Udu:

Survival in a

Harsh Land

AUDREY SMEDLEY

Nestled around a cluster of rugged hills about 20 miles south of the town of Jos in northern Nigeria is the village of Du, or Udu—the land of the Du people. As late as the early decades of the twentieth century, the nucleus of the village was located on the topmost slopes and interstices of the hill mass. By the middle of this century, however, most of the peoples of Udu had moved down from the hills and spread out north and south for several miles.

The peoples of Du are part of a large ethnic population now numbering over 110,000 who call themselves Birom and speak a language of the same name. Their habitat is a dry, flat plateau region consisting of savannah lands, dry scrub lands, and some minor sections of woodland spread across the center of Nigeria north of the confluence of the Niger and Benue Rivers. To the north of this area are the large Sudanic states of the Hausa peoples, whose origins go back some ten centuries. To the south are the peoples of the Guinea coast, where many forest kingdoms became rich and powerful largely because of the African-Atlantic trade.

Prior to the establishment of colonial rule under Britain, the Birom

Research for this work was made possible by a Ford Foundation Foreign Area Training Fellowship.

lived in dispersed villages, each of which was politically autonomous. They are just one of perhaps forty or fifty different linguistic and ethnic groups classified as plateau pagans to distinguish them from the Muslims and Christians. Not much is known of their origins. Many experts view the plateau as a refugee area populated by peoples who, over the past 400 years, fled into this barren land to escape the slave raiding and warfare which were common in much of the surrounding regions. Each group has its own legends and myths about its origins, and these appear to substantiate the speculations of historians and anthropologists in the area.

Since 1905, when Europeans discovered tin deposits on the plateau, the lives of the plateau peoples have been encroached upon and greatly affected by the presence of foreigners. Mines were established, and massive immigrations of peoples of other ethnic groups came from the south and north as well as other parts of West Africa. These newcomers changed the whole complexion of life on the plateau. Like many other peoples, the Birom at first resisted these changes; but the superior force of European-led military units led them eventually to accept the mining industry in their midst. With mining came a rapid alienation and depletion of their lands, depression of the traditional economy, their entry into a market economy, and their increasing dependence on wage labor.

Until the full-scale establishment of the mining industry, especially after World War I, the plateau area had been considered a backwater region. The soil is extremely poor compared to that of the richer surrounding areas, and it was subject to much leaching and wind and water erosion. Traditionally the Birom made a living by the practice of shifting (or swidden) agriculture. Under this system, weeds, brush, trees, and shrubbery are burned every year to give greater friability and mineral ash to the soil. After a few years of use, however, the farms are exhausted and the entire area must be left to rejuvenate, normally for a period three to four times the amount of time during which it was farmed. Swidden farmers also depend almost entirely on rainfall for moisture. But because of the leaching and erosion, the Birom, like others, have had to develop ingenious techniques such as the erection of extensive mounds and the fencing of fields with euphorbia (prickly pear) to contain the water.

In traditional times, the staple crop was acha, of which there were some twenty varieties developed by the plateau peoples. Acha is a hardy grain that thrives under unfavorable circumstances (for example, extremes of temperature and moisture)—conditions that would totally prohibit the growth of the nutritionally superior grains such as wheat, oats, barley, and so forth. With extra care and conditioning, most Birom can also grow small amounts of millet (both bullrush and finger millet), sorghum, beniseed, and very small amounts of maize. In addition, a large variety of tuberous crops is grown (yams, cocoa yams, cassava, small sweet potatoes, etc.) as well as many legumes (peas and beans) and cucurbits. However, none of these can be grown in great abundance because of the nature of the rainfall and the soil.

The Birom economy was a subsistence one; that is, they were able to grow only sufficient foodstuffs to maintain themselves, with little surplus for trade and none for the accumulation of wealth. Small livestock, goats, sheep, a few rabbits, dogs, pigs, and occasional horses (used for sacrifices) were the only sources of meat protein foods. This was supplemented by a variety of wild products: meat from wild animals, birds' eggs, lizards, crickets, certain types of rodents, and many wild leafy vegetables, berries, and nuts.

With the coming of the mining industry and the establishment of British colonial administration, little deliberate attempt was made to change the Birom way of life. The colonial administration was very remote and concerned primarily with pacification of the plateau region. Missionary activity was not very extensive in the villages nor very successful until after the Second World War.

But the alienation of their land to mining has forced many persons to engage in wage labor for varying periods of time, usually brief, throughout the year. Mining has not improved the Birom economy; in fact, it has exacerbated an already difficult situation and is slowly introducing changes, some of which (such as gambling, prostitution, confidence games, and alcoholism) are considered by the Birom to be undesirable. The vast majority of the villagers, however, have retained to a great extent their traditional cultural ways, values, beliefs, and practices. Those few who basically changed their life-styles long left the villages for the towns and a new type of identity. Even so, most have also retained some ties in the village, and frequent visiting back and forth exposes the villagers to news from the town and knowledge of town life.

The most manifest changes are in material goods, clothing, foodstuffs from the markets, and household goods. Gradually new ways of thought and new economic activities (construction work, tailoring, mechanical jobs, trading, and the like) are being interwoven with elements of traditional culture, and a heterogeneous rural culture of the plateau is emerging. My impression was that changes would be accelerating with independence (since 1960) and a growing political awareness on the part of young men.

Villages of the plateau are separated physically and culturally from the modern towns, all of which sprang up during or after the second decade of the twentieth century. And most people, foreigners as well as indigeneous groups, appear to accept the notion that there is a large sociocultural gulf between "bush" pagans who live in villages and "town" pagans.

It is about the women of the bush village that this paper is written. At the outset, it should be noted that what is being described and dis-

cussed here is the contemporary culture of the people of Du. This is fundamentally an indigenous African culture, some of whose elements have
been altered in the process of adaptation to new conditions. Where there
have been clearly distinguishable changes in certain practices, I have
pointed out the differences between the traditional and the modern.

But more than anything, this is a story of women who have long learned
to cope with the exigencies of a harsh and unpredictable existence. They
have accepted the changing circumstances of their lives philosophically, as
perhaps they have always accepted most of the conditions that have affected them. In this, they are no different from their men. Both men and
women view themselves as enduring a common suffering because of conditions which long antedate the coming of Europeans and other strangers.
Since that time, they have been and still are the victims of harassment and
exploitation. And of all the peoples of the plateau, the pagan groups appear
to be the most impoverished today.

The Birom say that they are a hungry people. Because of food scarcity
in an unproductive and difficult land, a predictable preharvest hunger
period during which everyone suffers, and—for many—no apparent means
of increasing their food supply, especially meat, they do indeed know the
meaning of hunger. It is in this context that we must view the women
of Udu.

WOMEN AND THE SOCIAL SYSTEM

Birom women spend the greater portion of their lives in homes in which
they were not born and usually have no blood kinsmen other than their
children and, later, grandchildren. By the time a girl is fifteen or so, she
is married and goes to live in the household of her husband. She returns
to her natal home only for visits and can never again be an effective member of her parents' and brothers' home, as there is no place for her there.
The Birom believe that a grown and once married daughter cannot sleep
in the same compound as her brothers on pain of supernatural penalty.
This may be perhaps an extreme accomodation to the incest taboo, but the
Birom observe it as a necessity for the smooth running of social relationships. (In a few very rare cases, a very old woman whose husband's kins-
people have all died and whose children are dead or away may move to
the compound of some kinsmen of her natal group, usually a much younger
man who indicates his willingness to support her. More commonly, however, such a woman prefers to remain alone, perhaps as the last surviving
member of her dead husband's household.)

So the most critical relationships that a girl has to face and adjust to
are those with her husband, her co-wives (if any), her husband's parents if
they are alive, and her husband's brothers, their wives, and their children.

It is with these people that she will spend most of her life. This does not mean that she loses contact with her own kinsmen or her identity as a member of her natal group. She is always a girl in the house of her fathers, though she may be eighty years old. And her brothers and other kinsmen will always be concerned about her welfare. But she is also a wife in another kin group, and this is her most important status/role.

To understand the significance of this custom—virilocality, or the custom of a wife going to live in the home of her husband wherever he may live—we must know something about the Birom social structure.

Like that of most African peoples, the Birom village community comprises subdivisions that are separate and distinct kinship groupings. These groups among the Birom are formed on the basis of the principle of patrilineality, that is, descent in the male line only. All children belong to the kin group of their fathers. A male child gains his identity, inherits economic properties, and succeeds to both secular and ritual offices in the male line. We call these groups *agnatic* groups (relationship through males) because they do not keep close genealogies or reckon all genealogical links to a common ancestor. Thus they are not organized as lineages, as in more tightly structured lineage-based societies. But the principle of patrilineality operates in the same way here as in societies with lineages. That is, discrete kin groups with nonoverlapping membership are formed. These are made possible by the exclusion of all children born to women members of the kin group.

Among the Birom, agnatic groups are corporate units with a name and identity in the village, a crest or symbol, and a leader or headman who can and does represent the group at public functions. The Birom call these groups by the term *lo* and usually specify which group by giving the name of the person presumed to have been the founding ancestor—the name by which all the members are known. It is easy to identify a *lo* if all the male members are living together in a single compound with their wives and children. But young men of a large kin group often live away, especially if they have several brothers with families and there are too many mouths to feed. Still, the ideal is that all male descendants of a founder (anywhere from four to seven generations away) should stick together— live, work, and play together. Like all other societies, the realities of Birom life do not always reflect its ideals, if for no other reason than that the ideals serve one set of goals or functions and the realities another.

Perhaps the most important corporate characteristic of the *lo* is that it is a property-holding unit. Vested in the *lo* members are rights and privileges regarding—as well as responsibility for—land, oil- and fruit-bearing trees, and some livestock. Land is the most important property, and the rights to it are derived ultimately from the ancestors of each *lo* who are thought to have first settled and farmed the sections of land now owned by the *lo*. Men inherit potential rights to the lands of their fathers.

Women do not inherit land, nor, theoretically, do they have rights to livestock or other basic economic properties. But in the Birom value system, every woman has the right to be cared for by some man who utilizes his inherited rights for women and their children.

The agnatic kin group is the essential referent for identifying the social roles of women. Beyond this, women have no social or political significance. Women do not and cannot hold political office, either as chiefs of villages, heads of wards, or as headmen of kin groups. Nor do women participate as leaders of rituals, most of which have some economic importance in terms of decision making regarding the utilization of valued and scarce resources. In theory, women cannot hold positions as counselors or advisers to men in positions of authority, although in reality—as we shall see later—they probably have as much influence as any man with respect to their husbands, brothers, and sons who are in policy making positions.

WOMEN'S WORK

As a result of a multifaceted ecological situation, the Birom have a complex system of landholding. First of all, in spite of the general infertility of the plateau soils, there are significant differences in soil fertility and humus content from region to region. The Birom pay close attention to minute differences in the soil and to the carrying capacity of different zones of land because this often means the difference between sufficient food and starvation. In general, the hilly areas or masses are more fertile because they contain more human and animal wastes and decayed vegetation and also because moisture can be better contained in their rugged terrain. The open plains are the least fertile areas, subject as they are to wind and water erosion and much leaching and consisting of hard lateritic topsoil.

Secondly, in traditional times, the Birom had a great need to defend themselves from slave raiding, horse raiding, and intervillage hostilities that normally took the form of skirmishes between groups of men of different villages. Virtually all villages were located in defensive sites, usually in the hills, and surrounded by natural barricades of densely planted prickly pear (often 20 to 25 feet high.) Not all villages were counted as enemies, but there were certain large, remote villages that had reputations for aggression, and there were regular struggles between Udu and the peoples of some villages. Thus among the important aspects in the ecological adaptation of the plateau peoples was the development of defensive mechanisms, reactions to sudden raiding, and the establishment of institutionalized systems of raiding others for horses, slaves, and sometimes women or food.

The Birom were able to cope with both of these complex problems by evolving cultural patterns, practices, and values which would render the dangers minimal and make the best of a bad situation. They divided the farm lands into three different types, with all kin groups necessarily having access to the farms and their products in these different zones. The three are *garden farms*, which are located around the compounds in the hill masses; *intermediate farms*, which are farther away on the lower slopes of the hills; and *bush farms*, which were traditionally out on the more open plains. The Birom diet reflects the carrying capacities of these three different types of farms. Tuberous crops (yams, cassava, cocoa yams, and sweet potatoes); peas, beans, and other legumes; cucurbits, melons, squashes, and leafy vegetables—all of which demand some care, weeding, and control of moisture—are grown in the small garden farms (plots usually no larger than $\frac{1}{4}$ acre and often much smaller). In the intermediate farms are usually grown three or four different types of acha plus the millets and some beniseed. The bush farm, however, is the chief source of acha, the valued staple, and here most of the varieties of acha are grown.

In traditional times, there were a number of taboos which prevented or separated women from the actual processes of growing acha; although porridge, beer, and all foods made of acha were prepared by them.

Men harvested the acha crops, thrashed and winnowed the grain, and stored the seeds. The strength and virility of a man was and still is measured in the products of his acha crop. During the threshing period, men work long hours beating the seeds from the stalks, and it is customary for women to dance and sing around them, mocking and challenging them with their songs, praising the strong men and taunting the weak. A good crop of acha is a man's pride and joy and a source of prestige. Women look up to him and other men respect him.

In the past, the agricultural tasks of women were confined to the garden and intermediate farms. Here were grown those crops—yams, beans, cassava, melons, and other vegetables—that demand better soil and more attention and care. Women, who are for much of their lives encumbered by pregnancy and child rearing, can more easily do the tasks of planting, weeding, watering, pruning, etc., in areas close to home and small children, and the children themselves help out in these fields. One important effect of this sex-linked division of labor is that protection for women and children is provided, since they are kept off the open plains close to home. It is clear, then, that the division of labor is a direct product of ecological conditions relating to warfare and the nature of the soil.

The division of labor was, in traditional culture, a rigid one. Virtually all important productive tasks were defined in terms of men's and women's work. Other relatively neutral tasks could be done by anyone, including children. This is still pretty much the ideal.

However, with the cessation of warfare and raiding and the periodic entrance of both men and women into mining activities, there has been some blurring of the customary division. Women are often seen working in the bush farms, particularly when their men are away, or they are employed in the mines. Most men will work at least a few weeks during both dry and rainy seasons as diggers in the mines, and some women have been hired from the 1920s as headpan carriers, transporting the ore from open mine sites to processing areas. This type of work, however, is extremely periodic and discontinuous. Some men and women have worked in the mines for only a matter of a few days. Men generally work every year for several weeks, just to get enough money to pay taxes and have an additional few pennies for buying meat in the market. Women, on the other hand, tend to work only during the period before marriage or during the first year or so thereafter. After the birth of her first child, a woman does not usually return to the mines. The Birom do not consider them a proper place for their women, although in hardship cases this work becomes a necessary source of income.

The traditional rigid division of labor by sex had an important cultural consequence for the Birom. For one thing, it separated women and men geographically for long periods during the farming season. If the bush farms were far afield, men would go in groups and spend several weeks preparing the ground and planting seeds in a large number of farms. Larger groups were naturally seen as more protective. If the bush farms were closer to the hills, men, again in work groups, would go out daily, starting before dawn and returning at dusk. During the dry season, men concern themselves with repairing houses, building new ones, thatching, clearing ground for storerooms, and making bricks. They also did and still do the weaving of doors, raincapes, storage bags, and other types of covers. None of these tasks are done in concert with the domestic tasks of women. Men go off on their own together, sitting under the shade of a favorite village tree or in the open yard outside the compound.

Women's work is mostly confined to the inner courtyard of the compound. This is the hub of the domestic unit. Here, every woman (except the newly married and those old women who have turned their domestic chores over to their sons' wives) will have her own hearth and cooking pots. Here will be found the mortars and pestles for the pounding of grain, the pots and pans of clay or metal or woven grass. There will be storage space or rooms for utensils and for water, and, of course, the food storerooms, which open onto the courtyard. Women of the compound generally work together, sharing many of their materials unless there is some antagonism or jealously. In these cases, women generally work silently and separately in an atmosphere charged with tension. When they are not tending their garden farms, fetching water or firewood, or—nowadays—going to market, women spend the greater part of their lives in the compound, surrounded by the numerous sleeping rooms, storage rooms, huts for animals, rainy-season cooking rooms, and the entrance hut—all of which they must care for. It is said of a good wife that she remains always in her *Ialla* (household or domestic unit).

Thus, in many ways, the lives of men and women represent separate and distinctly different spheres of Birom life. Yet even more important than the *differences* between male and female roles is the fact that the specialized activities of men and women are essentially *complementary*. Though separated both physically and socially, the tasks that men and women perform throughout the year are geared to and necessary for their respective activities. Both men and women recognize their dependence on one another.

Women are dependent on men to build and repair the houses, make the tools and implements of farming, build the yam ridges and prepare the ground for sowing, do the farming of the major cereals, and provide them with meat. Men are dependent upon women for the preparation of food (except on ritual occasions, men are prohibited from cooking, and there are mystical taboos against handling the cooking pots of women), for the growing and care of certain crops, for keeping the household, for feeding and tending to children, and for the transportation of foodstuffs and other goods. As we shall see later, there is a certain perhaps unanticipated inequality in the dependence relationships between men and women.

THE REARING OF A GIRL

Conditioning for the separate roles of men and women begins early in life. In fact, it may be said that the Birom distinctions between male and female begin with the rituals of birth, during which these differences are symbolized. If the child is a boy, the umbilical cord is cut with a special metal (iron) knife that is used to cut acha, thus symbolically associating the male child with acha. For girls, on the other hand, the cord is cut with a blade of grass or a bamboo knife. The afterbirth of a boy child is placed in a clay pot or calabash and then put high on the branch of a special cottonwood tree in the area of his paternal compound. The afterbirth of girls will be buried in the soil, usually during a special ritual of fertility. I found this to be still true even in families where the young adults were nominally Christians.

In terms of physical care, infants will not be treated differently on the basis of sex. Boys are much desired, as it is through male offspring that a man becomes the founder of a new patriline and thus gains some measure of immortality. Yet girls bring bride wealth and are looked upon with equal delight. Concern for the health and survival of all infants is shown, as nearly half of all children can be expected to die before the age of three. It is a sad statistic, but life among the Birom is harsh. Still, there are different emotional attitudes toward male and female infants; the same behavior is perceived and interpreted differently. The crying of a boy infant is a sign of a lust for life, a prognostication of his strength and virility in manhood. The frequent crying of a girl infant, unless she is ill, is—as often as not—interpreted as the beginning of a fretful and complaining personality. Since it is far more important for a girl to learn to get along with others than it is for a boy, adults are sensitive to these qualities in a girl. Girl children are also thought to be more vulnerable— that is, weaker and in need of protection. In boys what is looked for is strength, stamina, lack of physical deformities, and obedience toward their elders.

All children are trained from infancy to care for one another. Sharing and cooperation are such important values that by the time a child is three or four, sharing is a habit. I once saw a boy of four find a particularly large cricket. He hastened to the fire to roast it and subsequently divided it cheerfully into very small pieces for all of his age mates lingering nearby.

It is through demonstration, example, and instruction that children are taught the differences between men and women. Girls of four and five learn to care for small babies by carrying them on their backs. They are also instructed in how to carry head loads, how to sweep the yards and stack the yams, how to pound grain and prevent the chickens from eating it. Boys, on the other hand, do very little work until the age of about seven or eight, when they are taken in hand by the older men and taught the skills of farming. At this age, the differences between the sexes are made quite clear. One of the few times that I saw an African adult chastise a child by striking it was when a four-year-old boy, the baby of the family, kept insisting on trying to carry a head pan. Each time, his mother scolded him that this was not a thing for boys to do. Finally, fed up with his disobedience, she smacked him soundly and snatched the pan away. I never saw him attempt this again. Young boys soon learn that specific household chores are forbidden to them, although more general chores of fetching, handling of domestic animals, running errands, and the like are done by all children at the command of the adults.

Boys are sensitized at an early age and in subtle ways to have concern and affection for their sisters. A young boy of seven or eight in our compound frequently told me that he was "in charge of" the many girl children, some a few years older than he. This was especially true in the absence of an older boy or man. Girls frequently voiced the ideal that they should "obey" their brothers, but I found that they often did so only when they wished. However, girls are trained to depend on their brothers and seek protection from them. In spite of the usual bickering and arguing that goes on between siblings, there develops a strong affection between brothers and sisters which, as we shall see later, is bolstered by the fact that, as both children and adults, their roles are noncompetitive.

Before marriage, Birom girls lead lives that are fairly carefree and unencumbered. Although they must learn domestic duties, young girls are often told to go off and play "while there is still time." They well know that a girl's life changes drastically after marriage. Instead of the freedom to roam the village and play, she now has to accept near confinement in the compound and the domination of her husband and in-laws. Everywhere it is recognized that pagan women work hard, that marriage brings both an inferior status in an unfamiliar household and tremendous pressures to adjust to a whole new set of social relationships.

The Birom consider it important that a girl have a pleasing way about her. To this end, girls are deliberately and carefully instructed by their mothers and other older women in techniques that condition them to be both resilient and flexible. Alone in the compound during the day, women talk among themselves about the relationships between men and women. They tell young girls how to behave, how they must comport themselves in the compound and out in public (beyond the compound area). But most importantly, although it would never be expressed this way in the Birom language, they teach girls—both by example and instruction—how to handle men. For example, I have frequently heard girls in our compound told never to talk to a man when he is angry; wait until he is fed and given water. And they are taught always to be submissive and patient. In fact, patience is thought to be the most important quality in women, and those who lack it are ridiculed and shamed by other women.

Thus it is that girls are prepared for marriage and the psychology of women's roles by other women.

BETROTHAL AND MARRIAGE

In traditional times, by the time a girl was three or four, she might very well have been betrothed to a young teenaged boy. Nowadays, betrothal usually takes place much later, when she is about ten or eleven. Betrothals and marriages are arranged by the elders of the kin groups involved. Early betrothals were advantageous to the men of a girl's kin group, as the fiancé was expected to perform bride service—in the form of farm-help—every year until the marriage. In addition to bride service, a fairly heavy bride price was required; in the precolonial period, this price consisted of a horse and six goats plus the many gifts that must be given to a girl's relatives, both male and female. Nowadays, bride wealth is paid in cash, officially established at £16 at the time of my fieldwork. And bride service is still demanded and expected, although a young man with a fairly steady job or source of income may substitute for this service periodic gifts of money or grain or other foodstuffs.

Although all children were and are brought up to respect and accept the directions and decisions of elders, girls were never forced to marry someone completely against their wishes. This is too often a myth associated with societies in which marriages (because they are perceived as establishing a serious and permanent contract between two kin groups) are arranged by elders. Marriages are not taken lightly, and many calculations enter into such arrangements. If a girl absolutely refused to marry her betrothed, her kin group would feel a moral obligation to provide the other kin group with another bride, and generally one would be found. Also, another husband would be found for the first girl. However, the vast majority of girls accept the husbands selected for them because they feel that their fathers will have made the best choice.

As in all societies that have this custom, the bride price functions to legitimize the marriage. It is only by the full payment of a bride price that a man receives not only sexual rights to a girl and the right to her domestic services but also—and most importantly—the right to be the legitimate father (pater) of any children born to her. But there is more than just the right of paternity involved. In patrilineal societies where a child belongs exclusively to one set of kinsmen on the father's side, the bride price and the contract of marriage confers on that group the right to make a child one of its members. And even if the father dies, there is a custom called the levirate which recognizes the continued existence of the marriage contract and the kin group's rights. Under this custom, the widow will go to one of the "brothers" of her dead husband, and any children that she may bear thereafter still belong to the dead husband. He is always their pater though not necessarily their genitor.

Many marriages are contracted without the full payment of the bride price. Often initial payment is made with the remainder to be paid, by agreement between the elders, in installments. By ancient custom, a man thus may get a wife but not rights to the children of the union. A girl's own agnatic group claims rights to all children born before the full payment of the bride price. Retroactive claims can be recognized, however, depending on the nature of the relationships between the men of the respective kin groups.

The marriage ceremony itself was an elaborate affair, covering a period of several days, with the bride making several visits (including one in which she is "stolen") to the groom's home before settling into her marital role. Nowadays, such extended ceremonialism is generally omitted. As in all societies, this transition to a different social role is associated with many beliefs, some of both practical (or naturalistic) and supernaturalistic form. There are taboos, restrictions, values about proper behavior, etc., and the marital ceremonies provide an occasion for the reiteration of these beliefs and values.

WOMEN AS WIVES

The Birom do not have separate terms in their language for *woman* and *wife*. All girls who grow to maturity become wives at some time or another, even though in some cases the full bride price may never be paid for them. Since the bulk of any woman's life is spent within the compound of a husband's agnatic group, it is to the crucial relationships here that we must turn to understand fully the nature of womanhood among the Birom.

It is no doubt the case that, in a significant majority of human societies, the adult male holds the most important positions, exercises the greatest amount of formal power and authority, and is seen as the most important social element. This is certainly true in patri-oriented or patrilineal societies. Because of this and partly because of our own heritage and the conditions of our work, most ethnographers (male and female) tend to use the male perspective in their studies. As we are all aware, male ethnographers often cannot even talk in any depth to the women. So the views of what constitutes a "good wife" or "good husband" and the whole nature of the relationship between men and women are frequently colored with the bias of largely male informants and male ethnographers. While this surely yields valid information, it is legitimate and probably necessary to ask whether the male point of view on such matters as the qualities of a good wife is the same as the female point of view.

In my researches, I found that there are some differences in the views that men and women in Biromland hold of each other—differences in their concepts of the ideal and in their perceptions of real behavior. These were, however, primarily differences of focus and emphasis rather than explicit, substantive ones.

Both men and women tended to agree clearly on certain values. A fundamental and unequivocal one is that husbands are always dominant and wives must always be submissive to them. Within this general norm, however, men nearly always focus on domestic abilities as an index of a good wife. A woman should obey her husband and look after his needs, providing food and drink and attending to normal domestic and farming chores. A woman is adjudged a good wife if she stays in her compound except for periods of farming or fetching water and firewood. Keeping a neat household and running the many complex activities smoothly has a high priority among men. Although men tend not to be concerned, except secondarily, with personality factors, they do feel that a woman should be cheerful and maintain a proper demeanor around her husband, his friends, and his relatives.

Women, on the other hand, understandably value much more the ability to get along with mothers-in-law, co-wives, and the wives of other brothers. They are far more lenient with inefficiency or lassitude in household work. And they are highly critical of women who complain and nag or who are sullen, argumentative, and resentful of their work. Considered especially heinous are women who neglect their children. The Birom have a great love and desire for children and, to them, a woman who neglects or ill treats a child is radically abnormal. When I asked of women which was more important, taking care of their husbands' needs or those of their children, almost all refused to make the distinction and said both were equal. Yet in the practical realities of daily life, women invariably put their children first, feeding them from hidden sources and, when food is very scarce, sometimes at the expense of their husbands.

In the relationship of husbands and wives, compatibility of personalities is almost irrelevant to the jural or domestic stability of a marriage. Spouses need not be friends, although the atmosphere of the houshold is more pleasant if they are "friendly" in the sense of getting along well together. Love between spouses is strongly valued, and the idea of romantic love is gaining greater acceptance with greater exposure to external styles of life. But what the Birom appear to mean by love between spouses is that they should care about one another, not necessarily be "in love." In fact, to be in love—to be totally infatuated with another person—may have unintended consequences in the corrosion of other relationships. A number of Birom folk tales, some nearly legendary, document a strong belief that it is better to love wisely but not too well.

To care is to show concern for the other person's welfare, to do one's duties to the best of one's ability, and to avoid those situations which might initiate disputes and disruptions of the household. A woman says, "If he loves me, he will bring me food," or "If he loves me, he will clothe me," or "If he loves me, he will not beat me too much."

Men and women spend most of their lives in the company of their own sex where "good conversation" and companionship is valued. Although much depends on the personalities of the spouses, conjugal companionship is generally considered inconsistent with the work conditions of husbands and wives. But a curious factor in the husband-wife relationship is that the "social distance" between the spouses is predicated almost entirely on the childbearing status of the woman. The greatest differences between men and women are highlighted during the early years of marriage, when pregnancy and childbirth serve to enhance sexual roles. Women are never more completely subordinate to men than during this period.

As a woman grows older and becomes more secure in her position, the dominance of her husband tends to lighten. With menopause and in subsequent years, women reach a stage of "liberation" which virtually places them on an equal level with their husbands in many respects. They now have complete freedom of the village and can come and go as they like, especially if there is a daughter-in-law to do the domestic chores. And they are no longer liable to the demands of their husbands, who at this time sometimes complain about their lack of control of their wives.

It is correct and proper for a man to scold or even beat his wife should she be remiss in her duties. Women expect this and can usually anticipate when their actions will evoke this type of punishment. But men who beat their wives too often may risk losing them, and this is cited as one of the major causes of a woman's desiring to break a marriage. Yet in reality I have found that most men, rather than initiate a conflict that will result in the beating of a wife, will tend to ignore minor irritations, or they will complain and then walk away, expecting the wife to correct whatever is wrong. If a "talking to" does not work, then a beating might be in order, even though such behavior always carries the risk that the wife will complain to her paternal kinsmen, particularly her brothers, thus possibly provoking a major flareup between the two kin groups.

Perhaps the most critical relationships in any marriage are those between a young bride and other women of the household, particularly the mothers-in-law. In all human societies, no two households can be expected to be identical in their composition or their styles and modes of operation. New brides are expected to adjust to and learn the tempo and other idiosyncrasies of households already established and maintained by older women. The tenuous situation of a new bride is fraught with anxieties and potentially disruptive misunderstandings. So the Birom institutionalize the inferior position of a new bride and surround her with taboos and restrictions which have the effect of easing and facilitating her adjustment to the new household. Thus a new bride may not speak openly to her mother-in-law until the birth of the first child, when, with the onset of the first pains, she is expected to call out to the older woman, addressing her as "mother."

The Birom express the proper behavior of a new bride with the phrase *wa njiik*. The terms are not directly translatable into English but refer to a state of shyness, of silence and obedience, and an attitude of acceptance of her inferior position vis-à-vis the other women. With the birth of a child, the new bride is more firmly established in her new home. She now converses openly with the older women, with, of course, due respect for their age, status, and wisdom. Her own status is further strengthened when another new and younger bride is brought into the compound.

Thus although the Birom do not recognize the formal status of a first

or head wife and all wives are supposed to be treated equally in a polygamous household, there is still an informal but tacitly open pecking order
among all the women of a compound. The recognition of this hierarchy
is extended to neighboring and related compounds, so that when women
visit back and forth during their leisure times, deference is paid to older
women, those who are the wives of the headmen, those who have the most
children or have been married the longest, and so forth.

Now, in spite of the unquestioned authority of men over women, the
most important sanctions against improper behavior on the part of a
woman are the attitudes and evaluations of other women. In Birom society,
no married couple can ever be seen as an isolated or isolable unit. The
notion that a marriage is a private affair is completely alien to the Birom.
Relationships within marriage are open to the eyes of all, and new brides
especially come under close scrutiny, most particularly by other women.

It is women who talk about and judge the behavior of other women.
I can remember only rare occasions when I could elicit opinions about
women from men, and generally these were unmarried young men. I soon
came to realize that men did not usually know the opinions that women
shared about one another among themselves. It is essentially women who
pass judgment on who is a good wife and who is not, taking into consideration some of the most intimate behavior as well as many aspects
of behavior that would be considered trivial in our mobile society. I sometimes heard women, during afternoon gossip sessions, say of a particular
person that her husband should beat her because she is lazy or irresponsible
or difficult to get along with. And I can remember one occasion when
a young man (whom I knew well and who had stated to me that the Birom
should stop beating their wives) was literally constrained, albeit reluctantly,
to thrash his young wife by the pressures of the other women of the compound. He knew that his wife was indeed behaving badly by Birom
standards, but he had come under the influence of missionaries who had
taught him that wife beating was a savage practice.

In our own compound, the second wife of the headman was frequently
beaten because of her neglect of her husband. Her forgetfulness about
bringing him water and her preference to go off and have a good time
while neglecting the compound duties were for a time the source of much
gossip and scandal among the neighborhood women. It was not long before
these women had obliged me to see her from their point of view, in fact
turning to me on several humorous occasions for concurrence with their
judgment. "She deserves a beating, doesn't she?" In Biromland, I learned
never to underestimate the power of women's gossip.

Even little girls were aware of and participated in the formation of
local attitudes about certain women, and then, of course, had the most to
learn from the situations. Because of their freedom of movement and of

expression and their accepted presence everywhere, little girls probably knew more about what was going on in the village than any other persons.

Domestic disputes are generally resolved within the compound, sometimes by the women themselves and sometimes by the headman of the group. Those that cannot be settled among kinsmen are nearly always brought to the ward head, where a more formal procedure exists for ending conflicts of all sorts. During the almost two years that I lived in Du village, there were many occasions when husbands and wives brought their cases to Ben,[1] the headman of our compound and of the ward. He would hear the issues and attempt to conciliate or mediate the disputes. His advice was important not only because of his position but because he was considered wise in the ways of the Birom and eternally patient with people caught in the heat of argument.

However, I soon realized that far more effective than Ben's exhortations, condemnations, or suggestions were the undercurrent conversations of the women who were always present at these hearings. (In fact, men, women, and children from neighboring compounds would nearly always wander over, if they were not otherwise occupied, to hear what was going on.) Any woman involved in a domestic dispute, whether with her husband, a co-wife, or husband's relative, was ultimately far more responsive to the clucking noises of disapproval or words of advice directed at her by the other women. When Ben would finish the hearing with the last bit of advice and turn away to go into the compound, the women would emerge from their positions on the periphery. The older women, especially, would give their advice, and I was surprised at the number of times that it differed from the advice of the ward head. There would be a period of general chatter as the women prepared to go about their business; but the women had now taken over to either condemn or exonerate one of their own or simply to advise and teach her. In the ensuing discussion—including entreaties, debates, scoldings, and remarks of all sorts by young and old women—the ground was often laid for the real resolution of the problem.

If new brides come to love their mothers-in-law, as seems to be often the case, then an ideal situation is established from the women's point of view. In fact, this relationship is often the crucial element in the stability of many marriages. When I collected statistics on divorce, well over half the women interviewed said that if they loved their mothers-in-law, they would not break the marriage; and this was irrespective of their feelings about their husbands. There was also a close correlation between how well a young woman got along with her mother-in-law and complaints of wife beating. In traditional times, strife between a mother-in-law and daughter-in-law was a major contributor to divorce, and this type of strife often reflects or is reflected in strife between husband and wife. The biblical story of Ruth and Naomi is certainly not a unique one; it is probably acted out again and again in all patrilineal and virilocal societies.

At some time in her married life a woman may also become a co-wife; that is, her husband may marry a second wife or inherit a wife through the levirate. Ideally each wife has a separate cooking hearth and separate huts for sleeping and storage. The Birom come close to this ideal, with less than 5 percent of the women (excluding new brides who have not yet borne a child) living in compounds where they share a common cooking place. Still, women are jealous if a husband shows preferences among his wives, and they will argue and bicker over small differences in foods, over the uses of certain household properties, over children especially, and over many other matters.

Major disputes which lead to the breakup of a marriage usually occur early in the marriage. Divorces, which can be realized only when a new husband has been found for the girl, are far more common during the few years preceeding the appearance of children. (Divorce and remarriage always occur if a girl fails to conceive after about two years.) However, as we have seen, with the birth of children and the passage of time, the women of the household will have developed patterns of interaction and personal habits of adjustment to one another that avoid open conflict and contribute to the smooth running of the household.

In long-established domestic situations, I found that women in fact quite often come to like and even to love one another. The first funeral I witnessed in the village was that of an old woman in a neighboring compound. She and her co-wife had lived together, along with several sons, daughters-in-law, and grandchildren since the death of their common husband many years earlier. At the funeral the surviving wife was so grief-stricken and distraught that she cried out, "Oh, why did you leave me? Why did you not take me with you? You have left me alone!" Her children tried to restrain her, but she wept openly in their arms, striking and pounding herself and occasionally breaking away to throw herself on the ground in the dust. Friends explained to me, quite simply, that she loved her co-wife.

It would appear from a general outline of the structure of Birom society that women have peculiar disabilities because of their sex. One may be tempted, on the surface, to portray women as little more than slaves or chattel, as did many travelers and missionaries who knew nothing about the substance and processes of the daily life of indigenous peoples. From a purely formal perspective, women have no civil or political rights (but it is questionable whether terms of this sort can even be applied to the rights exercised by men). It is also true that women have no jural rights to the inheritance and control of property in land and livestock. Yet, their right to the *use* of these resources is never questioned. I have known several cases where the men of two kin groups argued heatedly over which group "owned" a particular plot of farmland. And while they carried on their argument from year to year, the women of these groups continued to grow their crops, sorting out the particular problems of sharing on the basis of kinship ties among themselves.

Perhaps of even greater significance is the fact that women have access to farmlands which are not available to their husbands directly. There are special plots called women's farms which are turned over to young women, or unmarried girls, sometimes by their fathers or brothers, sometimes by their husband's kin group after marriage for their exclusive use. Women also may borrow farms from their own agnatic kinsmen, from their mother's brother's kin group, and especially from their lovers. Nowadays some women rent farms on their own. A woman's rights to the use of such farms is never questioned, although permanent ownership remains officially in the hands of men.

The truth is that the realities of the woman's world in Biromland contradict their apparent low status, lack of rights, and seemingly great limitations on the personal mobility and freedom that which are so cherished in the Western world. Women have particular strengths which derive in part from their inferior status and from institutional aspects of the Birom economy.

Perhaps the single most important feature in assessing the strengths of women is their role in the domestic arena. The domestic unit is the vital economic unit among the Birom. It is a subdivision of a compound occupied by a man and his wife or wives and children. As such, it produces, stores, and manages its own food resources. Because only women do the cooking among the Birom, a viable domestic unit requires the presence of at least one able-bodied woman. Domestic units without adult, married-in women die out; if there are any remaining members, they will be scattered to reside among kinsmen.

There are several consequences of this fact. First, harmony within the domestic unit—which is absolutely essential for the smooth running of its economic functions—is largely in the hands of women. Women who run off and leave their husbands disrupt the entire economy of the household. Women are well aware that they can cause such a crisis situation even with the absence of a week or two. Second, this fact points out an imbalance in the dependency relationships of men and women. While men say that women are like children—fickle and incapable of caring for themselves and making important decisions, so that they must be under the charge of some man—women know that men are also dependent on them and that their dependence is greater.

Older men who are widowers and no longer capable of farming can no longer find wives. They must go and live in the households of kinsmen, where there are women to cook for them. When food is scarce, such old men are the last to be fed. One of the great fears that all men have as they get older is that they may outlive their wives. To this end, men prefer to marry younger women and, as indicated earlier, the institutions of long betrothal and later marriage for men tend to ensure that, even in a monogamous situation, the wife will outlive her husband. Men also find increased security by taking a second wife as they reach middle age. One of the more bitter areas of dispute between men and their sons concerns the choice of whether to use the slim resources of the kin group to obtain a young wife for themselves or to provide a wife for a son.

Women, on the other hand, have no such disabilities. Most women become widows at some time in their married lives and generally choose to remain in their husband's home rather than to remarry. This is always true if the widow is past childbearing age. Younger widows without children are always remarried. But the vast majority of widows with children will stay on to protect the property and status rights of their children. If they stay, they either go to a husband's brother in a levirate relationship or remain in their husband's domestic unit, farming and caring for themselves with the help of "lovers" (see below) and other kinsmen.

Older women continue their farming activities, particularly in small garden farms, and cooking for themselves long past the age of retirement for men. They also are the recipients of food gifts from many persons outside of their household—not only their children and children's spouses but also other kinsmen and "lovers." Widows can and do live alone for long periods of time nowadays because their children may take jobs outside the village. More often, however, they have with them a number of grandchildren of varying ages. Thus women have a type of economic independence that is not available to men. (Nowadays this custom is undergoing some change, but it will probably be another generation before the effects will be discernible.)

Elsewhere[2] I have argued that the exclusion of women from the traditional system of property rights and from the holding of secular or sacred positions of power is another source of the type of strength that women can exercise. This means that the roles of men and women are fundamentally noncompetitive and that women's ties to men are essentially complementary and affective rather than competing.

The complementarity of male and female roles is best expressed in the functioning of the domestic unit, where the innumerable but interdependent tasks are distinguished by sex. It is also manifest in the Birom ideas of the sexuality of men and women. Women are not seen and do not see themselves as passive participants in sexual activities, but they do see themselves as having a different sexual nature, with equal ability and rights to the enjoyment of sex. Because of this, women can and do use their sexuality for the benefit of themselves and their families, especially in the institution of *njem,* the traditional lover relationship described below.

Women have affective ties not only with their husbands but with a larger number of men whose loyalty and services they can command. Earlier I spoke of the strong affective ties between brothers and sisters. This is retained throughout their lives—with a few rare exceptions where a girl has been married outside the village and is too far away for her brothers to maintain constant surveillance of her welfare. In social anthropological studies, it is common knowledge that the in-law relationship is a potentially antagonistic one. A woman's brothers and father (if any are still living) will always be concerned with her welfare and that of her children even though they belong to a different kin group. They will readily come to her aid if they feel that she is being maltreated, or if, because of some disaster, her husband's kinsmen cannot provide her with food.

Strong, affective ties are also found between women and their sons. The desire for children of both sexes is great, and women express the feeling of a common bond among themselves because of the high infant mortality rate. Virtually all women have lost children either at birth or within the first three years of life. The average woman bears between eight and ten children during her lifetime. In the two generations preceding the time of this study, half of these children died in infancy. Women say that all women know sorrow because of the deaths of their children. So in those instances where children do survive, the ties between mother and child are very strong. While their daughters are always married away and the distance determines the nature of the mother-daughter interaction, sons normally remain in their father's compound and women see them as a source of sustenance in their old age. They say that sons will always feed them, and most women are pleased when their sons marry, as this means that they can eventually be freed from their housework as it is turned over to the new bride.

The influence that mothers have over their sons is probably substantial in all cultures. In Africa, from Egyptian times on, the influence of the "queen mother" has become institutionalized as a political position in those states classified as divine kingdoms. While the Birom were a tribal people who did not have centralized systems of authority, the mothers of important men were still thought to have a degree of elevated prestige principally because of their ability to influence their sons. The relationship that men have with their fathers is a fairly rigid one based on authority and subordination, but such qualities exist, if at all, only minmally in the mother-child relationship. Children generally are taught to obey their parents as well as all older people; as a son grows to manhood, however, the superior status of his sex takes primacy, and he learns to take an authoritarian attitude toward all women except the very old.

Because of the age difference in marriage, a mother in her early thirties frequently has a daughter who will be engaged and married to a man who was once the mother's younger playmate and for whom she may have been a baby-sitter. They will be "friends" of long standing, and the affective relationships of childhood will be carried forward into the new relationship of mother-in-law and son-in-law. Quite a few elderly widows in Udu had such a close relationship with their sons-in-law, men close to their age and some younger, and several were being supported almost entirely by these men.

Most revealing of the affective nature of ties that women have with men, especially nonkinsmen, is in the custom of cicisbeism, called by the Birom *njem*. Judging by the anthropological literature, this is a rare custom in human societies—although I suspect that it is not as rare as the literature suggests. Cicisbeism is the socially accepted and widespread custom whereby a woman takes a lover after her marriage. It is completely legal and traditional in those societies where it has been found. The Birom see it as both natural and necessary, claiming that all women have lovers (*rwas-njem*). They were always surprised when I said that this was not an accepted custom in America.[3]

Although the initial step in the establishment of an *njem* relationship is taken by the man who wishes to become her lover, each woman has the right to choose her lovers. Once agreement is reached, the lover pays a goat to the woman's husband and subsequently takes upon himself the traditional obligations of the *rwas-njem*. He must once a year bring meat to his mistress's family, he must help her with farming, he must feed her children if they are hungry, and he must bring his mistress oil for her body (especially necessary during the dry season) and other gifts and trinkets. Thus, his obligations to her are essentially economic and I would argue that, while the sexual component is important in the relationships, especially among younger women, the institution of *njem* is basically an economic one. The Birom women also recognize this, for when I asked about the reasons for this custom, the usual and most common answer was, "Who will feed my children?"

The women of Udu have peculiar strengths in their relationship to the various men in their lives. On numerous occasions I saw women influence their husbands to make decisions which were often contrary to what these men had originally intended. I have recorded cases where women helped to terminate long-standing arguments between men, both kinsmen and nonkinsmen. Women believe that they must support their men and that they also must do what is right in terms of Birom beliefs and values.

There is no doubt that the women of Udu are aware of their powers. Older women would often sit down with me for long hours, and some of them gleefully recounted events in which they either got their way in opposition to their fathers or husbands or were able to get men to do things for them. One old woman, while recounting the story of her life and marriages, told me that her classificatory fathers married her first to a man of Zawang, a village only a short distance away.[4] She, however, did not wish to be married that far away from her mother and sisters. Besides, she did not like the man. So she ran away . . . not once but six times! Each time her fathers took her back, insisting that it was a good marriage. After the sixth time, they realized that it would not work. So another marriage in Du village was arranged for her. As she told the story of her various flights, what she took with her, how she acted, and what she told her fathers (some lies), she and the other women around laughed heartily. There was general agreement that it was all right to deceive men as long as it was only a small deception and did not harm anyone.

Studies of preindustrial as well as industrial societies often point out that women usually represent the conservative elements in the social system. They seem to be more prone to maintain the status quo than are the men or younger people. In this sense the women of Udu are no different from other women. On several occasions, when I was investigating segmentation or the subdivision of kin groups that had grown too large and cumbersome for the resources available, I found the greatest resistance to my inquiries among the women (married in to the men of the group). While the men would ponder and attempt to answer the questions asked, women sometimes insisted that I should not ask such questions because I was dividing the group. They refused to recognize the already existing divisive forces. Not only that, but I found that women often knew more about the members of the group and how they were related to one another than did the men. It seemed at the time curious to me that women should be the ones who were most circumspect about the preservation of their husbands' kin group. But then, they bear the children for the group.

The realities of Birom life suggest that women have a vested interest in the maintenance of the system and particularly of their special roles and situations within it. One can conclude from this study that when the economy is so constituted that clearly distinguishable sex roles evolve as necessary for survival, then women themselves will obviously have reason for maintaining the structure of the society and the "inequality" of the sex roles. But such sex differentiation is more than a mere survival factor in the ecological circumstances of the Birom, since it has provided women with special opportunities and abilities for manipulating the social system outside of the competitive and more rigidly structured roles of the men.

NOTES

1. The name has been changed for the protection of my informants and my Birom family.

2. A Smedley, *Kinship and Social Organization among the Birom of Northern Nigeria,* Ph.D. thesis, University of Manchester, 1967. A somewhat revised version of this book is soon to be published.

3. A full account of this custom will be given in a separate publication.

4. A group of male kinsmen are called "Father" by a Birom woman because they share some of the obligations a biological father has toward his daughter.

Women in China: Past and Present

ALINE K. WONG

Introduction

An attempt to depict the Chinese women, their role and status in society, is by no means an easy undertaking. The Chinese women have undergone three stages of transformation—traditional, transitional, and modern—within a short span in modern history. At the turn of this century, gradually more and more traditional values and concepts came under fire for the first time as a result of Western impact. Subsequent economic and social modernization drives had worked their way into various dimensions of social life, including the traditional position of women. While the changes were in full swing, China was brought under Communist rule. The Communist revolution had not only stepped up the pace but also altered the patterns of social change. Under close government control, some aspects of Chinese society have changed beyond recognition. After two turbulent decades of radical social revolution, we begin to see a new modern womanhood emerging in China today.

Most writing in the West about Chinese women is about the traditional type of women. Recently, sinological research findings on the family institution have shown that the stereotype of the large extended family needs modification. So do some of the related features of the family organization. Thus the stereotype traditional Chinese women tend to

229

overrepresent the upper social class (for example, the gentry women) as opposed to the majority class (the peasant women). Likewise, much that has been known about Chinese women under the impact of modernization in the Republican period has an urban bias because it was mostly based on women in the more developed urban sector situated in the coastal provinces as opposed to women in the vast rural sector in interior China who were not yet exposed to modernization influences. It is equally difficult to talk about Chinese women under Communism today, partly because there are many information gaps and partly because the contemporary political and social scene is often too unsettled for impartial evaluation. Since the Cultural Revolution of 1966, almost no information has been published on this vital subject. It is very difficult to assess the net social effects of Communist rule on Chinese women because—it must be stressed —social change is necessarily a long process and many social institutions in China that were actually crumbling prior to the Communist Revolution only received a coup de grace at the Communist government's hands. Nevertheless, we feel that a fairly general picture of contemporary women in China can be drawn from scrappy information.

WOMEN IN TRADITIONAL CHINA

The Traditional Family and Discrimination against Women

The ideal of every traditional Chinese man was to have male children and set up a large family in which all his married sons and their families would be living together in one big household when he grew old. Within such a family, the oldest male member from the highest generation ruled supreme as the household head (chia-chang). He allocated the productive tasks to the individual family members and he also controlled the family's expenses. He saw to it that harmony reigned within the large household, which might sometimes consist of one or two dozens of people. However, families of such sizes were not common; in fact, they were found only among the wealthy gentry classes. The majority of the poor peasants had only a small piece of family land, frequently rented from a landlord relative, that could not support a huge household,[1] so that most peasant families consisted of five to six persons from three generations only.[2]

Traditional China was a male-centered society. The Confucian scholars taught respect for one's ancestors and laid great emphasis on the continuity of the family line. Confucius's disciple Mencius said, "There are three unfilial acts; the greatest of these is the failure to produce sons." Thus girls, from the day of birth, were subjected to lifelong discrimination, as so well described by a popular verse from the *Book of Odes* written some three thousand years ago: "When a son is born, he is laid down on couches, and is given a piece of jade to play with. When a daughter is born, she is laid on the floor, and is given a piece of tile to play with."

Confucian scholars viewed the social order as dependent on harmonious family relationships, which in turn were built upon the differentiation of age and sex roles. Thus some Chinese scholars, writing on the deplorable discrimination against women, said that "it all began with Confucius."[3] The traditional subjugation of Chinese women lasted for two thousand years, up to the eve of the 1911 revolution.

Socialization and Sex Role Differentiation

A girl probably enjoyed her happiest years in her family of orientation during infancy and childhood—although some girls suffered relative neglect and others became the victims of female infanticide.[4] In other cases, young girls might be sold as slaves if their parents were too poor to support them (they always preferred to devote their resources to bringing up sons). However, under most circumstances, a baby girl would receive from her mother nurturance and care probably in no way different from that of her brother. Discipline was relatively mild in the early years. At the age of three or four, parents began to make distinctions on the basis of sex, and discipline became slightly more severe for a girl. She was expected to absent herself from the presence of others, particularly from the presence of men. At the age of four or five, sex-role differentiation which would leave permanent marks on them was genuinely imposed on the lives of the children. Boys began to live in their father's section of the house, while the girls remained in the women's quarters and continued to be under the supervision and direction of their mother, who trained them for their future domestic roles. The boys of gentry families started receiving an education at an early age, either from private tutors at home or at the village school. Girls, however, never went to school, although a few might obtain some instruction at home if they were born into wealthy families and if they happened to be favorites with their parents.

A girl's relationship with her mother was always warm and affectionate, whereas her relationship with the father became constrained at an early age. Her awe and respect for her father, coupled with the strict incest taboo, created a lifelong pattern of distance and avoidance between father and daughter.

At the age of nine or ten, all joint play with brothers stopped and the girl was increasingly made aware that she was destined to marry out of the family. Then, during her early teens, she was more and more withdrawn from contacts with outsiders. She began to learn the manners of womanliness. She rose earlier than her brothers, dressed more neatly then they, helped in the kitchen, and often helped to take care of the younger ones. She played with fewer toys, did more work, talked more quietly, walked about more delicately. She was taught not to laugh but only smile; she would not look at strangers nor let herself be seen by them. She learned cooking, sewing, spinning, weaving, and embroidery. She was often reminded of the "Three Obediences and Four Virtues of Women" in preparation for her adult roles.[5]

Foot-binding

Beginning when the girl was four or five, the mother would start binding her feet, as every mother who wanted her girl to grow up beautiful and respectable would. Foot-binding was done by winding a long piece of cloth bandage around both of the young girl's feet, the tightness of the cloth being increased from day to day, until each foot was permanently compressed into a "golden lotus" shape.[6]

The practice of foot-binding had a long history in China, originating probably in the tenth century. The custom started in the imperial harem of the T'ang time, in connection with the gait of court dancers. It gradually spread from the north to the center and south of China and from the nobility to the commoners. By the early twelfth century, the practice had been widely adopted throughout the country. The Manchus were opposed to foot-binding but, during their centuries of rule, attempts at eradication were sporadic and unsuccessful. One Western observer wrote in 1835 that the majority of women in the large towns and cities as well as in the most fashionable parts of the country had their feet bound. He estimated that five to eight out of every ten females had bound feet, depending on locality and social class background—"with a tendency towards applying the bindings more tightly and rigorously as one went up the social scale."[7] On the other hand, women of the poorer classes, especially those in the south who worked in the fields, often went naturally barefoot. For the young girls with feet bound, "the effects . . . are extremely painful. Children will often tear away the bandage in order to gain relief from the torture; but their temporary removal, it is said, greatly increases the pain by causing a violent revulsion of the blood to the feet."[8] Women with feet bound had to assume a gingerly gait (because of the pain of movement) which was said to be graceful, and the feet themselves were said to have great sexual appeal for the men. However, there was no doubt that the bound feet had come to symbolize the subordination of the female sex, for the effect of the practice was to confine the women (especially the gentlewomen) to their own quarters. They could seldom venture outside except by being carried on sedan chairs. Thus the saying that "the girl does not go beyond her boudoir" equates staying home with feminine virtue.

Age at Marriage

In traditional China, girls were married off in their late teen years but were mostly betrothed at an earlier age.[9] Some girls from wealthy and powerful families might even be betrothed from the time of birth (*ch'i fu*) by parents who wanted to marry them later to the sons of their close friends or political allies. The age at which a girl was married varied somewhat with her family background. If she had come from a rich family, chances were she might be married at an earlier age.[10] On the other hand, there were also regional differences. For example, in the southeastern parts of China, it was the widespread custom among poorer families to acquire young girls into their families as foster children and future daughters-in-law (*t'ung yang hsi*). These girls would work for the families for a number of years before they were married to their intended husbands, without much formalism or ceremony. In these cases, the brides were frequently a few years older than the bridegrooms.[11] In their position as *t'ung yang hsi*, the young girls were often treated no better than slave girls.

Every traditional father considered it his obligation to find a suitable match for every one of his children. In regard to the daughter in particular, he would have totally fulfilled his duty as father upon marrying her off. A marriage was never taken to be a matter between the young individuals but was considered a family affair, involving serious considerations of the two families' social-economic standing, the sum of the bride price to be obtained, and the size of the dowry needed. Since the traditional marriages were entirely exogamous with regard to the patrilineage, the political relationship between the two clans involved also had to be taken into account. The consent of the boy or girl was unnecessary and any objection on his or her part would be condemned as an unfilial act.

Position as Wife, Daughter-in-law, and Mother

So "upon the orders of the parents and upon the recommendations of the go-between," a marriage was arranged and the girl was carried off (literally) to her husband's home. In traditional China, patrilocal residence was the rule. From the very beginning she was made aware of the authority of her husband, whom she might never have met before, and that of the other male members and senior female members of the family. It was after marriage that all the miseries of womanhood in Old China really began.

The duties of the married woman were to serve her husband and her husband's parents and to produce sons to carry on the family's name. She was not only subjected to the men in the household but was placed under the awesome authority of the mother-in-law. The harshness of the mother-in-law was well known in Chinese literature and folklore, and her formidable personality could be compared to that of stepmother in Western legends. Jealousy of the daughter-in-law's claim to her son's affection was a major factor in the mother-in-law's ill treatment of the younger woman. In part also, she was avenging the injustices that she herself had suffered as a daughter-in-law.

When a wife had incurred the displeasure of her parents-in-law, when she had fallen into disfavor with her husband, or when she had failed to produce a son, she would have to suffer the most disgraceful punishment inflicted on a married woman—she could be divorced unilaterally by her husband, who might very well be acting under parental pressure. The birth of a son might help to raise her position in the family and she would gain considerable power only when she became a mother-in-law, a widowed mother of a young son, or the wife of the head of the household.

Economic Dependence

However, the rigid division of labor between the sexes kept the woman's influence totally confined to the household and domestic affairs. Even in the home, her responsibility and authority were delegated by the male household head. The assignment of women to purely domestic affairs meant the extreme economic dependence of the female sex. This was true especially of the upper-class women and perhaps not so much of the peasant women. The peasant women had often labored in the fields during the peak periods of demand for labor; however, such work was never carried on regularly nor on a large scale. Work outside the household, in other words, never became the principal occupation of any women regardless of social class. Even in places where there were some well-developed domestic industries, such as the silk industry in central and south China at the end of the nineteenth century, women still had no control over the organization of such industries and never attained the measure of economic independence that female factory workers in recent times would. Women were further denied the available educational opportunities. "Lack of learning is a woman's virtue" was a well-accepted precept and a rationalization of men for the subordination of women. Her other virtues also offered the men the best advantages: quietness and obedience, industriousness and frugality, ability in domestic chores, "respect for the husband's parents, kindness to husband's brothers and courtesy to husband's friends."

HUSBAND-WIFE RELATIONSHIP

Since marriage was never considered to be the young people's affair, the husband-wife relationship was neither the strongest nor the most intense relationship within the family.

Romantic love was by no means unknown to men and women in traditional China, as witnessed by many popular love stories and love poems. The effect of the seclusion of Chinese women was to produce love mixed with tears and sadness.

> Chinese songs of love are songs of absence, of departure, of frustrated hopes and unquenchable longing, of rain and the twilight and the empty chamber and the cold bed, of solitary regret and hatred against man's inconstancy. . .[12]

Romantic love was seen as interfering with the young people's duties and obedience to their parents. It was therefore tightly controlled through segregation of the sexes and the institution of arranged marriage. Husbands and wives were not expected to have romantic attachments to each other even after marriage, although a growing emotional involvement and mutual commitment was common in the years after the union. Husbands and wives were not supposed to show affection for each other in public, or the women would be accused of improper behavior. The wife was expected to owe the husband complete obedience. In sex life, she was to submit herself without question. She was never to be the active partner or to show signs of enjoying the relationship. In the running of the household, she was to be the husband's helpmate.

Divorce

Under the Ch'ing law, there were seven grounds on which a husband could unilaterally divorce a wife. Such grounds were failure to serve the husband's parents and disobedience to them, failure to give birth to a son, dissoluteness of manners, jealousy, loquacity (i.e., talkativeness and quarrelsome conduct), malignant disease, and larceny.[13] Correspondingly there were only three grounds on which a husband had no right to divorce his wife: if she had participated in the three-year mourning of either of her husband's parents; if her husband's family was poor before the marriage but had become rich after; or if, after divorce, she had no home to return to.[14]

In spite of the above three grounds, however, the right of the husband to divorce his wife was in practice frequently exercised without the consent of the wife, and in any case a man could resort to concubines if he was not satisfied with his wife. In theory also, divorce by mutual consent was legally recognized when "husband and wife could not longer live together in harmony." In practice, a woman would never willingly agree to such a course of action, since a divorced woman was subject to a great deal of social sanction and would lead an extremely ostracized life thereafter. The legal position of the Chinese woman was such that she could not inherit any property, nor could she possess any apart from her dowry. There was no legal guarantee for her financial support after divorce. The disgrace suffered by the divorced woman and the man's opportunity to take concubines kept the divorce rate in traditional China very low.[15]

Remarriage of Widows

A widow had a claim to maintenance from her deceased husband's estate, but such a claim—being a moral, not a legal one—could only be exercised during her lifetime and was contingent on her good behavior and on her remaining unmarried in her deceased husband's family. The double sex standard in traditional China demanded not only that a woman should be a virgin when she was married[16] or that she should remain faithful to her husband after marriage but also that she should be a chaste widow after her husband's death. The doctrine of chaste widowhood had been officially upheld since the Ming dynasty, which started the practice of honoring chaste widows with official titles, the erection of memorial arches (*pailou*) over their native villages, and the exemption of members of their families from labor corvees. The doctrine of chastity and of chaste widowhood led to some cruel practices—for example, women who believed that they had been "defiled" by men other than their lawful husbands might commit suicide by dismembering themselves, and others engaged in the absurd practice of marrying the spirits of their dead betrothed. It was this sort of doctrine that caused Confucianism to be denounced by modern Chinese scholars during the new culture movement of 1917 as a "man-eating religion."

In practice, there were some remarriages among the poor, and it was not uncommon for poor boys to be married to widows mainly because the widows or their families would settle for a much lower bride price.[17]

Concubinage

The taking of concubines was frequently justified by the men as well as their mothers on the ground of the wives' failure to produce sons. However, very often this was not the only reason why men would take secondary wives in traditional China. Some sociologists contend that, lacking love in marriage and perhaps lacking satisfaction in sexual relationships with women who might actually have helped to bring up the husbands (as in the case of the *t'ung yang hsi*), men sought in concubinage an alternative way to love and gratifying sex.[18] The institution of concubinage was another indication of the men's freedom through domination.

The origin of concubinage may be traced back to the era of feudalism in China under which kings and officials were entitled to take concubines, the number varying according to their official ranks. Gradually the practice spread to the rich, who took as many concubines as they could afford as status symbols. Concubinage finally became so common even among the ordinary people that it was institutionalized and given legal recognition. The position of the concubine in the Ch'ing Code was always lower than that of the wife. This fact points out that Chinese marriages were not polygamous except in very special cases of *chien t'iao,* in which a man took on two or more wives for the special purpose of propagating the future generations of two or more branches of the family which had failed to produce their own sons. The concubine in the family was obliged to serve, obey, and respect the wife. Children born by a concubine owed their filial duty to the wife and not to their biological mother. The concubine was addressed by her own children as well as by the children of the wife as "sister" (*chieh*) or "maternal aunt" (*yi*). When the wife died, the concubine's children were obliged to mourn for three years, (just like the wife's own children), while they were obliged to mourn for their biological mother for only one year. (The wife's biological children would mourn for the concubine for only three months.) Furthermore, the wife's eldest son was heir to the household head's title of nobility and estate, but no such privileges were available to the concubine's eldest son.

The most common way of taking concubines into the family was by purchase through a go-between, and only poor peasants would give their daughters away as concubines. In some cases, men would take prostitutes home as secondary wives. Concubinage was a very well-established institution in traditional China;[19] however, its extent had never been great for obvious economic reasons.[20] Few men in rural China were rich enough to support several women as well as their sons and daughters. Thus the abolition of concubinage by the Republican and Communist governments in the twentieth century was of greater symbolic than numerical significance.

Prostitution

Prostitution went hand in hand with concubinage. Poor families sometimes sold their daughters as slaves, and they were often exploited by their owners and turned over to brothels. The dominance of males in Chinese society allowed them the freedom to visit courtesans' houses and brothels. Some of the courtesans were in fact similar to the geisha in Japan in that they were trained in music and literature—often accomplished ladies whose social skills added color to the amatory life of the scholarly class. Great poets and learned men had freely expressed their adoration for these courtesans throughout the ages. The "green boudoirs," as the courtesans' houses were called, were the places where men whose marriages were loveless could gratify their romantic impulses. "Patriarchal society has always seemed to require . . . some system of prostitution."[21]

By contrast to the courtesans, there were also prostitutes who came from families of outcast minority groups in the village community and who catered to the poor peasants, many of whom could not afford to get married until after they had accumulated enough money for a bride price. Some of them in fact remained single throughout their lives, and for them the lower-class prostitutes provided the major sexual outlet.

Cracks in the Conventional Image

The conventional image of the passive and subjugated women in traditional China needs to be modified in some respects. First, throughout the periods of traditional China, a number of women were able to rise above their ascribed statuses and achieve national as well as historical fame as scholars, poets, painters, and even warriors. A few had risen to political power as consorts and empresses. The stories of these remarkable women have been well chronicled by historians, retold as popular folklore, and studied by sociologists.[22]

Second, we have pointed out time and again in our description of traditional women that there were significant variations. Thus upper-class women in general were more subject to seclusion and economic dependence than were the majority of peasant women. Similarly, the age of marriage and the types of marriage entered into by gentlewomen were different from those involving the poor. The incidence of girl slavery and concubinage also differed according to social-economic status. And even though the Confucian code of ethics seemed to be universally adopted, the uneducated classes failed to follow many of its particular rules and prescriptions.

Third, many practices in connection with the mistreatment of women in ancient China were the result of economic backwardness and poverty rather than an expression of cultural norms and values. For example, female infanticide, the enslavement of girls, and the custom of t'ung yang hsi existed mainly because of economic necessity. As the material conditions and political stability in the village improved, these customs tended spontaneously to decline. One would suspect that the frequency of their occurrence would vary with wars and economic depressions.

Fourth, with regard to the conflicts between mother-in-law and daughter-in-law, many traditional women must have tolerated this relationship in the full hope that they would eventually vindicate the injustices they suffered when they became mothers-in-law in their turn. In fact, one can speak of a cycle of subjugation of the traditional woman—a cycle that would be completed when she became a mother-in-law, the widowed mother of a young son, or the wife of a household head.

Finally, the dynamics of marital relationships everywhere demand the adjustment of both husband and wife. The traditional husband might have symbolic authority over the wife, but the outcome of the sexual politics might very well be that the wife succeeded in henpecking the husband. In fact, popular stories were told about fierce, jealous wives and nagging wives who were the chief cause behind household divisions among married brothers.[23] Other stories told of kingdoms that were lost for the sake of beautiful women. In short, in spite of the institutionalization of women's subordination, the husband-wife relationship depended on the working out of individual personalities and the "war of the sexes." A generalized view of the position of traditional Chinese women is over-simplified insofar as it fails to take into account the psychological realities of the persons involved. It also tends to present an overly harmonious picture of traditional Chinese society.

Taking everything into consideration, the seclusion and secondary role of Chinese women were in many ways not dissimilar to the position of women in traditional Western societies. The division of labor between the sexes—the differentiation of instrumental and expressive roles between male and female—seemed to be a universal phenomenon. Even though foot-binding was peculiar to the women in China and was taken to be a symbol of their subordination, it should be remembered that the bound feet essentially represented sex appeal to Chinese men. In all societies and at all times, women had attempted to look attractive to men. Like those of their counterparts in the West, the role and status of traditional Chinese women gradually changed under the impact of industrialization and modernization, when educational and economic opportunities were made available to them, and when traditional attitudes toward the fair sex came under attack.

WOMEN IN TRANSITION—REPUBLICAN CHINA

The Feminist Movement

The Chinese women's movement is an integral part of the so-called family revolution in modern China, a process which started near the end of the nineteenth century and gathered great momentum soon after the turn of the twentieth century. As a result of contact with the Western world through trade and travel as well as through the efforts of Western missionaries, ideas of equality between the sexes and of democratic family organization began to be accepted by Chinese intellectuals. Talk of reform of traditional family institutions was in the air. On the other hand, the development of industries in coastal cities as well as in industrial centers inland provided the economic basis upon which young men and women could free themselves from parental control and, for the women, the basis of independence from male dominance.

Toward the end of the Manchu dynasty, opposition to foot-binding became more and more widespread; natural-foot societies sprang up everywhere with the help of Western missionaries and under both official and private sponsorship. Progress was slow at the start with conservative opposition mainly from the rural areas, so that success was not achieved until after the Republican government came into power. A series of decrees against foot-binding were passed by the Republican government, and serious efforts were made to stamp out the practice. By the early 1920s, it was reported that in some places the custom had died out completely.[24]

The beginning of women's participation in revolutionary movements could in fact be dated back to the T'aiping rebellion of the mid-nineteenth century, which had the abolition of foot-binding and the equality of the sexes as one of its major objectives. The participation of a large number of armed women in this unsuccessful revolution had become a legend. The involvement of women in the Republican revolution of 1911 greatly contributed to their own emancipation during the first two decades of the Republican period. The new constitution gave women the rights to be educated, to marry by free choice, and to participate in government.

The new culture movement of 1917 and the May 4th movement of 1919 subsequently gave another great impetus to the women's cause. Female students took an active part in both these movements. Various publications on the subject of modern womanhood appeared in quick succession and were eagerly read by the newly literate women in the cities. Women's rights organizations and women's unions began to appear under various labels. They helped not only to propagate the ideas of sex equality but actually helped thousands of girls running away from their families to find work and to obtain a modern education.[25] The Nationalist Civil Code, which contained the new family law, was promulgated in 1931. It established the freedom of marriage, the freedom of divorce, and equality of the sexes in marriage and family relationships.

Rising Status

The revolutionary activities of both the Kuomintang and the Communist parties in the 1920s carried the women's movement to new heights. Many women became party members, members of propaganda corps, political organizers, army nurses, and even soldiers. A few women served on the high councils in the coalition government, and many had joined the civil service. In the fall of 1919, the Peking National University admitted female students for the first time, and this was followed by coeducation in almost all schools and colleges. Women's occupations expanded considerably during this period, particularly in the cities. A host of other new social phenomena indicating the great changes in the social position of women also emerged:

> . . . the great popularity of athletics for girls after 1930, and in particular swimming for girls in 1934; the vogue for nude pictures . . . the coming of Margaret Sanger to China in 1922 . . . the introduction of contraceptive appliances . . . the publication of *Sex Histories* . . . ; the influence of Greta Garbo, Norma Shearer, Mae West, and Chinese movie stars . . . the great spread of dancing cabarets which came over China about 1928 . . . the permanent wave, English high-heeled shoes, Parisian perfumes and American silk stockings, the new high-slit flowing gowns, the brassiere . . . and the one-piece female bathing suit.[26]

All these came about in the large cities in a matter of thirty years.

A split in the women's movement appeared in the mid-1920s—one side becoming extremely political while the other withdrew from politics. The Protestants tended to go into social service and educational work and were discreetly neutral in politics. Members of the political section of the movement became involved with anarchists, left-wing Kuomintang members, and Communist party members, and they were actively engaged in student, labor, and peasant activities.[27] During the Sino-Japanese War (1937 to 1945), however, women belonging to both sections united in the war effort. Their political consciousness once again reached a high pitch.

It can be said that during the Republican period, the principle of sex equality was generally accepted by the urban intelligentsia—the upper and the middle classes. In place of traditional arranged marriages, modern marriages were increasingly being contracted under the new Civil Code. In the big cities, divorces became increasingly common.[28] The pace at which both educational and economic opportunities became available to women quickened, and women's appearance on the social scene (as contrasted with their former seclusion) was rapidly becoming an accepted fact. The changes in the position of women during these revolutionary decades were fast and far-reaching in their consequences for the social and cultural development of modern China. For out of these turbulent years were born some of China's greatest women leaders—leaders who are still playing very important roles in national politics as well as social and cultural reform in China today. Studying the life histories of these women, one can detect clearly the influences of Western religion (Christianity), modern education, and political involvement with the revolutionary movements of the first half of the twentieth century. Almost all of them were personally involved in the struggle for women's rights, and they were also pioneers in family reform.[29]

WOMEN IN CHINA TODAY

The Marriage Law Movement

The marriage law, passed in May 1950 as the first major law of the Communist regime and one of the fundamental laws of the People's Republic, was the culmination of a series of earlier efforts made by the Communist party in the soviet areas to bring about the socialist ideal of sex equality.[30] In place of the "arbitrary and compulsory feudal marriage system," the marriage law claimed to establish a "New-Democratic marriage system which is based on the free choice of partners, on monogamy, on equal rights for both sexes, and on the protection of the lawful interests of women and children" (Article 1). Husband and wife are described as companions living together, bound by law to love, respect, assist, and look after each other. They enjoy equal status in the home and have joint responsibility for the welfare of the family. They also have equal rights to choose their own occupations and to participate in social life. As necessary corollaries of the principle of sex equality, the traditional systems of polygamy, concubinage, interference with the remarriage of widows, and payment of bride price are outlawed. The freedom of divorce is guaranteed, and special provisions are laid down for the wife and children after divorce.

As we have seen, the 1950 marriage law was not the first attempt by a Chinese government to give the women equal legal status with men. The family revolution had started some three decades before the Communists came into power. However, the effects of this social revolution, together with changes in the position of women, had been limited to the urban areas and to the coastal provinces only. What the Communist party (CCP) did, right upon gaining power, was to extend the reform throughout the countryside and to turn it into a mass movement involving most of the female population. Thus within the first five or six years of the CCP regime, great efforts were made to implement the marriage law.

The marriage reform was taken by the CCP to be a major instrument for the socialist transformation of the whole society.[31] During the initial period of the marriage law movement, drastic measures were employed, in conjunction with the land reform of 1950, to shake up the old "feudalistic" order and to prepare the ground for the new socialistic society. There were reports of overenthusiastic cadres dissolving arranged marriages, returning child brides, forcing concubines to divorce their husbands and widows to remarry, and inflicting cruel punishment on the culprits. In some places, the marriage law came to be nicknamed the divorce law. As a result of the great social upheaval—as reflected in the large number of marital disputes, the number of suicides attributable to matrimonial difficulties, and the rising rate of divorce in these early years—the government became alarmed and soon took steps to subdue the tone and approach of the marriage reform. Since 1953 and especially after 1956, family peace and harmony rather than divorce and antifeudalism have been emphasized in official propaganda.[32]

The marriage law met a great deal of conservative opposition from the countryside. Even some party cadres responsible for its implementation needed periodical reindoctrination in the spirit of the law, as revealed in the official press. When the implementation of the marriage law was slackened in the second half of the 1950s, old practices reemerged. Thus, it was reported that, almost a decade after the establishment of the new regime, the practice of early marriage, arranged marriage, and the payment of exorbitant bride prices still persisted in many places in the country.[33] The marriage law movement of the early 1950s, however, should be considered as only one aspect of—as well as the initial phase in—the women's movement under the CCP regime. Other aspects of the movement included political organization and economic mobilization, with the latter taking precedence over marriage reform upon the launching of China's collectivization programs.

Political Organization

From the beginning, the CCP recognized the potential political strength of the women's movement. Systematic tactics for recruiting and organizing the women in the party's political maneuvres had been worked out since the soviet days. In April 1949, an All-China Democratic Women's Federation (ACDWF) was created as the leading organ in the nation's women movement. It was to become an important body in the drawing up of policies for the economic participation of women in accordance with national economic plans.

The ACDWF functioned through a system of elected women's representative congresses which included women delegates to the people's representative congresses, delegates from women's organizations, and delegates directly elected from among the female population by residential districts. Since 1950, every province, county, subdistrict, city, town, and village had a women's representative congress—so did every profession and occupation, organization, and school with women members. The membership of the ACDWF grew rapidly in the first few years. In 1950, it represented 30 million women; by 1953, its membership had grown to 76 million.[34]

Apart from the ACDWF, the women were also organized in peasants' associations and trade unions. In both these kinds of organizations they represented a large proportion of the total membership, and many of them were placed in responsible positions from the start.[35]

Economic Participation

Beginning with the First Five-Year Plan in 1953, women were greatly encouraged by the government to join in productive work on the grounds that economic participation would bring about a further rise in their social and economic status. At each stage of the agricultural collectivization process—from mutual-aid teams (MATs) to elementary agricultural producers' cooperatives (APCs) and on to the higher forms of agricultural collectives—the women were actively involved in the production effort with men. In early 1954, one-third of the members in the MATs and elementary APCs were women; in some places, the proportion of female membership was up to 40 percent, with many of them in responsible positions as chairmen and vice-chairmen of the cooperatives.[36] As the pace of collectivization was stepped up in 1956, the percentage of women members in the collectives continued to rise. For example, in the county of Wuchang, 61 percent of the female population had joined the APCs by the end of 1955, while 50 percent of the members in the 140,000 APCs in the province of Kiangsu were women.[37] By the middle of 1956, 80 percent of the female adult population had joined in agricultural production in Kiangsu.[38]

The number of female workers in the industrial sector was reported to have increased from 2 million in 1952 to around 8 million in 1959.[39]

However, up to 1958, a full-scale mobilization of the women in productive activities had not yet been called for. Much of the women's time was still occupied with domestic work. A new code of feminine virtues, wu-hao ("five virtues"), was expounded in official propaganda: "Good at harmonizing family and neighbor relationships, good at managing the household, good at educating the children, good at encouraging the family members to work and study, and good at one's own ideological studies." Domestic management was somewhat glorified as the necessary precondition for the male workers to concentrate on their productive tasks. On their part, female workers were exhorted to carefully schedule their time so that domestic work might not interfere with their economic activities, but the former was by no means to be neglected.[40]

The Communes

The full-scale mobilization of the female labor force came upon the establishment of the People's Communes and the Great Leap Forward in

1958. The communes were heralded as a new form of social organization in which complete equality of the sexes and total emancipation of women could be achieved. Large numbers of nurseries, kindergartens, communal dining halls, laundry service units, etc., were established in order to free the women from housework, thus enabling them to join in the production campaigns.[41] Official figures showed that, in 1959, the number of women who worked in the rural communes generally stood at 90 percent of the total female labor force. Whereas in 1957 the men worked an average of 249 days in the rural areas and women worked 166 days, in 1959 the figures were 300 days for men and 250 days for women.[42] In the cities, commune organization came at a somewhat later date (in some cities, urban communes were not established until the early part of 1960), but the same kinds of communal services were also provided so that, by mid-1960, 27 million women had become members of the urban communes and their labor was fully utilized in "street factories."[43]

The commune experiment, however, was short-lived. After the failure of the Great Leap Forward production campaign, the rural communes were reorganized. By the end of 1959, production had reverted to the earlier cooperative pattern and the radical tendencies in communal living had been checked. Similarly, the development of the urban communes has been halted since the middle of 1960. Thus the fears of many outside observers about the "disappearance" of the Chinese family on account of communal living proved to be alarmist. As the organization of production was decentralized, the family once again resumed many of its former functions and the women had to take back their domestic responsibilities.[44] As the national economic crisis deepened in the early 1960s, all talk of marriage and family reform was quietly dropped. When the new womanhood was discussed in public, it was only in connection with birth control and late marriage. In spite of the relative lack of information since the early 1960s, a general picture of the position of Chinese women right up to the eve of the Cultural Revolution of mid-1966 could still be drawn. Nothing much can be said about the subject after 1966 because of the information gap. In any case, the country has only begun to settle down from the great commotion of the past few years. The effect of the Cultural Revolution on the masses of Chinese women cannot be judged until a much later date.

Education and Occupation

The communes gave a sharp although short spur to the development of mass education in the countryside through the organization of literacy classes, which the peasants attended during their spare time. On the whole, educational development seems to have progressed at a slower pace than the other "social" developments. Thus it was reported that the illiteracy rate was 66 percent for rural area and 24 percent for cities in 1960.[45] No figures were available for the female population. However, it can be safely assumed that the illiteracy rate for females would be higher than that for the nation as a whole. The same would be true for the general level of education attained. Equal opportunity for boys and girls to receive an education had long been established in principle, even before the CCP came to power, but it would take some more time before the girls could catch up with the privileges that the boys had long enjoyed. Thus it was reported that in 1960 over one-third of the students enrolled in primary schools were girls and 23.3 percent of college students were women.[46] The figure for primary school education was much lower than that of most European and American countries or the U.S.S.R. in 1960; however, the figure for higher education compared favorably with the Mediterranean countries, Switzerland, the Netherlands, and Norway. It was almost on a par with the figures for West Germany and Austria, and was much lower than those of France, the United Kingdom, Sweden, and the East European countries.[47] In the area of higher education, many fields that were traditionally considered men's spheres now admit female students. For example, in Tsinghua University (China's leading engineering college), 26.2 percent of the students in civil engineering and 18.5 percent of those in electrical engineering in 1960 were women.[48] These percentages were higher than those of most European countries (East and West European) and lower only than those of the U.S.S.R. (where 52 percent of the engineering students were women in 1964 to 1965.)[49]

The participation of women in agricultural work has gone a long way from their traditional participation, which was confined to subsidiary occupations and helping in the fields during peak seasons. Today, 90 percent of the total female labor force on the rural communes is said to be regularly engaged in agricultural work, and the number and types of jobs these women do have increased threefold or fourfold. When the men are engaged in nonfarming activities at certain times, such as building water conservancy projects, the women take over the greater part of the work in the fields, doing most of the heavy work such as ploughing and sowing. Today women are trained to operate farm machines and to do agricultural research work. In the commune organization, women are playing an equally important role as functionaries. It was said that women served as chairmen or vice-chairmen of almost one-fifth of all the 25,000 People's Communes, and practically every production brigade had a woman leader or deputy leader in the early 1960s.[50] Most of these women leaders had been cited for outstanding work in production. Many also attended "red and expert" classes in ideological training.

"With the exception of certain kinds of work unsuited for women for health reasons, every branch of industry in open to women." The greatest number of women workers are in the textile and the light industries.[51] The number is also rapidly increasing in heavy industries such as iron and steel; locomotive, chemical and metallurgical works; and in new industries such as plastics and transistors. It was estimated that in 1966 there were 71,000 women engineers and technicians in the Shanghai textile industry, while about 200 were directors and deputy directors of factories.[52] More than 10,000 women were said to be employed in the steel industries in Anshan in 1966, and in that year blast furnaces began to be operated by women.[53]

In the professions, women have gained recognition as doctors, engineers, architects, artists, and scientists. In 1960, there were 10,000 women doctors, including medical research workers, in Peking—about 40 percent of the capital's total number of doctor's.[54] In Shanghai, around 50 percent of the medical and teaching staff were women.[55] Compared to the U.S.S.R. (where 76 percent of the doctors are women), China still lags behind, but she is far ahead when compared to the United Kingdom, France, Germany, Sweden, or the United States.[56] Just before the Cultural Revolution, an estimated 25 percent of college faculties, 45 percent of secondary school teachers, and 62 percent of primary school teachers in Peking were women.[57] The percentage of female staff in higher education was higher than that in most European (East and West) and American countries in the 1960s except for Romania and Poland. Again, China still falls behind the U.S.S.R.'s 36 percent, which tops the list.[58] Women in China accounted for 23 percent of the total research staff of the highly prestigious Chinese Academy of Sciences.[59]

Other occupations now open to women include the service industries, transportation, the armed forces, and sports.

Women in Politics

From seclusion under the traditional society, Chinese women have emerged to play important roles in public life from the local level up to the national level. The achievement of Chinese women in the political sphere has been most outstanding, even by comparison to the achievement of women in many advanced countries. There is a female political elite in China whose members are decision makers and important executors of national policies. Most of them have gained high position through seniority, especially through their long and devoted service to the Communist party since its earliest days. Some of them have been coworkers with their powerful husbands, striking examples of husband-wife teams. The most famous woman to emerge from the Cultural Revolution is Mao Tse-tung's wife, Chiang Ch'ing, who is now a member of the Politburo. Yeh Ch'un, wife of the former Defense Minister Lin Piao, was also a member of the Politburo, while Teng Ying-ch'ao, wife of Premier Chou En-lai, and Ts'ao Yi-ou, wife of Politburo member K'and Sheng, both serve on the Central Committee. Tsai Ch'ang, President of the ACDWF, is wife of the State Planning Commissioner Li Fu-ch'un.

Of the 3,000 deputies to the incumbent Third National People's Congress, 542 (or 18 percent) are women, (as compared to 10 percent in 1950 and 12 percent in 1958).[60] Comparable figures for England were 5 percent of the Members of Parliament in the House of Commons in 1967, and for France, it was 2.3 percent of the Deputies.[61] The Central Committee of the Chinese Communist party has 13 women as full members and 10 women as alternate members, or 8.3 percent of the total.[62] In addition, 1.43 million women—constituting 22 percent of the total membership—are serving as deputies on local people's congresses at various levels.[63] The corresponding figure for the United Kingdom in 1967 was 12 percent of the borough and county councils; and in 1965 for France, 2.4 percent of the municipal councils.[64] There are today about a million women members of the Chinese Communist party and 75 million members of the ACDWF.[65] Since the Cultural Revolution of 1966, women form 10 to 20 percent of the membership of the revolutionary committees at all levels—committees that have been set up to carry on the national revolutionary movement.[66]

Health and Welfare

The Labor Insurance Law (passed in May 1951) provides social security to workers in plants with more than 100 employees. It covers accident and death benefits and provides for dependents and for women workers. Women are now entitled to a fifty-six-day maternity leave with pay. All factories with more than 500 workers are to set up their own medical scheme, to be administered by the union. Under labor insurance funds, women industrial workers over the age of fifty and who have worked for fifteen years are paid retirement pensions of 50 to 70 percent of their wages.[67] Maternity hospitals and clinics and small-scale "health stations" for women and children have been established throughout the country. However, these medical and insurance schemes have not been uniformly maintained, and the government has not been especially strict in enforcing the provisions of the Labor Insurance Law in some places. Improvements in health standards and the expansion of medical services have also suffered setbacks from repeated economic depressions in the early 1960s and from the social political turmoil of the recent Cultural Revolution.[68]

Love and Marriage

Up to the eve of the Cultural Revolution, some customs pertaining to the traditional forms of marriage were reported still to be existing in some parts of the country. Arranged marriages, the demand of bride prices, and early marriage were still found. However, whenever cases like these arise, the young people involved are able to bring their plight to the attention of the women's organizations, the street committees,[69] the commune, and the party. Thus freedom of marriage is guaranteed. Concubinage has disappeared. On the other hand, due to the reaction which set in against the revolutionary excesses of the marriage law movement in its early years, divorce is now treated with much greater caution. Young couples are advised to look at their marriage with serious purpose and intent. "In choosing their marriage partners today, young people are more and more inclined to demand in the first place conscientiousness in work and in ideological study, as well as a progressive outlook."[70] The correct "class background" of the prospective spouse also figures as one important consideration.

The above quotation, however, should be taken to mean a norm rather than a statement of fact. For in practice we find a lot of deviation from the standard. In two letters from two girls to the editor of the *Chung-kuo fu-nu (Chinese Women)*, published under the title "Whom to Love" in the February 1964 issue, the conflict between the "ideal proletarian" standard for the choice of marriage partners and the "bourgeois" standard showed through most clearly. One girl was facing the dilemma of deciding between an activist—an austere but conscientious young man—and another "man of the world" who shared the girl's interests in dancing, movies, and going to restaurants. The other girl also expressed indecision over whether to switch to another boyfriend who was earning a better wage. In response to the editor's invitation to express their opinions, many readers wrote about their own experiences. As many as 2,000 letters were received, a number of which were printed in later issues between February and September of the same year. From these revealing autobiographic accounts, it was evident that in Communist China, even after twenty years of socialist education, many young women still want the same things as their sisters in the capitalist countries, namely, a good marriage, secure income, and happy family life. The fact that this is not an easy thing for the CPP to admit—much less tolerate—can be seen from what happened to the journal during the Cultural Revolution—the editor was fired and the journal suspended indefinitely.[71]

It is also evident that a companionship type of marriage relationship has sprung up between husbands and wives, especially among the educated and the professional classes, which is not very different from the conjugal relationship existing within the nuclear family in Western industrial societies. One husband expressed his view this way: "Working in two different fields, Pan Chieh [the wife, a radio announcer] and I [the husband, an engineer] nevertheless respect each other's work, and we understand that each in his or her own way contributes to the building of socialism. Time and again we discuss our work with each other. . . . Both of us try not to be self-centered, but rather make an effort to consider each other's interests."[72]

On the other hand, unlike the two-generational family in industrial societies, the three-generational family is still very popular in China today —if for no other reason than that grandparents can and do help with child care and the housework so that the daughter-in-law can work outside.[73] However, between the mother-in-law and the daughter-in-law, traditionally so antagonistic, there is a lot more love and respect than before. In any case, a harsh mother-in-law cannot possibly escape the severe criticisms of neighbors and party cadres.

Age of Marriage, Birth Control, and Family Size

The marriage law of 1950 set the age of marriage at twenty for men and eighteen for women. However, since the birth control campaign started in 1956 to 1957 and was reactivated in 1962, men and women have been encouraged to postpone marriage to a much later age—twenty-three to twenty-seven for women and twenty-five to twenty-nine for men.[74] Official propaganda has concentrated on the advantages of late marriage, including among these physical and emotional maturity and freedom to devote time and energy to work and studies.

Recent visitors to China have reported that contraceptives are freely available and that abortion is free and permitted on medical advice. Sterilization is becoming more widely accepted. After a trip to China in late 1962, Han Suyin reported, "Two or three children were now considered the ideal family. Among rural people, six children were thought enough. . . ."[75] The more recent reports in April-May 1971 indicated that the birth control campaign has produced great effects even in the countryside. "Two are considered the right number," generally speaking, and the largest family on one farm in a commune 20 miles outside Shanghai has only four children.[76] The small family size means that women can now devote more and more of their time to collective labor through the reduction of their childbearing period. The fact that some men (although still a very small number) are undertaking sterilization also shows a further progress towards sex equality.

Sex and Puritanism

The new "free and equal" relationship between the sexes is now governed by an intangible but definitely felt stress on puritanism and asceticism. Romantic love is considered to be bourgeois, leading to decadent habits and behavior. It is ironical, in a sense, that young men and women should have so much freedom and opportunity to mix together in work and studies but should be subject to such strict surveillance under the eyes of the party cadres and their peers. Although dating is allowed and has been reported to exist among young students and workers,[77] it is by no means encouraged, and any suspicion that they had engaged in premarital intimacies would place the couple under severe criticism. Cases of forced separation have been known to occur upon the detection of such illicit behavior.[78] However, pregnancies before marriage are not unknown.[79]

Prostitution as an organized activity has been stamped out. Neither love nor sex is allowed to occupy much of one's thinking, as they would interfere with work and studies.

> It sounds excessively Puritan, yet China is not, strictly, a Puritan country, because sex is not the simultaneously horrifying-fascinating topic that it is to the real Puritan in the Cromwellian or Victorian sense of the word; sex is not a near-obsession to brood over in private and condemn in public. It is, rather, that in China sex, though important, is not allowed to occupy too much time and attention; it has to be taken in the stride, kept in its place, and its place is the marital couch, over which the veils of privacy have to be decently drawn.[80]

The matter-of-fact attitude of the young men and women today toward sex—in attitude stripped of the commercialized titillation that is common in the West—has "shocked" journalists and visitors to China in the recent past.

"Where are the women?" one member of a Polish delegation to China was supposed to have asked, rather tactlessly, on one occasion in the mid-1950s. On account of their devotion to work and also for fear of criticism, the women have neglected their looks. For practical as well as economic reasons, the drab-looking blue tunic with baggy blue trousers has become the uniform that women wear in and out of their homes. Two basic hairdos—short straight cuts or long hair brought together in braids—have become universal. In 1956, a campaign to "look gayer" was launched to make the Chinese girls look more attractive. Speeches and newspaper articles urged the women to wear more colorful dresses and to vary their styles. The *Chung-kuo ch'ing-nier* (Chinese youth) are persuaded as follows:

> The majority of our people can now dress better than ever before. We are decidedly not against the wearing of uniforms . . . but let the youth of our country have not only beautiful minds but also a beautiful appearance. . . . Some people are still not used to seeing a well-dressed person. They consider her lacking in frugality and simplicity . . . but (these people) should know that we are promoting things beautiful, that beauty is a requisite in our living, an expression of our love of life.[81]

However, this campaign "to go gayer" has not, thus far, produced any major changes in the dress styles or appearance of women.

Conclusion

The New Womanhood

In spite of the paucity of information on the position of women in China, especially in the 1960s, two trends are definitely evident. First, the general rise in the social, economic, and political status of women is not only the "natural" result of economic development—as in the developed industrial countries—but also the "unnatural" result of ideological forces exerted by both the government and the women's organizations acting under party guidance. It is this ideological coloring which has given the Chinese women's movement its unique character. Second, a new womanhood is emerging that, with all its freedom and independence, also carries tensions and conflicts not unlike those experienced by modern women in most non-socialist countries.

Chinese women have advanced far beyond the frail, feminine figures they were in the traditional days. From illiteracy and seclusion within the family, they have come to participate fully in the national social, economic, and political life. The new woman is commonly portrayed in Communist art and literature as a robust, healthy-looking, and cheerful person whose bountiful energies are devoted to work and studies and whose unfailing loyalties belong to the production brigade, the commune, the militia, and the party. In spite of some measure of discrimination that women are said still to encounter in daily life,[82] they have now gained a sense of worth and self-respect and faith in their ability to change their own fate—qualities that had not been characteristic of women in the traditional society. They are also able to achieve social recognition as model workers, model peasants, inventors, leaders, and functionaries at all levels of the state and party machinery. Young women are considered as co-heirs of the revolution together with the men. The importance of their ideological purification was at no point more emphasized than during the Cultural Revolution, when millions of young boys and girls walked literally thousands of miles to the capital and the cities to pay homage to the revolutionary fathers. Today, young men and women volunteer to go to the countryside and the isolated outer provinces to do hard labor and "to serve the people." The women today are the brave new generation who compete with each other as "steel girls."[83] They also show a new concern over international affairs, especially the women's movements in other parts of the world.

Before the Cultural Revolution, "model wives" were also given some measure of social recognition. In place of traditional virtues like obedience and chastity, the new socialist woman is supposed to win respect from her husband on account of her industriousness, frugality, and correct party line. She is her husband's helpmate in his work and ideological studies. The good wife is one who manages the household so that the husband can devote himself fully to the tasks of socialism and the children can be brought up in the socialist tradition. However, it is evident that many modern women are no longer satisfied with the role of housewife, and many want both the economic independence and the status of workers in their own right. Consequently, employed married women are facing the same role conflicts as those that trouble modern women in Western industrial societies. The conflict between career and family life is nowhere more succinctly demonstrated than in the party's concern over this problem during the Cultural Revolution. It should be pointed out that the women's liberation movement was not an important part of the revolution in the mid-1960s, as it was during the land reform. (In fact, the leadership of the ACDWF remained relatively immune, though in the two-year turmoil the organization itself became paralyzed and its mouthpiece, *Chinese Women*, was—and still is—suspended. However, the Liu (or "revisionist") line of thinking with regard to the women came under attack. Liu was condemned for—apparently—taking a view that emphasized the incompatibility between careerism and homemaking. He was alleged to have said:

> The women comrades in general cannot do without (or invariably want to have) children. If women really desire to do something for the Party, it is better for them not to get married. . . . If they wish to get married, they should make up their minds, face the inevitable, and be determined to rear children. Let them not think about making a career.[84]

To this conflict between the demands of the profession and the demands of the home is added the conflict between the demands of the state and personal interests. In Communist literature, a woman's happiness is invariably depicted as the result of an inner transformation involving the pains of self-examination and self-denial. The happy wife is one who succeeds in adjusting her life patterns and thinking in accordance with the new society. It is only in this way that she can maintain her claim over the affection and respect of her husband. In a "typical" story called "The Wife," the central character Yueh-chen was worried about her husband's growing indifference because of his preoccupation with his career. She was even afraid that he might abandon her for a younger woman. At first she tried to make herself look more attractive in order to regain his love, but without much success. Then she decided to attend classes in the afternoon to educate herself. "Not too long after, she surprised her husband one night with her new literacy and even helps him copying figures." From then onward, she regained his affections and became known as a model wife.[85] Other stories tell of girls who are too busy to see their boyfriends, of pregnant women who refuse to take rest or maternity leave because of urgent tasks, and of others who would not complain even though they suffer from bad health on account of protracted hard labor. One gathers from reading these stories that

> . . . the greatest hero is he who exercises the greatest self-denial for the sake of Communism . . . one should progressively demand more of oneself and expect less of the others, so that one may ultimately approach the ideal Communist person—a cheerful automation whose one passion is love of labor.[86]

What are the women's own reactions to all these conflicting pressures? How adaptable are they to their new roles? The available information tells us of great enthusiasm for the new social order on the part of those who have made successful adjustments. But at the same time there are others who have not yet succeeded in doing so. There are still some women who, while wanting to follow in the footsteps of exemplary heroines, cannot do so on account of physical weaknesses or "bad class backgrounds." For those falling short of the ideal standard, there is often public shame and inner guilt. The reactions of Chinese women to the changes brought about by the Communist regime must have varied from social class to social class and from person to person. To the once illiterate peasant woman or the former slave girl, these changes have meant new-won freedom, education, social status, and self-respect; but such changes also involve incessant hard labor, increasing self-denial, group pressure, conformity, and, perhaps, loss of privacy. An outside observer's evaluation of the Chinese woman's present lot depends ultimately on his own ideological standpoint; but for the masses of women within China there is no choice—and neither is there any going back.

NOTES AND REFERENCES

1. J. Lossing Buck found that the size of the household actually varied with the size of the farm. J. L. Buck, "An Economic and Social Survey of 150 Farms, Yenshan County, Chihli Province, China," *University of Nanking Bulletin*, June 1926, p. 63.

2. Sociological and anthropological field research in the 1920s and 1930s in China showed that the ideal large family existed only among the upper classes and that the average size of the family for most people was between four to six persons. See Sidney D. Gamble, *Ting Hsien, A North China Rural Community*, Institute of Pacific Relations, New York, p. 24; C. K. Yang, *The Chinese Family in the Communist Revolution*, Harvard University Press, Cambridge, Mass., 1959, pp. 7–8; Olga Lang, "The Type and Size of the Family," in *Chinese Family and Society*, Yale University Press, New Haven, 1946, chap. 12.

3. "The progressive subjection of women followed pace by pace the increasing development of Confucianism." Lin Yutang, *My Country and My People*, The John Day Company, Inc., New York, 1935, p. 137.

4. Ho Ping-ti, in his *Studies on the Population of China, 1368–1953* (Harvard University Press, Cambridge, Mass., 1959), points out that infanticide was common in the historic past. The practice of female infanticide continued well into the twentieth century, as reported by Olga Lang, op. cit. However, without accurate census figures on the sex ratio at birth, it is not easy to assess the extent of this practice in the traditional society.

5. The "Three Obediences" called on the woman to obey her father at home, her husband after marriage, and her eldest son after the death of her husband. The "Four Virtues" required that a woman preserve her feminine qualities, be gentle in disposition and pleasing in appearance, be chary of speech, and be assiduous in the performance of her domestic duties.

6. See Howard S. Levy, *Chinese Footbinding, The History of a Curious Erotic Custom*, Walton Rawls, New York, 1966.

7. Ibid., p. 52.

8. Ibid., p. 52.

9. The *Book of Rites* (Li Chi) states that men should marry by the age of thirty and women by twenty or twenty-three under certain circumstances. But these figures were interpreted as maximum ages of marriage.

10. Data from Ting Hsien, for example, showed that while one-third of the males in the couples in families with less than 50 *mu* of land were married before they were fifteen years old, the proportion was 80.5 percent in families with 100 *mu* or more. In the latter group, 40 percent of the males were married when they were fourteen years of age. The effect of economic status on the age of marriage of girls was less striking but still very noticeable. Sidney D. Gamble, op. cit., pp. 43–44.

11. In Phenix village in Kwangtung Province, the age of marriage for girls was eighteen and for boys a year to a year and a half less. These boys and girls were married approximately ten years after betrothal. Daniel H. Kulp II, *Country Life in South China*, Teachers College, Columbia University, New York, 1925, p. 175.

12. Lin Yutang, op. cit., p. 158.

13. See Vermier Y. Chieu, *Marriage Laws and Customs of China*, The Chinese University of Hong Kong, Hong Kong, 1966, pp. 61–68.

14. Ibid., pp. 68–71.

15. Kulp found no single case of divorce in Phenix village, nor could one case be remembered by his informants. Daniel H. Kulp II, op. cit., p. 184. Gamble recorded two divorces among the 515 families that he investigated. Sidney D. Gamble, op. cit., p. 38.

16. On the second day of the traditional wedding, a female attendant would go to the bridegroom's parents and present to them a piece of white silk stained with blood as proof of the bride's virginity. In south China, the bridegroom's family would send roast pigs to the bride's family on the third day of the wedding in token appreciation of the bride's virginity.

17. In Ting Hsien, 14 percent of the women who had lost their first husbands remarried. Sidney D. Gamble, op. cit., p. 38.

18. The difficulty of sexual adjustment between a wife who has been a *t'ung yang hsi* and her husband is suggested by Margery Wolf, *The House of Lim*, Appleton-Century-Crofts, New York, 1968.

19. Concubinage enjoyed an interesting survival in the British Colony of Hong Kong. Up to 1970, the traditional marriage institution under the Ch'ing Code, which permitted concubinage, was still recognized by the Hong Kong government.

20. Concubinage was found in less than 1 percent of the families in Ting Hsien. Sydney D. Gamble, op. cit., p. 38. In Lang's study of 1,700 college and high-school students during 1936 to 1937, it was found that only 11.4 percent of the students admitted the existence of a concubine in the family. In another 5.8 percent of the cases, concubines were suspected though not admitted. Olga Lang, op. cit., pp. 220–221.

21. David and Vera Mace, *Marriage: East and West*, Doubleday & Company, Inc., New York, 1959, p. 116.

22. For studies of remarkable Chinese women of the past, see Florence Ayscough, *Chinese Women, Yesterday and Today*, Jonathan Cape, London, 1938.

23. For stories of jealous wives in ancient China, see Howard S. Levy, *Warm-Soft Village* (Dai Nippon Insatsu, Tokyo, 1964.) Sociological case studies of traditional families have also "uncovered" the fierce wife as contrasted with the conventional image of the docile female. See Lin Yueh-hwa, *The Golden Wing*, Kegan Paul, Trench, Trubner & Co., London, 1947.

24. Sydney D. Gamble, op. cit., p. 48.

25. See Anna Louise Strong, "Problems of China's New Woman," in *China's Millions*, New World Press, Peking, 1965, chap. 9.

26. Lin Yutang, op. cit., p. 170.

27. See C. K. Yang, op. cit., pp. 117–119. Also, Helen Foster Snow, *Women in Modern China*, Mouton & Co., The Hague, 1967, pp. 19–20.

28. Figures for divorce during the Republican period were fragmentary. It was reported that in 1930 more than 800 suits for divorce were filed in the Peking district courts, 30 percent of which were instituted by women; in Canton, there were 200 divorces in the same year. In Shanghai, 645 divorces were recorded in 1929 and 853 in 1930. Many cases of separation were effected privately without notification in the press or legal action, so that the actual numbers would be much larger than these figures indicate. Contemporary Chinese commentators were led to conclude that "Divorce is too cheap and easy nowadays in China." See Herbert Day Lamson, *Social Pathology in China*, The Commercial Press, Shanghai, 1935, pp. 532–533.

29. Autobiographies and biographies of ten of China's great women in the modern era are collected in Helen Foster Snow's *Women in Modern China*, op. cit.

30. For a detailed account and analysis of the earlier marriage legislation of the Chinese Communist party (CCP) in the Kiangsi Soviet and the border areas in the 1930s and 1940s, see M. J. Meijer, *Marriage Law and Policy in the Chinese People's Republic*, Hong Kong University Press, Hong Kong, 1971, chaps. 2 and 3.

31. Ibid., part II, chap. 5 to 8.

32. For the implementation and results of the marriage law movement in the early 1950s, see Aline K. Wong, "Changes in Marriage and Family Institutions in China, 1949–1969," in Steve S. K. Chin and Frank H. H. King (eds.), *Selected Seminar Papers on Contemporary China*, I, Centre of Asian Studies, University of Hong Kong, Hong Kong, 1971, pp. 152–161.

33. *Chung-kuo ch'ing-nien (Chinese Youth)*, no. 2, January 16, 1958, Peking.

34. See Chao Kuo-chun, *The Mass Organizations in Communist China*, Center for International Studies, M.I.T. Press, Cambridge, 1953.

35. By the end of 1951, more than 26.5 million peasant women had joined the peasants' associations in the east, central-south, southwest, and northwest administrative districts (i.e. about 30 percent of the total 88 million members of the associations). In some areas, the percentage of female members was as high as 50 percent. Women also accounted for 10 to 15 percent of the committee members, chairmen and vice-chairmen. *Hsin Chung-kuo fu-nu (New Chinese Women)*, no. 25–56, 1951, p. 16.
It was reported that, in 1950, 90 percent of the women workers in Tientsin had joined the trade unions, among these women, 260 became chairmen or committee members

of the union branches. Eighty percent of the female workers in Shanghai were union members in'same year, and 19.3 percent of the union officials above the basic committee level were women. *Jen-min jih-pao (People's Daily)*, March 13, 1950; *Chieh-fang jih-pao (Liberation Daily)*, August 12, 1950.

36. Lo Ch'iung, *Fu-nu wen-t'i chi-pen chih-shih (Basic Knowledge on the Question of Women)*, Peking, 1956, p. 42.

37. Hupei radio broadcast, December 14, 1955; *Hsin-hua jih-pao (New China Daily)*, Nanking, November 20, 1955.

38. *Kirin jih-pao (Kirin Daily)*, Changchun, May 14, 1957.

39. See *Ten Great Years*, State Statistical Bureau, Peking, 1960, p. 182.

40. "Work Among the Suburban Women," *Jen-min jih-pao*, October 12, 1956.

41. In a rural commune in Pihsien, Szechwan, 432 dining rooms were set up in 1958 to serve the 16,900 households (each dining room thus catering to about 40 households). 75,700 men, women, and children were fed by these communal facilities. In addition, nurseries and kindergartens were established. As a result, 17,000 women were "freed" to participate in economic production. This at once solved the labor shortage problem in connection with the production campaign of the Great Leap Forward. Chuan Nung-tiao, "How Commune Dining Rooms Serve the Peasants," in *Peking Review*, no. 2, January 12, 1960, pp. 16–17.

42. "The People's Commune Advances Women's Complete Emancipation," *Peking Review*, no. 10, March 8, 1960, pp. 6–9.

43. Henry J. Lethbridge, *China's Urban Communes*, Dragonfly Books, Hong Kong, 1961, pp. 22–23.

44. As Audrey Donnithorne, widely known authority on Communist China, has remarked, "The resurgence of the rural family as the basic unit of consumption and of a considerable part of production, has been the most striking feature in China's country-side. Its efficiency as an economic unit is due to the immediacy of the incentives to hard work and thrift and to the convenient way in which its multifarious aspects dovetail into each other. . . ." Audrey Donnithorne, *China's Economic System*, George Allen & Unwin, Ltd., London, 1967, p. 91.

45. George P. Jan, "Mass Education in the Chinese Communes," in Stewart E. Fraser (ed.), *Education and Communism in China*, International Studies Group, Hong Kong, 1969, p. 138.

46. New China News Agency (NCNA; English), "Women's Status in China," in *Selections from China Mainland Press* (SCMP), no. 2211, United States Consulate, Hong Kong, March 2, 1960, p. 12.

47. Evelyne Sullerot, *Woman, Society and Change*, translated by Margaret S. Archer, McGraw-Hill Book Company, New York, 1971, p. 179.

48. NCNA, "Women's Status in China," op. cit.

49. Sullerot, op. cit., pp. 192–193.

50. NCNA (English), in *SCMP*. "Women of Rural China on the Road to Complete Liberation," no. 2210, March 1, 1960, p. 7.

51. In the textile industry, over 60 percent of the workers in 1966 were women. NCNA (English), in *SCMP*, "Women of New China," no. 3654, March 6, 1966, p. 24.

52. Ibid.

53. *SCMP*, no. 3654, March 7, 1966, p. 29; *SCMP*, no. 2655, March 8, 1966, p. 24.

54. NCNA (English), in *SCMP*, "Peking Women Contribute to Science, Engineering and Medicine," no. 2215, March 8, 1960, p. 24.

55. NCNA (English), in *SCMP*, "Women's Role in Building Socialism in China," no. 2211, March 2, 1960, p. 13.

56. Sullerot, op. cit., p. 151.

57. NCNA (English), in *SCMP*, "Women of New China," no. 3654, March 6, 1966, p. 24.

58. Sullerot, op. cit., p. 155.

59. NCNA (English), in *SCMP*, "China Provides Opportunities for Women in Scientific Work," no. 2695, March 6, 1962, p. 34.

60. *Ten Great Years*, op. cit., p. 14; *Current Scene*, vol. 9, no. 1, January 7, 1971, p. 18.

61. Sullerot, op. cit., pp. 222–223.

62. *Current Scene*, vol. 9, no. 1, January 7, 1971, p. 18.

63. NCNA (English), in *SCMP*, "Women of New China," no. 3654, March 6, 1966, p. 24.

64. Sullerot, op. cit., pp. 222–223.

65. Estimates are made from non-Communist statistics. See Christopher Lucas, *Women of China*, Dragonfly Books, Hong Kong, 1965, p. 159.

66. Fung Hai, "Programs for Women in Communist China since the Cultural Revolution," *China Monthly* (Chinese), no. 87, Union Research Institute, Hong Kong, June 1, 1971, p. 11.

67. NCNA (English), in *SCMP*, "Progress by Women of China," no. 3175, March 5, 1964, p. 16.

68. In March 1971, the *Jen-min jih-pao* made some references to the prevalence of gynecological diseases among the female population today. In one production brigade in a commune in Rue-tung *hsien*, out of the twenty-seven female members twenty-three had gynecological disorders. Of these, twelve could not participate in collective labor. *Jen-min jih-pao*, March 3, 1971, p. 4.

69. The street committees or urban residents' committees were established in 1954. Their functions were public welfare, public security, arbitration of disputes, promotion of government policies, and "reflection of public opinion." Residents' committees consisted of elected representatives from residential units of 100 to 600 households. Women's work was given a special place in the operations of these committees, which were closely linked to the police and the court systems. See Franz Schurmann, *Ideology and Organization in Communist China*, University of California Press, Berkeley, 1966, pp. 374–380.

70. *Peking Review*, no. 11, March 13, 1964, p. 19.

71. These letters were fully translated in the supplement to the July 1, 1964, issue of the *Current Scene*, vol. 2, no. 36.

72. Hsi Kung, "My Wife," in *Chinese Women in the Great Leap Forward*, Foreign Languages Press, Peking, 1960, p. 88.

73. As recent as 1971, stories of exemplary heroines still made references to the presence of grandparents living in the same household. See "Women Guard the Coast," in *China Reconstructs*, vol. 20, no. 3, March 1971, p. 39.

74. Michael Freeberne, "The Spectre of Malthus: Birth Control in Communist China," in *Current Scene*, vol. 2, no. 18, August 15, 1963, p. 5.

75. Ibid., p. 9.

76. Tillman Durdin, "The New Face of Maoist China," in *Problems of Communism* (United States Information Agency), vol. 20, September–October 1971, p. 11.

77. See Charles Taylor, *Reporter in Red China*, Victor Gollancz Ltd., London, 1967, pp. 94–95.

78. See Christopher Lucas, op. cit., pp. 185–187.

79. The *China News Analysis* (Hong Kong), p. 7, reported on May 21, 1971 (no. 842) that many unmarried girls are applying for abortion in the cities (based on refugee information).

80. Myra Roper, *China—The Surprising Country*, Cox & Wyman Ltd., London, 1966, p. 87.

81. *Chung-kuo ch'ing-nien* (*Chinese Youth;* Peking), March 16, 1956. Also quoted in Christopher Lucas, op. cit., pp. 101–102. See also Liu Yi-fang, "Clothes Go Gayer" in *China Reconstructs*, no. 6, 1956.

82. For example, in the matter of equal pay for men and women, there were lots of complaints in the Communist press about the breach of this principle throughout the 1950s. Recently, however, the principle seems to be in practice generally in the communes. See *China News Analysis*, no. 833, March 5, 1971, p. 4.

83. See "Steel Girls," in *China Reconstructs*, no. 3, March 1971, pp. 36–37.

84. *Jen-min jih-pao*, March 11, 1968, p. 4. Liu Shao-ch'i, former President of the People's Republic, was deposed during the Cultural Revolution.

85. *Wen-yi yueh-pao* (*Literature Monthly*), February 1957, quoted in C. T. Hsia, "Residual Femininity: Women in Chinese Communist Fiction," in *China Quarterly*, no. 13, January–March 1963, p. 168.

86. Ibid., p. 174.

Eskimo Women:
Makers of Men

JEAN L. BRIGGS

Introduction

As I think about the Eskimo women I know, what strikes me most vividly
is the variety of their lives. There are women whose lives seem full of satisfaction and others for whom frustration is certainly the most salient fact
of life. Some women are busy, others have little to do; some take an active
part in the male world of hunting and traveling, others are wholly occupied
at home with children and other family members to care for; some rule the
household (including their husbands) with a vigorous hand and voice,
others are docilely obedient to husband, mother, mother-in-law, or older
sister. There are "good" marriages and "bad" marriages, and they are good
and bad for a variety of reasons. It is impossible to generalize about the
quality of a "typical" Eskimo woman's life without doing violence to the
realities of individual lives.

However, the variations of real life are the outcome of situations that
are experienced in their several permutations by many, perhaps most
Eskimo women, and, for that matter, by women in other societies. The
regularities on this level, not only within Eskimo culture but cross-culturally, are as striking as the variations in individual outcome. What are
the situations that seem most important in determining the quality of an
Eskimo woman's life? What are the sources of happiness and suffering?

261

What do Eskimo women want in life? What relationships are important to them and in what ways? What are the important events in their lives? On this level, generalizations can be made, and it is to such questions that this paper will be addressed. My purpose, like that of other contributors to this volume, is to add to our presently rather thin ethnographic knowledge of what it means to be a woman in various parts of the world. A comparison of women's lives in different cultures may enable us to discover the common denominators of "womanliness' and the limits of cultural variation. It should also give us insight into the reasons for the situations in which women repeatedly or variably find themselves.

My choice of questions, my perception of what the salient issues are in the lives of Eskimo women, is influenced by the problems attendant on the relationships between men and women in our own society. But one should be careful not to evaluate Eskimo behavior that looks similar to our male-female behavior in terms of Western values. The same behavior in two cultures may be differently rationalized and may form parts of different behavioral complexes, so that it has different meanings in each culture. We shall see to what extent the attitudes and values associated with the roles of women in Eskimo society are different from those associated with similar roles in our own society.

The life to be described here is that of women in contemporary Eskimo camps. These women and their families are the last exponents of a way of life that is rapidly vanishing. Most Eskimos now live in settlements built by white men, and their satisfactions and problems are to some extent different from those that I shall describe. As I have not lived in settlements for extended periods, I know little of the changes that are taking place there. I have lived primarily in two camps, that of the Utkuhikhalingmiut (Utku) in Chantrey Inlet in the Central Canadian Arctic and that of the Qipisamiut (Qipi) in Cumberland Sound (Baffin Island) in the Eastern Canadian Arctic. It is the women of these camps whose lives will be described here. They may be considered representative of traditional Eskimo women in the general areas where these camps are located. Moreover, although details of social organization, subsistence activities, division of labor, and attitudes vary from region to region, so that the reader must generalize with caution to other parts of the Arctic, nevertheless much of what I say will sound familiar to those who know Eskimo women from other areas, such as North Baffin, Hudson Bay, Alaska, and Greenland.

The Utku and Qipi camps are in many ways similar. Both are small: the Utku at the time of study numbered maximally about thirty-five and the Qipi about fifty; the numbers in both cases varied with the season and the year. Both the Utku and the Qipi are seasonally nomadic, and at all seasons their camps are at least 100 miles distant from their nearest neighbors, who live in the settlements of Gjoa Haven and Pangnirtung respectively. For both groups, these settlements provide the main link with the outside world, both Western and Eskimo. The Utku men come in to Gjoa Haven to trade generally about once a month during the winter and spring months, that is, between the end of November and the end of May, when the ice of Chantrey Inlet and Simpson Strait is solid enough to sled over. They do not all come at the same time but travel in groups of two or three, by dogsled—a round trip of four to twelve days, depending on season and weather. No Utku owns a skidoo or a boat with a motor. Thus during the summer and autumn, open water cuts them off entirely from Gjoa Haven, though they do have sporadic contacts with tourists who are flown in by charter plane to fish in Chantrey Inlet during July and August.

The Qipi men follow a similar pattern of traveling, in small groups, in to Pangnirtung to trade more or less monthly. But as they are well equipped for crossing Cumberland Sound, by skidoo in winter and by powered boat in summer, the trip is much less arduous for them than for the Utku and the periods during which they are cut off from the store are much shorter: a few weeks during the ice breakup in the spring and another a few weeks during freeze-up in the fall. During the winter some Qipi men who have relatives in Frobisher Bay prefer to trade there, though the trip overland, over the mountains, is a little longer and harder.

These trading trips are almost the only contact the two groups have with the outside world except for the tourist visits to Chantrey Inlet that I have mentioned. Individuals from both groups have been sent out to hospital and a few of the children in both groups have had a little schooling —the Qipi children in Pangnirtung and the Utku children in Inuvik—a town on the Alaskan border, where there is a large boarding school for Indian and Eskimo children. Women and children from both groups very occasionally go along on trading trips to Gjoa Haven and Pangnirtung, respectively, but rarely oftener than once a year and in some cases much less frequently than that. So on the whole, both groups live quite self-sufficiently in their camps, adjusting minimally to Western culture except for the incorporation of such material goods as are useful to life in a hunting camp.

Physically, life in an Arctic hunting camp varies greatly from season to season. The nature of one's dwelling, its location, the food one eats, and the manner in which it is hunted all change seasonally.

Both Chantrey Inlet and Cumberland are more or less on the Arctic Circle and thus have similar seasons of light and darkness. Twenty-four-hour daylight begins in late May and ends in early August. Winter days are short and sunless, but there is no period of total darkness, as there is farther north. On the shortest days it is light from about 9 A.M. to 2 or

3 P.M. This means that men are able to hunt all winter long unless they are housebound for a period by stormy weather, but storms that last more than a few days are rare.

Men tend to range more widely in winter than in other seasons, taking advantage of the hard-frozen snow and ice that converts land and sea alike into a highway for skidoo or dogsled. But the world of women and children is most limited in winter. Children play outdoors a great deal except on days of high wind and blowing snow, but they rarely wander out of sight of camp, as they do in spring and summer; they are always close enough to home so that they can run in and warm cold hands and feet if necessary. Fear of wolves and spirits, which are believed to lurk outside the safe circle of the camp, may be more intense in winter too, though I have no clear evidence that this is so.

Women stay indoors most of the time in winter. They may run across the way, sewing in hand, to visit for an hour with a neighbor, but one corner of a housewife's mind is always occupied with the domestic situation. Are the blubber lamps flaring and in need of tending? Is the bread (baking in a frying pan over the lamp) burning? Is the meat boiling? Are the children at home and getting into mischief? She may send a child to check once or twice, but before long she will herself go home to attend to things.

The traditional Baffin Island winter dwelling, in which the Qipi still live, is a wooden-framed, double-walled tent—in Eskimo, *qammaq*—with a thick insulating layer of dry Arctic heather between the two canvas walls. Additional warmth is provided by papering the inside with multiple layers of newspaper or sheets of magazines. Described in this way, these tents sound flimsy and shivery in the extreme; however, they are very comfortable to live in, even for one accustomed to western-style (modern) housing. They are draftproof and can be heated up to 70 or 80°F with just three seal-oil lamps.[1]

The Utku, on the other hand, live in unlined snow houses heated by fish-oil lamps, which are smaller than the Baffin Island lamps. Kerosene or gasoline stoves (Primuses and Colemans) supplement the traditional lamps when fuel is available, but it is still impossible to raise the indoor temperature above 30°F without melting the roof; consequently the outer door is opened when the temperature rises much above 28°F. A temperature of 28°F is not uncomfortable to live in once one's metabolism adjusts; but it does require that one wear warm clothes, and the latter are not always available to the Utku in sufficient quantity. Moreover, when fuel is scarce, when there is no stove, or when visitors (and their body heat) are absent, the iglu temperature may drop as low as zero, a temperature that even Utku consider uncomfortable ("Too cold to sew").

In May or thereabouts, both Utku and Qipi leave their iglus or *qam-*

maqs and move to new campsites some miles away from the winter sites. Here they set up tents on rocky ledges or gravel patches from which the snow has melted, and from then until September (in the case of the Qipi) or November (Utku) they live relatively mobile lives, moving from tent site to tent site as the spirit moves them. The distances moved may be as small as 4 feet if a woman feels like having a clean floor for her tent or as much as fifty miles if her husband thinks that hunting or fishing will be better somewhere else. During these seasons of warmth and light, the worlds of of women and children expand; there is no longer need to stay close to home to tend fires or to keep small children from freezing. People go for long walks over the tundra or across the now soggy sea ice, sometimes with the excuse of gathering a bit of food—tomcod or birds' eggs, seaweed, clams, or berries; perhaps to hunt for baby birds to "adopt"; or to picnic on bannock and tea, brewed on an outdoor fire. It is an exhilarating season, though it may also be a season of hardship if ice conditions make hunting difficult.

It is apparent that one major difference between the situations of the Utku and Qipi is economic. The Qipi are extremely well off compared with the Utku. Game is ordinarily varied and plentiful in Cumberland Sound; the Qipi hunt seal and harp seal, beluga, and caribou, and they supplement their diet with fish, birds, and eggs in season. Sealskins provide the main cash income, and a man is likely to take at least thirty skins to sell when he makes his monthly trip to the store in Pangnirtung. With the proceeds he buys ammunition, fuel, food other than meat, clothing, household equipment and supplies, and a variety of expensive items such as tape recorders, phonographs, shortwave radios, sewing machines, and so on. In addition, every adult man maintains a skidoo and a canoe with outboard motor, and four of the older men own whaleboats. The latter are used not for hunting whales but for moving families to the various campsites occupied by the group and for making the trading trips to Pangnirtung.

By contrast, the Utku live almost entirely on fish. Caribou are hunted intensively in the autumn for winter clothing hides; but a man is lucky if he gets eight animals—and perhaps another three or four during the rest of the year. A seal is an event. The families I lived with got two in the two years (more or less) that I spent with them, and that was by accident when the seal blundered into a fishnet. The Utkus' cash income comes from the foxes that they trap during the winter; but although Chantrey Inlet is good fox country, men do not bother to trap very many. Needless to say, the inventory of Utku household goods is considerably smaller than that of the Qipi. Shortages of fuel, ammunition, and store food are not unusual experiences for the Utku in any season; during the summer and autumn months, when they are cut off from Gjoa Haven, these shortages are chronic. But though these differences in standard of living strike the eye of the Western observer, I have no evidence that the Qipi are in any way more satisfied with their life that the Utku are with theirs. Neither group appears to envy the life of the other, though they are aware of the differences. They do, however, compare camp life with settlement life. Some members of each group would prefer the easier, warmer, more sedentary, and more commercial life of the settlement, but others see the advantages of life on the land: it provides better food, is more peaceful, and— odd though the words sounds to us when applied to the Arctic—it is cosier.

Both Utku and Qipi camps consist of kin: people one has grown up with and known intimately all one's life. When possible, the Utku even marry cousins who have been playmates in childhood.[2] Among the Qipi, households tend to be nuclear whenever feasible—that is, when sufficient building material (wood, canvas) is available. Utku households also tend to be nuclear during the summer, but in the winter joint iglus may sometimes be built by two lineally related familes. Thus one winter a man and his two married daughters shared two iglus with one common entrance. Added warmth as well as increased sharing of food and work may have been factors in the decision to live together in this way.

The Utku acknowledge no group leaders. Each household head directs his own household but no others. Among Eastern Eskimos, on the other hand, there may be authorities who are superordinate to the household heads. In the case of the Qipi, the elder—the father of them all—is such an authority. He does not exercise authority in everyday matters of whether or not to hunt and where and what; but in long-range decisions, such as whether to move to Pangnirtung or not, some people defer to his wishes. The deference is voluntary—no household head is sanctioned if he decides to make his own decisions in such matters; but phrased as loyalty, it is nevertheless consciously there. The ways in which women fit into the authority structure will be discussed below.

THE SHAPING OF FEMININITY

Perhaps the most fundamental question, and certainly the first, is: Does a girl child feel wanted? Eskimos have a profound love of children. They sometimes defend themselves against the fear of losing a newborn by claiming that a baby is not lovable until it gets fat, but this attitude only intensifies the mothers nurturance. Babies and small children are the affectional center of the family; their every need is attended to with immediate solicitude, and during most of their waking moments they are cuddled and played with by any and all adults and older children who may be present. There is a common belief that hunting societies in general and Eskimos in

particular formerly valued male children more than female. The logic of
this belief, of course, is that a boy grows up to be a hunter—a provider—
whereas a girl is only a drain on her parents' household until she marries
and moves away to be useful to her husband's household. The Netsilingmiut, who lived close to famine, gave support to this belief: they practiced
female infanticide and justified it in the terms just cited (Rasmussen, 1931,
pp. 140–141). Freeman (1971, pp. 1011–1018) thinks that this is not the real
reason for Netsilik infanticide; but his explanation, too, supports the view
that Netsilik men (if not their wives) preferred male children. In brief, he
argues that because the Netsilik wife was both indispensable and assertive,
her husband felt a need to reassert his dominance. If a daughter was born,
the father was not only disappointed in his hope for a helper but also en-
vied his wife *her* helper and companion, so he ordered that the child die.
I tend to doubt that Netsilik men have such a strong need to be dominant;
there seems to be little in their upbringing that would produce such a
need and very little other behavioral evidence that it exists. I will return
to these arguments later.

In any case, the Netsilingmiut appear to have been exceptional among
Eskimos; in most other areas infanticide does not seem to have been a
regular practice. Moreover, even among the Netsilingmiut, if a daughter
was allowed to live, there is no evidence that she was treated less kindly or
loved less than her brothers. Indeed, she may have been highly cherished
as a scarce and valuable commodity.[3] Contemporary Eskimo groups are, of
course, buffered by welfare and other government payments as well as by
income derived from the sale of fox and sealskins, handcrafts, and cooperative enterprises, so they no longer need fear starvation. In the isolated hunting camps of the Utku and Qipi, I have listened for remarks that would
tell me whether boys are more desired or more loved than girls, and I conclude that they are not. Mothers with several sons express a wish for
daughters, and mothers of many daughters are delighted by the birth of a
son. Children of both sexes are cuddled, cooed at, and praised by both
parents and by all other relatives as well.

Other fundamental questions concern the ways in which a little girl is
made to feel feminine. What does it mean to be feminine?

In order to understand femininity, it is necessary to understand something about masculinity as well, since it is partly by contrast with men that
a woman develops a sense of what she herself is. Though, as I have said,
babies of both sexes appear to be welcome, Eskimos do differentiate
strongly between the sexes even in infancy. Both parents look forward affectionately to the day when their little boy will bring home his first seal or
caribou, and they tell him about his future role as provider long before he
is able to understand. They also very early make him aware of his physical
maleness. Little boys usually run around indoors without pants until they

are between two and three years old and fully toilet-trained. In the Eastern
Arctic, where sexuality (and other feelings) are more openly expressed than
in the Central Arctic, parents and other adults admire and kiss a little boy's
penis and encourage him—sometimes teasingly—to display it, at least until
he is old enough to go fully clothed. In the Central Arctic too, a baby boy
is held upright and encouraged to arch his naked body toward the audience.
When he does so, people exclaim admiringly and say: "He is becoming
masculine!" Then, gradually, the teasing component in the attention paid
to the genitals intensifies until pleasure in self-display is replaced by embarrassment and modest self-protection. A child is thought to be naturally
shy when teased. One informant said that if a child does not respond with
shyness, his parents worry that he will not be "normal."

Girls have similar experiences, on the whole. They too begin to learn
about their adult roles, both social and sexual, while they are still babies.
Girl babies as well as boys are cuddled and caressed, and their genitals,
like those of boys, are kissed and admired by both parents. They are encouraged, as their brothers are, to display themselves, and when they arch
their naked bodies, adults exclaim affectionately: "She is becoming feminine!"

Also similar to the treatment of boys is the way in which sexual admiration gradually changes into sexual teasing, prompting the child to protect
instead of to display herself. But there is a difference in the form of the
teasing. In the case of the boy, his big brothers and other men tell him:
"Ugh! you smell like feces!" or "I'll pull your penis off!" And older boys,
roughhousing with each other, often grab jokingly at each other's penises
as if to pull them off. I was told that remarks of this sort are deliberately
made in order to teach children to be "careful" of their bodies. More
specifically, parents want children to be aware that they may smell. They
also want to discourage masturbation, in the belief that a child who plays
with his genitals may become homosexual. Girls may also be told teasingly
that they smell like feces, but then instead of being told that they will lose
their genitals, they are threatened with being seen, kissed, or (in the Eastern
Arctic) goosed. Another difference is that except in the case of the smallest
children, it is predominantly men who tease children of both sexes, so that
girls are subject to much more teasing from the opposite sex than boys are.
In the East unlike the Central Arctic, such teasing continues throughout a
girl's childhood, and if a girl is too shy about being teased, both men and
women will be amused. They may intensify their teasing for the fun of
seeing her flee in confusion. If she cries, however, someone may gently
chide her and try to reassure her: "You are too shy; it's no fun to play with
you. I wasn't serious—did you think I was serious?"

But fear is not the only reaction to this joking pursuit; it is enjoyed by
the same girls who are embarrassed by it. Qipi girls very early learn to

count coups. I have heard seven-year-olds comparing notes with their girl-friends: "I've been kissed by . . . [naming a number of men, boys, and even girls], had my breasts felt by . . . [naming others], and been goosed by . . . [naming still others]." Small boys count coups too: "I have kissed . . . [nam-ing girls], felt . . . [more names], and goosed . . . [still other names]." In the Eastern Arctic, children also experiment with intercourse when they are only five or six, and it is not always the boys who initiate the experiments. I have heard boys about ten years of age admit to being afraid of sexually aggressive girls. One informant from the Eastern Arctic told me that parents are pleased when children talk about their exploits; they take it as a sign that the child is normal. It is thought that if a child—especially a boy—is silent on the subject of sex, he might grow up to be dangerously aggressive sex-ually: "He is enjoying sex inside, but not bringing it out."

Such openness about sex is not found in the Central Arctic. Utku boys do discuss the subject freely among themselves, but girls do not. After an initial period in which they are teased about sex, it becomes a taboo sub-ject for them. As far as I know, girls rarely or never talk about sex and sexual games are not played even in adolescence.

I have said that a girl begins to learn other aspects of her adult role while she is very young too. Even before she can walk, a girl plays at back-packing dolls, puppies, or any other object that can be conveniently stuffed into the back of her shirt or parka, the way her mother carries *her* or, later, her younger sibling. These toys are nursed, toileted, bounced to sleep, and in every way treated exactly as a real baby is treated. By the age of five or six, girls have begun to baby-sit for real babies—siblings and cousins—in addition to playing with make-believe ones; but they often treat their real charges as make-believe, too, pretending to be their "mothers." They also play at butchering, cleaning skins, sewing, cooking, and tending lamps: all the adult skills that they will begin to concern themselves with in earnest as their strength and knowledge increases.

Boys, too, begin to play at masculine pursuits even as toddlers, running make-believe dogsleds or skidoos loudly up and down the floor or hillside and loading and unloading toy sleds. A one- or two-year-old may be held in his father's or brother's lap and helped to "shoot" a .22. And boys as young as five or six may, in good weather, accompany their fathers and older brothers on short trips by boat or sled.

These early learning experiences are presented to both boys and girls as enjoyable, and often they are so perceived by the children. When they rebel, it is usually not because they do not want to learn the particular skill in hand but because they happen to feel like having some other sort of fun at that moment. Pressure to learn a given skill at a given moment is minimal, especially in the Central Arctic; Utku children initiate much of their own education, and when they become bored, they are generally not criticized if they turn to some other activity. And even Qipi children, who are more frequently set unwelcome tasks, are at the same time often admonished to go out and play: "Because you're a child."

Often, boys and girls play separately—especially if playmates of both sexes are plentiful. Or, when they play together, children of each sex enact their appropriate roles: older girls "mother" their younger brothers or cousins, older boys "drive" or draw younger children on toy sleds, and (in Qipisa) boys and girls of more or less similar age frequently engage in sexual teasing. The playing of sexually appropriate roles is reinforced by adults who, when they see a boy behaving like a girl or vice versa, smile and ask: "Do you think you're a girl (boy)?"

Nevertheless, the sexual division is not rigid. Boys as old as nine or ten may occasionally play with their sisters and girl cousins at female games, including backpacking "babies." I have even seen one three-year-old taking turns with his five-year-old sister at "breast-feeding" a puppy. Similarly, girls as well as boys may play at driving dogsleds, or they may accompany their fathers on hunting or fishing trips in the vicinity of camp. Moreover, many activities do not appear to be the prerogative of one sex or the other. Boys and girls go tobogganing and sliding together or go off wandering in the hills to pick berries, chase lemmings, or stone ptarmigan. Girls and boys—together until puberty—may go swimming in little sun-warmed pools or inlets; and in the light spring nights both sexes, together or separately, may go off on long expeditions to collect seaweed, clams, or birds' eggs, and they may dare each other to scale sheer rock faces to test their skill and courage.

Some girls retain a taste for vigorous outdoor activity all their lives and some boys prefer sedentary pursuits to active hunting and traveling, but in general, by the time they are physically mature, each sex is fully occupied with its own work and a person has little time to indulge any taste he may have for the way of life of the other sex. Many girls marry at eighteen or twenty, and thereafter their time is taken up with caring for husbands and children; unmarried girls help their mothers or married older sisters to care for their men and their children. And young men, of course, are now full-time hunters and fishermen.

There are exceptions to this rule too, however, since Eskimos are pragmatic people. There is nothing holy to them about the sexual division of labor; neither is there, in their view, anything inherent in the nature of either sex that makes it incapable of doing some of the jobs that the other sex ordinarily does. So if a family is short of daughters, a son—often the eldest son—may be brought up to help his mother. In addition to being taught the usual male skills, he will be taught some female skills. Most boys baby-sit on occasion and run errands, but a mother's helper will do more. He may bottle-feed and change diapers, cook, wash dishes and clothes, run errands, and clean the house. Actually, most boys and men are capable of doing all these tasks in an emergency, as well as mending their clothes and tending blubber lamps, but they are not usually called upon to do so in the everyday course of events. One woman said that the difference between most men and those few who have been specially trained to be domestically helpful is that the latter tend to be much more helpful around the house when they marry.

Similarly, if a family has only daughters, a father may decide to bring up one or two daughters as hunters, so that they can help him and also that, if anything should happen to him, the family will not be left without a provider. Again, the older daughters tend to be chosen for this role. Such girls will go hunting with their fathers from the time they are small. To be sure, they also learn female skills, and eventually they marry and have children, but the masculine training they have received may show itself, according to the same female informant, in a tendency to be somewhat bossy toward their husbands.

Orphans of either sex also, of necessity, tend to acquire the skills of both sexes—partly in self-defense because they have no one to take care of them and partly because they tend to become camp slaveys, at the beck and call of anyone of either sex who needs a job done.[4] This situation is reflected in Eskimo folklore about the orphan who makes good—the equivalent of the youngest son in European tales—but it is not just a fact of folklore; several of the most competent Eskimos I know, both men and women, had been orphaned, and their competence was attributed to this fact. In one of these cases, that of a young woman who lived with a remote relative by marriage, it was evident that she was indeed called upon to perform a great variety of tasks, from baby-sitting and cleaning sealskins to hunting seal and caribou, even backpacking hindquarters of caribou—a weight much too heavy for most women—for long distances.

Attitudes toward adults who have the skills of both sexes seem to be slightly ambivalent. I have mentioned that "masculine" women are sometimes criticized for exercising authority inappropriately over their husbands. On the other hand, admiration is expressed for women who are good hunters. Men may seek their opinion not only with regard to matters such as illness and birth, concerning which women are thought to be wise, but also with regard to hunting and traveling decisions, which are usually made—nominally, at least—by men alone. One woman told me that her husband had married her because she was a tomboy, and he knew that she would be a good traveling companion.

Similar ambivalence seems to be shown toward men who have feminine skills. One woman told me, speaking generally, that parents who love a daughter very much and want her to have an easy life sometimes give her a husband who has been brought up as a mother's helper, so that he will help her in the house. But when I asked if she personally knew of any case in which parents had given their daughter such a husband, she told me about a widow who was trying unsuccessfully to attract the young man who was courting her daughter; it was not out of affection but in jealous spite that she arranged for her daughter to marry another, more "feminine" man. Another story I was told also seems to show a mixture of positive and negative feelings about feminine behavior in a man. The story was about a widower who adopted a baby and wore a woman's parka so that he could backpack the motherless child. I had the impression that my informant was both amused and touched by this behavior.

In sum, then, a girl learns a variety of lessons about femininity during her childhood. She learns that she is a sexual being and attractive to men —a fact that, in various degrees, both pleases and frightens Qipi girls and perhaps Utku girls as well. However, the reactions of the latter to sexuality are so much more subdued or suppressed that they are difficult to detect.

In order to keep this teasing in perspective, it is necessary to remember that Qipi boys (and probably Utku boys) learn similar lessons about their sexuality, and that they have similar mixed reactions to the teasing to which they are subjected. While they are usually not openly pursued by the opposite sex, they are often provoked into pursuing or are frightened away by sexually pointed remarks or gestures.[5]

Childhood for both sexes is also a period of training for adult life-styles that are in some ways quite different from one another—different in obvious ways, such as in requisite skills, modes of self-expression, and tastes, and different also in subtler ways, such as in rhythms of coming and going, of work and leisure, of activity and rest. I will describe the activities of a woman in more detail before taking up the complicated question of how Eskimo men and women evaluate their roles.

WIVES AND MOTHERS

Since most Eskimo women marry at least once, to describe adult womanhood is to describe marriage. However, it is extremely difficult to find out what relationships between husbands and wives are really like and what marriage really means to the partners. As one Eskimo woman said to me: "The only way to learn about Eskimo marriage is to disappear." I think I did "disappear" to some extent during the two winters in which I shared the iglu of my Utku adoptive family in the sense that they became very used to my presence, but my eye was to some extent always that of a foreigner, and my ear never developed to the point where I could understand conversations between husband and wife which they intended I should not understand. And in Qipisa, though I lived in a little room attached to the *qammaq* of my adoptive parents, I was always a "visitor," and my comings and goings through the main room always to some degree changed the tenor of the interaction there. So I make the following remarks with some hesitation.

Utku marriages are different in certain respects from Qipi marriages, young marriages from established ones, first marriages from second ones, and, of course, every marriage represents an idiosyncratic compromise between different personalities. Nonetheless, it is possible to make some generalizations both about prescriptions for marriage in these two Eskimo groups and about actual sources of marital satisfaction and strain.

One of the salient features of Eskimo marriage, and I think one of its strengths, is the clear division between male and female roles. Men are, of course, first and foremost hunters, but relatively little of their time is spent in the actual pursuit of game. More time is taken up with ancillary activities and household maintenance tasks. Men make, clean, and repair their own tools and equipment and those of their wives. Nowadays, a regular evening and "holiday" activity is the repair of skidoos; but even if the skidoo is in working order for once, there are seal and fishnets to be woven, dog harnesses to be sewn, *ulus* (semilunar women's knives), snowknives, and perhaps fishhooks to be made—as well as sleds, boats, tent poles, fish spears, ice chisels, harpoons, and a variety of other specialized tools. It is a man's job to repair stoves, lamps, and other household equipment. It is he who knows how to put a new handle on the pot, make a new lid for the teakettle, or bend the spout back into shape. In Qipisa, men feed the dogs; Utku men also are responsible for this task, though their wives and daughters may help. Iglu building is another male job, as are all other tasks that require more strength than a woman possesses: carrying a sack of fish back from the nets, bringing in loads of ice to melt for drinking water, fetching carcasses from the caches, and so on. Flensing and butchering are also done by men in Qipisa; Utku men butcher caribou, but smaller animals, including the very occasional seal, may be butchered by women.

Women are responsible for most of the physically lighter tasks connected with household management and, in addition, a very large proportion of the care of children devolves on them. They cook, wash, clean, and tend the lamps, but few of these tasks entail any time or labor. Once a day—or it may be more often if suitable meat or fish is available—a large pot is hung over the lamp (or put on the stove) to boil. This cooked meal is timed to be ready for the men when they come in from their outdoor work, but—as long as the meat lasts—it is also eaten by anyone else who happens to be hungry. The rest of the day, people just help themselves to whatever fresh or semifrozen meat is lying in the larder. Bannock is usually made once a day too, when flour is available. Otherwise, the only cooking is the frequent brewing of tea. Cleaning is equally untaxing: a wooden floor may be swept and occasionally washed, the dirty snow on an iglu floor may be replaced with fresh, cups may be washed now and again (not every day), and that is about all. Clothes washing is more time-consuming as it is done by hand and—if the family is large or there are small children—every day.

The most important and time-consuming jobs that women do—other than caring for the children—are preparing hides for sale or for use, preparing meat for storage, and sewing. Hide preparation is by no means light work. In the case of sealskins, the thick layer of blubber must be scraped off and then the skin must be washed, stretched on a frame to dry, and, when dry, scrubbed again with a brush or scouring pad. Caribou hides must have the brittle membrane first cracked by scraping with a dull tool and then removed by scraping again with a sharp blade. Cutting up meat for drying and gutting fish for storage in hollow stone caches are less tiring activities, but they can be uncomfortable when done outdoors with a cold wind blowing on wet hands. Women joke about the weather and suck on their hands to warm them, or they may periodically stop to drink a cup of tea.

When not engaged in one of these more active tasks or in feeding the baby, a woman usually occupies herself with sewing or knitting, just as a man most often has some small craftwork in hand. Nowadays, women buy most of the cloth clothes worn by their families, but they still make the fur clothes and the boots. Since boots, especially, wear out very rapidly, there is always some repair or replacement under way.

Some observers, watching women hard at work scraping hides while their husbands sit about drinking tea and relaxing or filing fishhooks, have had the impression that women do much more work than men—that, in fact, they are servants to their male overlords. But such observers forget about the times when the women are sitting comfortably at home in their warm qammaqs or iglus, drinking tea and chatting, while the men are out in subzero winds and blinding snow, trying to find a seal or bringing home a load of fish from a cache 50 or 60 miles away. They are also applying their own standards of "justice" to a situation that may be perceived quite differently by the actors themselves, a point to which I shall return in the final section of this paper.

The major irritant in the everyday life of an Eskimo woman is not that her physical strength is overtaxed (it is not) or that she is forced to work while her husband takes his ease—it is that the demands of children, especially infants, often conflict with the demands of other work. It is difficult to sew when a two-year-old tries to take away your needle or cries to be nursed and difficult to flense a seal when the three-year-old is experimenting with the flame of the blubber lamp. Mothers try to solve these problems by asking older daughters or other girls to baby-sit or by trying to nurse the baby to sleep. Sometimes, however, these tactics do not work: the baby cries

to come home or refuses to go to sleep. Then a Qipi mother may exclaim
in annoyance: "The baby is watching me! How willful he is when I want
to work!" And an Utku mother will smile and say: "How lovable and at
the same time how irritating my baby is. I will work when he sleeps."

The interdependence of male and female work is obviously complex.
When seal hunting has been good, women are extremely busy and may feel
somewhat pressed, because sealskins spoil if the blubber is not removed
from them within a day or two. They may also work long hours sometimes
if a man is in need of a new pair of boots or a new fur parka. In this sense,
the rhythm of their work is dependent on that of the men. But the men
are also dependent on the pace of the women's work. A man cannot hunt
until his parka is finished, nor can he move his family to spring camp until
his wife has finished making the tent. Each sex claims to be incapable of
performing the other's tasks and thus sees the work of the other as indispensable. As one friend said to me: "My husband and I make a good team;
when people come to consult him about [matters pertaining to his sphere
of competence], I never even ask what they talked about, but when [it's a
matter that I understand better than he does], I handle it." I have never
heard either sex rationalize his or her ignorance of the other's work in
terms of its being demeaning for the opposite sex to perform. Husbands
and wives both express pride in the fact that they have skills that the other
does not have; and occasionally they may show off their competence a bit
by teasing the other about his or her lack of skill: "Let me do that; you
don't know how; just look how clumsy you are." If the spouses are not
fond of each other, the teasing will be hostile; but often the tone is affectionate.

The separation between male and female spheres applies not only to
tasks but to decision making. It is sometimes said that in Eskimo families
the husband commands and the wife obeys, but this is an oversimplification.
A wife will say: "My husband is my leader," but she means this in a rather
limited way—especially in Qipisa. She means that nominally he makes all
decisions about hunting and traveling. He decides where the family is going
to live and when and with whom they will move. And if a woman wants to
accompany her husband on one of his trips in order to visit a relative, she
has to ask his permission. Sometimes, wives are made unhappy by their
husbands' decisions; but if they are sufficiently unhappy, they have ways of
letting the men know it. Often, moreover, a husband will consult his wife
in private—especially if it is a decision about which she is likely to have
strong feelings or pertinent information; thus the public statement that he
ultimately makes about "his" plans really represents a joint decision. In
the Eskimo view as well as in our own, it is the responsibility of the
"leader" to be sensitive to the wishes of those he leads. Moreover, as one
Central Eskimo man said: "One can't be happy if one's wife is unhappy."

In addition to deciding about hunting and traveling, Utku men also direct domestic affairs, more or less depending on temperament—their own and their wives'. In general, an Utku woman decides for herself how she is going to spend the day—whether she will make a pair of boots, go to gather twigs to tie into winter sleeping mats, or take the day off and go fishing. However, her husband may veto her plan if he sees fit, whereas the reverse is not true. I have never heard an Utku wife tell her husband how he is going to spend his day, and if she did, she would certainly be looked at askance. Moreover, an Utku wife tends to serve her husband in small ways more than he serves her: she may fetch his boots, cut up his meal of frozen fish if he feels lazy, pour his tea, and roll his cigarette. He less often does the same for her; though if she is doing something that cannot be interrupted, she may ask him to hold a crying baby or put it over the can to pee.

Qipi men, as a rule, are much more helpful in the house than most Utku men are, and women are much more directive to their husbands. Coming from the Central Arctic, I was startled to hear a Qipi woman tell her husband to turn over the bannock in the frying pan, take his two-year-old son out to visit, mend his small daughter's torn slacks, put some meat on to boil, or bring the clothes in off the line. But the husbands obeyed with good grace, and, later, a woman explained to me that in Qipisa husbands are leaders only with regard to hunting and traveling; indoors, the woman is the leader. Of course, in this case too, the leader must be sensitive to the moods and wishes of the led or suffer the consequences.

So far, I have stressed the separateness of male and female realms in Eskimo life, and this is by far the most visible aspect of the relationships between the sexes. Publicly, distance is quite rigorously maintained. One sees clusters of men standing down on the beach, or around a sled that is being loaded or unloaded, or playing cards in someone's house, or gathered around a skidoo that is being repaired; and there are seldom any women in these groups. It is always a cause of excitement when visitors are seen approaching camp, and almost everyone who can walk runs out to watch; but women cluster near the tents or houses, while the men stand more boldly, further down the slope. When the sled or skidoo or boat has come to a stop, it is the men who flock to greet the arrivals. Women go to shake hands only if the person who has come is a close relative or a good friend; otherwise they go home again, make tea, and wait to be visited. If men are talking together, women listen, and if women are talking, men listen. They do not ignore or deprecate each other's conversations; they listen with interest but they rarely join in. Among the Utku, men and women used to eat separately, and they still do when more than a few of each sex eat at the same time. So do Qipi when a hunter calls the whole camp together for a feast of raw caribou or seal. An Utku man explained that each sex feels freer to talk and laugh when it is alone: men feel that way about women and women (his wife agreed) feel that way about men.

But this somewhat formal public behavior makes it easy to overlook another important aspect of Eskimo marriage: a strong loyalty and companionship built of shared activities and experiences. I have mentioned the woman who told me that her husband said he had married her because she was a tomboy and would therefore happily share his life of traveling. And at home, when visiting neighbors have left and only the family is present, it is husband and wife who play cards or talk and laugh together. In Qipisa, one may sometimes find a man lying with his head cosily cradled in his wife's lap while she cleans his ears or plucks out his white hairs; sometimes it is he who performs similar services for her. Among Utku, late evening is the time for conspiratorial feasts of the scarce delicacies that one is reluctant to share with the neighbors. Food has tremendous emotional significance for Eskimos, so what is being shared within the intimate circle of husband, wife, and children is not just meat or rice or raisins—it is love.

Another sort of intimate sharing is less tangible, but one hears echoes of it when a husband and wife talk about their past life together: the death of a child; a famine they survived together; experiences they had on their first long caribou-hunting trek inland, "before we had children." Dreams, too, give one glimpses of the emotional interdependence between spouses: a man dreams that he is trying to go back to a place where he and his wife camped long ago because she wants to live there again. And most vividly of all, one sees this dependence in the loneliness that each spouse feels when the other is away for any length of time. Some men even complain of loneliness if their wives go out visiting for a few hours. Such a man may follow his wife to the neighbors' and "joke" that he is depressed because he was left all alone; or he may go to visit another neighbor, explaining that it is lonely at home because his wife is out. Women, of course, are used to being left alone for hours, since a man's hunting activities take him away from home whenever weather permits. But when he goes on a trading trip and is gone for several days, she too may begin to mope, and the neighbors will take notice and make an effort to keep her company to compensate her for the absence of her husband.

A woman's emotional needs, however, are by no means entirely filled by her husband. One of the most important sources of gratification for both spouses in an Eskimo marriage is children; and, conversely, a woman's unfulfilled desire for children may cause serious strain in a marriage, even when her husband is devoted to her. Children are playthings when small, companions and helpers when older, a much needed source of support when their parents are old. At all ages, a great deal of protective affection is lavished on them. Because the father is absent from home so much, most of the actual care of children devolves on the mother (until boys are old enough to accompany their fathers); but fathers help too when they are at home, and they enjoy cuddling and playing with their children as much as their wives do; indeed, mutual love for their children is an important bond between husband and wife as well as between each of them and the children.

Unfortunately, Eskimo marriages, like those in other societies, create tensions as well as satisfactions. Some of these must be evident from the preceding discussion. If spouses are ill-matched, so that they do not give each other companionship or appreciation; if for some reason they cannot have children; if the man is a poor hunter or his wife a clumsy or lazy seamstress—there will be trouble.

One major source of marital difficulty is jealousy. I have not mentioned sex as a source of gratification for a woman because I know too little about Eskimo sexual practices. We have seen that Qipi girls learn both to enjoy and to fear sexual advances and that Utku girls are taught extreme modesty. But how these early trainings are related to later satisfaction is unclear. Evidence is scanty and mixed and comes from widely scattered parts of the Arctic. Some women may fear the initial encounter, feeling embarrassed about self-exposure or anxious about unknown discomfort. Sexual approaches may at first also be seen as a threat to autonomy (Washburne, 1940). But these initial anxieties may dissipate readily; we do not know. With regard to established marriages, we find a variety of comments. Burch (1966, 1972), writing about a Northwest Alaskan community, says that both men and women claim that they sleep with their spouses primarily to have children and rarely for pleasure. He says that pleasure is experienced more often in relationships with exchange partners, and that both sexes have ample opportunity to initiate such relationships. A white man of my acquaintance who has lived for a long period in the Central Arctic says that there, Eskimo men do not consider themselves successful lovers unless they can please a woman, but I am not sure whether the reference is to wives or other women or both. David Stevenson (1972), who has lived for an equally long time in the Eastern Arctic, says that in the communities with which he is familiar it is sometimes women and not men who initiate spouse-exchange relationships. My own Central Arctic experience agrees with Burch's observation that it is not uncommonly the wife who takes a lover behind her husband's back.[6] The latter facts would seem to indicate that women value sex, but Burch's is the only clear statement that they actually enjoy it; he says that, by and large, they enjoy it more outside the marital context than within it. One indication that men expect women to enjoy sex, at least in some contexts, was provided by a Qipi man who expressed surprise when I refused his offer to find me a husband for the duration of my stay there. "Don't you *like* to sleep with men?" he asked.

However this may be, one thing is sure; both men and women tend to be extremely possessive of their spouses and extremely alert to any slightest suggestion of attention from third parties. One often hears gossip about jealous men who strike their wives and women who scold their husbands or who tear each other's hair out over suspected attentions to the husband of one of them. Whether or not the stories are true—and I suspect that they are sometimes exaggerated, since Eskimos are prone to exaggerate stories about aggression in general—they do indicate a concern with sexual fidelity and infringements thereof. Since Eskimos very easily interpret as potentially sexual any friendly exchange between adults of opposite sex, it may be that the social distance that obtains publicly between the sexes is in part a protection against such accusations.

The practice of spouse exchange might seem to contradict the view that spouses are possessive of one another, but only at first glance. Spouse exchange is a contractual relationship which is entered into with the full knowledge and often with the agreement of all four of the parties concerned.[7] The reasons for the exchange are various: sexual attraction; the desire to strengthen a friendship or an economic partnership; and, especially in former days, convenience. For example, if one man planned a long trip on which his own wife was unable or unwilling to accompany him, he might take another man's wife, leaving his own with the other man. Or the other's wife might want to visit relatives at a distance and would ask permission to accompany a man who was going in that direction. In any case, this sort of open and aboveboard exchange was not classified as infidelity and was not, as far as we know, a cause for jealousy.

It has been said that Eskimo marriages are fragile,[8] and it is true that many people are married more than once in the course of their lives. However, remarriage is by no means always due to conflict. Since the death rate is high,[9] it is not at all uncommon to lose a spouse while he or she is still young. Most of the remarriages that I know of have been due to the death of one spouse. However, divorce is also easy for both sexes (unless the couple has been married in church) and does occur, for all of the reasons discussed above and others.

The generalization about the fragility of Eskimo marriage applies most accurately to young marriages, I think. As one woman explained: "Young people have had no practice in being involved with another person, no practice in being concerned for another. People say that one should marry young, while one's mind is still soft and one can learn to be concerned."

I have said that Utku children are often betrothed at birth to cousins or other relatives and that they grow up together with their future spouses.

In some cases, prior knowledge of the other's idiosyncrasies may tend to ease the adjustment of marriage; but in other cases, young people resist marrying the person chosen by their parents. Then the adjustment if difficult indeed, and conflict with the parents may ensue as well.

In the East, marriage entails different problems. Here too, marriages are usually arranged by the parents, albeit later, when the children are nearly old enough to marry. Whereas Utku girls have little or no opportunity for sexual play before marriage, Qipi girls engage in a great deal of casual experimentation as well as, on occasion, more serious courting. "Sweethearts" are a major topic of conversation during adolescence, and already jealousy is rife. However, girls do not necessarily marry one of their sweethearts, and if they are required to marry a man they do not know well, they may look forward to the event with mixed feelings. One young mother, reminiscing with her friends about her marriage, said: "I was so frightened that I cried and cried, because Silasi hadn't been my sweetheart. Someday (and she laughed) I'll have a sweetheart—not Silasi."

There are other reasons too why, in spite of her desire to have a husband and children, a girl may look forward to marriage with some trepidation. It may happen, both among Utku and Qipi but especially among Qipi (who do not marry relatives), that a girl has to marry out of the community where her parents live. This is very likely to be experienced as a hardship, since ties between parents and children are extremely strong.[10] A girl's mother—and if her mother is dead, her father—is her staunchest ally. And allies are very important to people who tend to fear the worst from one another and to be afraid to ask for the slightest consideration, as is the case with many Eskimos.[11] Throughout childhood, one's mother has been a bulwark against the threatening outside world; in adulthood too, she will support one against others who criticize. One is not afraid to ask her for food or lamp oil if these are lacking at home; she will teach one how to live, how to sew complicated clothing, and how to raise one's children; and she is unfailing company when one is lonely. I once heard a middle-aged Qipi woman explain to her brother that his daughter-in-law was worried because she was not feeling well: "She is unhappy and no wonder: she has no one to talk to here, because she has no mother." And an Utku girl I knew who, because of various misfortunes, was still unmarried at the age of about twenty-six, refused two men who came courting her because they would have taken her to live in a distant community and she did not want to leave her father.

In later years, one may come to count on one's husband for support. Spouses are supposed to be loyal to one another and to present a public front of unanimity on important issues; indeed, disloyalty may be grounds for divorce. In many cases, as time passes, loyalties may become very strong indeed, capable of withstanding powerful abuse on the part of one spouse or the other and even community encouragement to dissolve the marriage. As one woman said: "The word *aippara* ['my spouse'; literally, 'my other'] means 'my other self'; it's a very strong word." At the outset, however, a woman may be uncertain whether her husband's support can be relied on, especially in case of conflict with his family, since, as I have said, his filial loyalty is likely to be as strong as hers. On the other hand, if a woman has had an unhappy childhood, she may find in her husband a friend from the outset. One such woman put it strongly: "My husband was the first person who trusted me." And another person said, speaking of an orphan girl who was the scapegoat of everyone in camp: "Now she has nothing at all and is abused by everyone, but if she marries, then she will have food to eat and clothes to wear; she will be able to buy things, and her life will be much better."

There is one more problem attendant on the first years of marriage that deserves mention here. I have said that, as in other societies, husbands and wives have to learn to tolerate each other's idiosyncrasies. But more than that, women have to learn to tolerate being housebound. Before marriage, girls help a great deal at home, but they are generally not responsible for the smooth running of the household. It is not they but their mothers who have to be sure that the lamps are burning properly; that the meat is cooked, ready for the return of the hunters; and that the teakettle is put on to heat when the children shout that the men are coming. Girls can visit their friends more or less at will; they may be recalled at any time to help with a given task but, job accomplished, they can leave again. Most of all, they are not burdened by having to be constantly attuned to the needs of a baby. For young mothers, some restlessness and irritability is mingled with the happiness of motherhood, especially on light spring nights when all their friends are out wandering in the hills or across the inlet. One girl sang a little song about it to her baby one day: "I used to roam all night in the spring, but now I'm always sitting still; I'm becoming an old granny, but I don't mind any more."

The middle-aged and elderly marriages that I have seen contain much more of the companionable warmth that I have described above. Elderly couples spend most of their time at home together, visited by their younger relatives and their children's friends but rarely visiting themselves. "They are tired and they should rest," I was told. Some Eskimos feel that second and subsequent marriages may be warmer and more mutually satisfying than first marriages. One woman said: "A man would do anything for his second wife." The spouses are "grateful to each other" for companionship and care in their older years.

There is increasing satisfaction, too, in seeing one's children grow up around one—the boys become good hunters and the girls skillful housewives. I have said that often there is much warmth in the relationship between mother and daughter. The relationship between mother and son may also be very close. One mother told me that when each of her two oldest sons married and moved away, she had difficulty in sleeping at night because she missed them so. She missed their jokes and their laughter, and the house seemed empty without them and their friends.

I had the impression in Qipisa—and the impression was confirmed by an Eskimo friend from the Hudson Bay area—that sometimes the relationship between husband and wife can take on some of the quality of that between son and mother. One middle-aged husband used to squat beside his two-year-old son in front of his wife's workboard, picking off bits of blubber to eat while she scraped sealskins. Another middle-aged man occasionally sucked from his small son's baby bottle as he lay resting on the sleeping platform. But the most vivid impression is that of seeing—almost every evening—a young mother lying on the sleeping platform, nursing her baby, while her husband lay curled around the baby's back, facing his wife. Each parent had an arm over the child. The girl was ostensibly putting the baby to sleep, but her husband regularly fell asleep too, and slept through the evening. Once, as she got up to resume her work, she looked down at the two sleeping figures and said, smiling wryly: "My two sons." She did not like it that her husband slept away the evenings and did not keep her company: "He's no fun to be with." All three of these women, incidentally, sometimes scolded their husbands as they scolded their children.

It would be interesting to know whether women, too, would like to see parents in their spouses. The father-daughter tie is strong—as evidenced by the number of daughters who are reluctant to leave their fathers when they marry. Nevertheless, on the face of it, I see little evidence of wives treating husbands as fathers, and the same informants who agree that men treat wives as mothers do not see the other situation.[12]

LEFT ALONE

Although many elderly marriages seem warm and companionable while both spouses live, the life of the aged can quickly become lonely and difficult when one of them dies. Sometimes even very old people remarry; but if they do not, they become dependent on the help of their children, who are often but not always kind. If they have no grown children they are really in straits, since loyalties tend not to extend far beyond the nuclear family. Enough help may be offered to keep the old person from starvation, but more than likely it will be offered grudgingly and the recipient will be sensitive to that fact. There are sanctions against neglecting the elderly. It is believed that the thoughts of old people are powerful, so that if such a person broods resentfully, he can injure the one who has harmed him. But fear that an old person will take revenge in this way is not always sufficient to deter those who would be unkind. To be sure, the accumulated wisdom of old people may be valued by their juniors; old men and women are often called on to advise in crises. However, the more feeble and inactive a person becomes, the less likely it is that his or her opinion will be sought.

Often an elderly couple or an old person of either sex whose spouse has died will adopt a grandchild for company and later to help him—in the house if the child is a girl or in hunting if a boy. But at best, old age is a time of crochets and rickets and is not looked forward to by either sex. In pre-Christian days old people to whom life had become distasteful or who felt that they were a burden on their children would ask the latter to help them put an end to it. Occasional people still do commit suicide, but the church frowns on it, so it probably occurs less often now than formerly.

THE WORTH OF A WOMAN

Much of what I have said so far about the lives of Eskimo women, their sources of satisfaction and dissatisfaction, their life goals, and the people who are emotionally important to them must sound familiar to a Western reader. The traditional world of Eskimo women is not so different from that of Western women or, for that matter, of women in many other societies. Women in both Eskimo and Western societies have traditionally been keepers of the home, while the men, dealing with the outside world, have provided the wherewithal for food, clothing, and other domestic necessities. This division of labor means that the house is the woman's territory and that she has the primary responsibility for arranging it, keeping it in good order, feeding and clothing its occupants, and raising the children.

Perhaps even more important, it means that she is the emotional center of the home, the source of warmth and affection, which is symbolized even more than in our society by the giving of food and physical care. It is to her that the children turn when the outside world is unkind; and if she goes next door to visit for a little while, her husband is sure to ask when he comes in from *his* visit: "Where's your mother?"—not because it was wrong of her to go out but because he misses her. I have suggested that some men seem to look for mothers in their wives; this pattern, too, should be familiar to Western readers and is indicative of the emotional importance of women in both societies.

Also related to the economic division of roles is the division of responsibility in the political sphere. I have mentioned the fact that a man is the nominal head of his family in the sense that he is its public spokesman, and that certain particularly visible kinds of decision—such as where to live—are nominally his prerogative to make as well as to announce to others. Women have their own domestic sphere of decision making, and men defer to their judgment in matters that pertain to that sphere. This, of course, is the public view of the situation. In practice, each sex may influence the decisions that the other makes. Sometimes they will consult each other privately; on other occasions the spouse who does not have nominal jurisdiction may take the initiative in making his or her views known, more or less indirectly. With regard to moving, traveling, and hunting, the man has the final say and may ignore his wife's wishes; as I have said, however, a wise man will not do so consistently. He will be restrained both by the Eskimo value that requires a leader to be considerate of those he leads and by his knowledge that his wife may make his life extremely uncomfortable if she is unhappy. Similarly, it is incumbent on a wife to heed her husband's moods and wishes.

One other way in which the role prescriptions for Eskimo men and women appear to run parallel to those for Western men and women has been suggested by Parker (1962, pp. 89–90) and Lubart (1970, p. 36), who say that Eskimo women as compared with men are allowed freer expression of their dependency needs. Though it is sometimes difficult to judge what behavior constitutes expression of a dependency need and therefore how male and female expressions compare with one another, I agree that dependency is a problem for Eskimos and therefore may be a source of conflict in relationships between men and women. This will be discussed further below.

Here the crucial point to be made is that the apparent similarities between the traditional role behaviors of Eskimo and Western women should not mislead one into assuming that the quality of female life is similar in both cases. This is the usual anthropological caution to the effect that one should look at situations from the points of view of the actors as well as from that of the observer. But it seems a necessary point to reiterate, especially with regard to the present subject, in these days of acute sensitivity to "male dominance." Western women, as we know, increasingly resent the clear division of labor and of authority that was traditional in Western society and their domestic, private, dependent role vis-à-vis men. Some, for complicated reasons, even resent the fact that they are sexually attractive to men. But the separateness of roles is not enough in and of itself to create dissatisfaction among the incumbents. To be unhappy with his lot, either a person must have learned to want something other than what he has or can have, or he must see that other people's roles are more highly valued than his own, or both. In other words, he must feel relatively deprived and/or relatively worthless. Therefore the important question is whether Eskimo women feel deprived or worthless as compared with their men.[13] I am not sure that the available data permit us to answer these questions, but we can at least look at the evidence pro and con.

Let us look first at what Eskimo women have traditionally learned to value—and I think it is necessary to distinguish between what they have learned to want for themselves and what they have learned to admire in others. A person may admire doctors or princesses, astronauts or mothers, and yet not want to be one.

So what have Eskimo women traditionally wanted to be? I think in most cases the answer is clear: mothers, and skillful wives of good hunters. They are not taught men's skills (with the exceptions that I have mentioned), nor are they directly taught to want them. A girl enjoys her own skills as play during her childhood, and the transition to adult responsibility is relatively gradual and, especially in the Central Arctic, unpressured. As a girl's competence develops, she is rewarded by being relied on to do her share as a functional member of the household. She may also be praised by both men and women, though praise of older children tends to be muted. Such children (both male and female) are considered to know that they are loved and appreciated without being directly told so. All these factors—association with play, appreciation, lack of pressure—should contribute to a woman's satisfaction with her role.

Women do, however, learn to associate the activities of men with all the most exciting events in their lives: the bringing in of meat and feasting, the return of a trading expedition, the arrival of visitors, and moving camp. Hunting, traveling, trading, and intercamp visiting are considered by both sexes to be among the most pleasurable activities in camp life, and men have far more opportunities to engage in them than women do. The glamour of a male life is vivid to women; they identify with the men and derive much vicarious pleasure from listening to the men's tales of their adventures and also from watching men hunt, when they do it within sight of camp or when traveling *en famille*. My question is: Do women actually want to hunt and travel themselves and therefore, presumably, resent being women, or do they value men the more because the latter are the source of all good things? Some women talk as if they do, to some extent, envy men the excitement, variety, and challenge of their lives; they imagine what fun it would be to be a man, to be free to travel and to visit other camps at will, wherever and whenever one chose. They enjoy taking a gun and going off after birds or hares, and they look forward to accompanying their fathers or brothers on occasional trips.

However, there is another side to male life which women are also vividly aware of—a difficult, rigorous, and sometimes dangerous side. A hunter and fisherman, obviously, must have many skills and strengths, not only knowledge of how to find and kill the game but also knowledge of the land itself: how to travel and find one's way in unfamiliar country or in a blinding blizzard or "whiteout," the peculiar Arctic condition in which a sense of perspective is so completely lost that it is impossible to see the ground under one's feet; how to build an iglu or keep warm without an iglu if necessary; how to melt ice for drinking water without a fire or make fire without a match. Eskimo men also need strength, patience, and endurance incredible to a white man: strength to heave a heavily loaded sled up over the jagged ice of pressure ridges or to right it single-handed when it overturns; to carry enormous loads of caribou meat, wet hides, household equipment, and possibly a three- or four-year-old child for miles across soggy tundra; patience and endurance to stand for hours motionless and freezing over a seal hole, waiting for the seal to come up to breathe so that it can be killed; to go without food and sleep for several days if necessary; or to walk 50 or 75 miles back to camp to fetch a skidoo part and then, after a cup of tea and a meal, walk back to the broken-down skidoo. All these male qualities have been described by others, but it is less often pointed out that most of them are qualities that Eskimo women do not have to have. And the fact that, by and large, they do not have them is an important factor in their view of male life. Camp women have traveled enough in their seasonal migrations and on trading and visiting trips to have tasted hardship and to be able to empathize with their men. Moreover, most women have lost men who were dear to them—fathers, brothers, husbands, or sons—in accidents. So although they may have fantasies about the fun and excitement in a man's life, they also know very well that they temselves lead much easier lives and that they are dependent for their very survival on the male activities that seem both more difficult and more dangerous than their own. It was this knowledge that made one woman say to me: "We want to do what we can to help [men] because they take care of us."[14] It was also this knowledge that led one of the same girls, who had remarked enviously that she would rather be a man, to grumble and complain when a male relative asked her to come sealing with him one day to help find breathing holes. A hunter's life is fascinating from a distance, but on closer view it is often wet, cold, monotonous, and hungry. One elderly man remarked in a regretful tone that in the old days, women used to help men hunt a great deal more than they do now. And when I asked why they no longer do so, he said: "They don't want to."

The other area of male activity from which women are excluded is that of public performance and decision making, and here too one must ask whether exclusion entails feelings of deprivation. What have women learned to want for themselves? The childhood training of both sexes teaches them first to enjoy self-display and then to fear it; the teasing to which they are subjected makes both boys and girls intensely sensitive to criticism and teaches them to withdraw silently in face of it. Under these circumstances, it seems likelier that men should envy women their privilege of retiring and not having to take responsibility for decisions that might turn out to be foolish and laughable than that women should envy men their opportunities for public self-expression. If there is envy on either side, it must at least be tinged with ambivalence. I met few camp women who were not extremely embarrassed and unhappy if required to express an opinion or state a wish in public. Of course, it may be that this reticence is due not so much to fear that one's opinion will be criticized as to knowledge that public performance on the part of a woman is unbecoming.[15] However, most men also exercise their public privileges with considerable restraint, withdrawing as quickly as women when threatened, for example, by older men or by strangers, no matter how slight the "threat" appears to a Westerner. If a man does not exercise restraint, he is labeled a showoff. Thus sanctions against self-assertion are applied to both sexes, not just to women.

To be sure, within his own family circle, a man may express his wishes more directly than his wife—except perhaps in Qipisa, and I am not sure how unusual Qipisa may be in this respect. But the indirect expression of wishes may be equally effective when others are attuned to this mode of communication, as Eskimos are. And again, if one expresses one's wishes indirectly, one is spared the risk of embarrassment in the event that one is refused or that the decision turns out badly. We have seen that men have the power of veto but that they are obliged to use it with discretion or take the consequences. The fear of being criticized by both men and women is a powerful motivation underlying the consideration of leaders for those they lead—in other words, the consideration of men for women.

The second factor that is involved in satisfaction—feelings of self-worth —is, of course, closely related to the first—feelings of deprivation—and is equally difficult to evaluate. What is the worth of a woman as compared with that of a man in the eyes of the Eskimo world and especially in the eyes of Eskimo men?[16] Do men devalue women?

It has been said that Eskimo women have less prestige—or at least less ascribed prestige—than Eskimo men (Parker, 1962; p. 90; Lubart, 1970, pp. 24–36). But I am not sure that Eskimo men and women themselves see matters in this way. The evidence seems to me a little unclear. On the one hand, differential prestige does not inevitably follow from differences in skill. It is not necessary that men should derogate women just because the skills of the latter are different, and I have no evidence that Eskimo men consciously do so. Men and women each have their own realm, as we have seen, and prestige accrues to excellence in each.

Women's remarks indicate that they like to feel needed, and they certainly have every reason to feel that they are needed—emotionally, sexually, and economically. I have mentioned their importance as the affectional center of the home, not only for their children but for their husbands as well in many cases. Moreover, the skills of women are as indispensable to survival as are those of men, and they are so perceived by men. Lubart (1970, p. 26) quotes a Baffin Island saying to the effect that "A man is the hunter his wife makes him." Without carefully fashioned fur clothing and waterproof skin boots, a man could easily freeze to death. To be sure, that is a little less true now that Western-style Arctic clothing can be bought, but Eskimo clothing is warmer and is still preferred by many men; even men who wear store-bought parkas admire the skill of a good seamstress. I was told that in the old days a man might commit murder to obtain a good seamstress as a wife, and that if a man froze his feet, it was his wife who was blamed. These stories may be apocryphal, but they express the value placed on the feminine craft of sewing. The question, "Which is better (or more important), a good hunter or a good seamstress?" is meaningless in Eskimo; both are indispensable.

Differential prestige does not necessarily follow from the existence of different spheres of decision making either. I have asked Eskimos, both men and women, whether men are considered to have more intelligence or better judgment than women, and I am consistently told no: men have better judgment concerning the things they have been taught and women have better judgment concerning the things *they* have been taught. The fact that the man makes certain kinds of decisions for his family and is its public spokesman is not rationalized in terms of his inherent superiority over the woman; it is just "appropriate" that way. Men may resent a woman's intruding on their male areas of decision making (and vice versa), but they are not threatened by women who publicly correct or elaborate their stories. More freely than some Westerners, they will openly admit to ignorance and ask their wives for advice, not only with regard to matters that pertain to female competence (the placing of a tent, the use of a particular fur) but also with regard to other matters. Moreover, dislike of female bossiness does not prevent men from appreciating women who acquire male skills; I have mentioned the admiration that is expressed for women who are good hunters and the old man's regret that women hunt as little as they do.

In our society, many men are ambivalent about marriage; they defensively derogate the institution even as they embrace it. Eskimo men do not do that. A particular man may derogate a particular woman or make her feel unwanted or unneeded, but I have never heard a man derogate women in general or marriage in general. It seems likely that this makes a considerable difference in a woman's own view of her wifely role.

BETWEEN THE LINES

So far, the evidence supports the view that Eskimo men do not derogate women. But the data I have drawn on consist largely of conscious statements, and behavior based on conscious views, concerning the worth of women. What about unconscious views? Is there any evidence that women are unconsciously devalued? Or are there any theoretical grounds for hypothesizing that such devaluation might exist?

To begin with the second question: It seems to me there are three possible reasons why men in any society might disparage women.

1. Disparagement could be a reaction to being mistreated by women in some way. For example, if women regularly make their sons or husbands feel weak, incompetent, or neglected, or if they regularly usurp male prerogatives, then one might expect men to fear and hate women and to retaliate in some way.

2. On the other hand, disparagement could be a reaction to a desire to remain dependent on a highly gratifying woman (or women). If such dependence were not considered proper in a man, he might need to compensate himself for giving it up, and one possible compensation is the rationalization that "women (or their ways of living) are no good anyway."

3. Similarly, a man might disparage women to compensate himself for a hidden desire to *be* a woman, in the event that he perceives female life to be more satisfying or easier than his own male life and thus enviable.

Other observers have said—or implied—that all these dynamics are found in Eskimo society. Lubart (1970) thinks that Eskimo men both envy women and want to be dependent on them. On the one hand, he hypothesizes that the vicissitudes of hunting are a constant threat to the male ego and that "one powerful mode of ego support lies in a form of male solidarity in which the female is derogated and her role reduced in importance" (1970, pp. 34–35). On the other hand, he considers that the long period of symbiotic attachment to the mother in childhood has created "deep and prolonged wishes to remain cared for . . . [and] marked enhancement of the need for female approval. Denial of this dependence, revelation of which could be embarrassing to the male ego, could take the form of male derision of the female role" (1970, p. 36). In other words, when a boy gives up a soft life in the shelter of his mother's affection and instead undertakes an arduous, dangerous, and very unpredictable life as a hunter, he may compensate himself by persuading himself that a hunter's life is, after all, more important and valuable than that of a "mere" woman.

A slightly different but related view is taken by Freeman (1968; 1971), who posits that the exigencies of decision making require that there be an ultimate authority; that this (for unspecified reasons)[17] must be the male, and that females pose a threat to this authority through their "assertiveness, indispensability, and . . . domestic autonomy" (1971, p. 1015). Thus in Freeman's view, as in Lubart's, Eskimo men feel weak vis-à-vis women and might be expected to take it out on the latter as a way of proving to themselves that they are not weak but strong.

Starting from the assumption that men do derogate women, Lubart argues further that because a person "unconsciously fears and projects a fearsome image of those whom he treats badly," men have a latent fear of women (1970, pp. 28, 35, 36). So the unconscious defense—disparagement—that men set up against their envy of women backfires, intensifying their fear of women. Paradoxically, disparagement and consequent fear of women might also be expected to intensify male dependence on women, since if one is divided in spirit between embracing and rejecting, the "embracing" self may fight the "rejecting" self and cling even more closely to what it fears to lose. Thus a vicious circle might be established: men disparage women in order to assert their strength and independence, but the disparagement has the unanticipated consequence of creating a fear of women which intensifies dependence on them—in turn increasing the need to assert independence by disparagement.

So far, disparagement has been seen mainly as a reaction to dependence and envy. The third explanation that has been suggested is that it is revenge for female derogation of men. The idea that women make men feel foolish and incompetent is implicit in Freeman's argument, which was outlined above. Rasmussen (1931, p. 191) and Freuchen (1961, pp. 86–87 and passim) are more explicit. They speak of the scathing tongues of women, which are freely directed toward men. Lubart agrees (1970, p. 27) and attributes this behavior to female resentment at being "exploited" by men. I have tried to show that there is little reason to believe that women perceive themselves to be exploited. However, it may be that they do to some extent envy the glamorous side of male life. A small girl's liking for self-display may also leave a residue that contributes to envy of men, in spite of (or perhaps even because of) later, very stringent training in self-effacement. In any case, if women do envy men and express it by mocking them, it is not impossible that men might repay them in kind.

This raises the possibility that derogation might be mutual, due to reciprocal envy. There is another reason, too, to expect that ambivalence might be entertained by both sexes, and that is the nature of Eskimo attitudes toward dependence. Lubart's suggestion that men may be embarrassed by their dependent needs has already been mentioned. He also notes (1961, p. 31) that an avoidance of close ties is characteristic of *both* sexes, as a reaction to the fragility of life and fear of loss. Elsewhere (1970, pp. 71–72; 1972), I have tried to show how Eskimo child-rearing practices create in all children this ambivalence about loving and being loved. Nevertheless, it is possible that dependence is more threatening to men than to women for the reasons already mentioned. A man's ambivalence may also be directed against women more than against men, since it is attachments to females that he has to throw off in order to grow up (if he does have to throw off attachments in order to grow up), whereas a woman has no special reason to direct her fear of affection toward men.

To sum up these arguments, then, one might expect to find tension between men and women on several grounds: (1) a male's need to bolster his ego; (2) reciprocal envy; and (3) ambivalence about affection and dependence, which is shared by both sexes but may be more pronounced on the part of the man. These arguments can be better evaluated after we have looked at the nature of tensions between men and women.

Is there, in fact, tension between the sexes, and if so, does it take the form of devaluation of women?[18] Lubart sees depreciation of the female by the male and her consequent resentment as important foci of tension in Eskimo society (1970, p. 34). In support of this view, he says that women do a "prodigious amount of work," processing meat and hides while their husbands sit around drinking tea and relaxing (1970, p. 26); that men are "dominant in the family . . . having complete authority with regard to hunting locations and camp movements" (1970, p. 26); that " 'use' is one of the words employed to denote sexual relations with a woman" (1970, p. 26); that traditional marriage (in Greenland) simulated kidnapping (1970, p. 29); and that one of the acts derided in song duels was " 'to be a crybaby like a woman' " (1970, p. 27). He also considers female infanticide an indication that men denigrate women (1970, p. 24), and Freeman (1968; 1971) too, as we have seen, hypothesizes that infanticide is an assertion of male dominance.

To support the view that men stand in ambivalent awe of women, Lubart points to Eskimo mythology (1970, p. 35). The two major deities are female, one the source of death from freezing and starvation, the other the provider (and sometimes withholder) of game. And various hero tales feature women who are cannibalistic or castrating.

Evidence that women resent their role Lubart sees in the high rate of adoption (willingness to give away one's children), the failure to romanticize pregnancy (1970, p. 29), the symbolism of "kidnapping" a bride (resisting marriage), and the ridicule or silent rejection with which women sometimes treat men (1970, p. 27).

Another author who argues at length that Eskimo women have reason to feel put upon is Parker (1962). He concludes that "in traditional Eskimo life, the woman's role carried with it more disabilities and less prestige than that of the man" (1962, p. 90), and he explains the prevalence of hysteria (*piblokto*) among females on these grounds. Parker draws on a wider variety of sources than Lubart, but his points in the main duplicate the latter's. He mentions that it is the man's prerogative to make decisions concerning marriage and wife exchange; that a woman (in East Greenland) serves her husband and "dread(s) to incur (his) displeasure"; and that (in Southwest Alaska) "all of the formally stated criteria for the achievement of prestige relate to the male role" (1962, p. 90).[19] He also makes two points in addition to Lubart's which are important to mention. One is that women may be physically abused by their husbands; the other is that the taboos traditionally applicable to women were more stringent than those applicable to men. A woman's offenses were regarded as more serious, and she was considered to have a greater power to contaminate (1962, p. 90).

The evidence that is cited to show that Eskimo men dominate and disparage their women can, then, be summarized as follows: men overwork women, exploit them sexually, and punish them severely for misbehavior—either by abusing them physically or by imposing taboos on them harsher than those they impose on themselves. Further, men destroy female infants, scorn female character, and arrogate to themselves all the important decisions and all the prestigious activities. Women, in turn, are said to react to this situation by symbolically resisting marriage, refusing to glorify pregnancy, giving away their children, making cutting remarks to their husbands, and—in extreme cases—rejecting them or becoming hysterical. Distress is ultimately expressed in the mythology, in which women destroy their tormentors.

Obviously, in compiling in this way the various pieces of data used by other observers of Eskimo culture, I have created something of a straw man and done violence to their arguments. No one author has drawn such a horrendous picture as this summary presents. However, even in their original contexts, many of these observations seem to be enthnocentrically interpreted. The problem is to separate the latter from other observations that are cogent and deserve to be considered carefully.

I have suggested alternative interpretations for some of the data, in particular those having to do with the division of labor, authority, and prestige. We should also be careful not to interpret Eskimo sexual codes in our own terms. It is true that, in many parts of the Arctic, a young woman's parents had the final say about whom she married; but the young man was equally subject to the will of his parents. As for being "kidnapped," Freuchen (1961, pp. 87–88) makes it quite clear that, on one level, at least, Greenlandic women enjoyed it: it was sexually exciting; it allowed them to put on a demure show of resisting advances that were in fact attractive to them; and it gave them an opportunity to be the center of attention in the community—an opportunity to say: "See how desirable I am." And the word *atuqtuq,* which Lubart translates as "use," does not, as far as I know, have the exploitative connotations that the English word *use* has in reference to a woman. It can also be glossed as "borrow" in opposition to "possess," and as "actualize" or "be in relation to" with reference to time and space. It is certainly true, as Lubart says (1970, p. 31), that pragmatic, utilitarian attitudes play an important role in Eskimo interpersonal relations; but, as he correctly observes, this is "a utility not based on crass use of one another, but rather on the exchange of 'utility potentials,' unabashed and without hypocrisy." Moreover, women are as likely to regard their husbands in utilitarian terms as vice versa.

With regard to Parker's point that Eskimo women fear physical abuse at the hands of their husbands, I would ask several questions, both about the circumstances in which abuse occurs and about the ways in which it is perceived. First, is it standard and approved practice for a man to strike his wife, or is it aberrant behavior? If the latter, it surely cannot be considered an indication that women in general are devalued, as it would be if women were considered "like dogs," creatures whom it is correct and even praiseworthy to strike.

Nowadays, physical violence of any sort directed toward anyone, male or female, is aberrant and strongly disapproved among Canadian and Alaskan Eskimos. It is not considered an appropriate way to demonstrate masculinity. I am uncertain about the traditional Greenlandic Eskimos; some of the literature from that area (Freuchen, 1961; Rasmussen, 1908, p. 56) sounds as if it were "machismo" behavior there, but it also sounds as if women rather encouraged it, on occasion. I have already mentioned Freuchen's description of the way in which Greenlandic women interpreted "kidnapping." To be sure, this refers to cases in which the violence was due to conflict over sexual advances, not cases in which the woman was being punished for behavior that had annoyed her husband. With regard to the latter—which also seems to have occurred in Greenland (Holtved, 1967, p. 147; Mirsky, 1937, p. 68) and perhaps elsewhere (Rasmussen, 1931, p. 191)—I would ask, first, how severe the "beating" was or was perceived to be and, second, whether it is perhaps ethnocentric of us to assume, on the face of it, that physical punishment is necessarily perceived as more vicious than verbal abuse or the rejecting behavior described by Lubart (1970, p. 27), which was the woman's means of punishing her husband. In fact, both are considered so bad that it is difficult to decide which is worse. Fear of physical aggression is indicated by the fact that Eskimos construe even a light slap as a severe "beating." Among present-day Canadian and Alaskan Eskimos, gossip concerning aggression that we would consider fairly mild is quickly blown up into reports of full-scale beatings.[20] On the other hand, verbal abuse is also feared. I have mentioned that Eskimo child-rearing practices rely heavily on teasing and thus tend to create personalities that are extremely sensitive to slights and to criticism. The fact, cited by Lubart (1970, p. 36), that Eskimo men who are rejected by their wives may become severely depressed and even commit suicide certainly supports the view that nonphysical forms of aggression are perceived as severe. In this connection, it is perhaps significant that Lubart does not say that women who are beaten by their husbands commit suicide.

The fact that men strike their wives and women criticize their husbands is, of course, good evidence of tension. But so far, I see no evidence that the tension is either caused by or expressed in a pattern of devaluing women. It could just as well be caused by vicissitudes of living together that are independent of cultural attitudes toward the sexes.

The remaining data are more difficult to evaluate. First, there is Lubart's observation that women are considered to be "crybabies." It is true that men and women are considered to have slightly different temperaments, and the perceived differences are both positive and negative. On the negative side, women are thought to gossip more than men and to be more bad-tempered (at least toward children), and men are thought to be headstrong and self-willed. These reciprocal accusations again suggest the existence of tension between the sexes, and this time the tension does appear to be expressed in derogatory stereotypes. But the stereotypes are reciprocal, not just one-way: men disparage aspects of female character and vice versa. Again we must ask, what motivates the tension? And who started it? We are not yet justified in assuming that men are the prime movers and women are merely retaliating.

What about the fact that the taboos imposed on women were more stringent than those imposed on men and that women were considered to be more contaminating than men? It may be true, as Parker suggests (1962, p. 90), that the regulations to which women were subject were experienced as frustrating. However, I do not think we can assume that they necessarily indicate that women were considered of less worth than men. Just the reverse may be true; that is, being subject to taboos may have been a price that women paid for being considered more important than men. A third possibility, which seems very likely, is that the taboos express an ambivalence about women—an ambivalence of the same sort that seems to be expressed in the myths about female gods, some of whom are good, maternal providers and others dangerously engulfing.[21] The possibility that women are regarded ambivalently will be discussed further below.

The datum most embarrassing to my argument is the female infanticide formerly practiced by the Netsilingmiut and perhaps by other groups as well. The Eskimos themselves explain it as an unhappy ecological necessity rather than as an expression of hostility toward females. Freeman argues that the *effects* of the custom are, indeed, ecologically adaptive and thus maintain the practice, but he thinks that the Netsilingmiut could hardly be aware of these long-range implications of infanticide. Therefore it is necessary to look for a cultural rather than an ecological *cause* for the practice. I am in accord with Freeman's attempt to separate effects from causes, but in the absence of other evidence of intense conflict between the sexes, I have difficulty in accepting the particular cause that he posits.

An alternative interpretation has been suggested by George Park (personal communication, 1972). He starts from the assumption (with which I agree) that Eskimos do not place the same absolute value on life that we do, so that children have to "apply for admittance"; they are not simply accepted on the ground that they happen to be born. If this is so, then it is necessary to ask why a girl should be given preferential admittance over a boy. Or, to put it in different terms, why should a boy be killed rather than a girl? Given the fact that, nominally at least, it is the father who makes the decision for life or death, two possible reasons for destroying male children come to mind: fear of one's successor or fear (dislike) of maleness. On the other hand, if these fears are not compelling—and they do not seem to be so in Eskimo society—a man might have strong reasons for allowing his sons to live. A man lives on in his successor; he identifies with him. Moreover, he enjoys his son's companionship and help on the hunt. A girl provides much less companionship for a hunter. One of her major values from the male point of view is sexual, and sexual behavior is disallowed between father and daughter. Therefore, given the pragmatic attitudes of Eskimo interpersonal relationships, perhaps one should see female infanticide as preferential acceptance of males rather than as preferential destruction of females, motivated by hostility.

The simplest explanation of all, of course, would be that Eskimos do perceive short-term ecological effects (more hunters in a man's family means more food for his family), even though they are not aware of the long-term effects of infanticide on the balance between population and resources. Thus perhaps more weight should be given to the Netsilingmiuts' own interpretation of their behavior.

In any case, as Park (personal communication, 1972) points out, regardless of the motivation for killing girl babies, the fact that women are in relatively short supply means that they are in a strong power position vis-à-vis men. A wife is likely to be treated with consideration and respect, since she is not easy to replace.

So far, we have been considering the evidence that is usually adduced to show that Eskimo men devalue women, and I have suggested alternative interpretations for some of the data. The data that have been interpreted as expressions of female resentment can also be seen in another light. For example, take Lubart's statement that the Eskimo woman's failure to romanticize pregnancy is an indication of ambivalence toward her maternal role (1970, p. 29). Might not a tendency to romanticize equally well be construed as an expression of ambivalence: a compensation for fear, distaste, or resentment? An unsentimental view of pregnancy, on the other hand, might indicate a realistic acceptance of its vicissitudes.

Lubart's assumption (1970, p. 29) that the high adoption rate characteristic of Eskimos indicates ambivalence concerning motherhood may also be susceptible of reinterpretation. I agree that children may be ambivalently regarded, but I have tried to show elsewhere (1972) that the negative side of the ambivalence is fear of loss, due in large measure to a high infant mortality rate rather than the mother's resentment at her lot as a female. It may well be true that a mother who gives a child away feels hostile to the child, but the hostility need not be the reason why the child is given away; it could be a way of dealing with the grief of separation. Denial and suppressed anger are common Eskimo reactions to unhappiness.

Finally, there is Parker's argument that Eskimo women who feel deprived or frustrated would be likely to express their feelings in hysterical behavior. He hypothesizes that hysterical behavior is correlated with a high expectation that dependency needs will be gratified. He suggests that Eskimo child-rearing practices create such expectations and that in Eskimo society, as in most others, females are "allowed greater (and less discontinuous) satisfaction of dependency needs" than men are (1962, p. 89). Hence, when their expectations are frustrated, they tend to become hysterical—to cry for help, in other words.

On the whole, this makes excellent sense. However, in order to explain the higher incidence of hysteria among women, it is not necessary to assume that women tend to feel more deprived than men do. Alternative explanations might be that dependent needs, of which hysterical behavior is a manifestation, are more threatening to men than to women, as Lubart thinks, or that—as Parker himself implies—men have a lower expectation that such needs will be gratified. It is not at all clear to me which sex has the greater freedom to express dependency needs. The division of labor is such that, when life goes smoothly, each spouse has tangible reason to feel cared for, being fed and warmed by the other. Women sit at home, comfortably sewing and visiting, while the men are out on the tiring and sometimes dangerous search for food; then, when the men come home, they have their turn at being cared for by the women who serve them. On the other hand, when things go badly, either spouse may perceive the other to be at fault and may blame or punish after his or her fashion. Quite possibly it is a mistake to phrase the question of freedom of expression quantitatively. A more productive question might be: Under what circumstances may men and women express dependence, and in what forms? For example,

Eastern Eskimo women feel freer to cry than men do—a fact that may be relevant to the choice of hysteria as a mode of expression. It would be interesting to know whether men who feel deprived express it through some symptomatology other than hysteria or through some means other than mental illness.

In sum, it seems clear that tensions and ambivalences, which are largely unconscious, do complicate relationships between Eskimo men and women, however mildly. They are visible in the mythology and perhaps also in the more stringent taboos placed on women. They may underlie the feeling that it is not manly to behave in certain respects like a woman (and not womanly to behave like a man)—a feeling that is expressed in reciprocal teasing and in negative stereotypes about aspects of male and female expressive behavior. Tension of some sort may also be one of the motivations underlying the publicly reserved behavior of each sex toward the other—behavior which one man explained by saying that men feel freer to talk and laugh with men, and women with women (Briggs, 1970, p. 92).

How are the tensions to be explained? We have seen that for other authors, male devaluation of women and female resentment and retaliation is the focal issue. I am not, however, convinced that mutual ambivalences are expressed either in depreciation of the woman's role or in behavior that is perceived, consciously or unconsciously, as exploitative. And if men are not exploitative, then women, presumably, have no reason to be resentful on that score.

We have not, however, disposed of the possibility that men and women may envy each other. In women, we have seen that envy might be aroused by the glamorous side of male life. It is also possible that, in spite of the costs involved in public performance, there may remain in adults of both sexes a residue of the liking for self-display that was engendered in them as small children, in which case women could envy men their public prominence. In men, envy could be related to the woman's easier and more protected life and to the greater opportunity allowed her for the expression of dependent needs—if her opportunities are, indeed, greater.

It would be interesting to know how many Eskimo women really wish they had been born men, and vice versa. People may symbolically change sex by giving their names to a newborn child of the opposite sex, thereby becoming that child. Theoretically, either sex may do this, but how often it actually happens, I do not know. Eastern Eskimos believe that an infant can change its sex from male to female at the moment of birth. Midwives see this happen occasionally; but it never happens in reverse—that is, the sex never changes from female to male. Might this indicate that it is men who wish to be women, and not vice versa?[22] The "effeminate" or "childlike" behavior that I observed among Qipisa men may be another indication that the desire to remain a child or to grow up female is strong.

"Effeminate" behavior is certainly also an indication that men have dependent needs. And ambivalence about dependence is, to my mind, the most critical factor engendering tension in intimate relationships on both sides, male and female. There are ample grounds for such ambivalence, even in the absence of exploitation. On the one hand, the mother is by far the most important nurturant figure in the life of an Eskimo child of either sex (Lubart, 1970, pp. 35–36; Briggs, 1970 and 1972). The period of nurturance and indulgence is long, and the mother may intensify the child's dependence by possessive behavior and by educational teasing, which is designed to make the child fear rejection and criticism from others—especially others outside the family. On the other hand, some of the mother's teasing in which she herself threatens withdrawal—her scoldings and also certain physically aggressive expressions of affection such as biting, pinching, and squeezing (Briggs, 1972)—frighten and anger the child and make him (or her) want to withdraw from the close affectional relationship. I see this as one of the probable bases of the strong value that adult Eskimos place on autonomy and self-sufficiency. As an Utku man said to me: "People don't like to feel uncomfortable; if one doesn't love too much it is good" (Briggs, 1970, p. 72). However, since the child still needs his mother and is very much rewarded by her warmth and care, one may imagine that his negative feeling toward her—his wish to detach himself—could be extremely threatening to him and could intensify his dependence and his need for her approval. And in fact, the emotional dependence of adults of both sexes on their parents seems to be extremely strong.

So far, what I have said applies to both sexes. It is necessary to consider, however, whether there are reasons why male ambivalence about affection should be directed toward women more than female ambivalence is directed toward men. The all-important role of the mother in child rearing does seem to be such a reason. We have seen the possibility that women are unconsciously considered more important than men; the deities are female, taboos imposed on women are more stringent, male infants may metamorphose into females at birth but not vice versa. All these facts could indicate the emotional centrality of the woman. So it is preeminently the woman from whom children of both sexes have to detach themselves, to the extent that a need for detachment is felt.

The question is, to what extent *is* it necessary for a man to throw off his attachment to his mother in order to grow up? To what extent is feminine or dependent behavior considered unmanly? Certainly, there are attempts to set up barriers between the sexes; we have noted negative stereotypes about aspects of male and female character and the publicly reserved behavior of each sex toward the other. Further, the public deference shown to men might perhaps be construed as compensation either for a painful separation or for a painful dependence on an emotionally strong and indispensable figure.

On the other hand, however, we have noted that in certain respects men seem less threatened by feminine behavior in men and by masculine behavior in women than are their Western counterparts, which might indicate that male egos are strong and unconcerned about dependence on women. Lubart argues that, as hunters, men must be more self-sufficient than women. But I wonder whether the "conflict" that we see between being a mature and independent hunter and indulging dependent wishes in one's leisure moments is an artifact of our own ways of conceptualizing personality. To us, "independent" and "dependent" behavior are seen as symptomatic of pervasive "personality" traits and thus as mutually exclusive rather than situationally specific traits which can coexist comfortably. Men do express dependent needs to an extent that is striking to a Western observer. I have already mentioned the "mother-son" quality of some Qipisa marriages. Dependence also seems to be freely expressed in relationships among young men, who engage in a great deal of close physical contact with one another, sometimes with sexual overtones. The fact that they engage openly in such behavior tempers what I have said about fear of dependence in general, and it certainly does not lend support to the view that men have greater dependency problems than women do.

Conclusion

Two rather different pictures on the relationships between Eskimo men and women emerge from the data discussed in this paper—one based largely on conscious ideology and behavior, the other drawing on unconscious material as well. The latter picture is considerably less clear than the former. In the conscious view, both men and women emerge as important, appreciated, and cared for. Nonetheless, it has been suggested that tension between men and women might be expected on several grounds: (1) a male's need to bolster his ego, (2) reciprocal envy, and (3) ambivalence about affection and dependence.

With regard to the male ego, I would say that particular men must certainly suffer from uncertainties about their competence and worth as individuals, just as particular women must suffer. Nevertheless, I see no evidence of systematic, institutionalized mistreatment of one sex by the other and therefore no reason to attribute unease to such a cause. We have seen that there may be grounds for a certain amount of envy on both sides but that, at the same time, there are strong rewards built into the roles of both men and women which, under ordinary circumstances, should keep the envy well in check. It would be interesting to know to what extent envy is actually felt, consciously or unconsciously, by either sex.

A great deal still needs to be known also concerning the strength of the ambivalence about affection and the cultural and idiosyncratic forms that it takes. How painful is dependence? In what situations is it legitimate for men and women to express it? Do men direct their ambivalence primarily against women, who are perceived as nurturant but dangerously powerful? Against whom do women focus their ambivalence? Do the rewards accruing to a man from a close relationship with a woman tend to counterbalance the wish to withdraw from her? In traditional Eskimo culture, ambivalence about dependence usually acts in a complex way to cement the relationship with the person toward whom one is ambivalent. But does it also motivate rejecting behavior on occasion? Or do the rewards of maintaining feminine approval (together with sanctions against aggression in general) tend to inhibit tendencies to behave hostilely toward women? The fact of being an independent, competent hunter must, of course, be rewarding in itself, thus lessening the need to compensate for separation in other, more destructive, ways. Separation can be an adventure.

But only further observation can clearly answer these questions. Meanwhile, my tentative conclusion is that in the traditional culture, though there may be a good deal of variation in the extent to which ambivalence about affection is a problem to individuals and variation also in the ways in which ambivalence is handled, nevertheless, in general, it takes rather benign forms and is not clearly directed toward one sex or the other. Whether it is directed by both sexes toward children is another question. Some of my data (Briggs, 1972) suggest that this may be the case, but again more observation is needed. In any case, I would rephrase one of Lubart's conclusions concerning potential sources of conflict in traditional Eskimo culture. Where he lists male dominance and female resentment (1970, p. 34), I would substitute ambivalence about loving and being loved. It is probable that the situation Lubart describes has arisen because of the experiences of men and women in contact with Western culture. But in the traditional culture, I see no conscious, institutionalized conflict between men and women and also—as societies go—relatively little unconscious potential for tension that is specifically directed by one sex toward the other. This is not to say that Eskimo interpersonal relations are free from conflict. They are full of conflict, but (to repeat) very little of the conflict seems to be institutionalized between the sexes.

NOTES

The fieldwork on which this chapter is based was done in the Canadian Northwest Territories over a period of nine years. In the Central Arctic, I have spent a total of thirty months, as follows:

1963 to 1965:   Seventeen months in Chantrey Inlet and four months in Gjoa Haven
       1968:   Seven months in Chantrey Inlet and one month in Gjoa Haven
       1971:   One month in Gjoa Haven
In the Eastern Arctic, I have spent a total of nine months:
       1970:   One month in Pangnirtung and one month in Qipisa
       1971:   Seven months in Qipisa
The fieldwork was supported by the Wenner-Gren Foundation, the Northern Co-
ordination and Research Centre of the Department of Northern Affairs and National
Resources (now the Northern Science Research Group of the Department of Indian
Affairs and Northern Development) of the Canadian Government, the National Institute
of Mental Health of the United States Government (Predoctoral Research Fellowship
No. 5 F1 MH-20, 701-02 BEH, with Research Grant Attachment No. MH-07951-01), and
the Canada Council (award from Isaak Walton Killam bequest to the Department of
Sociology and Anthropology of Memorial University of Newfoundland).
    The interpretive portions of this paper have benefited greatly from discussions with
the following colleagues and friends: Robert Bettarel, Minnie Freeman, Clinton Herrick,
George Park, Robert Paine, Ronald Schwartz, Victoria Steinitz, and Cato Wadel.
    I have used the ethnographic present to refer to the Chantrey Inlet situation of the
Utkuhikhalingmiut, although in the last few years they have gradually been moving into
Gjoa Haven and now seem permanently settled there. The Qipisamiut seem to be in
the process of moving into Pangnirtung, but about half of them still live in Qipisa as
of March 1972.

1. I refer to the traditional, shallow, half-moon-shaped Eskimo lamp with a wick a
foot or two in length laid along the flat edge.

2. At the time my study of the Utku was begun, the core of the group was an
extended family that consisted of two elderly brothers and their offspring of both sexes,
including three married or widowed daughters and the families of the latter. In addition,
there were four other men with their wives and children, who were related to the core
group in various complicated and relatively remote ways. The Qipi group consisted of
one elderly man, his third wife, and five married offspring (three daughters and two
sons) with their spouses and children, married and unmarried. In addition, the married
daughter of one of the elder's sons-in-law, together with her husband and children,
lived with the group.

3. I am indebted to George Park for this suggestion.

4. I am speaking here not of orphans who-were adopted in infancy but of those
who lo t their parents later, in mid-childhood. The former are often brought up with
as much love and care as the adopted parents' own children, but the latter tend to be
neglected and abused, as described here, even if they are nominally "adopted."

5. In the final section of this paper I will discuss attitudes toward affection in more
detail. Here I would like simply to note that there is an ambivalence about affection,
which may be involved also in attitudes toward sexuality.

6. Secretive extramarital affairs should not be confused with spouse-exchange relationships, which are openly acknowledged by all parties.

7. It is often assumed that it is the husbands who arrange wife exchanges, and
Freuchen speaks of a beating administered to a wife who refused to accept a visitor
(1961, p. 91). I wonder, however, whether in many cases the male initiative is not more
apparent than real. Mirsky (1937, p. 67) says that traditionally in East Greenland a
woman had as much freedom of choice as a man with regard to sexual partners and
could take the initiative in the game of "putting out the lamps." And I have mentioned
Stevenson's statement (1972) that in the north of Baffin Island, too, women might
initiate exchange or might act as go-betweens if their husbands felt shy.
    In most parts of the Arctic today, spouse exchange is no longer openly practiced.
Therefore it is difficult to know to what extent it still exists and how it is patterned.

8. Mirsky, 1937, p. 67; Lantis, 1960, p. 40. Spencer, however, speaking of North Alaska, says the reverse (1959, p. 251).

9. According to the *Annual Report of the Commissioner of the N.W.T., 1966–1967* (1967, p. 81), the average age of death in 1966 was 21 for Eskimos as compared with 62 for all Canadians. This includes infant mortality, which, according to the Economic Council of Canada (1968), is ten times the national average. Exclusive of infant mortality, the average age of death is 30.

10. This is not exclusively a problem of women. A man's ties with his parents are also strong, and since residence rules are flexible, it may happen that it is the man who has to move away from his home community. This, too, is experienced as a hardship and may weaken the marriage by creating counter-pulls. Two young men of my acquaintance—one an Utku, the other a Qipi—spent long periods of time away from their wives, visiting their mothers.

11. This fear is related to the stringent training in undemandingness that children receive. The training takes the form of persistent teasing rejection of the child's overtures and ignoring of his demands. It is described more fully in Briggs, 1970 and 1972.

12. It may, however, be significant that my informants are women.

13. One might also ask whether, in terms of some "objective" criteria, Eskimo women are deprived by comparison with men, but I do not consider such analysis relevant to the way life is actually experienced and therefore do not undertake it here.

14. Briggs, 1970, p. 108. Other aspects of the gratitude that women, more or less consciously, feel toward men are also described in this chapter, pp. 280 to 282.

15. This situation may be changing somewhat in the settlements, where women are exposed to other world views and life-styles. There, I was told, "women are beginning to speak up for what they want." Some, especially young women, have paying jobs, and others sit on village councils along with men.

16. I am assuming here, as elsewhere in this analysis, that men are the relevant reference group—that women do, in fact, measure their worth against that of men, rather than against some other category, such as older women, or other women of their own age and background. This assumption is almost certainly oversimplified; the truth is probably that women compare themselves with more than one reference group. But since Eskimos of both sexes do readily make comparative remarks about the other sex, I think it is fair to assume that men do, indeed, constitute *a* reference group for Eskimo women, as they do for Western women.

17. George Park suggests that perhaps the reason why men hold the final authority in so many societies is that physical force is the ultimate sanction, and men are generally bigger and stronger than women.

18. It is necessary to distinguish between the inevitable tensions that result from everyday interactions between individuals who happen to be men and individuals who happen to be women, and tensions that result specifically from sexuality and are directed toward men as a category or toward women as a category. It is the categorical, institutionalized attitude that we are concerned with here, the attitude that "women are no good" or "men are no good." This is quite different from saying: "I don't like Palak"—a particular man or a particular woman. In the latter case, the gender of Palak is irrelevant to the hostility.

19. He is quoting Margaret Lantis (1946, p. 246), who says that "a woman had no role *directly* [italics in original] in *relation to community affairs* [italics mine]. Hers were relationships with indivduals. . . . Hence only the men's roles are formally stated."

20. There is no denying that severe beatings do occur in the North American Arctic; but they occur usually under the influence of alcohol and, as I have said, they are strongly disapproved and feared. Holtved (1967, p. 147) says that among the Thule Eskimos, a certain man who was said to have been brutal to his first wife "had very great difficulty in getting married again."

21. The exact nature of the concept of ritual danger varies considerably across cultures. Radcliffe-Brown (1952, pp. 138–139) has pointed out that Polynesian societies, among others, see a fundamental identity between good-sacred (holy) and bad-sacred (unclean) things and may class them all together as "dangerous," in distinction from ordinary objects, persons, or states. The Coorgs, on the other hand, make a clear distinction between good-sacred and bad-sacred, seeing them as polar states (Srinivas, 1952, pp. 108–109). Eskimo may be one of the cultures that has a generalized, undifferentiated concept of ritual danger. In Netsilik, a Central Eskimo dialect, there is a word—*tiringnaqtuq*—that may be glossed as "spiritually dangerous." It describes a person who is subject to taboos. More precisely, a person who is in a spiritually vulnerable state or an act (such as murder) or event (such as birth or death) that places him in a vulnerable condition is *tiringnaqtuq*. Whether a further distinction is made between good-sacred and bad-sacred is not known.

22. An alternative interpretation that does not fit so nicely with my argument might, of course, be that women (midwives) value men more than women and thus wishfully "see" a male child in the first confused moment of the infant's emerging (Park, 1972).

BIBLIOGRAPHY

Annual Report of the Commissioner of the Northwest Territories 1966–67, Ottawa, 1967.

Briggs, Jean L.: *Never in Anger*, Harvard University Press, Cambridge, Mass., 1970.

————: "The Origins of Non-Violence," to be published in Warner Muensterberger (ed.), *The Psychoanalytic Study of Society*, International Universities Press, New York.

Burch, Ernest S., Jr.: "Authority, Aid and Affection: The Structure of Eskimo Kin Relationships," unpublished doctoral dissertation, University of Chicago, 1966.

————: Personal communication, 1972.

Economic Council of Canada: *Fifth Annual Report*, 1968, Ottawa, 1968.

Freeman, M. M. R.: "Ethos, Economics and Prestige: A Re-Examination of Netsilik Eskimo Infanticide," *Verhandlugen des XXXVIII. Internationalen Amerikanistenkongresses*, vol. 2, pp. 247–250, August 1968.

————: "A Social and Ecologic Analysis of Systematic Female Infanticide among the Netsilik Eskimo," *American Anthropologist*, vol. 73, pp. 1011–1018, 1971.

Freuchen, Peter: *Book of the Eskimos*, Bramhall House Inc., New York, 1961.

Holtved, Erik: "Contributions to Polar Eskimo Ethnography," *Meddelelser om Grønland*, vol. 182, p. 3–180, 1967.

Lantis, Margaret: *The Social Culture of the Nunivak Eskimo*, Transactions of the American Philosophical Society, n.s., vol. 35, pt. 3, Philadelphia, 1946.

————: *Eskimo Childhood and Interpersonal Relationships*, University of Washington Press, Seattle, 1960.

Lubart, Joseph M.: *Psychodynamic Problems of Adaptation—MacKenzie Delta Eskimos*, Ottawa, 1970.

Mirsky, Jeannette: "The Eskimo of Greenland," in Margaret Mead (ed.) *Cooperation and Competition among Primitive Peoples*, Beacon Press, Boston, 1937.

Park, George: Personal communication, 1972.

Parker, Seymour: "Eskimo Psychopathology in the Context of Eskimo Personality and Culture," *American Anthropologist*, vol. 64, pp. 76–96, 1962.

Radcliffe-Brown, A. R.: *Structure and Function in Primitive Society*, The Free Press, Glencoe, Ill., 1952.

Rasmussen, Knud: *The People of the Polar North*, Kegan Paul, Trench, Trübner & Co., London, 1908.

————: *The Netsilik Eskimos,* Report of the Fifth Thule Expedition, 1921–1924, vol. 8, nos. 1–2, Copenhagen, 1931.

Spencer, Robert F.: *The North Alaskan Eskimo,* Bureau of American Ethnology Bulletin no. 171, Washington, 1959.

Srinivas, M. N.: *Religion and Society among the Coorgs of South India,* Asia Publishing House, London, 1952.

Stevenson, David, "Social Organization of the Clyde Inlet Eskimos," unpublished doctoral dissertation, University of British Columbia, 1972.

Washburne, Heluiz Chandler and Anauta: *Land of the Good Shadows,* The John Day Company, Inc., New York, 1940.

Khmer Village Women in Cambodia:
A Happy Balance

MAY EBIHARA

One of the things I recall most clearly about my first nervous days of research in a Cambodian peasant village—as I struggled to adjust myself to an alien tropical setting, a blur of unfamiliar faces, and a language I could barely comprehend—is the old women. When I wandered timidly through the village, most people seemed to stand back and stare. But the old ladies smiled and greeted me, patted my arms, and drew me into their houses with graceful invitations. There they would offer me sweets, pat me some more, and speak to me slowly and simply as to a child, saying how nice it was that I had come to stay in their village. Filled with anxiety about my acceptance into the community, I clung to these expressions of hospitality like a drowning woman. The old "grandmothers" buoyed me through those difficult first weeks, giving a foretaste of the warmth and generosity that I would eventually receive from all the villagers; and I shall always be grateful for their kind welcome.

Village Sobay, located in central Cambodia, was the subject of a year's research in 1959 to 1960.[1] I settled into West Hamlet, one of the village's three divisions, a pleasant cluster of thirty-two wood-and-thatch houses set amid a verdant growth of palms, fruit trees, and other tropical foliage; and its 160-odd residents became the focus of my most intensive investigations as well as my friends and protectors. These villagers are ethnically and cul-

305

turally Khmer, the term for the numerically and politically dominant population of Cambodia;[2] they are representative of the majority of the country's population, who are similarly peasant cultivators. South of the village
stretches a quilt of rice paddies which are cultivated during the rainy season and constitute the basic livelihood of the villagers. In Sobay, however,
most families own only a small amount of land (about 1 hectare or 2.47
acres of rice paddies per household in West Hamlet); so rice is grown
mainly for subsistence rather than for the market and many people must
turn to miscellaneous part-time, cash-earning endeavors to make ends meet.
Villagers often remark, "We are so poor . . . life is difficult in the countryside"—and so it is in comparison to the relative ease and comfort enjoyed
by the middle and upper classes in urban centers.[3]

The village forms a territorial political unit under a headman who is
the lowest rung of an administrative hierarchy that fans down from the
central government in Phnom Penh. More importantly it is also, of course,
a social unit of kinsmen, neighbors, and friends bound together by long
years of association. And although there are few communal activities that
involve the village as a whole, its inhabitants identify with and feel loyalty
to their community. Sobay does not constitute a single religious congrega-
tion because its residents attend both the village temple and another a
short distance away. But they all share a common religious system which
is composed of Theravada Buddhism (the official state religion of Cambodia),[4] a folk religion with beliefs and rituals revolving around a variety
of animistic spirits and fragments of Brahmanism.

I shall try to give some impression of the lives of women in this village
society by describing five of them ranging in age from one to sixty. I selected
these particular persons primarily because they were special friends whom
I knew well. But despite this subjective choice, I believe that each is representative of her age group in most respects (and I shall note any ways in
which someone is unusual). Vignettes of these five, as well as their relatives
and neighbors, will provide some idea of the activities, conduct, and attitudes of Khmer village women from childhood to old age.

MIA*

Mia, a little over a year old, is the pet of the entire hamlet. While small
babies are always fussed over and passed from one set of arms to another
to be kissed, cuddled, and admired (even by adolescent boys), Mia has
passed this stage of infancy and would in our terms be called a toddler.

* In this and the following sections, I have altered personal names, but all other
factual information about individuals has been left unmodified.

But she somehow continues to attract more attention and smiles than others of her age. This is due not to exceptional beauty—although she is a pretty child with light brown hair finally beginning to cover a small round head, lively eyes, and an infectious smile—but to her alertness and charm. Her family, relatives, and neighbors derive endless amusement from the small repertoire of phrases and gestures she will give in response to questions such as "What year were you born in?" "Whose child are you?" "Where is grandmother?"—or to see her tiny hands twist in the air and feet stamp on the ground when one orders, "Dance, Mia!" Although still very young, she is thus becoming cognizant of various aspects of her culture: astrological signs she was born under, family ties and kin terms, the dances she will perform as a young woman to show off her grace. And even at this age she is beginning to be treated somewhat differently because of her sex. While babies are usually left naked and little boys often run about nude until the age of seven or eight, Mia is already dressed in a miniature sarong. Children of both sexes eventually develop a strong sense of modesty about keeping their genitals covered, but girls are taught this at a much earlier age and kept clothed in little skirts or trousers. Mia also wears a tiny pair of earrings (female babies have their ears pierced shortly after birth) and a little coin for good luck on a string around her neck, fore-runners of the more elaborate jewelry she will wear as an adolescent.

Mia is the first and still the only child of a young couple who live with her father's widowed mother. She holds the limelight in this household and will do so until another child is born. She is nursed on demand and may continue to be breast-fed for another two or even three years unless a younger sibling comes on the scene, although she now also eats various solid foods. She, like other young children, is constantly with her mother, who takes Mia everywhere she goes—whether to the rice fields, to temple ceremonies, or to bed at night—and is always ready to offer her breast, a lap, or soothing words.

But as Mia grows older, and especially if another child is born in the family, she will be propelled into a harsher world where she will be weaned, receive less undivided care and attention from her mother, accept discipline for misbehavior, and undertake some small chores. For some children this is a difficult transition to make; and the sudden withdrawal of attention plus sibling rivalry creates a petulant, sullen, or mischievous child who fights the younger brother or sister for the mother's eye. But as the child grows older, especially in the case of girls, the hostility toward the younger sibling is suppressed as she is given the responsibility of tending the little brother or sister and thus changes from competitor to surrogate mother. The village is full of little girls such as seven-year-old Laan, my next-door neighbor, who lugs her four-year-old sister astride her thin hip although her frail body staggers under the weight. But she, and even younger girls,

A typical one-year-old village girl.

take their baby-sitting duties quite seriously; they also find it fun, for it is not unlike playing with a live doll.

From the age of about five or six, children also move from their mother's side to more frequent association with their peers. Toys are scarce in village life, but there are many activities for active youngsters: fishing in the waterholes by the hamlet, a form of hopscotch played on squares scratched in the dirt, a bowling game using palm seeds as balls and pins, and the like. While it is not unusual to see play groups of both boys and girls at such pursuits, children tend to associate most with those of their own sex. Boys spend a good deal of time in gross physical activity: climbing trees, splashing in the rice paddies, or chasing each other around the hamlet. Girls, on the other hand, more often imitate adult activities: playing "house" in a small shelter made of cloth draped over some convenient poles; playing "restaurant" by selling meals of chopped leaves on pieces of broken pottery in return for "money" of torn bits of paper salvaged from my wastebasket; playing "temple" by kneeling with hands and legs properly folded and chanting replicas of Buddhists prayers; and, a special favorite of young girls, dressing up in scarves and borrowed jewelery to dance to music sung and drummed by obliging adolescents.[5] Thus, even little girls are conscious of the female role and feminine pursuits, and begin to emulate them from an early age.

KIM

Of the various youngsters who often came to visit me, Kim was one of my favorites. She is about fourteen, but still spindly and straight as a young tree, a bit gawky in her movements, very innocent and shy. In contrast to her friend Tua (another of my favorites), who is lively and even boisterous, Kim has a grave and gentle temperament coupled with deep intelligence. While Tua would bounce around my house poking at the typewriter or rummaging through the wastebasket, Kim would sit quietly but absorb all the conversation and activity going on around her. And when she came alone, we would have very earnest conversations about village events or what she was learning in school.

Because she is still considered basically a "child" and because her family is very poor, Kim does not yet have the beauty-parlor permanent that is a necessity for adolescent girls. Her hair, like that of Tua and other young

Two young Khmer girls, aged 13 and 10.

girls, is worn shoulder length and straight. At home in the village she appears in sarongs and simple blouses. (Although her breasts have not yet developed, she would be embarrassed to go nude above the waist as younger girls sometimes do.) When going to school, she exchanges her sarong for a short blue skirt, since Western-style dress is permitted for young girls. Older adolescents and adult women, however, would consider it highly immodest to expose their legs.

Kim lives with her parents and younger brother and sister in a small, shabby house built of palm thatching. Like other children, she has few definite chores apart from keeping an eye on her younger sister, collecting kindling for firewood, and helping to bring water from one of the hamlet's wells. She knows how to cook rice and a few simple dishes such as soup or grilled fish, and she has begun to learn how to transplant and harvest rice. But her mother does not yet require her to provide much help about the house or in the fields, partly because of Kim's youth and partly because a good deal of her time is taken up with school. For six hours a day, five days a week, nine months a year, Kim—along with other village youngsters between the ages of about six and sixteen—attends one of two public schools in the area. Kim has completed and passed the national examinations for *études élémentaires,* the first three grades, and has now begun her *études complémentaires,* which cover grades four to six.

Widespread education is a relatively new development in village life; prior to Cambodia's achievement of independence from French colonial rule in the mid-1950s, most peasants received limited formal schooling. By and large, only males received some sort of education at Buddhist temple schools or gained some literacy while learning scriptures during the period that they temporarily became Buddhist monks.[6] But females could not enter monasteries, and it was generally thought that girls needed no education beyond instruction by their mothers in essential domestic skills. This is strikingly evident in the fact that all women in West Hamlet over twenty-one years of age are completely illiterate; only two girls over the age of sixteen (both of whom grew up in other communities) can read and write Khmer.

But in recent years the number of public schools has expanded dramatically and education has been opened to both sexes. Girls as well as boys are encouraged to attend school and generally do so conscientiously and even enthusiastically. Parents realize that if their children are to step off the arduous treadmill of peasant life, they must have an education to enter nonagricultural occupations. Serious youngsters such as Kim perceive this as well. She has already gotten more education than her father did; and she feels—although she hardly dares to voice her hopes—that a career, perhaps as a schoolteacher, is not an impossibility.[7] Whether she or other village children will in fact be able to continue to the lycée or secondary school level is open to question. Probably most of them (including, I suspect, Tua) will not go beyond the sixth grade for a variety of reasons: because their families cannot afford to send them to Phnom Penh where the lycées are located, because the labors of adolescents are needed at home, because dreams of socioeconomic mobility can be achieved only by the hard reality of persistent drive and effort, and because girls in particular may be discouraged from further schooling by the likelihood that they will eventually become housewives who do not really need advanced education. (They may also be deterred by the hope that marriage to a well-to-do urbanite will enable them to leave the countryside and bring them advantages without the struggles a career might entail.)[8] Only one girl in the hamlet has begun studies at a lycée in the city. It is very uncertain that Kim will be able to follow in her footsteps.

Apart from her few chores and her studies, Kim still has time to play. She will often join girls of her age or her younger sister in various games and amusements. But conscious of her emerging adolescence, she rather prefers now to be in the company of older adolescent girls, listening to their gossip and chatter. She blushes when they jokingly claim that she has "a fiancé."[9] This is a common topic of teasing among children and adolescents; when Kim was younger, she—like other young girls—would react with anger or tears. But now, on the verge of leaving childhood to become a *kromom* (a female eligible for marriage), she is flattered.

NEARI

Neari, at eighteen, is most definitely a *kromom*. She attained this status a year or so ago when she began to menstruate and her figure, once as shapeless as her younger sister's, developed a real bosom and hips. In Neari's grandmother's time, the transition from child to *kromom* was marked by a special observance at the time of the first menstruation (which might occur any time between the ages of thirteen and seventeen). On this occasion, aptly called "entrance into the shade" (*Chol Mlop*), the girl was secluded in a darkened, curtained-off section of the house, forbidden to see any men (even her father and brothers), allowed to go outdoors only in the dark of night when the males of the village were asleep, and prohibited from eating meat or fish. This seclusion lasted several months (sometimes as long as a year), during which the girl passed her days learning feminine skills such as weaving or basketry. The "coming out of the shade" was celebrated with feasting of kinsmen and friends, offerings to ancestors and spirits, and several rituals similar to those performed at weddings, as if to signify that the girl was now ready to be married.

Such ceremonies have not been practiced in the village for some forty years.[10] But even without ritual observances, Neari's physical maturation is quite obvious. She is also considered to be one of the prettiest girls in the hamlet (although not *the* best looking because she is a shade too tall for a girl, her figure is not as plumply rounded as some of the others, and her nose is a bit too aquiline). Her hair, like that of other young unmarried women, has been given a permanent at the beauty salon in the nearby market town and falls in waves and curls to below her shoulders.[11] She dresses in an ankle-length sarong, often in brightly colored patterns, and some sort of blouse under which she modestly wears a camisole or brassiere to conceal her breasts. (Once at a festival, some strangers made rude remarks insinuating that Neari was not wearing a brassiere; her sense of propriety was so outraged that she almost came to blows with them.) Simple earrings and a necklace or bracelet are worn almost constantly, and on special occasions she, not her mother, wears whatever jewelry the family possesses.[12]

Neari is adult not only physically but in many of her activities as well. For the past few years, for example, she has worked alongside her mother in the rice paddies. While she cannot transplant or harvest rice as adeptly as older women, she can and does do a full day's work, particularly during the busiest seasons of cultivation when large cooperative work teams of women band together to labor on one another's fields in turn. She is equally capable of handling basic domestic tasks—as I know from firsthand experience because she, along with her cousin Saan, came to work for me as part-time housekeepers.[13] She can wash and iron laundry, sew simple blouses and mend clothes, keep a house clean and orderly, go marketing in town (selecting the best buys and bargaining skillfully), and cook even quite complicated dishes such as chicken curry with complex ingredients that must be prepared from scratch. Other girls her age are equally competent.

In addition to helping their mothers with such domestic and agricultural tasks, adolescents may also take occasional (and usually short-lived) part-time jobs to earn money. Neari's employment with me was, of course, unusual. More commonly, young women work as coolies, unskilled construction workers, on building projects at a nearby teachers' school; some girls in a neighboring village work as agricultural day laborers, transplanting and harvesting rice for people who need or can afford hired help. Neari and many other girls are allowed to keep the money they earn from such endeavors, although they usually turn over some or most of their wages to their families. Neari even owns property. Whatever she may buy with her earnings is indisputably hers; and, in addition, one rice paddy has already been designated as "Neari's field" and will be formally turned over to her when she marries. (Parents usually pass on major items of property such as land and jewelry to each child as he or she marries, although there may still be some property that is not apportioned until the parents die.)

Older adolescents are also conscious of behaving in a responsible and moral fashion. Neari is obedient and generally respectful toward her parents, accepting their decisions (even onerous ones) without the sulking, tantrums, or defiance with which her younger brothers and sisters often respond to orders they do not like. While she often still fights with her siblings, she also genuinely worries about their welfare and sometimes buys them treats with her earnings. She tries to maintain her reputation as a virtuous young woman: for instance, she worries about "shame" or "embarrassment" if she puts on too much powder or lipstick when she dresses up for special occasions, and she never goes out alone to distant rice paddies or abroad at night lest it be thought that she might have a rendezvous with some young man. Both parents and the girls themselves adhere very strictly to the rule that a young woman should be accompanied by some adult when venturing out at night or to isolated or strange places. For, apart from considerations of virtue, there is great fear of rape. While I doubt that rapists are as ubiquitous as the villagers believe, there are, in fact, periodic incidents—lewd remarks made by strangers, or the curious story of two young women in another village who were kidnapped and "made to be like wives" while visiting some other community—that lend some support to their fears.

Neari also realizes the import of the Buddhist belief that the number of meritorious deeds performed in this lifetime will affect one's position in the next incarnation. (As she said to me one day, half jokingly and half seriously, "I think I'll go to three or four Katun festivals [a major Buddhist ceremony] this year so I can be reborn as a rich American.") She has learned the major Buddhists prayers and chants, helps her mother prepare food offerings for temple ceremonies, offers her services when the temple requests aid in organizing festivals or work on construction projects, and adheres to the major Buddhist precepts for proper conduct in an effort to accumulate a supply of "merit" that will outweigh whatever sins she may commit. In addition to participating in Buddhist rituals, Neari and other adolescents take active roles rather than being mere onlookers at other ceremonies as well—for example, acting as wedding attendants at marriages or helping to give village festivals.

But despite their increasing seriousness, responsibilties, and ability to handle various tasks, adolescents are not overburdened with chores by their parents and still have a good deal of leisure. Young women often sit on an outdoor platform in the heat of the day or cluster at someone's house in the evening, gossiping, laughing, discussing clothes they'd like to have, assessing all the eligible young men they know, comparing themselves to other *kromoms* in the village, talking about their hopes and fears for the future, breaking out into popular songs. Sometimes groups of mixed sex will gather to banter and joke in the easy camaraderie born of long years of association, for many young men and women are related to one another or are, at the least, old friends who have grown up together. Neari's closest companions and confidantes are a few of the other village girls near her age. But she is also friendly with younger girls, such as Kim, and has a very easy-going, familiar relationship with her mother, one of her maternal aunts, and some of her mother's closest friends. While Neari feels a basic respect for her mother and the older women because of their age and positions, they are good-natured women who do not stand on formality and who permit Neari to gossip and joke with them much as she does with her peers. (This is not necessarily true, however, of all the adult women in the village, some of whom have a more reserved relationship with their children or younger people.)

One of the main concerns of Neari and the other *kromoms* is, as one might guess, the opposite sex. There are constant discussions and evaluations of the most attractive bachelors in the area,[14] endless gossip and teasing about "fiancés," and overwhelming excitement and meticulous primping before major Buddhist festivals or other events that draw large crowds and are therefore good hunting grounds for potential spouses. On such occasions, Neari and her friends, in bright pastel blouses and special silk sarongs, look like gorgeous birds of paradise; gold jewelry adorns ears, wrists, and necks; hair is carefully curled and arranged, faces are powdered and lipsticked; and normally bare feet are shod in sandals or mules. The young men, normally found in shorts or old sarongs around the village, are also transformed into dandies with pomaded hair, Western-style shirts, Western or traditional black silk trousers, shoes or sandals, and perhaps even prestigious sunglasses or a wristwatch. A good deal of subtle mutual observation goes on between young men and women at such events, and it is not uncommon for the overtly disdainful glances and casual remarks exchanged on such occasions to lead to marriage negotiations.

While young men and women come into contact under these and other circumstances, the general rule might be phrased as "Look, but don't touch." Premarital (and extramarital) sex is forbidden by one of the Buddhist precepts, and it is further thought that ancestral spirits frown upon and punish fornication. Actually, sexual ventures on the part of young men would be taken fairly lightly.[15] But Neari and the other unmarried girls are cautiously kept under surveillance and chaperoned, and they are well aware that loss of virginity before marriage would cause "great shame" and "bad-smelling talk." In fact, premarital sex does occur occasionally. Villagers spoke disapprovingly of a girl in another hamlet who was several months pregnant at her wedding and of another who disappeared on week-ends with a rich official from Phnom Penh. But such cases are fairly rare, partly because of the deterrents of adverse public opinion and the closeness of village life, which makes it almost impossible to keep anything secret. And Neari herself—although she has seen dogs copulating, teases her little brother about his penis, hears the sometimes ribald stories of adults, and uses a colorful village exclamation that can be roughly translated as "screw a widow"—remains innocent and uncertain about the exact nature of sexual intercourse and childbirth.[16]

Young Women

Most girls get married in their late adolescence or early twenties to young men in their early to mid-twenties.[17] Neari has already received several marriage proposals, brought by go-betweens on behalf of young men who had seen her in the village, at market, or at temple ceremonies. But her parents have rejected these offers, saying that she is still too young to marry, although another reason for their refusal to "give" Neari is that none of the suitors had promising enough futures. Neari herself does not feel ready to leave home; she is apprenhensive about the burdens of marriage and frightened of the pain of childbirth. Sometimes she and her friends laughingly assert that they intend to be spinsters, living as maiden aunts in the household of a married sibling. Yet in their heart of hearts, these young women know that they must get married, and, indeed, they want to do so—eventually. Having been born too soon to benefit from the expansion of public schooling and lacking any formal education, they have no alternative to marriage except spinsterhood. And if they wish to leave village life, as many do, the best that they can hope for is to marry men with nonagricultural occupations or professions who will take them away from the rice fields.

Villagers assert that marriages are always based on free choice; and that when a go-between sent by a young man's family proffers a marriage proposal to a girl's parents, the latter must consult their daughter, who is free to accept or reject the suitor as she wishes. Theoretically, parents cannot force a child into a distasteful marriage or prevent two people in love from marrying without incurring the wrath of ancestral spirits.[18] This ideal is indeed followed in many instances, with young men and women making the ultimate decisions about marriage partners, although their parents must still approve the match and handle the actual betrothal negotiations. However, in reality, parents often exert subtle influence over whom their child marries: for example, by obliquely mentioning possible spouses, extolling the virtues of one individual over another, expressing disapproval of certain matches, claiming that a child is not yet ready for marriage (as in the case of Neari), and so on. And some marriages are, in effect, actually arranged by the parents themselves. In such cases, children often acquiesce to parental wishes or opinions out of deference to the presumed greater wisdom of their elders, because they have neutral feelings about the proposed mate and no strong attraction to anyone else, or because individuals realize that not all marriages can be romantic matches but may have to be based on pragmatic considerations.

An excellent example of this involved Neari's cousin Saan. A young mechanic from Phnom Penh, visiting friends in the hamlet, saw and became quite taken with Saan. Saan herself did not find the young man terribly attractive, but her mother, Om, did. Om pointed out what an excellent catch he was: a nice young man with a good trade who would take Saan away from the poverty of village life to the big city. Furthermore, Om was a poor divorcée who could barely support herself and her family; Saan herself was, at age twenty, also a divorcée (she had made an early marriage at seventeen which broke up after two years because of incompatibility) and thus a bit less desirable than virginal girls. So Om accepted the fellow's marriage proposal on behalf of her daughter and Saan agreed to the betrothal even though she was torn with ambivalence. She realized that her mother's assessment of the situation was well founded, yet she was filled with distress at the thought of marrying a man she did not love as well as anxiety about moving to a strange place away from family and friends. Saan managed to postpone the wedding date three or four times. But in the end she was married, a beautiful but rather mournful bride. (I must hasten to add, however, that not all arranged marriages are so sad. Some are quite willingly accepted by the individuals involved. For instance, another girl in the hamlet had her betrothal engineered by her mother. But being a homely girl who was still unmarried at the age of twenty-five, she was delighted.)

Whether a betrothal is based on free choice or parental arrangement, certain considerations are taken into account. The young people themselves tend to be very preoccupied with physical beauty and handsomeness; there are endless discussions of who are the best looking *kromoms* and bachelors in the village, and boys have been known to fall in love at the mere sight of a splendid face and figure. But another and ultimately more important criterion is what villagers call a good heart or what we would term good character: a man must be hard-working, responsible, considerate, and not given to drink or gambling; a woman must be industrious, virtuous, even-tempered, etc. In addition, economic factors may be important: for instance, an individual from a poor family who stands to inherit little or no property may seek a spouse who is heir (or heiress) to sufficient rice paddies or other resources to make a living,[19] and many parents nowadays prefer men with salaried jobs to rice farmers as husbands for their daughters. Last but not least, astrological calculations are necessary. Each individual is born under certain astrological signs, and a couple's horoscopes must be checked to see if they are compatible; some combinations of signs are believed to indicate propitious unions, while others are held to forecast marriages that would be risky or doomed to failure.[20]

One significant aspect of the betrothal negotiations is the determination of the monetary gift that is given by the male's family to his fiancée's parents.[21] The exact sum is determined by bargaining between the two sides and, among villagers, usually ranges between 2,000 to 5,000 riels (roughly $60 to $140 at the official exchange rate in 1959, a not inconsiderable sum for peasant families). The amount depends partly on the financial resources of the man's family, but it also reflects on the desirability and attractiveness of the young woman. For instance, it was said that Priin, considered to be the most beautiful girl in the hamlet, could command a gift of 8,000 to 10,000 riels. On the other hand, less attractive women, widows, or divorcées would receive much less (e.g., Saan, a divorcée but still young and quite pretty, got 3,000 riels).

Assuming that all these considerations are resolved satisfactorily during the marriage negotiations, the "word is fixed" at a small engagement ceremony. It was once customary for the fiancé to render bride service for his future parents-in-law during the period of betrothal, working for them in

A young bride at her wedding going through one of the numerous rituals.

the fields and around the house to prove that he was industrious and reputable. But this tradition has begun to decline within the past decade, although a man may proffer help during the busiest seasons of rice cultivation if he lives nearby.[22] The wedding itself is one of the most extravagant, festive, and joyous of village ceremonies. Over a period of one and a half days, numerous kinsmen, neighbors, and friends gather at the bride's home for a series of rituals, feasting, dancing, and general merrymaking.[23] The celebration culminates as spectators throw seeds of the coconut flower on the newlywed couple and shout out: "Victory! Happiness! Health! This is a good day! We accept this fine couple!"

Srey, Neari's mother, has been married for twenty-one years. Her life has not been an easy one, as she has had to maintain a household with seven children on meager resources and labor in the fields with her husband. But she remains, at age forty, strong and cheerful. Although Srey has a volatile temper and lacks the serenity of some village women, she is generous, good-hearted, and irresistibly high-spirited. When I recall her face, I see it broken into laughter; I also remember her fondly as a rather fierce mother hen under whose wing I was herded to be fussed over, admonished, instructed, and protected as if I were one of her daughters.[24]

The transition from *kromom* to married woman involves not simply a change in status but an alteration in behavior that can be broadly characterized as a change from relative frivolity to seriousness, from light-hearted concerns to all the worries and chores of tending a family. Clothing and personal appearance reflect this change. Srey, like other married women, no longer uses cosmetics or wears jewelry; her hair is cut short at ear length, and permanents are a thing of the past. She dresses in sober (usually black) sarongs and a simple high-necked blouse or sometimes just a scarf wrapped in halter fashion; brassieres are discarded because her three-year-old still nurses, and nursing mothers or older women do not have to observe as much modesty about their breasts as do younger women. Another characteristic feature of the adult woman's appearance is lips and teeth that are stained from chewing betel,[25] a habit which is not usually practiced by adolescent girls or by men, who usually smoke cigarettes instead.

Srey married her husband, Buon, a hardworking, decent, kind-hearted man, when she was nineteen and he was twenty-one. They had known one another since childhood, for Srey grew up in East Hamlet Sobay and Buon in West Hamlet; while their attraction to one another was not passionate, they had always been fond of each other.

When they were first married they lived for about a year with Srey's parents (uxorilocal residence) before building their own house (neolocal residence). This is a very common pattern in village life. For although there is an old tradition that a young man should construct a new home for his bride, few have the money to do so. Therefore most young couples move in with either the husband's or the wife's family for a period of time that may range from a year to a lifetime.

Which household they go to depends not on any rules but on particular circumstances: which house has more room, which set of parents needs help with work, which spouse feels most strongly about staying at home, etc. But a high percentage of couples choose the wife's family, mainly because young women are more reluctant than men to leave the warm security of their homes where mothers can readily be called on for support, advice, and aid; correspondingly, many parents worry about seeing daughters move away from their protective surveillance and care. Young men, on the other hand, are not subject to chaperonage and given much more freedom to do as and go where they please; they are thus less timid about moving from home. But some of them, too, may remain with their families after marriage (virilocal residence) if—as in the case of Mia's father—aged or widowed parents need an able male around the house.

Villagers are, therefore, quite flexible about where a married couple may live. Some couples live neolocally from the outset of marriage. Others spend an initial period in uxori- or virilocality and then move into a home of their own for a variety of reasons: because they have saved enough money to build a house, or the wife gains confidence about running her own household, or the parental home becomes cramped as a couple bears children, etc. And still others decide on, or end up in, permanent uxori- or virilocality because of filial piety toward aged parents who need to be supported or because of continued dependence (financial or emotional) on parental aid. Such couples, though, usually inherit the house when the parents die, so they eventually get a home to themselves.

FAMILY RELATIONSHIPS

There are, then, two main kinds of family found in almost equal proportion in Sobay: the simple nuclear family, composed of parents and unmarried children, and the extended family, which is usually composed of parents, unmarried children, and one married child plus his/her spouse and their children.[26] It is important to realize, however, that such families are not immutable entities but often undergo changes through time. For instance, a nuclear family will become extended when a child marries and brings a spouse home, or an extended family will change to a nuclear one when the old parents die off. It is also not uncommon for a family to take in miscellaneous relatives—siblings, cousins, nephews or nieces, etc.—for short or long periods of time. So household composition in the village is quite varied.

The family is the most basic social unit in village life, its members bound together by various emotional, economic, moral, and legal ties. There are no organized kin groups beyond the household, nor are there any clubs, political parties, or other formal associations. So the bonds between husband and wife, siblings, and especially parents and children are the strongest and most enduring relations found in village social organization. Mutual affection, loyalty, support, and assistance are prescribed by general culture norms, religious precepts (based on both Buddhist teachings and the belief that ancestral spirits oversee the proper conduct of their descendants), and legal statutes. Real behavior does not, of course, always follow the ideal standards, but I shall try to give some idea of both.

Husbands and Wives

The emotional relationship between husband and wife naturally varies from couple to couple. For some, marriage seems to be mainly a matter of necessity or convenience. In such cases the spouses work and live together harmoniously but rather impassively, tolerant of one another but without any profound attachment. Other couples, however, such as Srey and Buon or Kim's parents, evidence deep mutual regard, loyalty, and trust. Overt displays of affection between husband and wife are not customary (one woman was quite nonplussed when her husband jokingly squeezed her buttocks in public, but she laughed and blushed with pleasure as well as embarrassment as she rebuked him for his audacity). Yet loving sentiment is obvious in the way that Kim's father calls his wife Old Lady Diamond, a private nickname he has made up for her; or the way that Srey worries over and pampers Buon when he is not feeling well; or the affectionate pride with which an individual talks about a spouse.

According to law, the man is *chef de famille* with almost absolute powers over household affairs and his wife and children (in precolonial days, he could even sell them into slavery) as well as certain prerogatives that are denied women (e.g., a man can divorce his wife on grounds of her adultery, but she does not have a similar right if he strays).[27] Buddhist doctrine also assigns a superior status to males. But a closer reading of both legal and religious statutes reveals that the woman, while certainly owing fidelity and obedience to her husband and possessing minimum legal capacity, is granted some rights and privileges. For instance, a man needs his wife's consent to enter a Buddhist monastery; a woman can initiate divorce proceedings; and a wife is owed food, shelter, and "material and moral" aid according to the law (Clairon, n.d., pp. 64–65) and respect and consideration according to Buddhist precepts (Burtt, 1955, p. 110).

In the reality of village life, the relative positions of husband and wife are virtually equal. Buon sees himself as the head of the household who is owed deference, respect, and obedience by his wife and children, and he gets angry (sweet-tempered though he generally is) when he does not get these. For instance, one day I heard him shouting at the top of his lungs that his frivolous wife had gone off to chat with her friends and did not have his dinner ready; another time I heard him yelling at his noisy children for disturbing a nap he was trying to take after a hard morning's plowing. Srey would concur wholeheartedly that her husband is master of the house. But she and other village wives are by no means completely docile and submissive creatures, for on another occasion I saw Buon bolt out of his house, pursued by Srey's fiery tirade because he had taken a few cents from the household cashbox—her domain—to buy some cigarettes without telling her.

In another household, a fascinating situation developed when Ek, a rather dapper fellow married to a slightly older woman, Luan, tried to take a young girl as a second wife. Polygyny and concubinage are legally permitted in Cambodia, so Luan had no legal grounds for objection. However, it is thought that a man should have the decency to obtain his first wife's consent to a polygynous match (she can sue him for divorce if he does not get her approval). Over a period of days, as we all breathlessly watched the drama, Luan subjected her husband to such a torrent of tears, remonstrations, reproaches, threats, and more tears that he finally caved in under the pressure and broke off with the girl. (Interestingly, exactly the same situation arose in the case of a man in a neighboring village who had similar thoughts of polygyny but also encountered an adamant wife. Many male villagers, empathizing with the husbands involved, thought it was rather a shame. But village wives felt a quiet sense of triumph for, after all, they would not want another woman around the house either.) [28]

Furthermore, a village woman such as Srey plays a critical, essential role within the family. She has primary responsibility for the care of children and the day-to-day household routine: cooking, cleaning, laundry, mending, marketing, and the like. She also makes mats and baskets, fresh thatching to repair houses, sometimes weaves scarves and sarongs, and helps to tend the fish traps, fruit trees, and small kitchen gardens which provide supplementary food.

The wife is a necessary coworker in the rice fields, for while men do the heavy work such as repairing dikes and plowing and harrowing, women do the sowing, transplanting, much of the harvesting, and the winnowing of rice. (Both men and women share the tasks of general maintenance of the fields and threshing.) She helps out also with the various part-time economic endeavors that many families must undertake to earn cash: for example, Srey boils down lontar palm liquid collected by Buon and churns it into palm sugar which is sold to traders; Kim's mother raises pigs for sale;[29] my next-door neighbor cooks noodle dishes and sweets to vend in the neighborhood; Luan runs a small roadside snack stand. The wife also wields an iron hand over the family budget and treasury, and she shrewdly handles the sale of rice, pigs, and foodstuffs (while males customarily deal with the buying or selling of cattle, chickens, and land).

A woman owns property in her own right, for in this bilateral kinship system[30] both males and females can inherit (or purchase) and transmit land, houses, trees, jewelry, cattle, etc. In fact, within the hamlet, more women than men own houses, village land, and rice paddies—the most important items of property—because of the tendency toward uxorilocal residence. Indeed, in some cases where the husband comes from another village, the wife actually owns *all* the major property in the family. The wife also exerts considerable influence, whether subtle or overt, on domestic affairs and important questions such as where to live (as shown by the preponderance of uxorilocal residence) or when and whom a child should marry (e.g., it is mainly Srey who thinks that Neari is too young to leave home; Buon is a bit more sanguine about the matter, but he feels that his wife knows best in this case). And finally, the wife assumes explicit legal authority over the household when the husband is absent, incapacitated, or deceased.

Women are kept busy by their various domestic tasks because the simple technology of village life makes such chores much more time-consuming than in our own society. Water must be hauled from wells, sewing is done by hand, meals take hours to cook on tiny clay stoves over wood fires, etc. Srey's life is a bit easier than it was for her mother or grandmother; for instance, she does not weave her own cloth but buys cheap fabrics, sarongs, and some ready-made clothes in town; a neighbor has built a crude winnowing device which Srey can borrow to save her the trouble of winnowing by hand; and just recently a machine-run rice mill opened down the road so that women no longer have to dehusk rice for cooking by pounding it in a mortar or grind their own rice flour between two stones. But all this has not meant any great increase in a woman's leisure time.

Still, while women are generally the first to rise in the morning and the last to get to bed at night, they do have periods during the day (except during the busiest seasons of transplanting and harvesting) to spend in the most common leisure activity of village life: sitting and talking with friends during the somnolent afternoons, when the tropical heat makes any strenuous activity foolhardy, or in the cool of the evening after supper and before bedtime, when everyone relaxes after the day's work. There are also periodic diversions. Srey and others faithfully attend all important events at the two local Buddhist temples. They look forward especially to the major Buddhist holidays that punctuate the year, not simply for the chance to earn religious merit but because they are gay, festive celebrations which offer a chance to see people from other villages, catch up on gossip, and be entertained. There are, too, other kinds of ceremonies in Sobay and other villages: weddings of relatives and friends, funerals, spirit medium séances, and harvest celebrations that break the normal routine.

Srey's life is not confined to the boundaries of Sobay. She goes regularly not only to the Buddhist temples but to neighboring communities to see relatives or attend ceremonies and to the nearby market town to buy necessities. And now that an expanded bus system has made travel much easier than before, when one had to journey by oxcart, she sometimes ventures even further afield to Phnom Penh or other distant places to visit her sisters or attend holiday celebrations.[31] On such excursions she may not be accompanied by her husband, although she customarily travels with some other persons (relatives or friends) for purposes of safety and "fun."

Parents and Children

Srey, with seven children ranging in age from three to eighteen, has the largest number of children in the hamlet. She welcomed the birth of each subsequent baby with great pleasure; for even though villagers often comment sadly that poverty makes it difficult to support their offspring as well as they would like, children are treasured for the gaiety they bring into a household. There is no special value attached to producing a great number of offspring, but the other extreme of barrenness is regarded as highly unfortunate and lamentable. Sterile couples commonly ask a niece or nephew or some other young relative to come live with them, while old couples whose children have grown up and moved away will have grandchildren visit them for weeks or months at a time.

There is no general preference for male and female children, although individuals may feel that one or the other is easier to raise. Some prefer girls because they are thought to be more obedient; others opt for boys who, it is said, require less money for clothes and jewelry. Neither are there any firm ideas about the proper number of offspring.[32] Statistically, however, the average number of children per couple in West Hamlet is 3.6. There may be several reasons for this relatively limited family size, which is lower than some estimates given for Cambodia as a whole (see, e.g., Steinberg, 1959, p. 31; Delvert, 1961, pp. 317–319).

First, West Hamlet women (Srey aside) seem to have a generally low birthrate.[33] I do not know why this is the case, because there are no means of limiting contraception apart from abstinence, which seems to be practiced only briefly before and after birth. Women know that contraceptive devices exist; Srey says that prostitutes and city women have "medicines" to prevent or abort pregnancies.[34] But, she continues, "We (villagers) don't know how to use such things; those women in Phnom Penh are lazy about having children." Moreover, abortion or, even worse, infanticide is abhorrent to devout Buddhists, for whom the taking of life is the worst sin. It may be that the long period of suckling children—up to the age of three or four—helps to limit births, although lactation is no guarantee against conception. But there must be other factors inhibiting fertility because there are many instances where children are spaced five or more years apart or where couples do not have children for a number of years after marriage (e.g., Mia was not born until five years after her mother had married); and several women have only one child after years of marriage.

Another reason for the limited number of children per family is infant and child mortality. Two children died during the year I lived in the hamlet—an infant several months old and a child of three, both succumbing to unknown illnesses. One villager estimated that one out of ten babies dies,[35] and about half a dozen women in the hamlet had lost children. Until recently villagers have not had easy access to modern medical aid (the closest hospitals and physicians being located in Phnom Penh, some 30 kilometers or 12½ miles distant) and have relied on traditional folk medicines and native curers who generally use a combination of rituals and herbal remedies. While such folk practices are often effective in treating minor ailments, they are usually useless against serious medical problems.

Other factors that may affect limited family size are the somewhat late age of marriage—in the late teens and early twenties—which means that some of the fertile years for female procreation are lost (cf. Nash and Nash, 1963, who suggest this as a factor influencing small Burmese families); and, according to Delvert (1961, pp. 320–321), a relatively high death rate in Cambodia for women between the ages of fifteen and forty-four due to childbirth traumas. I lack clear evidence for the latter, but within the past fifteen years, two out of four female deaths in the hamlet were relatively young women who died a year or two after childbirth, and it may be that they were weakened by the experience. Certainly difficult births must occur periodically, for I witnessed one during my stay. Kaiu, a woman of thirty giving birth to her first child, fell virtually unconscious after a hard labor with great hemorrhaging. Neither the traditional midwife, an old lady from a nearby village, nor a native curer could revive her. In desperation, the villagers sent for a government midwife, a woman trained at the special World Health Organization midwifery school in Phnom Penh who is stationed in the nearby market town. This modern midwife administered preliminary treatment to both Kaiu and the baby and then promptly arranged for them to be taken to a hospital in Phnom Penh. Mother and child returned a couple of weeks later, weak but recovered. Observing these events, I found it interesting that village women prefer to use the traditional old midwife who has delivered so many village babies and call upon the modern midwife only in extremis. But it is also important that they recognize the latter as a specialist who can cope with emergencies; and it is likely that her presence will help to decrease both infant and childbirth mortality.

Both the secular legal code and Buddhist precepts outline certain rights and duties that parents and children have toward one another (see, e.g.,

Clairon, n.d.; Burtt, 1955, p. 110). For instance, parents are obligated to protect, educate, and support their children, see that they make good marriages, and provide for their futures through inheritance. Parents are, in turn, given the right to exact obedience and respect from their children (using punishment when necessary), to approve or veto a child's marriage, to receive support in their old age, and a proper funeral when they die. The parent-child relationship sounds cold, strict, and formal when one reads such codes. But in the reality of village life, it is generally warm, indulgent, and flexible. Parents do indeed fulfill their various obligations to their offspring as best they can: for example, they provide children not only with necessities but also with occasional treats despite the strain on family budgets, worry about their getting adequate schooling and finding suitable spouses, attempt to apportion inheritance equitably, etc. But they also treat children with considerable permissiveness. Discipline consists mostly of verbal rebukes and threats that are not carried out, or, at most, light slaps on the body (severe physical punishment is thought to make a child "rotten"). And young children sometimes become openly defiant and insolent to their parents, although they generally behave respectfully and show deep filial piety when they become adult.

Of the two parents, children generally have deeper emotional ties and more intimate contact with the mother, who is the major source of sustenance and love. A father can also be affectionate, but usually he is openly demonstrative to his children only during their earliest years and becomes more authoritarian as they grow older. While neither Buon nor Srey is overly strict, Buon tends to be less patient and tolerant, quicker to chastise, and more demanding of obedience than is Srey. Relations between fathers and sons may become close as boys begin to work alongside their fathers in the fields and at various tasks. But the mother is always viewed as the warm and nurturing figure by children of both sexes. Several villagers tell bitterly of fathers who had been drunkards, wastrels, "bad characters," or who had abandoned their families (e.g., Buon's father deserted his mother when he was a little boy). But never did anyone speak ill of a mother. Once I asked some people if there were ever instances where children disliked their mothers, and they stared at me in amazement at such an inconceivable question. "No! Of course not! Children *always* love their mothers most of all!" While this reply could be viewed as simply a statement of an ideal, it does seem to be supported in practice; traditional proverbs also assert, "It is better to be deprived of a father than a mother, better to drown than be burned," or "A father is worth a thousand friends and a mother worth a thousand fathers."

The bond between mothers and daughters is especially strong. Close association begins in childhood (as we saw with Mia) and continues into adolescence as mother and daughter cooperate in household and other

A mother and her daughter.

chores, sharing common tasks and concerns. The young woman-to-be, at least before public schooling became widespread, learned virtually all she needed to know to cope with life as an adult female from her mother. And when the mother is relatively young or easygoing, there is great informality between mother and daughter that is more like a relation between peers than one between parent and child.[36] As I mentioned before, Neari jokes with, confides in, teases, and even chides her mother as easily as she does her friends. The intensity of the mother-daughter bond is further manifest in the high incidence of uxorilocal residence spoken of earlier, which is explained by the villagers as the result of girls' reluctance to leave their mothers—who can give them help, advice, and comfort during the rather frightening period of newlywed life and first childbirth.

Mothers and sons are very intimate during a boy's first years. Three-year-old Paa, for instance, the youngest and still the baby of the family, is rarely away from Srey's side. But as boys grow older they begin to loosen the figurative apron strings, as eight-year-old Sok is doing, running off about the village to play with his peers and becoming very impudent to both his parents. (His sisters, however, aged seven, eleven, and thirteen, tend to stick closer to home even when they play.) Sixteen-year-old Pol is even more independent of Srey, busy with school and proudly learning to plow and harrow the fields with his father. Sons continue to have abiding respect and deep affection for their mothers through adolescence and adulthood; but their activities and interests come to center more on male rather than female concerns, they are given much more independence and freedom than are daughters, and they are more likely to leave home upon marriage.

But the tie between parents and children remains strong even after children grow up and, as is often the case, move away. Efforts are made to maintain contact with one another: old people are often absent from the village for weeks at a time on visits to married children who live in other communities. Conversely, adult children (as well as grandchildren) pay return visits, especially during major holidays such as the New Year, which are traditional times of family reunion. Mutual responsibilities also endure. For instance, divorced or widowed offspring can always return to the parrental fold, while aged parents in need will be sent monetary support or taken into a child's home if no one has remained to care for them. And there is a strong moral obligation for children to provide a deceased parent with the finest funeral they can afford as a final act of respect and homage.

Siblings

The relationship between siblings is ideally one of loving harmony and mutual aid. Older siblings, it is said, should help their parents to provide moral guidance, support, and protection for younger brothers and sisters; and younger siblings should give respect and obedience to their elders. In practice, as might be expected, there is a good deal of fighting, name-calling, and even fisticuffs between young siblings. Quarrels often erupt between adult siblings as well. Villagers noted that conflicts between siblings were not at all uncommon, occurring sometimes for serious reasons (e.g., disputes over inheritance) and sometimes trivial ones. To take just one example, Buon has not spoken to his sister for several years, even though she lives only a few houses away, because of a fistfight between their sons and disagreement over which boy hit the other first.

Thus in contrast to the generally strong bond between parents and children, the relationship between siblings is more fragile and underlaid, in many instances, by an ambivalence that can be pushed into open hostility by one thing or another. But by and large, possible antagonism is restrained by the cultural ideal of sibling amity and the belief that ancestral spirits punish discord between close kinsmen. At best, siblings do fulfill the ideal, and ties are particularly close between siblings of the same sex. Srey and Om, for example, are usually inseparable, helping one another about the house and in the fields, sitting together in leisure moments. (Although they, too, had a small tiff at one point when their daughters, Neari and Saan, quarrelled, and each mother took her daughter's side.) The two also visit and receive visits in return from one sister in a neighboring village and another in Phnom Penh; but they see their brothers infrequently, even though one lives nearby. Siblings may also aid one another in various ways: for example, Srey has borrowed money from her urban sister, and one of Srey's daughters is sent to live for part of the year with yet another sister in southern Cambodia who has only one child and both wants and can support another youngster in the house. Even Neari, who battles constantly with her sixteen-year-old brother Pol, will shriek at him one minute and in the next minute tell me earnestly how she is saving up money to buy him a bicycle so he will not have to walk 8 kilometers (about 5 miles) to and from school every day. Siblings may also act as moral guides and arbiters for one another, especially when parents are no longer alive. For instance, Srey's eldest sister made a special trip from Phnom Penh to try to conciliate the rupture between Srey and Om and Neari and Saan, lecturing each in turn on their shameful behavior. In another household, Chek constantly harangues, pleads with, and scolds his younger brother to stop drinking, gambling, and philandering with women.

DIVORCÉES, WIDOWS, AND SPINSTERS

While marriage is the destiny of virtually all women, there are cases of women without husbands: some divorcées, a number of widows, and a few spinsters. Such women bear no stigma and are considered fully adult and full-fledged members of the community, but their lives may be somewhat different from those of their married counterparts.

Divorcées

Husbands and wives, at the very least, tolerate one another, because any serious dissensions can and do lead to divorce. Divorce can be initiated by either the man or woman and is fairly easy to obtain: one simply submits a written request to the local subdistrict office. This request is sent on to a court in Phnom Penh, and the final decree returns within a few months (unless a spouse contests the divorce, in which instance the case may have to go through court hearings). There is no disgrace attached to a divorced person unless he or she behaved abominably in the marriage and acquires a reputation for "bad character."[37] But there seem to be relatively few divorces in village life: there were only four in the hamlet in the past twenty years.

Reasons for divorce are variable. Both Saan and another woman divorced their first husbands on grounds of simple incompatibility. My "landlord" (the brother of Chek just mentioned above) was divorced by his wife because he was an irresponsible wastrel, squandering money on liquor and gambling and not supporting her in a proper manner. Om, Srey's sister, divorced her husband because he had a really "bad character" (it was said that he committed theft and even murder during a period of civil unrest in the countryside, and he was eventually ostracized from the village by his neighbors). Other grounds for divorce noted by the villagers are abandonment, adultery on the part of the wife (but not the husband),[38] repeated or serious physical attacks on the spouse or parents-in-law, conviction of a criminal offense, and refusal to have sexual relations for over a year (see also Clairon, n.d., pp. 69–70).

Upon divorce, each person takes back whatever property he or she brought to the marriage. Any common property acquired by the joint efforts of the spouses was formerly divided two-thirds for the man and one-third for the woman; but at present it is split equally between the two. (There are two interesting exceptions to this: all the common property goes to the wife if she has been abandoned or to the husband if the wife is guilty of adultery.) Custody of offspring, according to both village norms and legal statutes, is decided mainly on the basis of the children's ages or their own desires. Villagers say that children under ten or so years of age almost always stay with the mother, while those old enough to state a definite preference may choose whichever parent they like; or the father may ask for the older children if they and the mother do not object. Villagers stress that the personal preferences of the children are always respected and that usually *all* children opt to stay with the mother. This was indeed the case in all the divorces I knew of.

The husband is legally supposed to pay some sort of maintenance alimony to his ex-wife if she has not remarried and does not have adequate resources to support herself and the children. Among villagers, however, such alimony is rarely paid either because the ex-husband disappears or is too poor to pay child support or because the ex-wife goes back to be supported by her family or remarried quickly. The young divorcée almost always returns to her parents' household (or goes to a sister or an aunt if the parents are dead) until, as is highly likely, she remarries.[39] But the older divorcée without a family to fall back on and little prospect of remarriage often faces a difficult situation unless she has enough resources to support herself and her offspring. Om, for instance, divorced in her late thirties and now about forty-five, barely manages to subsist on a small plot of land and must send two of her children to live with a married daughter for most of the year.

Widows

Girls often play a game when they hear the distinctive cries of the gheko lizard, calling out *kromom* (unmarried or virginal woman) and *memay* (widow[40]) alternately to each successive croak (in a manner similar to our children chanting "loves me—loves me not" while pulling out daisy petals). Whichever coincides with the gheko's last croak is supposed to indicate what a girl's fate will be (or, if the game is played by a boy, what sort of woman he will marry).

Marriages are more frequently cut short by widowing than by divorce. I did not have enough data to calculate mortality rates or average life expectancy, but there were eleven deaths of adults in the hamlet in the past seventeen years. The age composition of the hamlet suggests that deaths become common when people reach their fifties and sixties and that relatively few survive into their seventies and eighties.[41] But some villagers die at an earlier age, for six persons had lost spouses in their twenties and thirties.

Like divorcées, young widows generally go back home to their parents or some other close relative. Next door to me, Em, a young woman in her twenties, had lost her husband a year or so earlier in a terrible accident when he fell from the top of a palm tree while collecting liquid to make into sugar. She moved in with her married sister's family, remarried before long, and she and her new husband continued to stay there because they were too poor to set up their own household. Remarriage is common for both widows and widowers in their twenties, thirties, and even forties for obvious reasons: a widow needs a man to work the fields and a widower needs a woman to tend the household, especially if he has children.[42] Although a widower with children is no bargain for an attractive young girl, he can usually find a spinster or divorcée in her late twenties or thirties who is willing to accept his proposal (this was the case with five widowers in the hamlet). And a widow with children who has her own property or is left executrix of her late husband's estate until her children come of age may be able to attract a man with little or no property of his own (I suspect this was true for Luan, the woman whose husband tried to take another wife).

Individuals left widowed in their late forties or later usually forego remarriage because their remaining days of fertility and hardiness are numbered and because they generally have children who are old enough to provide whatever labor is needed to support the family. In such instances, as I noted before, it is common for one of the children to remain at home after marriage and to assume, along with his or her spouse, much of the burden of supporting the household. This was true in Mia's family and numerous others.

The widow with children who does not remarry, although left with many difficulties, assumes considerable authority and responsibility. She is now recognized as the legal head of the household and administrator of her late husband's property. While she herself does not inherit anything from her spouse and must hold his property in trust for their children, she has the right to use that property and also receives title to one-third the common property.[43] (The widow without children, however, is left rather in the lurch because she receives only the latter, and her deceased hubsand's property goes to his parents or siblings.)

Spinsters

A few women never marry. Spinsters or "old *kromoms*," as unmarried women over the age of forty or so are called, are admittedly rare. There are only five in the entire village of Sobay (roughly 2 percent of the total adult female population of the community), one of whom lives in West Hamlet. Nom is a homely, stolid, taciturn, hard-working woman of fifty-one. I never had the nerve to ask her why she had never married, thinking it would be a rude question; but Srey told me that Nom had simply not been interested in any men or marriage. And perhaps the fact that she was from a relatively poor family and was probably not very pretty as a girl meant that she received few proposals anyway. But Nom has managed very well as a spinster and has even acquired a family of her own by "adopting" a niece, her niece's husband, and their two children, all of whom live with her. Nom is, for all intents and purposes, the maternal head of this household; her niece and nephew-in-law call her mother, just as their children think of her as their grandmother. It is interesting that two other spinsters in other hamlets of the village have the same arrangement as does Nom, with a niece assuming the role of daughter and living with the aunt after marriage. Such "ready-made" families provide these single women with support in their old age, and the situation is also advantageous for young couples who may be poor or orphaned. (Another spinster in Middle Hamlet has been incorporated into a married brother's household.)

Nom and the others just mentioned may be regarded by people as slightly eccentric because they have remained unmarried for one reason or another. But the general live-and-let-live attitude of village life accepts them with a shrug of the shoulders as full-fledged members of the community. There is, however, one unusual case of two spinsters in East Hamlet of whom Srey said, "They live together and work together like man and wife—they do not like men but only each other." While I doubt that these women engaged in lesbian sexual relations, there did seem to be a homosexual attachment between them. These two were considered rather strange by other villagers, but even they were not ostracized.

In a neighboring community there is an even more fascinating example of an unconventional, indeed highly aberrant woman whom I shall call Chia. She is also a spinster—but one with three illegitimate daughters. I saw her briefly once or twice—a small, gentle, sweet-looking old lady—and I could scarcely believe the things that Srey and Kim's mother told me about her. As best, as I can piece the story together, Chia had had illicit sexual relations with some man (or men?) in her village and borne *three* illegitimate children. While extramarital sex and illegitimacy are not considered absolutely heinous and unforgivable transgressions, neither are they condoned. They incur great gossip and censure—behind one's back, to be sure, since villagers are extremely reluctant to voice criticism directly to anyone's face. But nonetheless one would certainly know what was being said. So it took a kind of reckless courage for Chia to march down her deviant path, ignoring the whispers, raised eyebrows, disapproving looks, and turned backs that must have surrounded her. What is even more incredible is that she is suspected of having committed abortion or infanticide on even another child. But no one knew for certain, so no one dared to make a direct accusation; and again there was only hushed gossip. So, Chia lived to be a gray-haired old woman with a scarlet past, supported by her illegitimate daughters, and still looked at askance but not completely ostracized.

GRANDMOTHER MIEK

Miek, age sixty, is a typical *yeey*, a "grandmother" or "old woman." Like the other women past the age of menopause, her gray hair is cropped short in a brush only an inch or so long, a custom which neutralizes her sex (it is sometimes difficult for an outsider to distinguish between old men and women) and seems to symbolize, like the shaved heads of Buddhist monks, renunciation of worldly concern with physical beauty. She dresses in plain white blouses and black sarongs. Her body and face are gaunt, the skin pulled tight over her bones without a spare ounce of flesh; but she is still handsome and generally hardy. Grandmother Miek is a lady in the truest sense, a women of serene temperament and dignified bearing. She is not remote or aloof, for she is always ready to smile and, like the other "grandmothers" who greeted me on my arrival in the village, she radiates affection and consideration for others. But she is never boisterous, ill-mannered, or given to outbursts of temper or unkind remarks; her words and actions are informed by a deep intelligence and wisdom. People be-

An old Khmer "grandmother."

come somehow more composed and better behaved in her presence, and they know that they can go to her unhesitatingly in time of trouble for comfort and help.

Miek, like others of her generation, married at an earlier age than young women do now. At sixteen she became the wife of Peng, a spirited, industrious young man of twenty-two who was also born in West Hamlet. Unlike most couples, they lived neolocally from the start of their marriage because Peng had the financial resources and skill at carpentry necessary to build a new house for his bride. Miek bore two sons. One moved to Phnom Penh; but the other, Von, brought his wife to live virilocally. So the nuclear family changed into an extended one which eventually came to include Von's four children.[44]

There can be problems in such extended families when the younger couple chafes under parental authority, is cramped in small quarters, or feels burdened by the responsibility of caring for sick or aging parents. But Von and his wife, Sieng, are fortunate in several respects. The house is large enough to be curtained off into separate sections for each couple, and recently Peng and Miek, to give themselves more quiet and privacy, have taken to spending most of their time in a small structure (originally built as a granary) adjacent to the big house. Moreover, while Peng and Miek are still of sound mind and body and thus retain nominal authority over the entire household, the younger couple are given considerable independence and control over their own affairs. For instance, Von and Sieng keep their own stores of rice, prepare separate meals, maintain their own family budget, and make their own decisions on matters concerning themselves and their children.[45] Finally, both Von and Sieng are hard-working, even-tempered, responsible individuals who feel a deep sense of respect and filial piety for the older couple. (Sieng is an admirable daughter-in-law. Her temperament and character are remarkably like Miek's, so she works smoothly with her mother-in-law. She has great affection for her father-in-law as well, often weaving him scarves and sarongs of special color and design on her loom.)

Von does not think in terms of compensation for his efforts in supporting Peng and Miek, for it is considered only fitting that offspring should care for aged parents in their declining years, just as they were cared for as children. But Von will receive the lion's share of the rice paddies plus the house and all its furnishings, land in the village, palm trees, and jewelry as his inheritance. This is thought to be only fair because, as Miek says, "Von's duties have been so heavy," and the other son earns a good living in the city. It is also a good example of the way in which the concept of equal inheritance for all children is actually adjusted in practice to take account of varying circumstances. But such inequalities of inheritance are actually fair-minded attempts by parents to provide for those offspring who deserve or need a larger share than others.

Miek, like other villagers, is related to a great many people in the village as well as in other communities. There are no organized larger kin groups beyond the household, but individuals recognize a wide range of kinsmen on both the maternal and paternal sides of the family. Although they do not often keep track of exact genealogical links beyond first or second cousins, they will remember that "so-and-so is a kinsman" of some sort; and relatives by marriages (not only parents- or siblings-in-law but, say, a wife's sister's husband) are also included in the general circle of "kin." There are no rigid rules of behavior toward kinsmen beyond the family; the extent and nature of actual interaction between relatives is determined to a high degree by individual sentiments and circumstances, such that a person may be very intimate with one relative and not another. Nonetheless, there is a general feeling that one *should* be friendly toward

and assist kinsmen in various ways, and this norm is fulfilled in many instances. Relatives may, for example, exchange cooperative labor in rice
cultivation, give one another a hand in preparing for weddings and funerals, lend each other goods or money, or offer one another shelter.

Miek's household periodically includes miscellaneous relatives. Some,
such as the grandchildren who live in Phnom Penh, come for days or weeks
on pleasure trips. Others, such as a nephew from the city who stayed for
several months, come for more serious reasons, in this instance to recuperate
from a debilitating illness in the healthy country air. I have already given
several other examples of families who have taken in relatives. One important fact about such situations is that individuals who are ill, orphaned,
destitute, or otherwise in need and whose parents are dead or unable to
provide help will almost always join the household of a female relative:
usually that of an elder sister, mother's sister, or grandmother. For it is
not surprising that a person in distress would seek out or be rescued by the
closest substitute for a mother.[46] There is also the interesting custom of the
towaa or fictional kin relation: when an individual (usually male) must
travel or temporarily reside in a strange place, he will often ask someone
to informally "adopt" him. That "someone" is generally a woman who becomes known as a *"towaa* mother" and provides protection, companionship,
aid, and lodgings for her *"towaa* child."[47] Several women in the hamlet
have *towaa* children (e.g., Mia's grandmother has two); but Miek has had
more than all the rest put together, because her warm and generous nature
is widely known. So her household sometimes also includes *towaa* sons who
stay for varying lengths of time.

Miek is still strong and by no means idle. She can still transplant and
harvest rice with dexterity and speed born of long years of experience
(when large work teams of girls and women assemble for these tasks, she
and the other older women race ahead of the younger girls and tease them
about their slowness). Although her eyes are getting a bit weak and her
fingers a little stiff, she can still cook, help with housekeeping, make mats
and baskets, baby-sit with her grandchildren, and do other tasks to care for
herself and Peng and assist her daughter-in-law.

But with the main burden of subsistence passed on to the younger generation, old people such as Miek have increased leisure time. Part of this
leisure is used for extended visits to see her married son and grandchildren
in Phnom Penh. But it is devoted, above all, to religious activities. Mindful
that death and the final tallying of merit which will determine the next
incarnation are not far off and no longer weighed down by the mundane
worries of daily existence, the elderly turn their thoughts to spiritual concerns. Both men and women become highly devout in their old age: they
observe virtually all the ten major Buddhist precepts,[48] remain secluded in
meditation or go to the temple on the Holy Days that are similar to the

Judaeo-Christian Sabbath, and attend all temple ceremonies—lesser events as well as large festivals, staying on through all the prayers that younger adults often skip because they must get home to do chores. Such acts earn old people a great deal of religious merit in their last years of life, as well as respect from other villagers.

This necessity to earn merit weighs especially heavily on women. Buddhism considers females to be inferior to males, and to be born a woman indicates that one had accumulated only a limited amount of merit in the previous incarnation. Women are not permitted to become monks, the means whereby males can earn a tremendous amount of merit at one blow, and there is no comparable order of nuns.[49] Buddhism does not completely denigrate women, for it does preach respect for one's mother, consideration and loyalty to one's wife, and solicitude for one's daughters. But it seems to view women rather suspiciously as possible temptresses who may lure monks from their vows of chastity,[50] for monks are forbidden to be alone with women, to take objects directly from the hands of women, to glance immodestly at women, and so on. Thus, a woman starts out with several strikes against her and must work harder to compensate for them. This, plus the fact that dishes of special foods are one of the main offerings that villagers can afford to give to the monks, seems to account for the great preponderance of females at various temple ceremonies. Some of the lesser events are attended almost exclusively by women such as Miek plus a few old men.[51] Women, then, tend to be much more conscientious about their dedication to Buddhism throughout their lifetimes, in contrast to males— who generally become very devout only in their final years.

In addition to their devotions at the Buddhist temple, Miek and Peng are frequently called upon to participate in village rituals such as weddings. Peng is noted as an *achaa*, a sort of lay priest or "master of ceremonies" in the literal sense of one who knows how to conduct various rituals. Miek is also asked quite often to assume certain ceremonial roles—at weddings or betrothals—which must be filled by honorable and happily married women, for she has a widespread reputation for "good character" as well as knowledgeability about proper ritual procedures. Some women also act as religious specialists in the realm of the traditional folk religion. While almost all curers are male, there is one old lady in a nearby village who occasionally conducts curing rituals for Sobay residents. And spirit mediums, who once a year go into trance and are possessed by spirits of the dead who speak through their mouths, are almost always female.[52]

WOMEN IN SOCIETY

While the central government has a few women occupying ministerial or other posts, females do not hold formal positions of political authority at the village level. The elected offices of village headman and subdistrict chief, while not legally barred to females, have traditionally been held by men, and no woman would consider running for them. In fact, women were officially granted the right to vote only in 1956. They have accepted the franchise with great pride and enthusiasm (e.g., in an election for sub-district chief in which well over a thousand voters participated, about half the votes were cast by women); but they, like the male villagers, know little of national politics.[53]

In an informal capacity, however, women can exert some influence not only within the household but within the community. While all old people, male and female, are granted a certain amount of deference from younger villagers, some of them achieve special prestige and authority by virtue of their exceptional "good character" which fulfills all the ideals of behavior, their reputation for wisdom and good judgment, and their ability to direct and organize people when the need arises. Peng is one of these, and so is Miek. While she does not carry as much weight as her husband, she is acknowledged by all as a wise and admirable woman, called upon for ad-vice on personal as well as ceremonial matters, and her opinions of people and situations are given serious consideration by both her husband and her neighbors.

During Miek's lifetime, the status of women in the society at large has undergone some changes, as it had in preceding centuries. The chronicles of early travelers to Southeast Asia indicate that women occupied high and honorable positions in the ancient kingdoms. A Chinese envoy to Angkor in the thirteenth century speaks of women holding posts as court astron-omers and astrologers, judges, and palace guards, and notes further that women were skilled at commercial activities, given considerable freedom and mobility from an early age, and granted prerogatives in dress that were not allowed to males (see Pelliott, 1951). Several writers also believe that the ancient Khmer were matrilineal[54] and that the present-day tendency to uxorilocal residence is a survival of this earlier system.

But after the fall of Angkor the position of women—at least as it is delineated in the legal codes—declined for reasons that are not altogether clear. After the fourteenth century, females were viewed as legal minors who could be sold into slavery by their husbands to pay their husbands' debts, could not bring suits in court, received only one-third of the common property upon divorce, etc., although they were granted some rights and protection under law. During the period of French colonial rule, which lasted from the mid-nineteenth to the mid-twentieth century, the subordi-nate position of women was maintained. Although debt slavery was abol-ished, the French Napoleonic Code, which had some influence on Cam-bodian civil law, also considered females as subject to the authority of fathers and husbands (see Thierry, 1955, for more details on the preceding).

The legal position of women in modern-day Cambodia is still inferior to that of males in several respects, as I have already noted. But it is important to recognize that the contemporary civil code (see Clairon, n.d.) does attempt to protect females in many ways and treats them more equitably now on matters such as the division of property upon divorce. Moreover, after Cambodia achieved independence in 1955, women were granted the franchise and the right to hold political office (Steinberg, 1959, p. 122).

It is also important to remember that legal codes do not necessarily indicate the actual position of females in the day-to-day reality of life, especially in village society. The preceding discussion of Srey, Miek, and others lends support to the assertion made by many writers that Khmer women, as well as women in other Southeast Asian countries, possess substantial authority, independence, and freedom.[55] Of particular significance in this respect is, I believe, the indispensable economic role played by village women. The peasant wife and mother does not simply tend the children and household; she actively contributes to the material support of her family by helping to cultivate the rice paddies and by engaging, when necessary, in various part-time pursuits to earn money.[56] In the village division of labor, the roles of Southeast Asian men and women are "complementary" (Hanks, 1963, p. 444; Khaing, 1963, p. 116) and essential to one another. Women also traditionally manage the household budget, marketing, and some commercial transactions; these responsibilities not only reflect their financial acumen but bring them into contact with the world outside the village.

The status of women is enhanced also by the bilaterality of Khmer kinship, which gives equal weight to both the paternal and maternal sides of the family and permits women to own and transmit property in their own right. Moreover, while men are theoretically dominant within the household, the local sociopolitical structure, and the realm of Buddhism, we have seen that mothers are the focus of deep emotional attachments, that women can exert influence in varied ways (see, for instance, the high incidence of uxorilocal residence and the limited amount of polygny), and that females are important in the actual performance of Buddhist doctrine and ritual. The village women have also long had freedom of movement outside the home, not only within the village but beyond to the temple, the marketplace, and other communities.

At the present time, the main role played by adult village women such as Srey and Miek is as wife-cum-mother (although this role is, of course, multifaceted in village life). But the younger generation of Kim, Srey's younger daughters, and Miek's granddaughters may, with adequate education, have the possibility of an alternative or additional role in some sort of career. Education, with the new horizons it opens, is perhaps the most important change that has come into the lives of village girls, and it may affect the future status of Khmer women in general as more of them become capable of entering various occupations and professions. Even those girls who do not think in terms of a career still harbor hopes of leaving village life by marrying men who are not peasants. In short, the younger generation of female villagers aspires to geographical and socioeconomic mobility, and many of them may well succeed in finding lives that are less arduous than those of their mothers and grandmothers. Finally, if Western ideologies concerning the equality of women filter into Cambodian culture, Khmer women in the future may be granted more equality under law and greater participation in local and national government.

APPENDIX

Urban Women

I am hesitant to discuss the position of urban women because my knowledge of their lives is so limited that I fear making misleading or erroneous statements. Although I have seen hundreds of city women on the streets of Phnom Penh, I have actually met less than half a dozen of them, and then in only brief encounters.[59] Thus many of my remarks must be taken as tentative inferences drawn from very limited data rather than as definitive statements. Moreover, the fact that urban women belong to different socioeconomic strata makes it even more difficult to generalize about them.

In Phnom Penh, the major city in Cambodia, one encounters Khmer women as coolie laborers on construction projects, "water pullers" (parts of the city have no plumbing and water is brought to homes in huge wheeled drums), snack sellers, domestic servants, bar girls, prostitutes, store clerks, secretaries, teachers, midwives, radio announcers, actresses, singers, operators of various businesses (e.g., stores),[58] and a few government bureaucrats or officials.[59]

Some of these jobs clearly fall into the category of unskilled labor and are filled by lower-class urban women who, like their village counterparts, must work to help support their families. Other occupations, however, require some education or training and are probably held by women from varied backgrounds. Some may have come from peasant or urban lower-class homes but were able to take advantage of government scholarship or training programs. I imagine, however, that most are from middle- or upper-class families that could afford to give their daughters a secondary school or perhaps even college education.[60] Upper-class women obviously do not *need* to work, but there are some who choose to do so—perhaps because they have unusual ambition or have been influenced by Western ideas that a woman with talent and intelligence should utilize her abilities.[61]

I have no information regarding job discrimination against women except for one statement that industrial wages for women average 25 percent less than for men in the same positions (Steinberg, 1959, p. 178). I would hazard a guess that women would meet strong prejudice only in the realm of high government. It is true that aristocratic women have held honored positions as queens, princesses, and royal consorts since the time of the ancient kingdoms and may well have wielded some influence in such positions. But after Cambodia achieved independence, the king became only a symbolic head of state; real political power was vested in a constitutional administration with a premier, cabinet, ministries, assembly, etc.[62] So far as I know, women have yet to acquire top-ranking positions of authority in this new national government. This may be due also, however, to lack of motivation and drive on the part of females to pursue demanding careers, for women are similarly rare or nonexistent (to my knowledge) in professions such as law, medicine, the natural and social sciences, etc. (But actually, there are relatively few Khmer men in such realms.)

It is my impression that most middle- and upper-class Khmer women lead purely domestic lives with no outside occupations.[63] They may do so for several reasons: because there is no economic pressure to work, because they have no desire to pursue careers outside the home, or because they may feel that it is a mark of prestige *not* to work. I would speculate further that in households where wives do not work, there is a much clearer delineation, as well as separation, between male and female spheres of life. Obviously there is still complementarity between the roles of husband and wife in urban families, but the situation differs from that of peasant men and women who labor alongside one another and share various tasks.[64] The nonworking urban wife's primary and almost exclusive function is to tend the household and children. (Note, however, that in relatively well-to-do families it is domestic servants who do most of the actual housework, cooking, marketing, etc.) On the other hand, the urban husband has a job away from home (in an occupation with which the wife may have no contact) and bears the main burden for financial support of the family.[65]

There is some evidence that urban men may have more social life of their own outside the home as well.[66] Americans often commented on the fact that Khmer officials almost never brought their wives to parties given by diplomatic personnel (although I am certain that urban women attend strictly Khmer social events). Urban husbands are also more likely to have extramarital amorous interests. Men have ready access to the company of bar girls or prostitutes, and if there is at least a modicum of truth in gossip, a number of them also have adulterous affairs or keep concubines.[67] Polygyny, too, is evidently more common among middle- and upper-class men in Phnom Penh than it is in the countryside.

I do not know if urban women have the degree of authority and independence enjoyed by village women. It may be impossible to generalize on this point because there is probably variation among individual families and different socioeconomic levels. But I suspect that many nonworking urban wives may be somewhat more cloistered than their village sisters. City women undoubtedly venture outside their homes to shop, attend the Buddhist temple, or visit relatives and friends (and those with servants certainly would have more time for such activities than village women). But I think that they would feel less free to wander around the city in the way a peasant woman can roam about her village;[68] that the daily routines of well-to-do women occur largely within the confines of their villas and apartments,[69] in contrast to village life where most activities occur outside the house and allow a woman ample opportunities for contact with others; and that, as I suggested before, urban women may be restricted from accompanying their husbands to certain events (e.g., parties with foreigners) or places (e.g., bars).

Bilateral kinship structure[70] and nuclear or extended families occur in the city as well as in the village. The urban woman doubtless enjoys authority within the domestic sphere, charged as she is with the major responsibility for surveillance of children and supervision of servants; and she has the same legal rights to own property, initiate divorce proceedings, etc., as do village females. I suspect, however, that urban men, particularly in the upper social strata, may wield a stronger hand over their wives and families than do village men. My impression is that relationships within upper-class families may be somewhat more formal and strict, that the father may be more of a patriarchal and authoritarian figure, and that husbands have more freedom to come and go or do as they please.[71] But I am not at all certain that these conjectures are correct, and urban wives may well wield more power over their husbands than I give them credit for. Whatever the case may be with respect to the urban woman's relation to her husband, she undoubtedly receives great respect and affection from her children and plays a crucial role in their lives. In the end, despite the possibility that she may have somewhat less voice and freedom than her village sisters, the urban wife-and-mother still occupies a critical position in her family.

NOTES

1. Sobay is a pseudonym for the community I studied under the auspices of the Ford Foundation Foreign Area Training Fellowship Program. Although I shall use the ethnographic present, I must emphasize that my account deals with Cambodia of a decade ago and that conditions have undoubtedly changed considerably in the past few years because of warfare. For greater detail on various aspects of life in Sobay, see Ebihara, 1964 and 1968.

2. About 15 percent of Cambodia's population is composed of various minority groups such as the Chinese, Vietnamese, Cham, tribal groups, etc., whom I shall not discuss.

3. A few families in West Hamlet own 2 or more hectares of paddies and are considered to be "people [who have] enough" and do not have to scrimp as much as the "poor people" who comprise the majority of households. But there are no class distinctions within the village itself.

4. Theravada (or Hinayana) Buddhism, which is dominant in most of mainland Southeast Asia and Ceylon, considers itself to be closer to the original, orthodox Buddhist doctrine than the Mahayana Buddhism of China, Japan, Korea, and Tibet.

5. Boys may also participate in such play, but they are usually very young ones who are roped in by their older sisters. Boys sometimes imitate adult male activities, such as plowing, but they do so relatively rarely.

6. Among the Khmer it is customary for males to become monks at some point in their lives. In Theravada Buddhism, monkhood need not be a permanent commitment; therefore most village males enter the monastery for a period of a year or more during their youth and then resume secular life.

7. Village children are encouraged in such hopes by what they see at a nearby normal school, where many young men and women from rural backgrounds are being trained at government expense to become public school teachers, in return for a promise to spend ten years in the public school system.

8. It is estimated that only 16 percent of secondary school pupils in Cambodia are female (Ward, 1963, p. 56).

9. The term used, *song saa,* literally means "fiancé" and is also sometimes used to refer to lovers. But in this context it is comparable to the way children in our own society tease one another about having boyfriends or girlfriends.

10. There is still a sort of survival of the concept of "the shade" in the feeling that menstruation should be concealed from and never mentioned in the presence of men. I was once roundly chastised by some women for inquiring about the *Chol Mlop* ceremonies in the presence of males.

11. The village women were distressed that I, an unmarried young woman at that time, cut my hair almost as short as a boy's (because of the heat) and made no effort to curl it. They were much relieved when, toward the end of my stay, I let it grow out.

12. Villagers customarily put any cash savings into jewelry rather than in banks. So jewelry serves an important function aside from mere ornamentation.

13. I might note that Neari and Saan were selected by the villagers (not me) to be my housekeepers—not on the basis of any special skills they had, but because they were both from poor families who needed money.

14. While girls may acknowledge the handsomeness or good qualities of young men in the hamlet, the latter are generally dismissed as possible marriage partners because they are too much like brothers or old chums. (And boys feel much the same about the girls next door.) People in other communities, however, arouse much more romantic interest. This is one of several reasons for a high incidence of village exogamy (marriage to someone outside the village), although about one-quarter of marriages involve village endogamy (marriage within the community).

15. But opportunities for young men to have premarital sex are limited. It would be very difficult and risky to find a sex partner in the village, and there is little money or chance to frequent prostitutes in the city. So they speak rather wistfully of desiring sex but not being able to get any.

16. Unmarried young women and males are not permitted to witness childbirth. Indeed, I was firmly forbidden to do so, although villagers allowed me to do many other things prohibited to their own young women.

17. The minimum *legal* age for marriage is fourteen for females and seventeen for males, although one can apply for special dispensation to marry earlier (Clairon, n.d., p. 56).

18. It is believed that ancestral spirits (*meba*) frown on any serious discord within the family or between kinsmen and will punish offenders by causing some innocent member of the family or kindred to fall ill.

19. This is another reason for the high percentage of village exogamous marriages; land holdings in West Hamlet have become increasingly fragmented and limited with each successive generation of inheritance.

20. For charts of favorable and unfavorable astrological combinations, see Porée-Maspero, 1962.

21. This money is used to buy clothes and jewelry for the bride and to help defray the expenses of the wedding ceremony, which are borne by her family.

22. Villagers attribute the decline of this custom partly to weakening tradition and partly to the fact that more village girls became engaged to men with nonagricultural occupations which do not permit time off to render bride service.

23. For details of the marriage ceremony as well as birth, first menstruation, and betrothal rituals, see Porée-Maspero et al., 1958.

24. Many other villagers assumed a very protective attitude toward me because I was, at the time, young, unmarried, and female and thus considered much more vulnerable than a male would have been under the same circumstances.

25. Actually, the women chew a quid made from bits of areca nut and a sprinkling of lime wrapped in a betel leaf. This concoction, which has a mildly stimulating effect, produces reddish saliva which stains the mouth.

26. There is no rule with respect to sex or birth order about which child remains at home after marriage. Statistically, however, it is most often a daughter. Occasionally, there may be two married children in residence, or a widowed or divorced child with offspring, or a married niece or nephew.

27. For details on the legal position of wives in Cambodia, see Thierry, 1955; Clairon, n.d.; Daguin, n.d.

28. Indeed, in Cambodia as a whole, polygyny is quite rare (an estimated 1.6 percent of recorded marriages in 1952) and appears to be limited generally to relatively wealthy men (Thierry, 1955, pp. 157–158). For legal statutes regarding polygyny and concubinage, see Clairon, n.d., pp. 51–55.

29. The raising of pigs and chickens for sale is looked on askance by very strict Buddhists because the taking of life is regarded as a cardinal sin, and these animals are nurtured only to be eventually killed for food (even though the villagers themselves never do the actual slaughtering). It is thus interesting that the care of pigs and chickens devolves mainly on women; for while this may be a matter of pure expediency in the division of labor, it may also reflect the fact that women hold a lower status in Buddhism than do men.

30. In a bilateral system, there is no special emphasis put on either the male or female line, such as is found in patrilineal or matrilineal societies. Rather, both lines are given equal weight: for instance, inheritance can pass from either or both parents to both sons and daughters; individuals have the same kind of relations and obligations to kinsmen on both the father's and mother's sides of the family, etc.

31. In a study I made of villagers' journeys outside Sobay (Ebihara, 1971), I was struck by the fact that women traveled almost as much as did men to a variety of places.

32. Steinberg (1959, p. 77) states that five children is considered the ideal number, but I never encountered this notion.

33. A crude estimate of the birthrate in West Hamlet is, in traditional demographic terms, 21.25 births per 1,000 persons or, on a smaller scale, about 3 to 4 births a year for this population of about 160.

34. Men know of the existence of condoms but view them as a means of preventing the transmission of venereal disease rather than contraception.

35. Cf. Delvert (1961, pp. 320–321), who estimates about 12 percent mortality before one year of age.

36. Nash, 1965, p. 151 ff. notes a similar situation among the Burmese.

37. A divorcée, however, usually commands less of a monetary gift from the groom's family when she remarries and generally has a less elaborate wedding than someone being wed for the first time.

38. Buon admitted to me that he had once had a brief affair with a woman while working in Phnom Penh. But he was overcome with guilt and shame afterward (not to mention a dose of venereal disease) and confessed it all to Srey. She was furious (and still gets mad to this day when she thinks about it), but she forgave him.

39. According to law, a divorcée must wait ten months from the date of the final decree to remarry. This practice is designed to avoid any questions about the paternity of a child that might be born after the divorce (Clairon, n.d., p. 58).

40. The term *memay* is also used to refer to divorcées.

41. This accords with Delvert (1961, pp. 320–321) who, on the basis of limited figures, suggests that most deaths occur after the age of fifty-five.

42. There are no rules regarding when a widow (or widower) may remarry, but villagers say that it is customary to wait several months after the death of one's spouse (see also Clairon, n.d., p. 58).

43. For other legal statutes concerning widows, see Clairon, n.d., pp. 128–130; Lingat, 1952, vol. II, pp. 130–135, 169–170; and Thierry, 1955, pp. 117–118, 145–146.

44. A fifth baby was one of the children who died during my stay. A sickly infant from the start, she survived only three months.

45. Where, however, the old parents are ill, senile, or widowed, the extended family is more likely to operate as a single unit with one granary, one budget, communal meals, etc.

46. Some individuals may go to "father figures" such as an elder brother or uncle, but this is relatively rare. Out of eighteen cases in the village where families took in kinsmen other than grandchildren, sixteen involved relatives of the wife. Similar situations are reported for Malaya, Java, and Burma (see Djamour, 1959, pp. 63–64; Geertz, 1961, p. 34; and Nash, 1965, p. 153).

47. A *towaa* sibling relation may also be formed by two very close friends, who will then consider one another's parents as *towaa* parents.

48. The first five precepts which all villagers try to observe more or less constantly are as follows: do not kill living things (including animals), do not lie, do not steal, do not engage in immoral sexual relations, and do not drink intoxicating beverages. The last five (do not eat after noon, do not sleep on a raised bed, do not indulge in sensuous activities such as dancing, do not wear cosmetics or jewelry, and do not touch money) are usually followed only by old people, or the extremely devout, or on Holy Days.

49. Leclére (1899, p. 425) speaks of "nuns" or women who voluntarily observe vows similar to those taken by monks; but I never encountered any. Some old village women, however, go to live at the temple to serve the monks or to stay in seclusion to meditate and pray. I should note also that it is thought that some of the merit earned by the monk is supposed to accrue to his parents.

50. Zadrozny (1955, pp. 342–343, 345–346) notes that the idea of females possessing dangerous sexual powers occurs also in Khmer folk beliefs and folklore.

51. For instance, at one event, females outnumbered males about four to one. The women ranged in age from adolescents to old ladies, while the men were all middle-aged or elderly.

52. Why this is so, I do not really know. But it is interesting to note that the spirit medium is an essentially passive figure, one whose body is taken by spirits to use as a

channel for communication with the living. The medium can convey messages and confer good luck, but she does not control the spirits or possess any ritual knowledge that can influence or sway events—as does the curer, a type of sorcerer who can kill people (the latter are very rare, and they are always male). These ritual specializations are, then, perhaps consistent with the general notion that, in theory at least, males are active figures of power while females are more passive creatures.

53. Ward (1963, p. 65) notes that the same is true for Burmese and Thai women.

54. See, for instance, Coedès, 1953; Thierry, 1955; O'Sullivan, 1962. I believe that the Khmer kinship system has always been basically bilateral, but it is interesting to note that different degrees of cousins are defined in terms of sharing the same female ancestress (e.g., first cousin = "one grandmother," second cousin = "one great-grandmother," etc.).

55. See, e.g., Thierry, 1955, p. 155; Steinberg, 1959, p. 79; Burling, 1965, p. 2; Ward, 1963; Khaing, 1963 and 1967, Hanks, 1963.

56. Women are also essential coworkers in villages that pursue various cottage industries. For instance, I have seen women cooperating in the production of pottery and bronze ware, and women are the primary producers in villages that specialize in weaving.

57. For some of the information I am indebted to Mr. and Mrs. Dale Purtle, who served several years with the foreign service in Phnom Penh and therefore had more occasion than I to come into contact with urban women.

58. A number of upper-class women are also said to be the legal owners, if not actual working heads, of companies or real estate registered in their names by Chinese husbands. Much of the upper stratum of Cambodian society is Sino-Cambodian because of considerable intermarriage between Chinese and Khmer; until recently, Chinese were classified as aliens who could not legally own property (see Willmott, 1967). Khmer-Chinese marriages are relatively rare at the village level.

59. There is also one librarian that I knew of, as well as a number of young women (primarily, I believe, from the upper class) who comprise the Royal Cambodian Ballet, a troupe which performs classical Khmer dances only for the royal court or on state occasions. Khmer women doubtless hold other occupations as well, but I have listed only those that I or the Purtles definitely knew of. It should be noted that many varied jobs in the city are held by non-Khmer women, notably Chinese and Vietnamese.

60. Some upper-class girls are even sent to France for part of their education.

61. For instance, I met one woman, the wife of a wealthy import-exporter, who translated documents from Khmer into French for a project devoted to the compilation of Khmer customs; another young woman, who had some schooling in the United States, worked in a United States Information Agency library.

62. The monarchy was abolished and Cambodia declared a Republic in 1970. A parenthetical but interesting note is that under the recent conditions of warfare, women have evidently been drawn into military service. I would guess, though, that females serve with "home guard" sorts of units and not with active fighting troops.

63. Ward (1963, p. 50) states that in various Asian countries it is common to find gainfully employed women among the poor and fairly well-to-do (who are educated and freed by servants from domestic chores) but not among the middle range or the extremely wealthy.

64. I might note that, in the village division of labor, there are some tasks that men or women do exclusively (e.g., a woman would never plow a field). But a number of other chores can be performed by either males or females either as a matter of course (e.g., harvesting rice) or in times of necessity (e.g., a woman *can* drive an oxcart if she has to).

65. That is, unless the wife is wealthy in her own right and may derive some income from property holdings or remittances from parents.

66. Certainly village men could also be said to have some "social life" of their own in the sense that they often gather together to talk among themselves, apart from women. But they are rarely beyond easy reach of their wives.

67. Clairon (n.d., p. 51) states that "Le concubinage est de 9 à 10% en ville," although it is not clear what the percentage refers to. A concubine is distinct from a first- or second-rank wife and, although recognized by the law, is not owed the various obligations due to a married spouse. (Her children, however, are entitled to inheritance from their genitor.) See Clairon, n.d., p. 55 for more details.

68. Very wealthy women may, however, have considerable mobility. For instance, one woman had a chauffeur-driven car at her disposal, and I heard of one royal princess who often traveled to Europe and other countries.

69. As an example, one day I stopped by the home of an official and found his young wife, who did not have children, puttering aimlessly around her apartment with nothing to do but wait for her husband's return. Khaing (1967, p. 347) suggests that urban Thai and Burmese women lead more sheltered lives than village women, and Swift (1963, p. 283) posits the same for aristocratic Malay females. Ward (1963, p. 77) suggests that, by and large, women in lower socioeconomic classes generally have more freedom and a higher status within the family than do those in the upper classes. On the other hand, unmarried Khmer girls in the city may enjoy somewhat more freedom than young women in the village. Steinberg (1959, p. 83) states that there is some dating among college students in Phnom Penh, and, as I noted before, some girls may be sent away to school.

70. One exception is the *baku,* a group which has traditionally served as priests for royal court rituals, who are said to practice patrilineal descent (Aymonier, 1900, vol. I, p. 63). Aymonier also noted (pp. 61–63) a patrilineal emphasis among royalty and their descendants; but I do not know if this is still the case.

71. These surmises are based only on impressions and inferences. I think that notions of proper decorum and etiquette may prevail more in upper-class families than in the easy give-and-take informality of village life. One middle-class man told me of the strict discipline imposed upon him as a child, which was quite unlike what I saw in village families; and some sources (e.g., Monod, 1931, p. 32) speak of upper-class children having to kneel properly and fold their hands before their parents. It is also possible that the authority of the urban male is strengthened by the fact that his wife and children are dependent on him for material support, and he may have significantly more dealings with and knowledge of the world outside the home than does his wife. By contrast, the village woman, while certainly less well educated and sophisticated than her urban counterpart, may know and deal with just about as much of the external world as does her husband.

BIBLIOGRAPHY

Aymonier, Étienne: *Le Cambodge,* E. Leroux, Paris, 1900.

Burling, Robbins: *Hill Farms and Padi Fields, Life in Mainland Southeast Asia,* Prentice-Hall, Inc., Englewood Cliffs, N.J., 1965.

Burtt, E. A.: *The Teachings of the Compassionate Buddha,* American Library, New York, 1955.

Clairon, Marcel: *Droit civil Khmer,* E.K.L.I.P., Phnom Penh, n.d.

Codès, Georges: "Le substrat autochtone et la superstructure indienne au Cambodge et à Java," *Journal of World History,* vol. I, pp. 827–838, 1953.

Daguin, Arthur: *Le mariage cambodgien,* Lucien Dorbon Librairie, Paris, n.d.

Delvert, Jean: *Le paysan cambodgien,* Mouton, Paris, 1961.

Djamour, Judith: *Malay kinship and marriage in Singapore,* Monographs of Social Anthropology no. 21, London School of Economics, Athlone Press, London, 1959.

Ebihara, May: *Khmer,* in F. LeBar, G. Hickey, J. Musgrave (eds.), *Ethnic Groups of Mainland Southeast Asia,* Human Relations Area Files Press, New Haven, Mass., 1964.

————: *A Khmer Village in Cambodia,* University Microfilms, Ann Arbor, Mich., 1968.

————: "Inter-Village, Village-Town, and Village-City Relations in Cambodia," Paper delivered to the New York Academy of Sciences, 1971.

Geertz, Hildred: *The Javanese Family,* The Free Press of Glencoe, Inc., New York, 1961.

Hanks, Lucien and Jane: "Thailand: Equality between the Sexes," in B. Ward (ed.), *Women in the New Asia,* UNESCO, Amsterdam, 1963.

Khaing, Mimi: "Burma: Balance and Harmony," in B. Ward (ed.), *Women in the New Asia,* UNESCO, Amsterdam, 1963.

————: "Burma and Southeast Asia," in R. Patai (ed.), *Women in the Modern World,* The Free Press, New York, 1967.

Leclère, Adhemard: *Le Bouddhisme au Cambodge,* E. Leroux, Paris [1899].

Lingat, Robert: *Les régimes matrimoniaux de sud-est de l'Asie, essai de droit comparé indochinois,* vol. II, Publications of the École Française d'Extrême-Orient no. 34, E. de Boccard, Paris, 1952.

Monod, G. H.: *Le Cambodgien,* Larose, Paris, 1931.

Nash, June, and Manning Nash: "Marriage, Family, and Population Growth in Upper Burma," *Southwestern Journal of Anthropology,* vol. 19, pp. 251–266.

Nash, Manning: *The Golden Road to Modernity, Village Life in Contemporary Burma,* John Wiley & Sons, Inc., New York, 1965.

O'Sullivan, Kevin: "Concentric Conformity in Ancient Khmer Kinship Organization," *Bulletin of the Institute of Ethnology,* Academica Sinica, vol. 13, pp. 87–96.

Pelliot, Paul: *Memoires sur les coutumes du Cambodge de Tcheou Ta-kouan,* Librairie d'Amerique et d'Orient, Paris, 1951.

Porée-Maspero, Eveline: "Le cycle des douze animaux dans la vie des Cambodgiens," *Bulletin de l'École Française d'Extrême-Orient,* vol. 50, pp. 311–366.

Porée-Maspero, Evaline et al.: *Cérémonies privées des Cambodgiens,* Commission des Moeurs et Coutumes du Cambodge, Editions de l'Institut Bouddhique, E.K.L.I.P. Phnom Penh, 1958.

Steinberg, David et al.: *Cambodia, Its People, Its Society, Its Culture,* Survey of World Cultures Series, Human Relations Area Files Press, New Haven, Mass., 1959.

Swift, Michael: "Men and Women in Malay Society," in B. Ward (ed.), *Women in the New Asia,* UNESCO, Paris, 1963.

Thierry, Jean: *L'évolution de la condition de la femme en droit privé cambodgien,* A. Portail, Phnom Penh, 1955.

Ward, Barbara (ed.): *Women in the New Asia,* UNESCO, Paris, 1963.

Willmott, William: *The Chinese in Cambodia,* University of British Columbia Publications Centre, Vancouver, 1967.

Zadrozny, Mitchell (ed.): *Cambodia,* Human Relations Area Files Subcontractor's Monograph no. 21, Human Relations Area Files, New Haven, Mass., 1955.

Women in Philippine Society:

More Equal Than Many

HELGA E. JACOBSON

This essay is concerned with the role of women in Philippine society. Its basic aim is not to answer the question "are women oppressed?" or even "to what degree are women oppressed?" but rather to explore the roles and spheres of interest that are properly women's in a non-Western, largely nonurban and nonindustrial setting. The growing literature concerned with women's roles and rights seems all too frequently to assume that all women in all societies are by their nature and circumstances "oppressed." This seems to me to be a more than somewhat ethnocentric view. The intention here, then, is to counterbalance this view with some information about a situation in which women traditionally and today have honored roles and duties and a right to respect as full members of society. Their spheres of interest, control, and activity are perceived as being different from those of men, but it is essential from the outset not to confuse this difference with inferiority. It is important to recognize that many kinds of activity are cooperative, and the fact that men and women make different contributions to society does not automatically provide for the higher status of men.

I intend to show through this general exploration of the role of women in Philippine society how the balance is established and maintained. In order to understand the context of Philippine society, it is necessary to know something of its geography and history. This background is especially important in the case of the Philippines, as the country is frequently assumed to be so Westernized that traditional values and behavior have long since been replaced. However, traditional values and behaviors are still strongly maintained. Finally, it is important to note that the Philippines is a complex society; complex in the sense that it includes different cultures, languages, and degrees of modernization. The general focus here is on the lowland, Christian Filipinos who are the dominant group. Given the shortage of basic information, an essay of this kind can only be exploratory; but it is hoped that, by bringing what information there is together, some contribution to our understanding of the role of women in non-Western society in general and Philippine society in particular can be achieved.

THE SETTING

Covering an area of some 500,000 square miles of the western Pacific Ocean is the archipelago of the Philippines. The total land area is 115,000 square miles, and it is composed of some 7,000 islands. Not all of these are inhabited. The major land and inhabited areas are found in the principal regional divisions, the island of Luzon, the Visayan Islands, the island of Mindanao, and the Sulu Archipelago. The setting is one of considerable diversity. In terms of ethnic composition, the population is predominantly Malay, with Chinese, Spanish, American, and Japanese additions introduced at various points in history.

Philippine history is frequently regarded as being unusual in the Southeast Asian context—in contrast to its geography, which is typical. Nevertheless, in relation to the factors of colonial rule and the introduction, spread, and absorption of a nonindigenous religious system, the Philippines is by no means unique. In that the colonial rulers were the Spanish and American and that the major religion is Roman Catholicism, it is, however, different from the rest of the Malay world of Southeast Asia.

In the sixteenth century—after the Filipinos had experienced earlier contacts with Muslim Malay, Indian, and Chinese traders—the Spanish conquest introduced Roman Catholicism, which has been the dominant religion ever since. The end of the nineteenth century saw the beginning of some fifty years of American rule. After the Japanese occupation, during the Second World War, the effectively independent Republic of the Philippines emerged.

Because of this history of contact and rule, it is often stated that "the Philippines is the least oriental country of the Orient" (Wernstedt and

Spencer, 1967, p. 2) or assumed that the Philippines has developed "a culture which owes as much to the Occident as to the Orient . . ." (Fryer, 1970, p. 165); in other words, that the traditional life of the Filipino has been substantially altered if not in many senses lost.

However, in spite of this history and the recurrence of the view that much of traditional culture has been lost, this paper is written from the standpoint that traditional Filipino values, beliefs, attitudes, and institutions are still and have always been very much a part of the local setting. The situation is much less "a mask of Asia" (Farwell, 1967) than it is a mask of the West. This is not to deny that other influences are present and that other traditions have been incorporated—particularly religious ones, but rather to stress the foundation on which they rest.

Philippine society today is still predominantly rural. Some 70 percent of the population live outside the cities (Hollnsteiner, 1969; Fryer, 1970, p. 83). In 1965 the population was 32 million (Fryer, 1970, p. 3). The urban population is distributed in cities of differing sizes throughout the archipelago. The major cities are the metropolitan Manila complex, which in 1970 housed about 15 percent of the total national population; Cebu City, the second city of the Philippines and about a quarter the size of Manila; and Davao City, the third rapidly expanding urban center on the island of Mindanao. Administratively the country is divided into provinces, municipalities, and barrios, with chartered cities forming autonomous administrative units.

Barrios are the smallest units in the political and administrative hierarchy. Socially they are frequently divided into *sitios* or hamlets. These are the units to which people generally feel they belong. Except at times of national crisis, and not even always then, the sense of national identity or recognition of membership of an independent state is not strong in the Philippines. Local and provincial or regional loyalties tend strongly to be those that come first.

Regional variation is considerable in relation to cultural patterns, linguistic differentiation, geographic and climatic characteristics, economic development, and local products. My concern here is primarily with the first two sets of variation. Cultural patterns and social organization are far from uniform throughout the archipelago. In the north, on Luzon, are the groups that have been least influenced by the Spanish conquest, American rule, and the advance of Christianity, although this is a picture that is gradually changing (see, for example, Dozier, 1966). In the south of Mindanao are the remaining Muslim minorities who have preserved many aspects of their traditional social organization along with their religious beliefs. Between these two extremes are the majority of Filipino farmers, fishermen, and workers. They are divided by language and localized interests and differentiated by a variety of rules and local traditions not as yet fully described or understood. For the purposes of this chapter, it will be necessary to treat this situation as far less differentiated than it is in practice.

A brief description of the language distribution and variation will serve here to provide the setting of the various groups which will be described or mentioned. The 1960 *Census of the Philippines* lists some 70 languages. Of these, 39 languages have more than 10,000 speakers and 31 languages are spoken by more than 50,000 people. These language groups are not entirely localized, but there is a strong tendency for local and provincial boundaries to be drawn along language lines. The national language is Filipino, a slightly modified form of Tagalog—the mother tongue of some 21 percent of the population. The national language is learned and spoken, in addition to their own local language, by many more people than this. The dialect with the largest number of speakers is Cebuano, which is spoken as their mother tongue by 24 percent of the total population. Its speakers are centered in the Visayan area. In addition, approximately one-third of the population is able to speak English. Spanish is spoken by only a very small number of people.

Apart from delineating local boundaries and defining where people belong, this language pattern has an additional significance. The strong retention of local languages indicates something of the degree to which Philippine traditions themselves have been maintained. Although English is now used for many public and official communications, the various traditional languages have retained their currency as the languages of daily communication in household, village, city, and marketplace. They carry the traditional unwritten literature, myths, legends, and stories and are the sources of the many proverbs and sayings which direct everyday actions. Neither Spanish nor English have become in any sense substitutes; they have remained predominantly the languages of schooling.

IN THE RURAL PHILIPPINES

Prior to the Spanish conquest, Philippine social organization consisted of numerous small autonomous units. They were internally little differentiated in relation to relative wealth and status and were on the whole self-sufficient subsistence units. Their external relations with other units of a like kind were of alternating patterns of warfare and alliance. Only in the areas of Muslim influence did different patterns emerge. In these situations a number of such units were subject to one ruler. The reason for noting this early form of social organization is that it provides the initial setting in which the traditional role of women in Philippine society can be understood. It is against this background that differentiation and change have taken place. In traditional Philippine society, women take a full share of responsibility and have a critical role in the process of decision making concerning themselves and their families (Infante, 1969). Kroeber defines and summarizes this in the following way (1919, p. 83):

> Women are socially the equals of men. This is clear from their position in marriage, descent, and the holding of property. The division of labor between the sexes is on a physiological rather than a social basis.

The same point is made by Benavides, a Filipina and a university graduate and teacher, who says of her country (n.d., p. 1),

> A close and impartial study of Philippine affairs will reveal that our women . . . have contributed in a large measure to the building up of our present economic and social structure; for unlike the women of most oriental countries, they were not confined to a life of sheltered ease. They have always participated freely in commercial, religious and political activities.

A little later in this chapter I will show more precisely what this participation actually means and which aspects of women's traditional role have most influenced the course of development. In the contemporary situation there is, of course, a great deal of variation to be found according to whether the setting is rural or urban and in relation to differences in regional development. However, the general point remains the same (Fox, 1963, p. 364):

> The relationships between men and women in Filipino society and the roles they assume are remarkably equalitarian. The stereotype is that men dominate the society—sociologists have even called Filipino society "patriarchal" —but in reality women as well as men enjoy and assume social, economic, and legal freedom. The Filipino in both the traditional and modern setting is a dynamic and aggressive member of society.

In order to clarify what this means to the quality of life of women in the Philippines, I want now to look at some specific situations. Although these are, strictly speaking, neither typical nor representative, they will serve as examples. Through these examples it will be possible to understand more accurately the nature of the woman's world, the spheres in which she does effectively participate and make decisions, and the kinds of opportunities in work and leisure that are open to women.

It is worth noting that as a specific topic of study the role and position of women in the Philippines has so far rarely been documented in any detail. This is not to suggest that the topic is never discussed but rather that it is usually discussed in general rather than in particular. Among the more specific studies that have been undertaken are those of Castillo and Guerrero (1969) and Fox (1963). These will be referred to where relevant, but since this essay is in no way intended as a survey of the information available, I will not attempt to cover the same general ground.

The first situation that I want to discuss in some detail is that of Barrio Malitbog in Central Panay, an island in the Visayan region of the Philippines. The barrio has been studied and described by Jocano (1968 and 1969), from whose work the following discussion is taken. What I shall do here is to use his description of life in Barrio Malitbog to provide a setting for making some statements about general rules of behavior.

The spheres of activity of boys and girls, men and women, are segregated; different tasks are performed and considered appropriate, different behavior patterns are expected. This segregation of spheres of activity begins early in childhood and continues through life. In Malitbog, for example, among young children, there are games which boys play and games which girls play. Spinning tops and kites serve as playthings for the former and dolls for the latter. Girls are told to keep away from boys when they play these games. Too much involvement in boys' games would call forth teasing from parents and relatives and older children. Any boy showing signs of wanting to play with dolls would be similarly treated (Jocano, 1969, p. 47).

Differentiation according to sex in other spheres begins with participation in work, which comes with late childhood or *nakaluad* (Jocano, 1969, p. 47). Boys help in the fields—watching the carabao (water buffalo), plowing, harrowing, fetching water, and cutting firewood; girls take care of younger siblings, help in the kitchen, and generally assist their mothers about the household as their brothers help in the fields. Girls can also assist with some tasks in the fields, but only those defined as being appropriate to their sex (Jocano, 1969, p. 47). To transgress this rule would again call forth a teasing commentary. As puberty approaches, the behavior pattern appropriate to each sex is more clearly defined; shyness and decorousness is expected among girls and respectfulness from among boys.

With adolescence comes recognition as an "adult person"; adolescents are known as *hamtung*, or full-grown persons. It is now appropriate to begin to think of marriage. At this stage new rules come into being along with the recognition of sexual maturity and age. The adolescent is entitled to greater respect and obedience from younger siblings and younger members of the community. This is accompanied by the undertaking of a greater share of responsibility, and in this context differences in the roles of boys and girls emerge clearly. The boy will now assume a far greater share of the work load on the farm and will become responsible as another provider in the family. He may take part with his parents in the process of decision making on family matters. His sister, however, holds a position of lesser responsibility, though she can substitute for her mother in various domestic activities. Her voice is always secondary to that of her brothers (Jocano, 1969, p. 61). There are two points to note here: first, that both parents are involved in making decisions about the family; second, that a female takes full social responsibility later than a male. This has to do at least in some measure with different perceptions of their sexual roles and of the meaning of maturity.

The primary criterion in selecting a bride is chastity; a girl is always warned to be careful in relationships with boys and her freedom of movement is restricted accordingly. A girl who loses her virginity or who loses her reputation cannot make what is regarded as a good marriage. Boys, on the other hand, are expected to seek after adventures. In any case, by the nature of their tasks, they are expected to be about the barrio—working, drinking, serenading their girlfriends, and in general spending time with their contemporaries in the more public social activities. Girls will also meet each other as they go about their tasks, but these are much more related to and confined to the household. The difference in attitude and freedom of movement is summed up by one villager as follows (Jocano, 1969, p. 62):

> When Malam Ang's wife complained about their son's passing the night with his friends in sitio Agsiw, her husband said, "He's not a woman that you should keep him here. Moreover nothing will be lost—turn him upside down and he is still a man."

The emphasis on premarital chastity and the emergence of different rules of conduct for adolescent boys and girls is quite likely the result of Christian influence. Reports from early observers in the Philippines and some studies carried out in northern Luzon support this conclusion (Infante, 1969). Prior to the introduction of Christianity and the development of codes of conduct consistent with it, it is probable that girls enjoyed a greater degree of freedom prior to marriage than they are allowed today. The following rather amusing story gives an impression of what this meant (Infante, 1969, p. 30 and Cawed, 1965, pp. 15–16):

> Several newsmen took the trip up to Bontoc (northern Luzon) in search of eye-catching and novel realities to report on. After having almost lost a head among them, for the interference of one in a religious ceremony . . . they invited themselves to a visiting session at a young girls' *olog*.[1] Another one of them took a young maiden to fancy, and in the course of the evening's conversation sought to kiss her. Little did he think that he would end up with a bloody face all scratched by the indignant young girl and her *olog* companions. And still he had to be thankful that he did not come across the young man to whom she was betrothed or that he was not pushed by the girls into a ten foot pig pen generally found in front of the *olog* [and]

separated from it by only a narrow path. For according to a guide, boys who misbehave with the girls of the *olog* are pushed into this pen!

This example fits with the statements that women were "socially recognized as the equals of men." What this recognition of social equality meant and indeed still means is that women were regarded as fully competent to make decisions about matters that concerned themselves. They were not totally subject to rules made about them and without consultation. Although now premarital chastity is a stringent requirement and private or essentially unsupervised association between the sexes is not permitted, rules governing the choice of a marriage partner are still not at all rigid.

The ideal age for marriage is thought in Malitbog to be approximately twenty for a boy and eighteen for a girl. Courting, which takes the form of serenading and visiting, is a rather public affair. The final selection must be approved by both sets of parents, but the initial selection can be made by the individuals themselves. Boys and girls meet at harvest time, at barrio dances and fiestas, and at baptisms, weddings, and wakes, so opportunity for meeting is not lacking. In addition, the local school is a meeting ground and may set the stage for later courtship (Jocano, 1969, p. 68). The fact that marriages take place by preference between people who are related and share barrio membership means that both the parents and the young people know who is available and are frequently acquainted with them. With marriage and the establishment of a family, both men and women take their place as responsible adult members of the community.

The preceding description of adolescence in Malitbog suggests that there are differences in status between adolescent males and females. Although Jocano (1969, p. 60) says that both are regarded as "full-grown persons" in that they are now able to marry and raise a family, the final stage or recognized social maturity has not been reached—namely, that of being married and therefore fully socially responsible. Sexual maturity and social maturity are in fact clearly distinguished, and this has consequences for both sexes. Young unmarried men are regarded as "unreliable," but this changes as soon as they get married (Jocano, 1969, p. 75):

> Most informants are agreed that as soon as a man establishes a family of his own, he can be relied upon for so many things. He will think twice before doing anything bad.

The notion of being married and of establishing a family are closely tied together. Children are conceived of as gifts from God, divine blessings on the couple for living a "clean, obedient, and pious life" (Jocano, 1968, p. 213). To be married and childless is a cause for concern, and childless couples will frequently adopt a child—often a nephew or niece. For a woman, the final arrival at full social maturity is occasioned by the birth of a child, for then she can take her share of responsibility for the raising of the child and subsequent children. Her responsibility increases over time as the household becomes larger. The children must respect both parents and respond to their authority, as illustrated by the following incident (Jocano, 1969, p. 78):

> When Husi, ten, woke up to find that his pet chicken was eaten by the pig he was very angry. He started beating the pig . . . After a while, his mother called him to stop . . . [but] he continued to beat the pig.
> Later his mother called again. "Will you stop chasing that pig?"

Husi, however, would not stop and shouted back at his mother. While this was going on his father returned from fetching water and overheard the boy answering back. He then beat the boy with a piece of stick saying "You should learn better than to answer your mother. You should be ashamed to the neighbors for doing that. They might say I am not teaching you good manners" (Jocano, 1969, p. 78).

The normal condition in adult life is to be married. In sharing a household and raising children, men and women cooperate and their spheres of authority are complementary. In his study of Malitbog, Jocano notes that bachelors are the objects of fun and village ridicule. They are called by derogatory nicknames such as *agi,* effeminate; *warat buras,* without genitals; *matalaw,* coward (Jocano, 1969, p. 64). However, being a spinster is not considered shameful. "I have decided to become a spinster" is frequently given as an excuse when turning down an unfavored suitor (1969, p. 64). Neither men nor women can accomplish full adult status without marrying, the men because, not having assumed responsibility for a family, they are seen as being "unreliable"; the women because they are not able to function as fully responsible members of a household. In this sense both are socially marginal. However, it is possible to compensate for this marginality by acquiring responsibilities in the extra-household world —that is, by engaging in productive activity of some kind. Thereby it is possible to become responsible for resources and to control of them; for example, men may control land as farmers and women may control commercial enterprise as traders.

Finally, I want to look at the question of household management. The extent to which the wife "manages" the household is most clearly shown through the budget, which she handles and controls. For example, ". . . in the rural Philippines the wife controls the family pocketbook and has an important voice in all family decisions" (Madigan, 1968, p. 11).

This finding is supported and the situation is described in more detail in a study of decision making among farm families carried out by Guerrero (1966; and Castillo and Guerrero, 1969). She notes that joint husband-wife decisions were reported for buying land, borrowing money, and deciding what to plant; buying farm tools was the prerogative of the husband and household furniture that of the wife (Castillo and Guerrero, 1969, pp. 25–26). On the question of controlling not only the budget but actually holding the purse strings, Castillo and Guerrero have the following comment to make (1969, p. 26):

> Generally speaking, even where farm related matters are being decided upon, although the wife is never the sole decision-maker, she is consulted and exerts influence especially where additional expense is involved in adopting a new farm practice This is inevitable because in the Philippines the wife is the family treasurer. In interviews with farmers in eight barrios, 91 percent indicated that the wife holds the family purse and only 3 percent that it is the husband who performs this function. When asked about the normative angle "who should hold the family money?" the percentage of respondents assigning this function to the wife increased from 91 to 93 percent. Incidentally, this practice is not peculiar to farmers. [The study referred to here is that of Feliciano, 1966, pp. 428–437.]

This management of the household has two very important consequences: first, it defines a specific sphere of authority and decision making in which it is appropriate or proper for women to engage; second, it makes it possible for women to engage in a variety of commercial, entrepreneurial activities, on a small scale outside the household, in relation to organizing the family budget and consumption. The freedom of movement created in this way is important to understanding the occupations and opportunities that have become open to women with economic development and change and in the urban area. That the view of women as industrious and as managers of the household is a general one is reflected in a popular motif in Philippine folk tales. There are a number of stories about the lazy husband and the industrious wife (Fansler, 1921, p. 237; Aquino et al., 1969, pp. 1–5).

In the Philippine rural context, spheres of activity, tasks, and appropriate behavior are differentiated according to sex. This, however, does not preclude active cooperation and joint decision making. There are in addition some shared activities both within the household and extending beyond it—that is, into work in the fields. What this means is that part of the routine day-to-day activities and decisions involve cooperation, and this—together with the sharing of responsibilities for household and child ren—means that women play a critical and socially recognized role in rural society.

Finally, women also enter the public world in their capacities as healers and traders. In the sphere of traditional medical practice, women play an important part as healers (called *shamen* in Infante's description of women's roles in early Philippine society) and as midwives. In addition, they work as traders, often contributing substantially to the household income. Myrdal, in writing of this pattern and its consequences, notes (1968, p. 1132):

> Not only do women enjoy higher social status in Southeast Asia, but prejudices against women's work are usually less pronounced. . . . in Southeast Asia . . . much small trading is done by women. As a result, a larger proportion of economically active women there work on their own. . . .

The point is further documented by a study carried out in Barrio Tarong, an Ilocos Barrio in the northern Philippines (Nydegger and Nydegger, 1966). There, women who earn money other than in the agricultural sector do so through working as traders. "This activity ranges from (looked down on) fish peddling to acting as middlewomen in expensive jewel purchases" (Nydegger and Nydegger, 1966, p. 35). In this situation all but two of the women traders were either widows or spinsters. Trading thus provides for women who have little land and need the resources to support themselves and their families, whether of orientation or procreation. That is, widows are likely to be supporting their own children, while single women may well be supporting or aiding the support and education of younger siblings, nephews and nieces, or even cousins. Other occupations for women in Barrio Tarong were those of weaver, seamstress, laundress, midwife, and embroiderer (Nydegger and Nydegger, 1966, p. 35). This pattern of small-scale trading or the running of small stores is characteristic not only of the rural areas but is also found in the cities. There as a primary occupation, it provides additional resources for married women as well as single women and widows. More often in the city, it serves as a secondary source of income.

The range of occupational roles and situations open to women, then, takes them well outside the domestic sphere. Coupled with their managerial functions, this has made accessible a wide range of additional opportunities that come with economic change and development.

Finally, a word about the kinship system of the Philippines. It is bilateral; that is, relationships are traced through both men and women and descent is reckoned through both the father and the mother. The general implications of such a system are not relevent here, nor are the specific details of its structure. What is important is the light that this kind of reckoning of relationships and descent throws on the social organization and the role of men and women within it. First, men and women can form relationships in their own right. A woman does not have to depend on a husband, a father, or a brother for recognition or the right to form alliances. As a person—whether a wife, mother, daughter, or sister—

she establishes and maintains her own network of ties. Second, in the reckoning of descent bilaterally is carried the implication that both males and females inherit. The traditional situation has, of course, been modified by Spanish conquest, American rule, and modernization, but this fundamental right has nonetheless not been alienated. Women can hold and inherit land, act as executors of estates, and take their part in family businesses of many different kinds.

In the kind of society depicted here in the rural Philippines, disadvantaged people are clearly not by definition "women." They are people who deviate from the general or proper pattern whether they are men or women and who are to be pitied for their lack of success or bad luck. No special circumstances make women more to be pitied or less lucky where they fail in life or in some specific endeavor.

THE URBAN SETTING

The growth of cities and the social changes that come with urban development and economic differentiation have created new opportunities and new situations in which people must find their way. What I want to consider here is the way in which women's traditional roles permit them to move into this new and different world. I shall select the situations which show this rather than attempt to give an account of all areas and levels of society.

In the previous discussion, the woman's role has been defined as manager of the household and sharing the responsibility for the upbringing of the children. This means that she in no sense occupies a subordinate role. The point to consider here is how far this remains the case in changed living circumstances and where different and new occupational and educational opportunities exist. If we consider first those people who are able to take advantage of these new opportunities, it becomes clear that in her managerial capacity the Filipina maintains and extends her traditional role. Writing of her experience as a career housewife in the Philippines, Arce-Ortega (1963, p. 368) says,

> My husband and I contribute fixed amounts to the family budget. The rest is my responsibility—how much for this, for that, etc. So unless I want a big headache I stick as strictly as possible to carefully planned spending. My little whims and fancies are taken care of by my pocket money. The same goes for my husband and his personal fund.

Some interesting light is also thrown on the situation by a government survey of workers in small-scale industries in the Philippines (1960). Among the questions asked were a set relating to certain decisions concerning family matters:

Matters for decision	Who makes the decision		
	Father	Mother	Total
Choice of residence	236	127	363
Money expenditures	94	250	344
Education of children	144	152	296
Friends of children	47	58	105
Choice of mate	47	44	91

If we look at the pattern of response in the above instances, it is clear that women make a considerable contribution to how things are decided in the family. Although, in the majority of cases, place of residence was chosen by the man in the family in relation to the job opportunity open to him, a significant number of women made the decision for their husbands, and this was also in relation to the work situation. The situation concerning household finances can be seen very clearly as the woman's responsibility. In the three other situations that concerned the investigators, the responsibilities were rather evenly divided. What this underlines is that in the family sphere, women, as wives and mothers, have a considerable degree of control over household decisions, the children, and their future.

One final point to note from this study is that of the question of "choice of mate." This was a study of small-scale industries, and the fact that "choice of mate" was seen as an important sphere of family decision making is interesting, since it is indicative of the maintenance of traditional patterns. Because marriages are less arranged than. approved, this pattern and the traditional progress from courtship to marriage can be followed. What it means is that an unsuitable marriage partner will be vetoed but that suitable matches in relation to people who have selected each other pose no problem. The effect of the existence of a wider range of possible marriage partners in the urban areas will be discussed later.

Because women control household affairs and resources in a very direct way and because traditionally they also work and trade, it has been possible for women to move outside the household in situations of new economic opportunity. In the city, a great many women work as professional career wives and in a variety of other occupations as well. They run small sari-sari (variety) stores, bakeshops, dressmaking establishments, and beauty parlors. Many of these are run from the home. In addition, there are a great many women teachers, nurses, clerks, and factory workers.

The Philippines is unusual in that it educates almost as many women as men (Boserup, 1970, p. 120). Three factors make it possible for many educated women to utilize their training; the availability of domestic help, the sharing of households, and the fact that many small business enter-prises can be run from the home. In the city, a great many women rely on domestic help for aid with the housework and care of the children. Conditions for household help are not always good, and increased oppor-tunities for one sector of the female population sometimes come at the expense of another. However, maids, it must be stressed, are also members of a class which includes houseboys, guards, gardeners, and other servants. Reference to this point will be made again later.

In some households, other members of the family may take over some of the responsibilities that a working wife and mother cannot carry if she also works. Many households include parents, siblings, or nephews and nieces who can share some of the household duties. In middle-class families these will be of the planning or tending variety and will not involve the heavier household chores, which will be the tasks of a maid or houseboy. Finally, many of the small business enterprises are run from the home, so that both sets of duties can be carried out. In these situations relatives or servants when present, will also assist.

Two other features of the urban work situation need to be noted here. First, a great many people, both men and women, do more than one job in order to raise the family income and maintain a middle-class though not highly elaborate level of living. For example many women in Cebu City, where I did my research, will work as teachers for half the day. Local schools work on a split-shift system to make maximum use of space and to prevent classes from becoming too large. When school finished, the teachers would return to another occupation—running a small restaurant, bakery, store, hairdressing or dressmaking shop, or poultry farm. Most of them had maids who could aid with the care of children and household tasks. One of my friends remarked one day that the common room at her school was "like a marketplace" on days when people brought in their goods for sale or exchange. It is important to recognize, second, that in this situation no loss of status comes from carrying out a wide variety of different tasks. The maintenance of an adequate standard of living (not based on con-spicuous consumption) and the ability to provide at least the same standard for the children, are crucial. In addition it is important to note that men also will do jobs "on the side" in order to contribute a larger share to the family budget (Jacobson, 1969, n.d.).

So far discussion has been of those people who are able to take ad-vantage of the economic opportunities offered by the urban environment, principally in those situations in which women work—that is, essentially in middle-class contexts. Specific information about other spheres is harder to find. However, one study of the lower-class Cebuano family does show that the patterns considered so far are maintained even where the resources to be managed are scarce (Liu and Yu, 1968, p. 123):

The dominant pattern in the lower-class Cebuano family shows the wife to be autonomous in four out of the seven household task areas listed, namely: family health, money control, food preparations, and child control. However, she is also the executor of another family task: schooling of the children.

Again, this shows the continued exercise of the women's managerial role in relation both to household tasks and care of and arrangements for the children. Women's roles in the sphere of commercial activity are fairly easy to define, and some account of what this means has been given. Myrdal, in his general study, notes that in the Philippines "there are few prejudices against women engaging in productive work . . ." (1968, p. 496).

The question that now arises is that of the roles of educated women in contemporary Philippine society, the opportunities open to them, and the other effects of education. Detailed information about the numbers of women in professional occupations is hard to obtain. However, from the information that is available, it is clear that women in the Philippines form a rather high proportion of those receiving higher education who have the opportunity to take up professional occupations (Myrdal, 1968; Boserup, 1970). In the Philippines, 21 percent of all personnel in clerical and administrative positions are women (Boserup, 1970, p. 125). If the number of women in all professions is looked at as a percentage of all professionals, then the total proportion is 51 percent (Boserup, 1970, p. 126). Between one-fifth and one-quarter of all doctors in the Philippines are women (Stauffer, 1966, p. 118), and a high proportion of optometrists, pharmacists, and chemists are women (Fox, 1963, p. 356). In addition, many women work as schoolteachers and nurses. Although this reflects a Western division of labor within the professional sphere, it should not be assumed too readily that status and prestige are accorded in an identical manner. In the Philippines professional occupations, because of the resources needed for the training, recruitment from the middle-class sector is high. A profession also brings with it considerable prestige, regardless of the actual position, both because of the initial advantage and the additional benefit of success in the occupation. In connection with receiving a higher education, it has been suggested that women face a special problem. According to Fox (1963, p. 356), many men will hesitate to marry a woman with more education than they have for fear of being said to be "under the *saya*" (the traditional women's costume, a wraparound skirt). He suggests, therefore, that women tend to choose professions requiring less education. However, he also notes another emerging pattern (1966, p. 357):

> There are certainly emerging particular 'types' of marriages within the professional group; female pharmacists, for example, marrying male doctors with the wife then managing the family-owned chemist shop. In the rural areas, marriages between teachers are common.

Suburban housing, Cebu City. The carabao belongs to a local farmer.

This situation is worth considering in a little more detail. For a man to be seen as being "under the *saya*" clearly reflects the dominance of the woman in the situation, and this is evidently seen as being undesirable. Ideally the contributions, duties, and responsibilities in a household should be shared. In the traditional situation and the contemporary rural sector, this can be maintained, for men and women live and work in the same spheres. Occupational differentiation is not great. Since women control the household budget (i.e., hold the purse strings), if there is to be a status differential, then the preferred direction is for the man to be of higher status, otherwise there would be too great an imbalance. That a leveling mechanism operates where possible is attested by Fox in the passage quoted above.

In the cities, where there is increased educational opportunity (for those able to take advantage of it) and considerable occupational differentiation, the same values are operative. Among the largely professional middle-class population of Cebu City, it was rare for women to marry men with lower educational attainment than themselves. The pattern was for marriage to take place between those of the same educational level or for the man's attainment to be higher (Jacobson, 1969, n.d.).

Similarly, in San Pedro Village, a middle- and upper-middle-class suburban community in Makati (a commercial and residential development adjacent to Manila) where I recently completed a study, among the

98 women for whom there is information, only 8 had married men with lower educational attainment than themselves, 39 had married men with the same level of educational attainment, and 51 had married men with higher educational attainment (Jacobson, n.d.). The majority of these women had a university education. Boserup (1970, p. 120), as has already been noted, points out that the Philippines educates almost as many women as men. Does the pattern that is illustrated here reflect a situation in which women are denied the opportunity to use their skills?

The answer to this question must be understood in the general context of Philippine economic development. Although it is true that the Philippines educates almost as many women as men, the meaning of this must be understood. The majority—that is, approximately 70 percent of the Philippine population (about 35 million in 1970)—live in the rural areas, as has already been noted. In practical terms, this means that very few of them have access to schools above the primary level (Jacobson, 1969, n.d.). Very few people from the rural areas have the opportunity to attend high school and even fewer to attend college. Those that do obtain a high school and/or college education are exceptional.

Because the Philippine economy is an underdeveloped one, there is a further problem. There are insufficient job opportunities for people with higher levels of education. Industrial and commercial expansion is not sufficient to provide for the numbers of educated Filipinos who leave school or college each year. The Philippines also has a very high birthrate and has had for a number of years. This means that more people than the country can accommodate are continually entering the labor force. This problem exists for all those who receive an education, both men and women, and for all those who do not as well. Educated women form half of a small educated (even an overeducated) population that is now facing difficulties. How many women, then, are able to utilize the education they receive? Data for the whole of the Philippines are not available; however, the following information from Makati serves to illustrate the situation (Jacobson, n.d.).

In San Pedro Village, of the 98 women about whom there is information, 48 were not working at the time of the study. Among these are some who had already retired and some who were planning to start some kind of a business. All except 6 had had some college education, and the majority had completed a college-level education. Among the women who were working, 50 in number, 26 were employed full-time, most of them in the occupation for which they had been trained—that is, as doctors or teachers, for example. Some were running businesses, beauty parlors, bakeries, or real estate agencies. There were 11 women working at their primary occupation, and these had, in addition, a subsidiary business interest in which they were active. Finally, 13 women were occupied part-time or were involved in small-scale business enterprises, usually on their own (Jacobson, n.d.). This situation is probably fairly typical of the middle- and upper-middle-class situation in the urban areas. That working women are able to employ domestic help has already been mentioned, as have the other circumstances which make it possible for them to be away from the house. There are no day-care centers in the Philippines, but again this must be understood against a background in which welfare services are generally inadequate and where the family still provides an additional and viable alternative. In those cases in which women do not work, it must be emphasized again that, since they run the organization of the household and manage the budget, their role is still regarded as an important one.

This point is also made in the Castillo and Guerrero study (1969, p. 26). After discussing budgeting in farm households, they note that ". . . Even among highly educated professionals this control of the budget by the woman in the household is almost a universally accepted norm."

During my study in Cebu City, I found that when I asked people who was the household head, very frequently the woman's name was given even when her husband was also a full member of the household and employed. When I asked about this pattern, I was told that it was because the women "run the house" and deal with the budget. This makes clear what the rules about the division of labor and spheres of authority in fact are. It also underlines the fact that the household does not have a "head" in any strict sense but rather that there are well-defined spheres of authority and decision making which are equally important and appropriated by the man or woman according to the situation and type of decision required.

A case for discrimination against women is difficult to sustain in the general context of Philippine society, either rural or urban, unless it is assumed that managing a household is of itself sufficient to constitute both "discrimination" and "oppression." However, there are situations in the developed sector of the economy that do pose problems. Women are noticeably scarce in the corporate enterprises at the managerial and executive levels. This is reflected in the San Pedro village case of those who had professional occupations or occupations involving the commercial sector, more women than men obtained aid from close relatives or worked in family businesses; that is, 19 women as opposed to 10 men (Jacobson, 1972, n.d.). Though it is important to note that men are also assisted in this way, the proportion of women utilizing these connections is absolutely greater, as fewer were working. When all the occupations of all the working women are considered, 29 out of 50 working women utilized family connections in setting up or obtaining their positions in business, whereas only 26 out of 93 working men used such connections. What this suggests is that for women the aid is more essential in obtaining such positions. For men, it is helpful but not essential to be able to utilize connections.

Studies of managers and entrepreneurs in the Philippines also reflect the bias, as they assume without question that all such people are men

(Carroll, 1965; Bennett, 1971). However, if the definition of entrepreneurs and perhaps managers were extended to include some of the differentiated small-scale businesses that are found throughout the urban areas, even this picture might change. The sectors in which there is the strongest evidence for some level of discrimination against women are those surrounding the Western, often American-introduced, large corporate enterprises. These businesses bring with them their structures, their male personnel, their ideologies, and their rules about the proper division of labor. In general, the areas in which there is the strongest evidence for a bias against the employment of women are those which have taken their development and ideology from abroad.

A very interesting account of the manner in which a woman makes her way into and around this commercial world is given in a novel by L. C. Quirino entitled *Like the Wind I Go.* Clearly autobiographical, the novel shows how a woman built a fairly large financial empire—the alliances she had to form, the responses she received from her male colleagues and competitors, and the way she maintained her business and personal life. Often romantic and sometimes overwritten, it nonetheless provides an interesting and useful insight into the development of the postwar business of the Philippines.

Nonetheless, the situation for the majority of women able to take advantage of education and professional training is adequate. Discrimination in the spheres of educational and employment opportunity is strongest against those people who do not have the resources to take advantage of either.

In conclusion, it is important to stress again that the people discussed in this context are those who are able to take advantage of economic development, industrial growth, and the changing opportunities provided by urbanization. They are a small sector of the total population, and not the whole of the urban population either. Many people living in the cities, particularly those living in the metropolitan Manila area, are excluded from the benefits of urban and industrial growth. The residents of the slum and squatter areas do not have the educational and employment opportunities open to the middle-class sector of the population. What this implies is that where women suffer disadvantages, they do so as members of a disadvantaged class. It is not primarily their status as women that determines their disadvantaged or "oppressed" state.

The fact that women can and frequently do find work as maids or in home industry of one kind or another means that they have, in some sense, a greater range of work opportunity open to them in the urban setting. The skills they bring to the city from the countryside are more flexible in this respect than are those of their husbands, sons, or brothers and lend themselves to modification and use in the new setting. The household then remains the focus of a woman's managerial control and provides her with a place in the new environment from which she provides the family with an organizational and stable base. This does not mean that such families are then well placed economically or that their situation is in any sense adequate. Under these circumstances both men and women suffer the effects and consequences of poverty, but women have slightly greater resources with which to begin to combat them.

OUTSIDE THE HOUSEHOLD

The fact that women share agricultural activities, act as managers of the household, and work as traders means they can move rather readily from the strictly domestic sphere into other social situations in the wider social context. I want now to look at these situations in general and then in relation to the contemporary scene.

On the whole, there is very little information about the role of women in the community other than as they are engaged in commercial activities, either in the rural context or in the early Philippines. It is therefore difficult to work out the general rules for the participation of women in other spheres. However, Infante (1969) does make some interesting points in her study of women in the early Philippines and I want to take up two of these here (1969, p. 159):

a. Women were as likely as men to be the victims of headhunting raids.

b. High ranking women could exercise considerable influence even though they seldom held the control of government.

Among the communities of the early Philippines, headhunting was a rather widespread practice. Communities aligned themselves according to relationships of hostility or alliance, and any member of a community defined in the latter category was liable to be killed. For the purposes of both attack and subsequent revenge, women were equally liable to be killed, either in a raid or as they happened to be caught going about their business outside the community. The importance of this point for the discussion here is that this suggests rather strongly that women were fully recognized as social persons both in the domestic sphere and outside it. Even if being equally liable to being killed seems a dubious privilege, it must be recognized as a significant indicator of the status of women.

Women do not, and did not, depend exclusively on their roles as wives and mothers for their recognition as members of the community; they were regarded as social persons in their own right. It is perhaps worth noting in this connection that in both Cebuano and Tagalog the pronoun meaning "he" and the pronoun meaning "she" is the same, *siya*. Again, this would point to the recognition of both sexes equally in their capacities as social persons. There are, of course, in addition a variety of different ways in which the sexes are socially distinguished, and I shall turn to those shortly. What this argument shows is that both sexes have an equal right to social recognition; differentiation follows after that.

The second point that Infante (1969, p. 159) makes also has some interesting implications. She herself suggests that the function of high-status women in the early Philippines was to set an example to others that they could use their initiative and influence to show what should be done, especially in the context of women's role in the spread of Christianity (1969, pp. 152–158). Pigafetta, in his description of Magellan's landing in Cebu and his conversion of the local population, notes that the Queen came with forty-two women to be baptized (Infante, 1969, p. 153). Again, one can ask what relevance this has for the contemporary situation. It suggests that, in spite of not formally governing, women traditionally had a recognized public role to play and could properly exercise influence. Today, they can do more than that. Women are elected to congress and the senate of the Philippines. They serve on barrio councils and as barrio captains. They act as school principals and heads of university departments, and they teach at all levels of the school hierarchy. Although the political sphere and government bureaucracy is dominated by men, there is nothing to prevent women from taking a greater share of political responsibility. In the recent election (November 8, 1971), a group organized to protect the polls and ensure people's freedom to vote was strikingly effective and utilized a large number of women at all organizational and operational levels.

However, it is important to note that not all women in the Philippines view their position as I have presented it here—that is, as a situation in which women have a great deal of choice and freedom of action and opportunity. Some are ambivalent and others are organizing toward making changes. Ambivalence and a rather traditional view of the power of the Filipina is reflected in the following quotation by a woman who is a professional journalist (Kalaw, 1970, p. 148):

> But being a woman who cannot in all her 23 years recall an instance of male cruelty and who for a time derived sadistic pleasure from seeing men's faces redden in humiliation and defeat, one is moved to purr with the Pussycat and at the same time to cry with a growing number of valiant young Filipinas, *Makibaka*. . . .

Makibaka is a women's liberation organization which is now growing, predominantly in Manila. The organization is composed of students, professionals, workers, and peasants; it includes both men and women (*Philippine Free Press*, December 1970, p. 148). Among the activities of the

organization mentioned in the little information I have available is picket-
ing a beauty contest "to expose the inanity of treating women as commercial
commodities to boost capitalism" (*Philippine Free Press*, December 1970,
p. 148) and assisting in a strike of Carriedo shoe store workers who earned
2.75 pesos for fourteen hours work (there are now some 6 pesos to the
dollar).

Two important features can be seen from this limited information
about Makibaka. First, it is essentially a political movement aimed against
capitalist—usually recognized as foreign or imperialist—enterprise in the
Philippines. As such it is related to other movements of the same kind
that are also beginning. Second, it includes men and women and one of
its aims, as stated in the article, is to improve working conditions for
people in general, not just for women as an especially disadvantaged
sector of the working population. This supports the arguments, made
earlier, that stress the fact that problems such as lack of employment
opportunity are generally felt by both sexes.

These examples are inadequate to a proper understanding of the problem, but they do suggest that difficulties are arising for women in conjunction with industrial development and "Westernization." That is, in
reaction to the importation of Western, particularly American values into
the Philippines. It is to be hoped that as economic development continues, the new situations will accommodate the values of the already
existing situation rather than attempting to change everything in the direction of a productive, strictly Western or North American industrial social
world in the Philippines.

THE SPHERES OF MEN AND WOMEN

In the earlier section on social organization in Barrio Malitbog, I noted
that there is segregation of spheres of activity. This pattern of association,
of male with male and female with female, which begins to be stressed
early in childhood is perhaps most emphasized during adolescence and then
continues throughout adult life. One of the striking characteristics of the
social scene in the Philippines is the extent to which members of the same
sex congregate together. Except among small children, it occurs in most
public social situations regardless of age.

Accompanying this pattern of grouping is a different style in personal
interaction. People talking to each other stand together more closely than
I, for example, coming from England, am used to. Striking too is the fact
that as people talk and walk together they will also casually walk arm
in arm or hand in hand. This pattern is found among both males and
females but very rarely indeed between members of opposite sexes.

A study of students ranging in age from nursery school through to
sophomore college level, carried out at the University of the Philippines,

showed that students at all levels chose friends of the same sex and age (U.P. study, pp. 29–30). Liu (1968, p. 120) in his study of the lower-class Cebuano family notes the existence of the *barkada,* which are cliques or perhaps gangs, depending on age and circumstances (Hollnsteiner, n.d.), formed by selected members of one sex only. They seem to be most characteristic of masculine society but can form among girls or women also (Liu, 1968, p. 120). However, it has been suggested that among girls such groupings are more common prior to marriage than following it. Marriage for the woman generally takes her into a different pattern of friendship association in connection with her household responsibilities and the new kinship ties she may then have also to take responsibility for. In both cases there is as yet very little information about the operation and formation of either group at any stage in the life cycle. What this underlines, nonetheless, is the pattern of segregation by sex in the context of friendship ties and general social life.

In addition to the patterns of relationships involved in the formation of this kind of friendship pattern, there are different patterns of activity involved. In the rural areas, the times and places at which men and women socialize differ. Women, for example, do not congregate in public to drink, and men do not meet in the course of shopping for household supplies or doing the washing. In the city the same is true, but in addition there are different and increased opportunities for using leisure time and a greater variety of situations in which friends can meet—movie houses, bowling alleys, tennis courts, and so on. In the context of Cebu City, in which I lived and worked, the following summary further defines some of the differences in patterns of association (Jacobson, 1969, p. 143):

> Women predominantly meet their friends at work, in and around the city, and in their own or their friends' homes. A higher proportion of women than men meet their friends at church or in conjunction with church activities. For men, the pattern of association at work, and in and around the city, is similar but there is a greater emphasis on activities taking them away from the home. Higher proportions of men, as compared with women, meet their friends for some specific activity which ranges from sporting activities, at restaurants, or at meetings. As more men have business activities which take them out of the city, a larger number meet their friends in the course of these as well.

In all these situations the pattern remains the same. In the responses to my questions about meeting friends, where women named a male friend it was always someone whom they would meet in some official capacity. For example, a doctor, lawyer, or priest. Alternatively, the man would be the husband of a woman friend and the couple would be mentioned together. Men, on the whole, did not specify in this context meeting female friends at all except in a few cases in which they were very clearly work associates.

If a man and a woman are seen together too frequently, this occasions both rumors and teasing, all strongly implying the existence of an intimate relationship which is seen as being a sexual one.

Friendship, then, can be seen as a relationship between members of the same sex; relationships between people of opposite sexes are generally assumed to be of quite a different character. That is, they may either imply intimacy and therefore be sexual relationships, or they may involve a business or contractual relationship. The latter must initially be understood in relation both to the kinds of obligation involved in the recognition of a friendship tie and the spheres of business activity traditionally open to women.

The full recognition of a friendship relationship between people who are not kinsmen involves very strong permanent obligations (Hollnsteiner, 1964; Lynch, 1964; Jacobson, n.d.). Stories of people meeting with accidents in public in the Philippines and being totally ignored and left to help themselves are legion (Pacana, 1958, pp. 29–30). An explanation of this is that to involve oneself would create an enormous burden of indebtedness for the aid given. It is therefore preferable to both parties to avoid this kind of commitment whenever possible and to enter such relationships with due consideration.

People do try to reduce the number of such maximal obligations in most situations. There are, of course, in addition, some in which you will try to maximize the number of people indebted to you. In other situations the aim is to have friends among whom the honors are more or less even; these would be casual friends, one's peers, and most of one's daily associates (Hollnsteiner, 1964; Jacobson, n.d.). Whichever kind of friendship relationship is involved, it precludes relationships between members of opposite sexes. The only type of relationship open then is what can be defined as a contractual one—that is, one involving some kind of a business relationship or commercial exchange. Since women traditionally worked as traders and healers, any exchange falling under these headings would be permissible. Outside of these spheres there would be problems. This kind of ruling can be extended into the new occupations of the urban sector as well. In addition to the definition of the type of relationship that is appropriate, there are rules defining tasks as being properly appropriated by men or women—tasks which are recognized strictly as noninterchangeable unless in some sense accompanied by a change of sex. Before turning to a consideration of differentiation according to tasks, it remains to note that relationships between men and women are strictly not to be defined as friendship; they are business, commercial, or contractual relationships and characteristically would terminate with the conclusion of the transaction. This is not to suggest that such relationships are in any sense unfriendly, only that they follow rules of restricted relevance and endure only during the exchange. They may, of course, be recurrent. Women, therefore, can follow a variety of different occupations in the urban business sector as long as they observe these rules in the relationships they have with men. Men must also observe appropriate behavioral rules towards women.

I want now to consider the allocation of tasks and their relationship to the definition of the spheres appropriate to different sexes. Clearly at the domestic level women are responsible for the household organization and management. For a man to take on these functions would be to call very seriously into question his masculinity, which perhaps explains the mockery of bachelors in Malitbog. Hart, in his study of various aspects of homosexuality in the Philippines (Hart, 1968, p. 229), notes that

> Most household chores are woman's work, e.g., daily marketing, preparing most foods, cooking, washing, and ironing, cleaning house, etc. A man may perform some of these duties occasionally, or when his wife is ill, but rarely regularly.

Here it is important to stress that while housework may be regarded as unmanly, what this means is that it is appropriate to a woman, not that it is inferior. A man who regularly performs a woman's work is not by definition inferior but rather different, as will be shown further below. Similarly, if a woman engages in activities inappropriate to her sphere, she will be defined as being masculine, or like a man.

Trading, small-scale marketing, and weaving are all women's occupations. The heavier work in the fields and around the house is properly appropriated by men. Where someone of either sex regularly carries out an inappropriate task, there is always the consequence of the recognition of a changed sexual identity. What is involved here is not a definition of a social problem but the recognition of a changed role and therefore identity. This may but need not involve homosexuality as we define it. Hart in his detailed study of the subject (Hart, 1968, pp. 216 and 236), points out that

> Bayot, lakin-on and bakla lack the clamorous condemnatory meaning of the English terms, homosexual, lesbian, or transvestite. Filipinos often translate these as "sissy" or "tomboy". . . . The various meanings of these terms vividly contrast with usage in the United States where as Sechrest and Flores comment, "Homosexuality is such a grave concern that it must be kept a non-overlapping term."
>
> The typical attitude towards the bakla (or Cebuano bayot) is "one of fairly good natured amusement." They are "teased and bantered with, but not detested and beaten" [Sechrest, 1966, p. 33].

The importance of noting this here is that while in relation to the appropriate tasks sexual identity is strictly defined, anyone who crossed the boundary does not become a social outcast. It also emphasizes that there is more flexibility in the system than might otherwise appear. In a sense it is a matter of choice; men may undertake women's tasks, the only risk is that of being ridiculed. Further, in relation to the role of women in the modernized sector of the Philippine economy, it calls attention to the fact that as long as women follow occupations that can be recognized as being consonant with their traditional ones, there will be no problem. They have freedom to move in the new and in the public sphere provided they follow the proper rules. What this means is that while women may become doctors, pharmacists, and optometrists, it would perhaps be less appropriate for them to become engineers. There are, in addition, occupations which are in some sense "sexually neutral" and can be followed by either men or women. Teaching would be one of these. In these situations women can operate as women by maintaining their feminine quality, i.e., by presenting themselves as female while carrying out the task or working in the particular occupation.

Finally, I should add a note about education and change. One of the characteristics of the educational system is that it provides new and greater opportunity for men and women to meet. At most levels there are shared classes, though some private schools and universities are segregated by sex. This is undoubtedly having some effect, as is the sharing of offices and factory floors where such meeting occurs. So far there is little that one can say definitely about the long-term effects of new institutions of this kind, and much more research needs to be carried out. My observations here relate to the situations which I know at first hand.

At the universities there is a tendency for segregation by sex to break down in the process of day-to-day association. The result of this is less the emergence of couples as a part of the social scene than the appearance of mixed groups of young people. Such groups, both during work and leisure, are becoming far more commonplace, especially in the major urban centers. This means that there is a far wider circle from which a marriage partner can initially be selected. Family approval and making an appropriate choice, however, remain very important. Courting still remains a public rather than a private affair, and seeking too much privacy violates rules of proper behavior. Even in the new situations which have come into existence, these traditional rules remain strong.

Conclusion

Starting from the widely held assumption that in the Philippines men and women are social equals, I have tried to show what this means and how it is to be explained in relation to social participation, spheres of activity, and appropriate behavior. It is clear that the role of the woman in the Philippines today can be seen against the background of her traditional place in society. Her freedom of movement in contemporary Philippine society is in part the result of the existence of traditional occupations outside the household and in the religious and economic spheres. As well as being wives, mothers, and sisters, women also were healers and traders. In addition, they took their place in agricultural work. Within the household, women, through their control and allocation of the budget, act as managers and therefore have the right to a voice in the process of decision making. The recognition of this managerial capacity, as clearly defining a woman's sphere of interest, is important to recognition of her as an equal social person. At this level it is ability and sex that determine the sphere of interest and kind of responsibility appropriate to women, just as the same criteria determine rights and duties of men. Ultimately this is what social equality means.

NOTE

1. *Olog* is the term for young girls' sleeping quarters, which were a common feature of village organization in the earlier period. These served as a gathering place and a place where girls were visited by their suitors or betrothed partners.

BIBLIOGRAPHY

Aquino, Gaudencia V., Bonifacio N. Cristobal, Delfin Fresnosa: *Philippine Folktales,* Alemar, Phoenix Press, Quezon City, 1969.

Arce-Ortega, Angelina: "A Career-Housewife in the Philippines," in *Women in the New Asia,* UNESCO, 1963.

Benavides, E. R.: "The Filipino Woman's Social, Economic and Political Status," *Philippine Life,* Cultural Foundation of the Philippines Series, n.d.

Bennett, Alfred B., Jr.: "Managers and Entrepreneurs: A Comparison of Social Backgrounds in Philippine Manufacturing," in Frank Lynch and Alfonso de Guzman II (eds.), *Modernization: Its Impact in the Philippines,* V. IPC papers no. 10, Ateneo de Manila Press, Quezon City, 1971.

Boserup, Ester: *Women's Role in Economic Development,* George Allen & Unwin, Ltd., London, 1970.

Carroll, John J.: *The Filipino Manufacturing Entrepreneur: Agent and Product of Change,* Cornell University Press, Ithaca, New York, 1965.

Committee on Human Development: "Friendship Choices among U.P. Students," *The Education Quarterly,* pp. 17–32, 1964.

Crisostomo, Isabelo T.: "Imelda for President?" *Philippines Free Press,* Dec. 12, 1970.

Castillo, Gelia Tagumpay and Sylvia Hilomen-Guerrero: "The Filipino Woman: A Study in Multiple Roles," *Journal of Asian and African Studies,* pp. 18–29.

Dozier, Edward P.: *Mountain Arbiters,* University of Arizona Press, Tuscon, Arizona, 1966.

Fansler, Dean S.: *Filipino Popular Tales,* American Folk-Lore Society, Kraus Reprint Co., New York, 1969.

Farwell, G.: *A Mask of Asia,* Frederick A. Praeger, Inc., New York, 1967.

Fox, Robert: "Men and Women in the Philippines," in Barbara E. Ward (ed.), *Women in the New Asia,* UNESCO, 1963.

Fryer, Donald W.: *Emerging Southeast Asia: A Study in Growth and Stagnation,* Georgia Philip and Sons, Ltd., London, 1970.

Hart, Donn V.: "Homosexuality and Transvestism in the Philippines: The Cebuan Bayot and Lakin-on," *Behavior Science Notes,* vol. 3, pp. 211–248, 1968.

Hollnsteiner, Mary R.: "Reciprocity in the Lowland Philippines," in Frank Lynch S. J. (comp.), *Four Readings on Philippines Values,* IPC papers no. 2, Ateneo de Manila University Press, Quezon City, 1964.

————: *Urban Development in the Philippines: Trends 1970–2000,* prepared for the Presidential Organizing Committee on University Development, Ateneo de Manila, Quezon City, Sept. 15, 1969.

————: *Manila Microcosm: Leadership, Belonging, and Viewpoints in a Tondo Neighborhood,* Institute of Philippine Culture, Ateneo de Manila, Quezon City (forthcoming publication).

Infante, Teresita R.: *The Woman in Early Philippines and among the Cultural Minorities,* University of Santo Tomas Press, Manila, 1969.

Jacobson, Helga E.: *Tradition and Change in Cebu City: In a Philippine Provincial City,* Cornell University, unpublished Ph.D. dissertation. To be published as *Tradition and Change in Cebu City,* University Monograph Series, Wake Forest, North Carolina, 1972.

————: *Patterns of Friendship in a Philippine Provincial City,* IPC publications, Ateneo de Manila Press, Quezon City (forthcoming).

————: *San Pedro Village Makati: A Study of a Suburban Community in the Philippines* (in preparation).

Jocano, F. Landa: *Growing Up in a Philippine Barrio,* Holt, Rinehart and Winston, Inc., New York, 1969.

Kalaw, Lorna M.: "Our Lady of the Jet Set," *Philippines Free Press,* Oct. 10, 1970.

————: "We Wanna Be Free," *Philippines Free Press,* Dec. 12, 1970.

Kroeber, A. L.: "Kinship in the Philippines," *Anthropological Papers of the American Museum of Natural History,* vol. 19, pp. 69–84, 1919.

Lynch, Frank, S. J. (comp.): *Four Readings on Philippine Values,* IPC papers no. 2, Ateneo de Manila University Press, Quezon City, 1964.

Liu, William T., and Siok-Hoe Yu: "The Lower-Class Cebuano Family: A Preliminary Profile Analysis," *Philippine Sociological Review,* vol. 16, pp. 114–123, 1968.

Madigan, Francis C., S.J.: *The Farmer Said No,* University of the Philippines, Community Development Research Council, 1968.

Myrdal, Gunnar: *Asian Drama,* Pantheon Press Books, Inc., New York, 1968.

National Economic Council: *Social Implications of Small-scale Industries in the Philippines,* Statistical Survey C.P. 60106, 1959, Manila, June 1960.

Nydegger, William F., and Corinne Nydegger: *Tarong: An Ilocos Barrio in the Philippines,* Six Cultures Series vol. VI, John Wiley & Sons, Inc., New York, 1966.

Pacana, Honesto: "Notes on a Filipino Rule of Conduct: Noninterference," *Philippine Sociological Review* vol. 6, no. 6, pp. 29–30, 1958.

Rama, N. G.: "Imelda, the Presidency, the Nacionalistas, and the People," *Philippines Free Press,* Dec. 19, 1970.

Stauffer, Robert: *The Development of an Interest Group: The Philippine Medical Association,* University of the Philippines Press, Quezon City, 1966.

Wernstedt, Frederick L., and Joseph E. Spencer: *The Philippine Island World: A Physical, Cultural and Regional Geography.* University of California Press, Berkeley, Calif., 1967.

In Reality:
Some Middle Eastern Women

LOUISE E. SWEET

> One of the respondents said that he decided to leave with his family when [a soldier] asked him about the ages of his daughters: "I was frightened, that they might do something to them." When this man was asked why his relatives had stayed, he said, "Because they don't have any daughters. . . ."
> The families who left their homes often left some member of the family behind, to look after the family home and property. The men of the family, those of military age, would leave and take with them the womenfolk and the children. Older men could stay behind, as caretakers and guardians. In some cases, older women could stay behind, too. (P. Dodd and H. Barakat, *River without Bridges*, Beirut, 1968, pp. 52–53).

Introduction

Nothing seems to be more difficult than to persuade the commercial Western world that Middle Eastern women were never powerless or oppressed or subordinated *as women* any more than their brothers in traditional Arab, Kurdish, Persian, or Turkish society or in the tribal nomads' camp, in peasant villages, or in urban communities and whether Muslim or Christian. Many of those activities which once were performed by women *within* a distinctive lineage-based householding political economy, with a strong, complementary division of responsibilities between men and women, now have become "public" professions and occupations. When, as in the past, the "domestic sphere" of social life is the center of resource control, then indeed the place of women is important. Thus, the Western observer may see women engaging in the traditional "householding" contexts of management, production, midwifery, counseling in the family meeting, and directing and participating in village or community affairs. Their competence, their professionalism (in medicine, architecture, law, and politics), their self-confidence, and their occasional ruthless aggressiveness surprises the Western observer, if he *is* observing at all. But the old myth that seclusion, the veil, legal bias toward corporate lineage control of property (usually misinterpreted as a male advantage) are facts or symbols of the low status of Middle Eastern women of whatever rank or class continues to perpetuate misunderstanding. Moreover, international political biases of many colors enter into the resistance of Western scholars. And these are further compounded by elitist, old and new, collaborators from Middle East societies themselves who echo the "myths" for their own reasons.

Therefore I cannot hope to convince in a brief essay here. But I have lived at length and closely with some Arab and Persian families and in village and urban contexts in the Middle East and have visited many others. Perhaps, therefore, the most salient illustration from some considerable depth of field experience will be more suggestive of the sources of the remarkable gutsiness of Middle Eastern women than esoteric argument.

In the thoroughfares of a Muslim Oriental city today there is still no safer identity to possess than that of a woman—a woman who does not otherwise cue herself by dress or behavior as a Westerner or a local commercial prostitute (a European invention?).

The major points I wish to illustrate here are as follows: First, traditional Middle Eastern societies draw clear boundaries between social units, and there are good historical and environmental reasons to explain this. I present these in a brief introduction to the Middle East as a "high-stress" area. Second, the extended family, the corporate lineage, and the tribal or ethnic enclave are boundaries of security: *within* them economic production and exchange do not operate according to the commercial processes of the market, and the division of labor between men and women is complementary. Third, within such boundaries, families as units are more frequently *ranked* in relation to each other than they are placed in an economic class relationship: kinship, language, religion, etc., provide links that override economic differences. *Between* such boundaries vertical patron-client relationships—as between landlord and peasant—may hold; yet even these relations include an etiquette and mutual obligations which do not resemble at all such commercial relations as those of employer and employee do. Last, when the anthropologist has lived *within* such boundaries as Middle Eastern people do, the status of any individual, male or female, becomes that of the family in the larger system; the roles of so-called power and authority become "speaking chief" roles for the familial and client constituencies they represent; and women and marriage are fundamental mechanisms in forming alliances between families and tribes.

Mechanization of economic production in agriculture and crafts and the displacement of subsistence agriculture by widespread cash cropping have in the past century begun to dissolve the old ways. For reasons given here, as Middle Eastern women emerge from the protective boundaries of past society, they bring with them a long tradition of responsibility for the performance and management of social and economic activities and of manipulation of political relations between the segments of society. The ancient etiquette of modesty, demurity, and deference in public places simply does not mean low status at all.

The major context in which I discuss the lives of Middle Eastern women is drawn from the Syrian plains village of Tell Toqaan, where I lived from 1953 to 1954. At that time the village bore fewer traces of departure from tradition than it does, perhaps, today: there were absentee landlord-peasant combinations, there were a few independent peasant freehold families, and there was the Shaikh's household, a Homeric social unit in which the three wives of the Shaikh dominated.

AN AREA OF HIGH STRESS AND THE PROTECTION OF WOMEN

The Middle Eastern area in which the Syrian village of Tell Toqaan is located is a peculiarily high-stress zone. All regions of human occupation have more or less stringent ecological boundaries demanding unique adaptive mechanisms for survival, such as the extreme cold of the Arctic and the extreme dryness of deserts. The Middle East shows a considerable variety of these: barely habitable deserts; limited distributions of areas of fertile soil; overabundance of water in flooding deltas, marshes, exotic rivers, and torrential tropical rains; rugged mountain ranges; and cold highland plateaus. Its position linking continents rather than lying at continental extremes increases these environmental hazards because of frequent invasions, colonizations, conquests, migrations. The expectable consequences include epidemic diseases, interethnic and intersectarian competition, and extreme population pressure. The resulting ethnic and cultural mosaic seems intricate and fragile, and the lines of fracture appear to be deeply etched. Hence, it is in the Middle East, more than most other areas, perhaps, that women are "hoarded" and "protected" and caught between fertility demands and population control mechanisms such as war. Women have many very subtle and sometimes very distressing functions to perform in the interests of the survival of their kin groups and of society. This, it must be recognized, is often if not always in their individual interests too. Many women whom I have known have been aware of it, and many men have too.

One routine example of the protection of women, often misinterpreted as "oppression," is that urban and often village women rarely enter public shops except in the major capitals of the "modernized" Middle East such as Cairo, Beirut, Istanbul, and Teheran. In Tell Toqaan and other villages I have lived in, most adult women never did. They might send their children to buy or to sell, but they did not themselves go. When, however, an itinerant peddler brought a pack sack or truckload of printed textiles or household utensils to Tell Toqaan, many women hurried to see the goods spread out in a side lane of the village.

In the Levant and indeed all of the Middle East, market places are among the several locations where all the diverse and competing ethnic groups meet; they are dangerous places, as is the battlefield, the *majlis* or political meeting place, and the reception ceremony—wherever strangers, traditional rivals, or outsiders may be encountered. The dangers are real, for here is where lethal fighting and feuding break out.

However, one explanation for the protection of women which seems largely to be for public consumption, for outsiders, is that found written in the sacred literatures of Judaism, Christianity, and Islam. It is expressed by men especially, and sometimes even by women: women are weak, prone to aggressive sexuality, nonrational, and so forth, and hence must be "disciplined" or "controlled." Westerners, even social scientists, interpret this control as invariably oppressive, but I think this is a rather naïve distortion. When one has lived closely with a Middle Eastern family and community for an extended length of time, it is the propaganda value of such statements that is most impressive. Daily experience finds too much variability in both men and women and in their relations to each other to allow one to agree that this viewpoint is to be interpreted, therefore, as an actual belief in or evidence for the inferiority of women. Rather, it has a positive, adaptive function: it is an attitude consistent with boundary defense of a social system composed of relatively exclusive social units (familial or household)[1] more or less densely packed together in the living spaces of camps and of compact villages and crowded urban quarters.

WOMEN OF THE SHAIKH'S HOUSEHOLD: TELL TOQAAN, SYRIA, 1953 TO 1954

An examination of the relationship of Middle Eastern women to their society may become clearer if we begin by presenting in detail their position in one village and then consider the many variations from this particular example.

The village of Tell Toqaan, Syria (1953 to 1954), is similar in structure to many other Middle Eastern villages of the plains insofar as it is composed to a considerable proportion of tribesmen, headed by a Shaikhly family. Present also are peasant families, but it is in the internal organization and management of the Shaikhly household that the roles and statuses of women become clear. Some 120 persons of the village were members of the Shaikhly household, a little over a third of the whole community. Of these 67 were males and 53 females; the individuals in both categories were distributed from infancy to unemployable old age and many of them were children. The Shaikhly household is more accurately understood, however, as a clearly bounded societal unit composed of some twenty full-family subunits, a number of broken ones, and only a few isolated individuals without local kinsmen. Within it births, marriages, and deaths took place during the year that I lived there (1953 to 1954), as though it were a small society almost complete in itself.

The whole Nuri group was both ranked and stratified. The Shaikhly *family* members were the possessors and top-level managers of the property of the whole unit. For all but their fellow tribesmen (Bu Layl) they were the aristocrats or upper class of a ranked rather than stratified society, for all Bu Layl shared the ideology of a common descent and a common tribal membership. Fellow tribesmen of the Bu Layl in the village were thus clearly of lower rank than their Shaikhly family and numbered five other families than the Shaikh's. Other members (fourteen families) of the Shaikhly household, however, were of diverse origin and attached to it by clientage, customary contracts of partnership or incidental labor, or—in the case of a "refugee" mother and her baby—by the sheer charity of traditional sanctuary.

These members of the household provided labor for such occupations as personal slave (attendant and bodyguard); chauffeur or driver of the automobile or, more importantly, the tractor; foreman of the farmhands; shepherd of the local flock; and a gardener (he specifically grew vegetables in contrast to the other agricultural workers who plowed, sowed, and harvested the grains, legumes, and forage and cash crops). Most of the working members of the household, however, were engaged in a variety of jobs from general agricultural labor to building houses and making repairs, food processing, and the making of household or other equipment (tent screens, trays, clothing).

The sexual division of labor had little overlap, but the mode of membership in the Shaikh's householding unit was recruitment by family, so to speak. A few families, in fact, had no adult males and the clientage position was in fact held by the widow or divorced women (also a mother) and her children. Women were equally active with men (or perhaps more so) in the production, processing, and maintenance activities of the Shaikhly household.

The property resources of the Shaikh's household were various and dispersed. About a third of the fertile Tell Toqaan lands belonged to the Shaikh's lineage in the name of the Shaikh, and there was also lineage-held land in other villages of the tribal unit. There were the Nuri flocks, said to amount to several thousand sheep, which were kept in the grazing zones well to the east of the village by shepherding families attached to the Shaikh's family by customary contracts. A flock of about a hundred ewes and their lambs was maintained in the village for local household needs. The Shaikhly family owned a residence in Aleppo, where some members of the family stayed much of the time. It was quite clear that while ownership might be legally invested in the individual person of the Shaikh and that inheritance would follow state-stipulated legal process from father to sons, every member of the *whole* household, from members of the Shaikhly family by kinship and marriage to those members by contract and alliance, identified closely with that ownership by enjoying right of access to the resources as they needed them.

The property of the Shaikhly household in land and flocks thus provided all the food staples for the members of the participant group, in grains, milk and milk products, meat, and vegetables. Cash crops of cotton and sesame, surplus in animals, and animal products which were sold to the markets made it possible to purchase from those markets those things not available in the household production, from an automobile and tractor with attachments to factory-made textiles and toys. Most luxury items were essentially status items and were initially found chiefly in the possession of members of the ranking Shaikhly family, males and females alike. The individuals often gave such trinkets or small items away after displaying them for a few days. That the production of the Shaikh's household was not at all profit-oriented and was not in any sense a commercial enterprise is suggested by the fact that his farmhands and tenants cultivated only as much of his lands as were deemed necessary for household supplies and the cash income for fashionable luxuries wanted for the coming year. The Shaikh was, in fact, criticized for not cultivating all his arable land; his critics were thrifty peasants in the village who were not associated with his household.

From ·the uninitiated outsider's point of view, it would appear that the Shaikhly household was supported by the casual labor of a considerable number of men, women, adolescents, and even children who came and went, between their homes in the village and the Shaikhly compound, haphazardly to ask for some needed items for themselves or "on command" when the elderly slave, the foreman, or some other messenger of the Shaikhly household required help or service. However, it became clear to me that one-third or more of the people of the village "belonged" to the Shaikh in the sense of being members of his household as an economic unit, and that the work or production and maintenance proceeded according to the need of the whole, and especially of the core Shaikhly family itself.

While some claimed at first, for my benefit, that the farmhands and casual laborers of the household were recompensed in money as wage laborers, they in fact received food, protection, solution of grievances, supervision of marriages, and other services of *noblesse oblige*. They also provided many other services, some of which will be indicated below, outside the economic ones to the Shaikhly family. They were not employees in any contemporary market-system sense of the term but were attached as families to the household membership. The women in particular signified this in their brightly colored chiffon headbands. Political allegiance, however, tended to reflect kinship closeness more strongly than economic dependence.

The Shaikh's own family, regularly occupying his large house and open compound in the village, included fifteen persons: himself, his three wives, the younger children of these women (two boys and five girls), two young sisters of the Shaikh for whom he was responsible, and the young son and daughter of a deceased brother. He maintained a house in Aleppo where his mother and oldest son lived; an older daughter was at a boarding school. He himself could hardly be called a resident of either the village or of Aleppo, however, for he traveled widely and spent much time in Damascus in the interests of his own small splinter tribe of Bù Layl. However, he was not, like Odysseus, absent for many years at a time. (This "Odyssean" pattern is characteristic, however, of many Middle Eastern village households whose men emigrate to work overseas.)

Although the Shaikh was more often absent from the village than present in the first part of 1954, Tell Toqaan was still the center of his economic enterprise. Perhaps the main reason for his absence was the political disturbance in Syria that year. In any event, the daily round of activities went on in the village. The affairs of his household in the village and the eastern grazing area were managed by his wives, especially the senior wife, A., his patrilateral parallel cousin (a daughter of his father's brother), and S., another more distant "cousin." The two women, together with his third and ·youngest wife, contrasted among themselves in personality. However, these differences I would consider to be strongly influenced by their respective ages and roles in respect to kinship closeness or family of origin and the behavior expected of them in respect to these criteria.

A. was the eldest and most reserved, a woman of dignity and good judgment in the eyes of others. As first wife, as closest cousin to her husband, she occupied her role and status well; but she was also said to be unfortunate in that she had no sons, only four girls. It seemed clear to me that, in spite of her failure to produce sons, she still held her primary status in the Shaikh's household and the village securely and apparently her seniority, first cousinship, and managerial expertise outweighed the lack of sons.

S., the second wife, was aggressive, ebullient, energetic. She marched about the village directing activities, from weddings to housebuilding, for the benefit of the Shaikh or for the workers themselves. She did this with such authority that she reminded me very much of the head of an order of Roman Catholic nursing nuns—a woman I know personally—who functioned in a highly responsible managerial role at the head of a network of hospitals reaching across the United States. Perhaps the analogy was facilitated by the remarkable similarity in costumes. I found that, in my own gallery of powerful personalities, the same nickname fit them both: Lady Bulldozer. In the village, S. was generally regarded as strong, and fortunate too, for she had borne two sons as well as daughters.

F., the third wife was still very young and shy, but with the self-assurance appropriate to a young lady of higher status, in the whole of Syrian tribal society, than any Bu Layl: she was one of the many daughters of an important and powerful tribal Shaikh in Syria in those days. She also had a small son, less than a year old. On one of my first visits to the village, before I had moved in to live there, I was invited to luncheon at the Shaikh's house. Although I was a woman, the situation was handled courteously and with ease. The Shaikh ate with me and F. sat with us, too shy to eat much at all (very proper behavior, from which she could depart after I had taken up residence and had become a familiar figure in the community). The eldest son of the Shaikh served us.

Strangers, especially men, probably never saw the three wives, and if they were Westerners, they had probably never heard of their existence. If they *had* heard of them, the three women's lives would have been explained to the Westerners thus: "Of course they did not work; as high-ranking tribal women of a preindustrial system, they had no education in the literate urban sense; they always stayed, as was proper, inside their compound and never went out; and they had given the Shaikh many children, especially three sons." The uninformed Western translation of this, however, would be: "These are idle, illiterate women; their only function is to bear children, preferably males; they are probably bored by isolation and restriction of movement, without knowledge of any kind; probably, therefore, they are conniving and jealous of each other. They do nothing."

But the more accurate understanding is very different. The first account, given above, of the wives of the Shaikh is supposed to indicate to the knowledgeable stranger or outsider that the Shaikh's household is so high in status and well-to-do that there is no need for his wives, daughters, and sisters to work. Their very "invisibility" is also evidence of their value and high position, as well as of the Shaikh's; thus, the status of his whole household is validated. The very talk of envy and jealousy among wives is part of the propaganda underwriting the prosperity of the whole household. When naïve Westerners believe otherwise (Protestant missionaries and casual travelers are especially susceptible and have long lamented the unhappy situation of women in polygynous households), the gap of understanding between systems is complete. Such talk is to be understood very differently indeed.

In daily life in Tell Toqaan, all women moved as they wished or needed to about the village, the wives of the Shaikh as well as lower-ranking women in the household and all other women of the peasant households. Escorts generally accompanied the highest-ranking women, much more for sociability and prestige than for protection. In the event however, that strangers or military police approached the village, women and children vanished, and not without good historic reason—as the chronicle of every village in the Middle East would demonstrate. But apart from such occasions, women circulated freely about the village. They also went off to visit kinsmen and friends in other villages or to the city, in accordance with cultural constraints whose significance can hardly be interpreted as a state of imprisoning oppression. Visiting patterns among women, as among men, are formalized, and in Tell Toqaan it was as important that the Shaikh's wives visit me as it was that I visit them. Each of the three came with an entourage and in order of seniority. Their visits were climaxed by that of the youngest wife, who brought a yearling lamb. (It was, as is the custom, presented to me tail first, to display its prime condition by the evidence of the firm fatness of its tail!)

Such life-cycle ceremonies as weddings, births, circumcisions, and funerals were community affairs and brought the women of the village out into public participation according to their roles, status, and kinship or household alliances. One especially well-attended celebration at which I was present was a night of dancing in honor of a marriage. On this occasion the universal participation in the great circular *dabké* dance was moving and exhilarating; nearly everyone took part, and everyone was indeed present. The *dabké* affords many styles of performance. Adult men and women move erectly, with dignity and intensity, while the young bucks prance and stamp with gusto, often with one or two of the earthy, bold, and boisterous older peasant or tribal women among them meeting their every challenge with vigor. The adolescent boys and girls sort out their special friendships and budding mutual attractions shyly, straight-faced— a youth moving into line beside a girl he has well-known hopes about.

The Shaikh's wives and sons attended the wedding dance at Tell Toqaan, and the sons and daughters joined the *dabké* circle even if the wives did not.

In the daily round of life, women and girls—like men—are evaluated for their diligence, and diligence in a householding economy like Tell Toqaan's means a long work day. Men and women, boys and girls, work at a steady although not a killing pace. They generally work sociably and sometimes cooperatively, depending on the task.

In a high-ranking polygynous family like the Shaikh's, the women's tasks are managerial and are divided among them, but on at least one occasion I sat with the three wives while they worked together braiding wool yarn and rolling it into the long *sbagg* or tethering rope used in milking a flock of sheep. The talk, as usual, centered upon village and family events. Meanwhile their children, the youngest sisters of the Shaikh, and some youngsters of village women who were helping with the wool played in a group near us with an assortment of toys from the city. When a small-scale quarrel over a tricycle developed, the three wives put down their work and bustled out to the children. Each mother extracted her own and drew them aside, remonstrating and reassuring but not scolding nor berating. The childhood conflict was cooled off and the women returned to their handiwork and chatting. Their husband was well-known and locally praised for his even-handed attention to his three wives, as befitted a Muslim. They had no reason, as far as I ever was aware, to be at odds with each other. Indeed, the three wives of the Shaikh remain with me, each a distinctive individual in her own right, as people that I am glad to have known. Their roles and responsibilities in their large household were clearly marked out for them.

A., the senior wife, may be regarded as the "first vice-president" of the Nuri household and overseer of all activities while she was in the village. Her chief responsibility, however, was to go east in spring with the flocks and to supervise the lambing, milking, cheese processing, wool shearing, and marketing of surplus products beyond the needs of the household for the coming year. She knew the tasks in detail since she had been brought up to know them, as her daughters were being brought up at the time I was in the village. She supervised the work of men and women who actually handled the manual tasks, but nearly every one of these she could also perform (shearing is probably the exception). Like any *mu'allim* ("master craftsman"), she could evaluate performance critically and meet crises with decisive action insofar as traditional husbandry practices were able to cope with them.

When A. was not in the village, S. took over as "second vice-president." She supervised not only the feeding of twenty to fifty people a day but also the household's agricultural and shepherding activities in Tell Toqaan.

She received the *wakiil* or foreman, the laborers, and those seeking temporary employment. She decided where the itinerant gypsy band might camp
on its visit to the village, and she provided food and shelter for travelers
passing through if they had no contacts in the village. She allocated overnight camping space and shelter for the lambs in a tent especially set up
for them, a tent set aside for any shepherd peoples that might be moving
east to the spring grazing. Regularly also, she saw to the preparation of
food supplies to be sent east to A.'s camp. S. also supervised and participated in village weddings, housebuilding, and the care of sick people—
including an anthropologist. She did so briskly, decisively, and with great
good humor. She kept up a surprisingly rapid pace of work, as necessary,
and there was never any question as to who was in charge, even though
the decisions might come through an intermediary and be phrased as "the
wish of Shaikh Nuri," who had not, in fact, been present for many days.

Two of the Shaikh's four children, both girls, lived in the village, as
did two of his young unmarried sisters. Of these four, two were youngsters
under ten and two were young women roughly between fourteen and sixteen. The Shaikh's twelve-year-old son also lived in Tell Toqaan and went
to school with the other children in the school of the Imam (the Muslim
religious leader). The activities of these girls gives some idea of the process
by which such competent and commanding women as the Shaikh's first
two wives might be trained.

All the Shaikh's children played with their own age groups in the village
and all attended the Imam's school. The youngest girls accompanied the
older village girls and women out to help milk the flocks twice a day. The
older girls, with their peers and friends among the village girls, brought
water and straw to the village midden, where the older women were making
fuel from a combination of manure and straw, or to the men who were
making mud bricks for construction. They did not do the manual work of
mixing, however, since this was one of the status barriers of the householding division of labor. To what extent and depth of sentiment there
is a "value" barrier of taboo or defilement for such manual labor has never
been adequately determined; it may scarcely be discussed, so it may carry
as sharp an effect as food taboos. Certainly the sons and daughters of the
Shaikh were everywhere deferred to in gentle ways, but they were also
instructed by the village women and watched over by the village men. And
they were partnered in games of tag and helped in making model houses
and toy furnishings by their peers, the peasant and tribal boys and girls.
They were all, together with them, regarded as "sons and daughters of the
Bu Layl and of Tell Toqaan."

One of the Shaikh's older daughters visited the village in early spring
(February); she was perhaps seventeen and was said to be in boarding school
somewhere to the west. In Tell Toqaan she wore the tribal village girl's

formal dress—a long black gown, simple headcloth and gamp, with a bright chiffon headband indicating alliance or membership in the Shaikh's household—with a subtle crispness of style. Hand in hand with a village youth of her old playmate set, she strolled on the village threshing ground, and the village women smiled that the two young people still liked each other. She was the belle at an evening wheat-grinding bee where the elders, village men and women, quietly sat at one end of the long room of a peasant's house, chaperoning. These elders instantly noted whom she favored and to whom she spoke among the young people. She spoke to everyone; in fact, she knew everyone and each parent was greeted with the proper kin term of courtesy. This was a demonstration of her social competence before a panel of judges—the adult membership of the Shaikhly household and the village—whose opinion she deemed important regardless of their economic status relative to hers.

Thus far, I have dealt primarily with the women and girls who filled the highest status roles in the Shaikhly household of Tell Toqaan, and I have tried to indicate that their roles call for a wider range of competence and function than has been generally recognized in Middle Eastern ethnology. In such an economy, domestic tasks are by no means the nuclear family housekeeping chores characteristic of a commercial industrial society. For one thing, women are far more active and interactive socially; in the rural village or nomadic camp, they are not at all confined. Even in the urban setting, "confinement" or "seclusion" are by no means imprisonment. But most importantly, the activity of women—whether management and supervision or the production and maintenance tasks of the peasant women—is as necessary to the success of the household operation as the sources of energy, whether men or machines, are in an industrial enterprise. In a householding economic unit such as Shaikh Nuri's, women at *all* levels more often participate in decisions than do individual employees below the management bureaucracy in a commercial enterprise.

For another point, it is obvious that the size of a village householding unit, such as the Shaikh's in Tell Toqaan, is such that most of the time its members are close together, know every issue that arises, and are vulnerable to the results of any decision. Everyone, even children, may indeed speak up. Even when the eldest of the Shaikh's wives moved east to manage the milking and shearing of the flocks, communications were maintained and she was regularly supplied, as she requested, with food staples from Tell Toqaan prepared under the second wife's supervision.

In the smaller peasant households, the joint or extended family usually provided a number of women—wives of brothers, daughters-in-law, and widowed or unmarried women—who worked more or less amicably together. A peasant woman with sons but no daughters was hard put to get all her work done, especially if she had no female kinsmen in the village, for mother-and-daughter or sister-and-sister combinations were most often the stable and compatible task teams (by observation and expressed preference and acknowledgment). Within all households in 1953 to 1954, much of the decision making about economic, social, and ceremonial events could still take place according to custom. That is, there were few surprises, and innovations were coming into Tell Toqaan slowly; the mature women were well practiced in the problems and answers of village life. Conflicts might occur between households over trivial issues and result in brief verbal fireworks and minor missile exchanges (clods of dirt) between the women, and these women were more ceremonially self-righteous (or family status-righteous, to be accurate) than truly competitive for survival. Indeed, it was, rather, among men of the families and lineages that the blood of feuding might be spilled and had been upon a very few occasions in Tell Toqaan history.

Tell Toqaan seemed in 1953 to 1954 and still seems to me in 1973 to have been and to be unique in its combination of social heterogeneity and—still at that time—lack of severe internal conflicts. Perhaps the lack of conflict stemmed simply from its smallness as a community (about 320 people), and its distance from urban centers, and the fact that it had adequate land. Even the so-called structural incompatibilities of some role dyads (e.g., mother-in-law/daughter-in-law) called forth little of the friction and not much of the anticipatory rhetoric that I saw later in urban families and mountain villages in Lebanon. I did not come across, in Tell Toqaan in 1953 to 1954, any "permanent" hostilities among women in any of the available roles, familiar or societal. At the same time I found no named roles with unusual import outside familial (mother, wife, etc.) or conditional (widow, girl) ones except for *Shaikha* (the female equivalent of *Shaikh*, political or religious) and *Hajjiya*, the female equivalent of a Muslim man who has made the pilgrimage to Mecca. But it is, I think, noteworthy that among the women of Tell Toqaan, regardless of rank and status, I encountered few who were not bold, outspoken, competent, and argumentative within the accepted contexts of etiquette (involving age, kinship, and social status). Most were quite ready to comment later that only the proprieties of the "public" situation kept them silent and seemingly demure.

Thus when a decision is made in a traditional Middle Eastern social unit, the spokesman may be a most distinguished man in role and status, but he is more apt than not to be voicing a consensus to which women have lent their weight. He will be a fool not to have listened to his mother, his aunt, his sister, or his wife, for it is they who know and manage the welfare of the internal or interior components of the social units (family, household, lineage, village) for which he is the minister of external affairs. The complementarity of the sexually defined roles in the Middle East invests both realms with access to responsibility, experience, social competence, and the authority of demonstrated good judgment. The competence of its women are an element in the power of any lineage and household unit in traditional Middle Eastern society, as are the number of its men and their competence. In the Middle East, power is vested in lineage and patron-client groups, not in individuals.

Last, we may turn to the little understood problem of sexual relations between men and women in the societies of many villages of the Levant. Here I prefer to generalize from observations and discussions with Middle Easterners rather than to make particular references to the several communities and many families I know more or less intimately.

Perpetuation of the family unit through time requires offspring, and the fecundity of the women is relevant. It is a value many but not all women hold fully as strongly as the men of their households, and it is consistent with a preindustrial economic and prescientific medical tradition. Young men and women are equally interested in who their future spouses will be, and, while the group interest comes first, they will know well—from direct acquaintance as well as report and discussion—the qualities of the person they marry. Many criteria enter in and I have known men to be rejected by girls regardless of their prosperity and status because of their known bad temper.

In some areas, virginity may actually be a rather rare attribute among girls in general, not only of the peasant class, and the sexual services expected of maids and servants for the men of high-status urban families is well known. There is a traditional village custom involving public ceremonies that assert the virginity of the bride—and most often these are no more than public ceremony; that is, they serve to indicate that the marriage is satisfactory to both parties (both families of the spouses as well as the young couple). As folk tales and proverbs indicate, the public display of a cloth stained with blood at the consummation also means that the male is sexually competent. That it may really *mean* nothing but the conventional acceptance of the marriage by and for the families so joined, as well as the community, could be tested if we knew how frequently it is chicken or pigeon blood that is daubed on the cloth. At the level of the peasant classes and even certain urban middle classes in the Middle East, premarital sexual experience may be frequent. In some communities where marriages are not easy to dissolve even in case of infertility, it is not unusual for a young man to test the fertility of his potential wife and for her to allow him to do so *if* indeed she considers that he will make a good husband—one who will provide the kind of household she wants. Such an arrangement may even include an agreement that both may have independent "private" lives, including extramarital affairs, while the family line is duly perpetuated and maintained in their mutual interest. There is much more to the "double standard" of the Middle East than the West is aware of, needless to say.

The ideology of the Middle Eastern economy does indeed emphasize the necessity for its women to produce legitimate offspring for the household unit. It is precisely the independence of the household unit managing its property for its livelihood and continuity that makes comprehensible the values of modesty, seclusion, and virginity of its females. When the society is a stratified one, the burden of closer adherence to the norms of the society bears more heavily upon women the higher they are in status. The most exclusive families of some Arab nobility are well known and praised for the number of unmarried women in their families, women who have remained single because no man of equal status and close enough kinship was available. This says nothing, however, about the private lives of the unmarried women. Sexual deprivation or freedom is not as relevant to their status and role as their economic competence and political usefulness in alliances—together with their reproductive function—the sentiments of the sacred texts notwithstanding. Moreover, to ask why appearances must be so kept up and hypocrisy be so obvious is, it seems to me, to underline what is essentially a sociocultural difference of kind in pattern, structure, or whatever may be the easiest way to put the matter. Societies organized chiefly around the importance of kinship ties are not comparable to market-based industrial systems in these ethnocentric moralistic terms.

Management duties, as described earlier, demand social maturity, and it is the ability to be a competent manager that is a chief personal criterion in selecting a wife. Moreover, in the preindustrial Middle East, the division of labor is such that women are necessary in a well-run householding unit of whatever scale of organization and production or mode of livelihood. Women are an important part of the labor force, and in this type of economy there are fewer ways to secure women for these functions than men. Usually the manual tasks performed by women are done as a complement to the work their husbands do as retainers or cultivators or in animal husbandry. It is the lower-ranked or statused husband along *with his family* who is recruited into a Shaikh's household unit by the several means mentioned earlier. However, managers as such can usually only be married, and in fact marriage is the predominant way to fill out the need for female labor in a household.[2]

The adults of the peasant household that I lived in in Tell Toqaan amused themselves at length arguing whether, in a household with three sons and no daughters, the husband should acquire a second and younger wife to help the first or whether a wife should be sought for the eldest son. The factors leading to the second choice were logical; perpetuation of the household through looking forward to the third generation was preferred to multiplying the potential number of brothers who would inherit. This small household had only enough land for two sons and already the third and youngest, then nine years old, was acquiring by encouragement the idea of moving to the city to become a *taajir*, a trader.

One final example may be given. In Kuwait in 1959 I learned that the eldest son of a Shaikh of a shepherd tribe had worked for an oil company for a number of years and had invested his oil company earnings in the then most important property—sheep and goats—of his community. He found it necessary to take a second wife simply because of the increase in the management and performance of women's work that occurred upon increasing his household property.

In this section on the internal organization of a traditional or preindustrial Middle Eastern household and the roles and statuses of women within it, I have endeavored to set forth and emphasize the importance of women to such households. This importance stems from their contributions in the areas of labor, management, procreation, and child rearing. Women may not be refused their desires with impunity, it may be said, and they have many ways to secure what they want through manipulation of custom (cf. Mohsen, 1967) as well as by simply refusing to fulfill any or all of their functions. Depending upon the legal code of the local community, if they have means to secure sole control of property, they also wield openly acknowledged power in the local community. None of the Middle Eastern communities excludes women or makes it absolutely impossible for them to achieve this; that there is no general movement to secure sole control of property is not surprising. The important unit of survival is a society, not a class, and the *household unit* of men and women and their ascendants and descendants, client families, and the like, is just that—a society. Young women in their own family of birth are participating members, and their feelings and attitudes are not usually of being subjugated. Even in families of great stress, when the father is "hard" or "shiftless" or powerless from illness, it is more important for the household to maintain solidarity than to defy or abandon the one who fills the role of protector of the gate, no matter how poorly he seems to do so. A role without an incumbent leaves its "system" handicapped.

In summary, we may say that in the range of family patterns in the Middle East a status hierarchy is usually present. It is not, however, insightful to conclude that because men's sphere is on the periphery of the social unit, performing defense and negotiation to maintain its security, that therefore the interior roles of women are inferior in status to all men, unless one is working from the definition that power is the decisive component of status and that power is control over personnel resources through formal structures and organization. Let us not confuse power with the playing of roles in formal ritual and ceremony—or, as Fried says, with the fuss and feathers of prestige.

Moreover, demographic imperatives have been forgotten until recently, as well as the economic and the ecological. In some areas of anthropology at least, there continues to be a recognition of the fact that any human group requires, in order to survive—whatever the source of energy or mode

and organization of its application—some women of at least normal intelligence. What is the demographic requirement? It depends upon the
nature of the technology of survival and the abundance of resources. Apart
from reproduction imperatives, what is there? Access to the skilled intelligence of the society—a social product. The women's managerial and task
roles in traditional village and householding units in the Middle East seem
to me to be much closer to promoting, in general, the development of
individual ability and dynamic and social personality than do women's
isolated domestic or subordinate clerical statuses in the Western commercial industrial system.

I have asserted that Middle Eastern society does not in social reality
subjugate and degrade *women per se,* even peasant, slave, or "minority"
group women either from a Western ethnocentric or an Eastern ethnocentric viewpoint. In my opinion Eastern preindustrial or industrializing
societies provide far more latitude for personal development and access
to positions of responsibility and power than do Western societies. After all,
two effective and dynamic heads of state, Madam Indira Nehru Ghandi and
Madam Bandaranaike, have no counterparts in the industrial West and
are prime examples for Westerners to note. Within the Middle East, as the
countries from Morocco to Afghanistan industrialize their technoeconomic
bases and revolutionize their social orders, it is women who have emerged
to fill roles of daring leadership and of professional responsibility in the
arts and sciences, with little if any resistance from their fathers, brothers,
or husbands. The protestations from men are mild rhetoric at most.

I should like to present, last, a brief sketch of one more remarkable
woman I have known, 'Umm Khaliil.

'UMM KHALIIL, THE MOTHER OF KHALIIL

At least once a week I went in the evening to eat supper with a family
living in Beirut. When I was depressed and tired I looked forward to it;
we all complained and then we would cheer each other up. The Haliims
are the heart of a much larger group of kin who live in apartments scattered around Beirut. But every day they are all in contact with each other,
visiting, phoning, coming to eat at Mother and Father Haliim's, or perhaps
going to Nadia and Saliim's or Nuriyya and Yunis's. Once in a while I
would go along when we went out to a public restaurant. Most of these
evenings, however, we ate at Mother and Father Haliim's, and I made
notes on every bit of food on the table and took down the recipes for
malfuuf or *kubbi 'arnabiyya* from 'Umm Khaliil. My "field notebook" is
now full of her recipes and she is the best cook I know.

But there is a good deal more to 'Umm Khaliil than her excellent cooking. When we gather at the table, her status in the family emerges. One
has to have visited many times, however, to have become as close as a

stranger can to that exclusive Middle Eastern group, the family, to understand this.

Ordinarily, Khaliil, the Haliim's oldest son, joins us at supper; he comes early enough to play a little while with his two young daughters. (They live with his parents and oldest sister now that his marriage has broken up and he and his wife have separated.) Then we sit down for a little while and drink a glass of beer or wine to relax. Perhaps Nuriyya and Yunis come for supper too, perhaps joined by some of the many cousins also living in Beirut or cousins from Wales or Canada. It is rare, in fact, for only the minimum number of family members to be present. However, if Khaliil has come when we sit down at the table, he takes the place at the head of the table, for he has now been designated head of the family by his father. Abu Khaliil, the father, has retired from most of the obligations of family head—visiting the sick; arranging appointments for jobs, dentists, doctors, lawyers for all members of the family (including all those cousins in Beirut, Tripoli, and in the vicinity of Saida); giving aid; attending marriages and funerals; and negotiating everywhere necessary on behalf of perhaps fifty to seventy-five people, including those who are abroad. At his parents' home, Khaliil sometimes must arbitrate between the family and the youngest of the two maids; she is "too independent" sometimes in her handling of Khaliil's daughters or in other tasks. Nora, the old family servant, is now too aged and feeble to do any work, but she continues to live with the family, does little hand tasks, and slips securely away, slowly, as the years pass.

At the table Abu Khaliil, the elderly father, sits next to his son on Khaliil's left, and I, in guest status, on Khaliil's right. 'Umm Khaliil sits next to her husband. The oldest daughter sits next to me unless others are present; then they are seated according to their status and the daughter moves to sit beside her mother. But if Khaliil, now ceremonial head of the family, is not present, his mother, 'Umm Khaliil, sits at the head of the table no matter how many others come, for she is *de facto* head of the family and has been so for many years.

'Umm Khaliil's advice prevails in all family decisions within the core group, even though the "voice of decision" is ceremonially expressed, after discussion, by Khaliil, the oldest son. But each day she is consulted on family disputes throughout the network of related families. On one especially mad and hilarious evening at the Haliim's—we laughed about it afterwards, after it was all over—'Umm Khaliil settled two family disputes of close kin by telephone, directed Khaliil on how to take the young maid to task, and brought to an amicable conclusion a husband-wife difference that had been so severe that they had spent the afternoon there at her insistence so they might discuss the problem in each other's presence. She and the whole immediate family were also deeply and delicately involved in negotiations with the most powerful priest of the church to which they belonged in arranging for the dissolution of the oldest son's marriage, a problem that took them to the patriarch of the community. 'Umm Khaliil was unquestionably the chief judge and arbitrator for a wide network of kinsmen, the chief strategist in negotiations with the "outside," and most surely the best cook.

But 'Umm Khaliil's activities do not stop with "family" business. She is active in the Palestinian cause through both church and formal political organizations of women. Their objectives are, of course, to raise money and secure clothing for the displaced peoples of the camps. But their activities are not narrowly focussed. 'Umm Khaliil's societies organize festivals and parties as well as group sorties by bus to religious sanctuaries and charitable institutions in various parts of Lebanon and Syria. The Greek Catholic ceremonial calendar is one framework upon which the women exercise their capacity for public pressure as a group. One of the leaders among them is 'Umm Khaliil.

The Haliims are a "middle-class" Greek Catholic Arab family, Palestinian refugees of 1947 from a prosperous business in Haifa. In Beirut, the sons and sons-in-law are businessmen and junior executives, salaried men of moderate means. The younger women work, married or unmarried, as secretaries, saleswomen, or housewives. 'Umm Khaliil, whose English and French are present but rudimentary, has traveled widely—Brazil, North America, Europe. Handsome, composed, warm, graceful in her courtesy, deferential to husband and sons in the smaller courtesies, she is considered the heart and soul of the family. But most importantly, the flow of social energy, if we may put the reciprocity of interaction this way in a Middle Eastern family, is not merely centripetal nor centrifugal but in continuous oscillation among them all. And 'Umm Khaliil is foremost in stimulating the continuity of interaction of all the family's members—of maintaining its solidarity and the firmness of its boundaries with the greater society. Beyond the family boundaries, she is active in other contemporary mechanisms of pressure and influence in Levant society.

NOTES

1. I use the term *household* here in the technical sense first noted by Aristotle and briefly developed by the economic historian Karl Polanyi (1944). It will be illustrated and exemplified by the household of Shaikh Nuri of Tell Toqaan in this paper.

2. It is not by any means the only way. For example, a man's sister or aunt may prefer, rather than to marry, to manage his household and property in his absence if his wife is not available for some reason. In some cases women "sacrifice" themselves for their male kinsmen in this way and are especially honored and respected (Sweet, 1967). Moreover, I have encountered many women in peasant villages with no interest in marriage or children—women who did not find it difficult to ignore the "norms" or to give only token conformity.

Ascendant Societies

Onondaga Women:
Among the Liberated

CARA E. RICHARDS

If you must be born a woman, try to be an Onondaga. Iroquois culture is one of the few in the world where the average parent is not disappointed when the child born to them is a girl. Historically, the relatively high status of Iroquois women is well documented. Descent was traditionally traced through the women, land belongs to the women, and chiefs are appointed by the women—who theoretically can depose them at will. This means that female children are important to a family, the opinions of women carry weight, and women have some legal and political power. Even after four hundred years of contact with the male-oriented European culture and its American descendant, Iroquois women still maintain their high status and may even have improved it somewhat. For example, women today sometimes use the non-Indian legal system (especially the family relations services) to increase or establish control over the men.

"Women's lib" movements should not find many converts among the Onondaga. Onondaga women are already liberted. They feel no shame in being women, and any men who try to exploit them do so at their own risk. This does not mean that women and men have identical roles—far from it. It means that Onondaga women possess a proud tradition; they take pride in their role and their sex. If a role is closed to her, it is not because she is inferior; it is because maleness is an essential part of the role. For her to try to be a chief would be as ludicrous as for her to try to be a father or as foolish as for a man to try to be a clan mother. But clan mothers appoint the chiefs, tell them what to say, and can remove them if they do not perform properly, so a woman can hardly feel inferior because she is restricted by her sex to being a clan mother rather than a chief. Onondaga is one of the few places in the world where a comment about a family with only one child would probably be that they are "lucky it's a girl."

What is expected of an Onondaga woman? Her role has changed through time, of course, just as roles change in all societies, but it continues to differ from the role of the non-Indian woman. Let us follow some of the changes as they occurred in the life of Mary Pierce.[1]

Mary was born on the reservation on February 11, 1900. She had some trouble when she applied for her social security benefits, and consequently she knows her birth date, which many women of her generation do not. No one during Mary's childhood ever felt it was very important. Mary's mother was an Onondaga, so of course Mary is an Onondaga, even though her father was Oneida. Mary does not remember her real father because he stayed around only long enough to sire Mary and her older brother (Mary's only full brother) and then went to Canada. Mary has several half brothers and sisters, two older and three younger. Mary's mother was more fortunate than most in that only three of her children died in childhood.

Mary's stepfather (the father of her three younger half siblings) is the only father she ever knew. He was a good, steady man who lived with the family until his death in 1945. Mary's mother died in 1948, and her death was a real blow. Even after all these years, Mary misses her. She has often said, "You never get over missing your mother." Funny or interesting things happen and Mary still catches herself thinking she would like to tell her mother about them.

Mary was born at home, with a local health nurse in attendance. That was something of an innovation because in those days most women still used only the services of a midwife—usually a relative. The home itself was a typical frame farmhouse. Of course this was before the time of electricity, piped water, or heating. Mary remembers the cold winters and how she enjoyed helping in the kitchen because the wood-burning stove made it the warmest room in the house.

Most of her earliest childhood memories are blurred and indistinct. She spent a lot of time playing with friends, most of whom were female relatives. A few things stand out sharply, however. She remembers watching the men play lacrosse in summer and snow snake in winter. She also remembers how frightened she was at some of the ceremonies. When the false-faces beat their rattles on the outside walls of the Council House during midwinter ceremonies, she always climbed up to the top bench and huddled against her mother, just as her great-granchildren do with her today. She used to hide her face when the false-faces raced through the door and tried to overturn the stoves. She remembers her oldest half brother standing with other young men and wrestling with the false-faces to protect the stove. Her uncle—her mother's brother—usually collected the chewing tobacco from the spectators, along with smoking tobacco and occasionally a few cigarettes, to give to the false-faces when they calmed down. Her stepfather was never present—or rather he *was* present as one of the false-face dancers, but since he was disguised with a mask and strange clothing borrowed from other families for the occasion, she never recognized him until she was much older.

When Mary was eight, her mother sent her to Carlisle Indian School in Pennsylvania. She enjoyed the experience, even though she was far away from home. There were a lot of other Indian girls there, some from Onondaga but many from other Indian tribes in the West. For the first time she began to feel a sense of Indian identity that set her apart from the non-Indian world. She became aware she was an Indian, and was especially proud to be an Onondaga and one of the Six Nations.

While she was at Carlisle, Mary was converted to Christianity. It was natural under the circumstances, but actually her basic beliefs remained almost unchanged. She reinterpreted Christianity unknowingly, so there was little conflict in her own mind. In later years, her knowledge of Christianity helped her to understand some of the puzzling behavior of white people.

Girls at Carlisle were often sent out as servants into non-Indian homes. Mary learned a great deal about white people and about their housekeeping methods this way. She was also taught—along with the standard school subjects—how to sew and cook. Later she put some of what she had learned to use in her own home, but more of it was useful in helping her earn a living in the non-Indian world.

Mary stayed at Carlisle only until she was twelve. Then her mother needed her help at home, so she returned to the reservation. Under the influence of her mother and other relatives, Mary quickly gave up Christianity and returned to the Handsome Lake religion with its meetings at the Council House—or Longhouse, as the whites called it. Her mother taught her to make the ceremonial foods—the corn mush that had to be fed to the false-face masks and the ubiquitous corn soup. She loved the smell and sound of the corn soup boiling gently in the metal wash boilers on the stove at the women's end of the Council House all during the long ceremony. Every family brought a container, and at the end of the ceremony, they were all placed together on the floor while some of the men (two to hold the wash boiler and one to serve) shared out the soup, putting a ladleful into each container in turn, round and round, until the containers were full or all the soup had been shared.

Cooking the soup warmed the Council House, so that even in the coldest weather of winter the wasps would come out of the eaves, fooled by the heat, and circle lower and lower over the heads of the participants. Sometimes they dropped directly down on someone, causing a flurry of activity, but she had not heard of anyone being bitten during a ceremony. She always watched them warily, but maybe the wasps responded to the incense of the Indian tobacco that sent out clouds of smoke each time the main speaker tossed a handful into the fire at the appropriate part of his speech. Its pungent fumes made her cough sometimes as a child, so perhaps it affected the wasps. Or maybe they enjoyed the singing and dancing. The heavy, rhythmic crash of the large snapping-turtle rattles on the bench between the singers—underscoring the high, tight voices of the men—always gave her a feeling of strong satisfaction, even today. One of her brothers had been a singer for years, as was her son John, and she was proud to see that one of her younger grandsons liked to sit on the bench with the singers and match their words and motions. It was good to have family members taking part. She was sorry that all her own children had not shown more interest, but at least the grandchildren were supporting the traditions.

Mary had her first child when she was seventeen. It was the result of a rather casual affair. She still saw the man occasionally, but she had no particular interest in him. He was a Christian. His wife had tried to get the baby, of course, but Mary did not want to give it up. She had to when she married George, however. No man wants to raise a child that is not his. It is too hard to control and will not take correction. The child says, "What are you telling me that for? You aren't my real father!" Mary remembered with some shame how she had said that once to her own stepfather, who had been a good, kind man, and how hurt he had been. He had never disciplined her again, but Mary's mother had been even stricter with her to make up for it.

Mary's mother raised Mary's son after she married. Mary had had almost two years with the boy, living at home with her mother, but then she had gone out to work, cleaning houses for different white women each day. It was not hard work, it paid well, and she was free to come and go pretty much as she liked. Usually the white women just told her what they wanted done and then left her alone to do it. If she found one who stayed around all the time, looking over her shoulder, she just did not go back again. When she wanted to do something else—take a trip to another reservation, attend a ceremony, or when she just did not feel well—she could always get someone to substitute for her. Most of the white women did not mind as long as their houses were cleaned.

Since Mary was a good worker and reliable, she had as many jobs as she wanted and brought in a good income to the family. It was easier and safer to leave the boy with her mother than to try to take him with her on the bus and always be worried about his breaking something in the strange house or getting lost. On the reservation he could run around all he wanted and could never get lost because there was always someone who knew who he was. He was related to most of the people on the reservation one way or another. People would feed him and look out for him even when he was not with his own grandmother.

She missed that boy. Even though she had left him with her mother when she married, she had still loved him and had seen him whenever she could. She had cried hard when he was killed during World War II. But her son had fathered a child of his own—a boy—before his death. She had raised the boy, named Cookie; and since he was very like his father, it was almost like having her own again.

When Mary's son had enlisted, his wife, Marie, had come to her instead of going to her own mother. Mary was not surprised. Everyone knew that Marie's mother drank a lot and did not take good care of her grandchildren. Once a child had been hurt accidentally while Marie's mother was in a drunken sleep. A neighbor had managed to find Mary and together they had hired a taxi and taken the child to the hospital emergency room. When they got back, Marie's mother did not even know they had been gone. Since then Marie had been afraid to leave the children with her mother and brought them to live with Mary.

After Mary's son was killed, Marie ran wild for a while. She got pregnant and finally decided to marry her lover. He was a good man. When he took her to live with him, he was willing to take the youngest child, a girl, who was still just a baby. But the boy looked too much like his father and Marie's new husband did not like him, so Marie left the child with Mary. Mary would have been happy to raise them both, but of course, a girl should be with her own mother if possible. That was a long time ago.

Now Cookie had been in the Army himself and he and his sister were both married. They had already made Mary a great-grandmother five times. Marie's wildness had not upset Mary. She had been pretty wild herself and knew Marie would settle down once she was a bit older. Youth was a time for wildness. If it did not come out then, it might later, and that would be much worse. Most of the young people calmed down once they had a few children and a steady mate. *She* had.

After she began living with George, Mary had had a son almost immediately. She had lost him, though, after only a few months. The boy died very suddenly during the night although he had not seemed sick or anything—just a few sniffles the day before. Even after all these years, Mary sometimes wondered if her sister-in-law had not had something to do with the death. Helen was suspected of being a witch even then, young as she was, and she had sure hated to see her brother married. One day when Mary was out of the house, Helen had thrown all Mary's clothes on the floor and cut most of them into ribbons. Some of the clothes had been very pretty; perhaps that was the trouble. Helen was always accusing Mary of feeling superior because she had been educated at Carlisle and knew more about the non-Indian world than George or any of his family. Helen also accused Mary of trying to get back with her first lover—which was not true —because she went to church now and then.

Mary tried to deal with the situation by getting drunk and fighting Helen, but the second time she drank too much and could not remember exactly what she had done. She must have made quite a bit of trouble, though, because when she woke up the next day, she was in jail. The judge put her on probation because it was her first offense, so she missed her best chance to learn a good profession. (She had heard others say that in prison they taught women how to be beauticians, which certainly paid better than cleaning house for lazy white women.)

The final break with her in-laws came when she found out that Helen was procuring women for George and encouraging him to take on lovers. When Mary learned that, she insisted they go into a place of their own. They moved into the upstairs apartment of Alice Webster's house, and only a few weeks later the baby died. Everyone had been sure at the time it was Helen's fault. Even Mary, who was skeptical of the talk about witchcraft because of her Christian training, could not help wondering, because the death had been so sudden and inexplicable. The white doctor they took the body to could not explain it either. Mary's mother had insisted on holding a special ceremony to protect Mary, and although Mary was skeptical of the value of that too, she cooperated for her mother's sake. Afterwards Mary had to admit she felt a bit easier in her own mind. She decided she would feel even better farther away from Helen, so she had persuaded George to move into town. They had lived off the reservation for over two years while George worked at a variety of jobs and she cleaned houses. Sometimes she helped other Indians clean the big fraternity houses at the university. That was hard work but good pay—and fun, too, because she was working with other women. They had a lot of laughs.

Finally, she got pregnant again and she and George decided to move back on the reservation. It was cheaper and they both felt more comfortable there, even though Mary missed some of the conveniences they had had in the apartment. George had not really wanted to move back very much. He liked being close to places where he could get beer, but Mary had insisted. George did not oppose her very often when she made up her mind to do something—he knew better, although neither one of them liked to fight. If she pushed him too hard, he just walked out, and so did she if he gave her too much trouble. One time he did not come back for two days and she decided to be a little more careful in the future, because he was a good man and she did not really want to drive him away. He seemed to feel the same way about her.

Eleanor, the child conceived in town, was still living. She was a big comfort to Mary and always had been. In the last few years, Eleanor had taken over a lot of the heavy work involved in the Longhouse ceremonies. Mary had been a clan mother since 1950 and was a faith-keeper long before that. She enjoyed cooking, serving, cleaning up for all the doings, and the feeling of being in the center of what was going on. She also enjoyed the bingo games, dinners, and other things that the clan mothers or faith-keepers had sponsored to raise money for the Longhouse; but in the last few years the hard work had begun to tax her strength.

It was harder for her to travel around with the ceremonies than it used to be, too, even though cars and roads were better. It took only a few hours to go places now that used to take a day or more. She had been quite a traveler when she was younger. She was working and had her own money, so she used to go off whenever she felt like it. George sometimes got mad when she would not take him, especially if he was not working and did not have the money to go himself. He was usually good-natured about it though. That time she was sick and just went off to visit some of her relatives in Canada without even telling anyone where she was going, he came after her, even though it took three days to find out where she was and he had to leave the kids with her mother till he got her back. Whenever family members got together, they still teased her about that and laughed at the trick she had played on everyone.

Eleanor had become a faith-keeper five years ago and since then had taken over many of the tasks Mary had always done. For example, Eleanor almost always prepared most of the corn for the soup. She was one of the few people on the reservation who still had a wood-burning stove, so she had the wood ashes to boil with the corn to hull it. A few people had tried lye to hull the corn, but Mary was a little afraid of that. Some of the women were careless about rinsing the corn afterward. Some others tried to save work and used canned hominy, but it never tasted right to Mary.

On the other hand, Elsie, born two years after Eleanor, had always been a bit of a disappointment to Mary. She had been sick a lot, with earaches and sore throats. A white doctor had finally persuaded Mary to take Elsie to the hospital and have her tonsils out. Mary had to admit that it had helped the sickness, but she still never could really understand Elsie the way she understood Eleanor. It was a good thing they had turned to white medicine instead of having a medicine society cure Elsie, because Elsie had turned Christian when she was about fifteen. She would never sponsor a ceremony now, and everyone knew that if you did not sponsor a ceremony occasionally for the society you belonged to, there would be sickness.

Elsie was hardly like an Indian at all. She had finished high school and had even taken some business school courses. She had a good job working in a nursing home. She had a good husband and a fine family, so Mary was happy for her, even if they did not understand each other very well. Of course those things were true of many of the young girls today, and yet they were still Indian in every way. But Elsie had married a white boy and moved off the reservation. That made a big difference. Mary did not see much of her or the children anymore. The white boy was a nice young man and did not seem to be at all ashamed of his Indian relatives the few times the families were together, but Elsie always appeared a little uneasy. It made Mary sad.

Elsie's children were quite thrilled at being part Indian, although they did not look Indian at all to Mary. One was dark-haired, but two of them were blond and blue-eyed, like their father, and who ever heard of a blue-eyed Indian? One of the old women on the reservation told Mary that the youngest child looked a lot like Mary's paternal grandfather, who was half white. Of course, old people were always seeing resemblances in children. It was a source of vicious gossip sometimes.

Mary's friend Louise had had a lot of trouble about that when they were all much younger. Her last child had been very different in looks from the other six, and no one could be convinced that he had the same father. It made a lot of trouble between Louise and her husband. People said that the youngest child looked more like Raymond's brother. Even Mary had to admit that he did, but she defended Louise because she was sure Louise would have told her about it or even have asked her help if she had been carrying on with her husband's brother.

Today, with so many of the young women driving cars, they did not need much help to carry on; but when she and Louise were at that age, it was pretty hard. People could see you and find out what was going on too easily. Cars made a lot of difference. She knew several men who had not liked it at all when the school put in a driving class for adults. It had been the most popular class for young women, and some men said it was because wives wanted to run around while their husbands were at work.

Mary suspected the men were sometimes right. She knew at least one woman who used her car that way. Betty kept offering Bob rides day after day every time he stuck his nose out of the house and eventually, of course, he gave in. No man could resist that kind of pressure. Bob's mother tried to make Betty quit, pointing out that Bob was a married man with several children, and Bob's wife even beat Betty up once, but Betty kept on. Of course her own husband had run off to Canada. Maybe if he had stayed home it would not have happened, but Mary was not sure. Betty was tough. It was easy to understand why her husband ran away to Canada.

Mary thought perhaps another reason the men did not like women learning to drive was that now some of them kept the car during the day and their husbands had to ride the bus to work. Mary felt that it would be fairer to let the men drive to work one day and let the women have the cars the other, but some women were selfish and wanted the car all the time. They did not care how hard it made life for their husbands. Maybe that was why so many men were complaining. Mary felt that people in her generation had been more considerate of one another.

In 1928, Mary had had her only living son. John, whom everyone called Bunny as a result of a childhood fondness for stuffed rabbits, was a very satisfactory child. He was strong, healthy, and very tough. However, he kept wandering away from home. She worried about it at first, but a white doctor once told her Bunny was a real throwback to the old Indians and would never get lost because the old ones had an instinct for direction. Bunny never did get lost either.

Now that he had grown up, he was a valuable Longhouse member and Mary thought the doctor must have been right. He was an old-fashioned Indian. At the midwinter doings he danced with the false-faces, but the rest of the time he was a singer. He knew all the old songs and went around to all the other reservations regularly, learning new ones. There were so few real Onondaga singers around any more that he was very much in demand. It made it hard for him to keep a job because he had to leave so often to sing.

John was lucky he was a good construction worker. When he was younger he never had any trouble finding a new job—provided any construction was going on, of course. When he wanted to work on a high building, he told everyone he was a Mohawk because all the white men thought Mohawks were the best high-steel workers in the world. John knew plenty of Onondagas that were just as good, but who had ever heard of Onondaga high-steel workers? It did not matter; the white men could not tell one Indian from another, and Mohawks he worked with thought it was a good joke on the whites.

Mary was worried about John these days, though. He was getting too old for the heavy construction work, and it was more difficult for him to find a job each year. He had never worked long enough for any one firm to be eligible for a pension, and he was too young to qualify for social security. She did not know what he was going to do in the future. He was beginning to drink more heavily and Mary suspected the problem was beginning to worry him, too.

A friend of John's, only a few years older but not so strong, had been out of work for more than two years and was existing by doing odd jobs around the reservation and getting welfare. Louie, the friend, was very unhappy. Just last month his house had burned down and he had almost been caught in the fire. John thought that was a sign, and he had been trying to persuade Louie to have a ceremony or at least to see a fortune teller about it, but so far Louie had refused. He had been drinking heavily the night of the fire, and he was still drinking.

Louie went into town any time he had money and bought cheap wine. Sometimes he found people who would buy him drinks in the bar. Mary was afraid that he would be killed some night walking home. White men, and even some of the Indians, drove much too fast through the reservation, especially when they had been drinking. The chiefs had tried to get the speed limit lowered through the most settled part or at least to have the limit that was already there enforced. The sheriff's office had been sympathetic, but the state had refused to listen. Now there were rumors that the speed limit would be raised "because people traveled that fast anyway." It made Mary angry. People had already been killed, but the state did not seem to care at all. Just two nights ago, one of her nephews told her that he had almost hit Louie, who stepped out from the side of the road right in front of his car. Elroy had been sober, and had swerved sharply so that he just missed Louie. Then Elroy and his wife had taken Louie home because he was blind drunk and crying about how sad he was. The next time Louie might not be so lucky. Mary did not want to see John get like that.

Fortunately John's wife, Rebecca, had turned out to be a good woman. Although Mary never thought it would last when they were first married, John's wife had stayed with him a long time. Mary had never heard such fights, but Rebecca was tough. One time she hit John over the head with a chair. That was the first time Mary had called the police. But after her second child, Rebecca seemed to calm down some. She stopped drinking and running around to bars, and she and John began staying home more. John began to treat her better. Once, when Rebecca was sick, Mary went over to their house to see if she could help, and there was John, doing the wash. Mary was going to yell at Rebecca for asking her man to do that work even if she *was* sick, but John said she was asleep and did not even know he was doing it. John often helped sort clothes and did the ironing if Rebecca did not feel well. A lot of men did things like that, especially if they got along well with their wives. It was all right if they wanted to do it, but a woman should not be so lazy that she would let a man do her work when she was able to do it herself.

Mary knew John was not ashamed of what he was doing. Of course, he would expect some teasing if any of the other men saw him (and he would tease any man he saw in the same situation), but Mary did not know anyone who would really be ashamed except some of the young boys who had picked up a lot of white notions. Everyone in the older generation knew that there were obligations wives had and other obligations husbands had, but it never made a woman any less a woman to do the job her husband was supposed to do or a man any less a man to do his wife's work; it just made the partner who was not doing the job look bad. More people would gossip about the lazy one.

Young people today spent a lot more time with whites than she ever had, though, and picked up a lot of their funny ideas. That was probably one reason why things seemed to have changed for the worse lately. White people did not have any sense of right or wrong, it seemed. She read now and then in the papers of women who killed their own babies or beat them so badly that they had to go to the hospital. She had never heard of such things happening on the reservation. Even if a baby had no father, there was always someone who wanted to take care of it, the way her mother had taken care of her first son. She could not imagine killing a baby. To her, it seemed barbaric.

Rebecca was an old-fashioned wife and Mary admired her for it. She would not even let John cook, although he knew how well enough. (Rebecca often pretended though, that he was unable to cook, telling other people that he would starve if she did not cook for him all the time. That way she let them know she was taking proper care of him.) They had a fine family of seven children, and only one—a boy—had died (of pneumonia). He had been sick and should have been taken to see the doctor, but the reservation health center was only open once a week and Rebecca just did not have the money for a taxi into town at that time. (John had smashed up his car, and neither one wanted to ask a favor of the neighbors, because they were quarreling.) Anyway, the boy got worse, and when they finally got him to the hospital, it was too late. Mary thought sourly of the reservation clinic. As people said, "You can only get sick on Thursdays."

It had been better when the nurse was around all the time, even though some of the young women had been offended when she came into their houses and started cleaning up. Those younger women did not know that the nurse was really acting almost like an Indian. Nowadays, when young women spent time with each other, they just sat and talked or watched television, so nothing got done around the house. In the old days a woman never just went in and chatted; she always pitched in and helped with whatever the other woman was working at. That way more work got done when women went visiting than when they stayed at home, and everyone felt good about it. Now there was gossip about lazy women.

Some of the old people felt bad when that nurse left. The nurse who took her place was scared to death of Indians and never set foot outside the office even if someone called for help, so not many people noticed when they stopped opening the clinic every day. They noticed now, though, when they got sick and had to go into the city for a doctor.

John's oldest boy had finished college and was working for a company in New York City. Mary had objected when he wanted to go to college because she had seen too many Indians turned into white men who came back and cheated their own people. Her daughter had turned away from her people because of education. But it had not happened to her grandson. He won out and went to college; yet every time he was near the reservation, he came to the ceremonies, and he even made a special trip for the mid-winter doings. He always danced, and Mary thought he was one of the best dancers she had ever seen. (Everyone knew Onondagas were the best dancers of the Six Nations, although the Mohawks did not like to admit it.) Robert often helped with the Fireman's Fair in summer, too. He performed the strenuous dances two or three times a day and seemed to enjoy it. When he was in college, he played lacrosse for the school, and now he helped with the team when he was home.

Rebecca had just told Mary that Robert was going to give up his job and come back to live on the reservation all the time, but Mary found it hard to believe. It seemed too good to be true. If he did come back, he would be a big help in some of their battles with the state. With his education, he would know when someone was trying to cheat them and, more important, he would be able to talk to them in ways that would command respect. Mary hoped Rebecca was right. She sometimes thought that most of this younger generation was going to get a college education. It seemed like everyone was going or planning to go. She hoped that they all turned out as good as Robert.

The Fireman's Fair was quite a bit of fun and a lot of work. It raised a lot of money to support the volunteer fire company on the reservation. There was always a big crowd of people from town who came to watch the Indian dances and buy all sorts of souvenirs. Indians worked all year to make things to sell at the two fairs, the Fireman's Fair and the State Fair, which was usually held a week or two after the Fireman's Fair.

Mary herself did not do much beadwork anymore, but she usually helped out at the clan mother's booth where they sold corn soup, corn bread (the Indian kind, with beans in it), and hot scones. Some of the women brought apple pie, which was popular with the whites, but Mary felt that the clan mother's booth should be reserved for traditional Indian foods and that apple pie therefore did not really belong there. She did not say much, though, because the younger women seemed to to want to change things, and the Fireman's Fair was not really a traditional Indian ceremony anyway.

Mary had to chuckle when she thought of the way the Indians fooled people at the Fireman's Fair. David, one of the officials of the Fireman's Association and a Christian, always gave a speech explaining the "traditional" dances to the visitors. "Traditional" indeed! Mary was not sure whether David would know a traditional dance if he saw one. He had never been inside the Longhouse to her knowledge. In any case, at the last Fireman's Fair, none of the dances had been more than a year old as far as Mary could recall. They had all been invented by an Onondaga-Potawatami who had spent years with a touring show and knew what kind of dances would please the white crowd. The young men enjoyed the joke and cheerfully practiced several hours to be sure of their parts in the "traditional" dances. The white people got their money's worth anyway, because even

Mary enjoyed the dances. They were colorful and exciting. The real sacred dances probably would have bored people since they were less energetic, and the colorful costumes, borrowed from Western Indians, were not usually permitted inside the Longhouse.

The State Fair was a little different story. The white men involved in that usually knew more about real Iroquois culture, and they turned direction of the Indian Village over to serious older Indian men and women who were usually more interested in presenting authentic Indian life than in putting on a show. The men were reluctant to show some sacred things to the casual visitors, but they tried to select material that was at least authentic. Of course, they did not always know themselves. Mary remembered one or two exhibits put on as "authentic" by sincere Indians that she felt had been quite incorrect. She had read as many of the old books as anyone, but things she had learned from the old people did not always agree with the books. Most of the books seemed like the Seneca way of doing things rather than the Onondaga. Nobody seemed to write about the Onondaga ways of doing things. It was important because when people did the wrong thing in ceremonies, sometimes the spirits got angry. Then they made people sick.

Year before last had been a bad one for sickness. Nothing had gone right. There were questions about the midwinter ceremony, with people saying important parts had been left out of long prayers or that parts had not been said correctly. Some people even felt the ceremony should be done over so people would not get sick. But putting on the long midwinter ceremony a second time was so much work that people were reluctant. Perhaps they should have. Mary was not sure. Some parts had not seemed quite right to her, but her memory was not what it once had been, so she just could not be certain. Her son John had come to her house one night after he had been drinking. He cried and said he was afraid because he did not think he had remembered all the songs correctly. Mary thought he had, but again she was not sure, so she did not support either side in the argument. In the end, people just left things alone or held their own private medicine dances to ward off danger.

Sure enough, the year had been a bad one. A lot of old people had died —more than usual—and even some of the children died, which had not happened in years. The trouble seemed to be on the whole Six Nations, though, not just on Onondagas. Twice the owl-hooting messenger had come to her house to announce the death of some chief on one of the other reservations. The men who died had been good men—strong supporters of the religion—and they had died before their time, so everyone was upset. Some blamed it on the new pressure to vote in state elections. They said that was breaking the treaty obligations, and would give the state a chance to break its part of the bargain even more than it already had.

That, along with other changes, was held to be responsible for the changed relationship with the supernatural, so everyone was in trouble.

That fall, however, they had had some very good Six Nations meetings (at which the recital of the Code of Handsome Lake was given). When the group came to Onondaga on its biannual visit, the doings had been unusually well attended, the preaching was exceptional, and even the social at night—after the preaching and public confessions were over—had been lively. Everyone was pleased and impressed. Then, that winter, the midwinter doings had been very good too, so everyone relaxed. No one had the anxious, uneasy feeling they had had the winter before. It had been a good year, and so far this year was going well. Mary was relieved that the religion stayed strong even though so many things were changing.

Mary was very much aware of the changes that had taken place on the reservation during her lifetime. She had seen electricity come to the community, so that now there was scarcely a house without it, and most had television sets, refrigerators, and washing machines too—in spite of the fact that piped water had spread much more slowly. Most houses used well water, and people hauled water to fill their washing machines. She herself had had a chance to put an electric pump in her well and pipe the water into her house. Her white son-in-law had gotten an estimate and had offered to pay for the whole thing as a Christmas present one year, but she had refused. She did not like the idea of all that metal in her well. It was one of the best wells on the reservation, with the best-tasting water. Many of her neighbors used it in preference to the piped water which was available from a spigot in the Longhouse yard. The metal in the pump would surely spoil that good taste, so she was willing to put up with the inconvenience of an outhouse and the need to haul water.

Actually, her daughter and grandchildren (or great-grandchildren) did most of the water hauling anyway. Some of them always stayed with her. Currently, living in her house besides Mary and her husband were Eleanor and her three youngest children and Eleanor's oldest daughter's two small children. (Alice had left her husband and decided to go to college. She was off somewhere in Montana, living with a cousin and working until she could earn some money to go to school and decide where to go.) Mary's nephew (a half-sister's child) was staying temporarily because he had had a fight with his wife. Mary's older half-brother had been living with them since he was widowed four years ago. He was vigorous, but his mind was not as clear as it had been and Mary tried to keep track of him through the local children. When her nephew went back to his wife (as he probably would do because he missed her), Mary thought that one of John's sons might move in. He had been fighting with both of his parents lately over a girl he had been seeing and might decide he could get more peace at Mary's house. She was glad she had a big house. There was always room for more. She had folding cots and plenty of extra blankets.

The house had been small when they first bought it but George did not want to do anything about it because they did not own the land it was on. The land belonged to Mary's uncle (her mother's brother), and after he died Mary was given the rights to the land during the distribution of his goods at the Dead Feast. No one could challenge their right to the land or the house after that, so George had gone to work expanding it for their children and grandchildren.

George had settled down in his later years. There had been a brief spell just before World War II when he had been playing around a lot, mostly with white women in town. He delivered coal then, and more than one woman took advantage of him to avoid paying the coal bill. She found out about it when he lost his job because his accounts never balanced. She scolded him so much that he was goaded into knocking her down. She had been furious and warned him that if he hit her again she would either kill him or have him put in jail for six months. Through her housework for white families she had learned a great deal about the white legal system, and she knew that family court was always hard on the men, especially when they hit their wives. More than one Onondaga man spent time in prison because of an angry wife. Sometimes Mary thought it was a bit unfair. One of her grandsons was paying support for a child that Mary was sure was not his. But as he said, a girl only has to point her finger at a boy and he has to pay, even if he never had anything to do with her, because the court always believes the girl.

The threat made George leave her for about four months, but when he found out that there was no one who would put up with him the way she did, he came back. He missed the grandchildren, too. He was much better with children than she was, especially when they were little. One time when Elsie had been so sick and feverish that she could not sleep, he sat up with her all night, holding her in his arms. Mary thought she could never have done that. She would have gone to sleep and let Elsie fall.

Lately she and George had found a lot of pleasure in discussing the old ways and people who were now long gone. The young people were good, most of them, but they had forgotten so much of the old ways. Now it was possible to go over to someone's house and never get a bite to eat, even though you were there for hours. That never happened in the old days, even when the same people showed up day after day right around meal-time. People laughed at them, of course, since their laziness was so obvious, but hardly anyone refused to feed them, and the few families that did hide food or changed their dinner hour came in for scornful comment themselves. Mary still offered food to anyone who was in her home for more than a few minutes. She was not going to let new ways keep her from doing what she knew was right.

A lot of the ceremonies had changed too or were not being held any more, especially the small ones individuals held for the different medicine societies. She could not remember the last time an eagle dance had been held, and there had been something wrong with one of the funerals two years ago. A young boy died, and of course that was always the worst anyway. Even though everyone naturally cried when someone died, people felt much worse if it was a young person. The boy's father, Ted, who was one of Mary's clan nephews, had been broken-hearted. It was his oldest son, and they had spent a great deal of time together. Ted told her once that he gladly would have died in the boy's place if he could have, because he had lived most of his life but his son had just been getting started. The boy's mother had been dreadfully upset. She was accusing Mary's sister-in-law of having witched the boy to death. She did not say so openly, of course, but she was hinting at it all the time, and the gossip had naturally reached Mary.

Since Mary was in the opposite moiety from the boy, she had been asked to take charge of all the funeral arrangements. One of the younger clan members had actually done most of the work because Mary had been sick, but she had supervised as much as she could. Everything had been fine right through the midnight feast of the first all-night vigil, after the body had been returned from the funeral home and was resting in the coffin in the front room. The television had been turned off as soon as the coffin was brought in, and all the mirrors were turned to the walls. People began to gather for the wake and at times one of the chiefs exhorted the family to control their grief so that they too would not get sick, since the community needed them.

When the midnight feast was served (and, in fact, at each meal while the body was in the house), a plate of food was prepared and placed on the coffin, under the gauze that covered the open part (or else someone turned back the gauze). Everyone remembered good manners and no one had accidentally given the customary words of thanksgiving after the midnight feast. (That would have been insulting to the family of the dead boy, since it would have been like saying thanks that the boy had died.)

Then, after the family had gone to bed, the watchers had begun to play games. They had played the right ones and had taken turns around the circle in reverse—as was proper for games dedicated to the dead. But they had not used the right counters. The usual counters for the games were beans; but at a wake, cloth should be used. Someone remembered that, but instead of using useful squares of cloth, which could be made into quilts or something like that, they had used narrow strips that were good for nothing. Mary had not been there—she had left right after the meal because she was still sick—or she would not have allowed it to happen. The thing that disturbed her most was that in years to come, people at funerals would say, "That is the right thing to do, that is the way the old people did it." A lot of changes had come about that way. Young people remembered, all right, but they remembered things the old people did wrong as well as the ones they did right, and no one was left to tell them which was which. That is why Mary felt it was so important for the old people to do things *right!*

Of course some things were still carried on properly. Her brother had had a dark dance only a year ago, after his wampum string—the one that showed that he was a clan chief—broke. He, at least, knew that that was a bad sign and took the right precautions. It worked, too. He had not been sick a day since he had that ceremony. Another friend of hers had been told by a fortune-teller to hold a peach stone game. She did, and she, too, had been a lot better since.

Mary was glad that her brother had been so prompt to respond to the bad sign. She would not want anything to happen to him. Not only was she fond of him, but he was a good chief. She did not like his alternate— a distant cousin—very much, even though she had appointed them both. Still, it would be difficult to replace either one. Few of the younger men in her clan were interested in the job of chief, and most of those that were interested were irresponsible boys or could not speak Onondaga or both. That is why she had had to appoint a relative she did not like as alternate in the first place.

Her son John would make a good chief, but she would be criticized if she chose him, because clan mothers sometimes had to scold their chiefs or threaten to remove them to make them support the position they were sup- posed to. Everyone knew a mother could not scold her own son properly. Her nephews—now that was a different story. Mary's half sister often sent her grown boys over to Mary to get a lecture, and Mary always did a thorough job. A white friend who had been present at one of those scold- ings told Mary afterward in a joking way that she had talked to the boy "like a Dutch uncle." Mary wondered if the Dutch had the same custom.

One good change Mary had noticed was that the young people today were more interested in Indian ways than they had been when Mary was a young mother. Mary was happy to see that some of them were trying to get Onondaga taught in school. What a change that would be! Mary re- membered how often she had been hit by teachers for speaking Onondaga, even outside the classroom. One of the young men had started a project of writing down all sorts of memories and predictions made by the old people. He was particularly interested in recording the proper way to perform the ceremonies. Mary liked that because it was one of their own Onondaga boys who was doing it. She got a bit irritated at the white anthropologists who were always coming around asking questions. It made her feel like an animal at the zoo. They were all so nosy. Apparently their mothers had never taught them elementary manners or they would have known it is improper to ask direct questions. But then, white people were ignorant of the strangest things.

Mary had to chuckle when she remembered the mess that one white girl had caused. The girl had been staying with Susan, one of Mary's friends. Susan brought her to several ceremonies. She seemed like a friendly person, but she had been very foolish. She had danced at least three times directly behind one young man and then another two or three times directly in front of another man. Both of the men were married, and naturally their wives were very annoyed. One of the wives had a terrible fight with her husband over it and ordered him out of the house, even though he protested that he had done nothing to encourage the white girl. Unfortunately, his wife had seen him talking to the girl before the doings, so naturally she did not believe him. Susan said she had talked quite sharply to the white girl about her behavior, and the girl had been totally amazed. She had not had any idea she was going to cause trouble. She had danced near the men because they were the only ones she knew and they had invited her to dance.

Mary believed the white girl, although some people did not. Mary had had a lot of contact with whites, and she knew how differently they thought about a lot of things. The young girl probably had not recognized the signs that certain men gave to show their interest in her. She did not know that she would have to arrange the dates with the young men if she returned their interest—or at least Susan said she did not know. After she learned, she stayed away from the Indian boys. Mary was glad, because when an Onondaga married a white girl, his children were lost to the reservation—they had no rights to the land anymore. Of course, that was also true if an Onondaga man married anyone but an Onondaga woman. The child belonged to his mother's people and had no rights to Onondaga land. If the mother was Onondaga, it usually did not matter. Even though the rules said they would lose their rights to land if their mother married white, Mary could not think of any case where this rule had been enforced. Everyone knew that if the mother was an Onondaga the children were Onondagas, no matter what the rules said.

Mary felt sorry for some children whose mother was a Canadian Mohawk and whose father was a United States Onondaga. Nobody would accept the children. In the United States, the Onondagas insisted that these children were Canadian Mohawks, after their mother, and the United States government usually went by whatever rule the Onondagas accepted. The Canadian government, on the other hand, traced the line through the father, so the Canadians insisted that the children were United States Onondagas. Consequently the children were unwelcome everywhere. They did not even have a nationality. The parents always compained, but Mary felt they should have thought of that before they had children. It was their fault, not the children's.

This coming fall the Six Nations meeting was coming to Onondaga again. Mary was looking forward to that. In fact, she thought that this year she might travel with the preachers and visit all the different reservations they went to. She had not done that for years. George might even want to come along, and they could compare notes on the past and present ceremonies or how the Onondagas matched up against other reservations. The trip would be a physical strain and Mary did not know for how many more years she would be up to it; better go while she was still feeling good.

The thought of death did not particularly frighten Mary. She was a happy woman. She had plenty of work to do, whenever she felt like doing it. She was still in demand for housecleaning work because she was healthy and strong. This gave her a source of funds that kept her independent. She was surrounded by her family—children, grandchildren, great-grandchildren, and swarms of clan relatives—so she never lacked company. She did not need anyone to take care of her, but if she did, there were a lot around who would be glad to do it. Her husband was still alive and had become a valued companion in their old age. She had had a good life and was content. She was an Onondaga woman.

NOTE

1. The name is fictitious but typical of reservation names. The story of Mary Pierce is a composite of episodes and recollections of many reservation women. None of the events is fictitious, but the composite is. There is no such person as Mary Pierce, and her life does not duplicate in detail that of any single real woman on the reservation.

Conclusion

CAROLYN J. MATTHIASSON

Westerners frequently assume that all societies are organized on the basis of male dominance, that men are "naturally" more prestigious than women, and that male pursuits are more valued by society than those of women. The social sciences have encouraged this belief. Statements assuming that men are the ones who have always exercised a dominant role in warfare and in the political and social spheres of all societies are common. A current example of this thinking is found in Claude Lévi-Strauss's *The Elementary Structures of Kinship* (Lévi-Strauss, 1969, p. 117; original 1949). We begin to wonder whether or not the majority of ethnographic reports have simply ignored the less apparent but powerful political influence that women have had on their societies.

POWER AND INFLUENCE

Before discussing the uses of power and influence in various societies, the reader may wish to have a concise idea of how power and influence are used in this book. Marc J. Swartz, Victor W. Turner, and Arthur Tuden define power as one of a number of ways of securing compliance with

421

obligations (Swartz, Turner, Tuden, 1966, p. 18). Anthropologists have defined power in a variety of ways. The Swartz, Turner, and Tuden definition is, perhaps, broader than many other definitions and one which may be applied to whole systems as well as to individuals within a system. All the definitions of power emphasize the potential use of threats or sanctions to enforce power. However, some definitions incorporate force as a necessary component of power, whereas this definition does not.

Influence is distinct from but often involved with power. Influence is a way of directing personal or group behavior. It may be defined as a form of persuasion in which someone in leadership capacity convinces others that a proposed plan of action is in their own best interests. This process is free of threats, bribes, or sanctions (Swartz, Turner, and Tuden, 1966, p. 21).

Iroquois matrons, for example, have held obvious political power in Iroquois societies. This power includes the right to select all tribal chiefs. Iroquois matrons also have the right to dismiss chiefs that do not please them. In traditional times, matrons decided the fate of war captives. They could effectively cast the ultimate vote for or against projected warfare, since women were responsible for provisioning a war party (Brown, 1971, pp. 152–156).

Among the patrilineal Birom of northern Nigeria as well as in other patrilineal societies, women have considerable influence over their sons. In such societies, as a father aged and his authority decreased, the strong attachment of sons to their mother would give her considerably more power through control of her sons than their father could command either by himself or through his sons (Michaelson and Goldschmidt, 1971, p. 339). This power is never official and that may explain why it is so often unrecognized; however, it is nontheless effective.

Riegelhaupt has also suggested a way in which women may have considerable informal political power. Portuguese law excludes most women and many men from participation in the political process, since the right to vote is limited by various conditions—among them literacy and the payment of a poll tax. Throughout the rural farming communities men work in the fields and women sell produce to customers in urban centers. Information passes through women's communication networks, from customers in cities to rural wives and then to rural husbands. In Portugal as in many other agrarian countries, political action at the regional or national level is accomplished through knowing someone who can "pull strings." Contact is made with influential urbanites through the ties established by women vendors or through a woman's former employers. On the local level, village women put pressure on the wives of the community's appointed officials to accomplish political change (Riegelhaupt, 1967, p. 123).

African village women in many regions of this vast continent run their own associations and institutions and often have their own religious cults.

These are complementary to those of men and necessary for tribal unity (Paulme, 1963, p. 4). Even in tribes in which women do not have associations or formal political authority, such as the Birom, women take it upon themselves to criticize, or exonerate other women in village disputes. Sometimes they take a position in direct contradiction to that of the male village elders.

Aline K. Wong's discussion of traditional China and Doranne Jacobson's analysis of North and Central India both deal with peasant groups organized in patrilineal descent groups in which women have no formal political authority. In both India and traditional China rural women had little interest and no role in formal village politics. However, in the villages of Syria and Lebanon, also areas of patrilineal descent, women may head households, participate in village politics, and lend their weight to various factions (Aswad, 1967, p. 145). Louise Sweet has also observed that while Middle Eastern men may serve as clan, family, or lineage spokesmen, they would be fools not to have consulted with their wives and female relatives as well as their male kin in any issue of concern to the unit they speak for.

It might be a more accurate assessment of power structures to state that although roles of formal political power or social authority are more often held by men, informal power is held by women. The activities of women "behind the scenes" have generally gone unrecognized. This is confusing formalized prestige with effective decision pressure. Until recently, the question of women's participation in nondomestic contexts has not been in vogue as a topic of interest to anthropologists. Given the variety of data which suggest that women do participate politically in various ways, there seem to be grounds for a reevaluation of the relationship of women to formal and informal power structures.

STATUS OF WOMEN

The question of the status of women in society is a many-faceted one. In dealing with status cross-culturally, it may shed some light on the position of women to examine in detail the situation of women within the household and the effect that the domestic position of women has on their overall status.

We begin the examination of the domestic status of women with a look at women in manipulative societies. Eileen Maynard mentions that Guatemalan Ladino women are often exploited by men. Palín wives frequently are abandoned—with small children to support—by their husbands. These women, in spite of their hard circumstances, remain cheerful, resourceful, and closely tied to their children. Mothers are the focal points of their families. Families that have been abandoned by the father cannot follow the strongly patriarchal form which is the Guatemalan ideal pattern. Therefore, despite the cultural ideal of patriarchy, a substantial percentage of Ladino families are mother-centered.

The majority of women in France, regardless of class, also find themselves from birth and through marriage in patriarchal families. Both they and Guatemalan women have developed ways of dealing with men to achieve modest desires. Deceit is the most common device used by women of Guatemala, and among French women, careful circumvention is the mode. In France, the status of women within the home is secondary. Because husbands are a permanent part of the domestic scene, they are able to wield a degree of authority that Guatemalan Ladino husbands consider their right but do not always attain because of their frequent abandonment of their families.

North American families—in Canada and the United States—originate out of differing ethnic backgrounds, social classes, and regions and therefore display a variety of structural types. The dominant ideology is that most families are organized on the basis of a modified patriarchal family organization. This assumption needs qualification. Among Midwestern United States rural families, Gallaher found that while older couples tended in the direction of patriarchality, especially in terms of decisions and purchases, younger ones followed an egalitarian pattern (Gallaher, 1961, p. 109). Families in the coal mining regions of the United States followed three patterns—patriarchal, matriarchal, and democratic (Lantz, 1958, p. 153). Lantz suggests that up to the time of his study, social scientists had for some reason either avoided thoroughly examining American family structures or had been biased in their examination, since so little mention had been made in the sociological literature of the existence of mother-centered families in North America (Lantz, 1958, p. 153).

A study of working- and middle-class wives in Philadelphia indicated a pattern which differs by social class (Rainwater et al., 1962). Working-class husbands tended to be more dominant in some areas and less so in others. Approximately half of the wives made decisions in financial matters, making both major and minor purchases. One-third shared responsibility in financial affairs, and in the remaining cases the husbands controlled the purse strings. On the other hand, middle-class families in this study tended to share decisions regarding major purchases, with the wife being given a monthly allowance for household purchases and the husband handling more complex financial matters such as savings, investments, insurance, etc. (Rainwater et al., 1962, p. 90).

In working-class homes the husband is the most central figure. He is viewed as the reprensentative of external forces against which wives have no control (Rainwater, 1962, p. 78). Working-class life-styles tend to reinforce the wives' feeling of powerlessness, since women live lives separate from their husbands, not sharing interests in work or leisure activities.

Philadelphia working-class males and females live sexually segregated lives in comparison to their middle-class counterparts. Husbands' employment is of greater concern and more a part of life for middle-class wives, who often hear husbands' work-related problems and who more often interact with coworkers and their wives. In addition, in this particular study, middle-class husbands and wives tended to spend more of their recreational time with each other than did working-class families, in which the pattern is for husbands to go off hunting, fishing, or socializing with other males, leaving their wives at home (Rainwater, 1962, p. 85).

Despite the assumption over the years of the inevitability of the assimilation of ethnic groups in the United States and Canada, immigrant populations still retain much of their viability. This is especially true of their domestic life. Due to a variety of patterns in their countries of origin, the position of women in the home differs among various North American ethnic subcultures. Japanese-American families still retain some of the aspects of family structures found in rural Japanese society. In both Japan and the United States husbands and fathers hold positions of authority and leadership. Wives and children are expected to be obedient and respectful toward male family heads. The Japanese-American family is more male-oriented than many white, urban, middle-class Protestant families (Kitano, 1969, p. 66).

Mexican-American families in past decades followed a strict separation of male-female roles, with girls and women performing household tasks and boys and men doing outside work. Both rural and urban families followed this division of labor. Decision making has never been based on a strictly patriarchal model among Mexican-Americans. Mothers made daily decisions about children and household matters, while husbands and wives decided jointly on major purchases. Mothers also normally punished Mexican-American children. Over half the sample of Mexican-American respondents in a University of California-Los Angeles study mentioned their mothers as having the greatest influence over them. In Los Angeles 13 percent of the respondents and in San Antonio 8 percent of the informants claimed equal influence of both parents (Grebler, Moore, Guzman, 1970, p. 360). Information of this nature makes it difficult to claim that women were low in status within the family among Mexican-Americans in the Southwest except as an ideal in the minds of male informants. Joint decision making in financial matters with mothers supervising their children and household affairs is also the most frequent family pattern among Mexican-American families in Milwaukee, Wisconsin (Matthiasson, 1968). Higher-income Mexican-Americans in San Antonio more often stated that they were influenced by their mothers, which negates the possibility that the ideal of male authority may have been more easily attained among those persons who were better off financially.

South Italians, like Mexicans, have a stated ideal of male superiority within the home. However, in actual fact, mothers appear to have been the central figures within the family both in terms of prestige and as the keepers of the family finances (Covello, 1969, p. 219). Italian-Americans in East Harlem continue the tradition of idealized male dominance over wives, sisters, and daughters (Covello, 1969, p. 358).

Thus, as the previous data have indicated, among several Euro-American societies the woman is generally the central figure in the home. She is frequently the person who controls the family budget, buying what is needed by the family. Another pattern, common to middle-class North America, is joint action in financial matters. Joint decision making or decisions by the wife are the most frequent ways in which family decisions are made.

On the domestic scene in North America, middle-class wives and women of some ethnic groups do not take second place to men, as women do in France. Domestic equality of middle-class women in North America has led to the widespread but mistaken belief outside North America in the liberation of women in North American society as a whole. However, North American society shares some of the qualities which characterize the manipulative societies in this volume.

Westernized society has tended to blur distinctions between some sex roles and to emphasize others. Both men and women may be teachers, social workers, laboratory technicians, and workers in service occupations, but in North America doctors are generally men while women are nurses. Men become dentists; women, dental assistants. Few women become architects, lawyers, or engineers. Women are rarely found in police work, fire fighting, truck driving, carpentry, or other skilled trades.

North American society has not been open to women's equal participation in the professions and higher-echelon occupations. Until the turn of the century, careers for women outside the home were considered not quite respectable. In the Canadian civil service, 80 percent of the 55,000 women employees are in lower-level jobs as clerks and typists. Only 8 percent of professional employees are women (University Affairs, April 1972, p. 12).

In the United States, it is still customary in business to hire women only as secretaries and in other lower-level occupations, excluding them from executive positions. A recent survey indicated that 98 percent of nongovernmental jobs paying $13,000 or more are held by white men (Newsweek, April 10, 1972, p. 72).

Women's contributions to society, either as housewives or in careers, are not viewed as important by many members of Western society. An example of the low prestige of the North American housewife is summed up by the phrase "she is just a housewife." This implies that a woman so described is not capable of doing anything else. On the other hand, the phrase "career girl" is used to describe a woman of any age who works outside the home. This phrase implies that such a person has not become socially mature and is somewhat abnormal. One never hears a man described as a career boy or man nor is "just a" applied to any occupational group other than low-status ones like those of garbage men, ditchdiggers, or other manual laborers.

Domestic labor, either in one's own home or for hire, has low prestige in Europe and North America, whereas in non-Western society women's labor is necessary to the household economy (Ward, 1964, p. 79). Among the middle and upper classes in Europe, it was customary in the recent past to hire domestic help, thus freeing the wife from contributing to the running of the household and freeing men in these classes from dependence upon women.

Women in North and Central India hold a position of authority within the home in relation to disciplining their children, food production, and managing the family finances. The wife is the person who holds the purse strings and doles out the money. Husbands and wives discuss major purchases, which—although made by men in village areas—are made by wives in urban centers. Wives are instrumental in choosing spouses for their children through their communication networks with women in other villages. However, the joint family in India has a profound influence on the autonomy of young wives and their relationships with their husbands. In the early years of marriage, a young woman has almost no authority within the household. A woman's domestic authority increases as she becomes older and as her mother-in-law declines in vigor.

Women are economically necessary to Amahuacan men in the growing of corn, the basic food staple, and the cultivation of all other vegetables and fruits as well as the grinding and cooking of corn. In addition, women cut and haul all the firewood used for cooking. However, the indispensability of Amahuacan women does not appear to have given them a position of authority or equality either within the family unit or in other relationships with men. On the other hand, men are feared by women and other men since men express their own hostilities and those of their community through sorcery or murder.

Lau women are subject to the authority first of their fathers and later their husbands. As in North and Central India, women reside patrilocally. A young bride entering the family is subject to the dictates of her mother-in-law. Here also a woman's domestic authority increases with age. Both Lau men and women believe that women are inferior to men. Spatial arrangements within the houses and the family canoe reflect the lower status of women. However, Lau women have developed mechanisms which permit them to defy the authority of men. Women can curse their husbands if they are newly married and want a divorce or—if desperate—they may curse themselves. A woman can also flee to the woman's seclusion area to avoid work, a beating, or consummating a marriage. A village can be thoroughly disrupted if a woman feels so mistreated that she gives birth in the village rather than in the birth hut. The village becomes polluted and the men must leave it until it has been ceremonially purified.

POSITION OF WOMEN IN COMPLEMENTARY SOCIETIES

The position of women in the home in many non-Western societies fits more closely with their actual status in society than it does in Euro-American and other manipulative societies. In many non-Western societies, social roles of men and women are complementary. Each performs tasks which are essential to and hence valued by the opposite sex. The societies in this volume which are complementary are the Birom; the Eskimo; the Philippine; the Khmer of Cambodia; and the Arabs, Christians, and Druses of Syria and Lebanon. In order to understand the implications of complementarity it is necessary to examine the domestic position of women in non-Western societies.

An Eskimo woman is the central figure in the home, and her husband is completely dependent upon her and her labor. "A man cannot hunt until his wife has finished working on his clothes. Camp cannot be moved in the spring until the wife has made the tent" (Briggs). On the other hand, wives are dependent on husbands to provide food. Consequently both value the skills of the other.

In decision making, the Eskimo husband may be the nominal leader in decisions involving hunting and traveling, although he often consults his wife privately before announcing a decision. If a wife is unhappy about a decision, she lets her husband know. In the eastern Arctic, women are the decision makers within the household, although this is not as true in the central Arctic.

Khmer women of Cambodia may say that their husbands are the masters of the house. However, women in fact retain control of certain areas of the domestic sphere; for example, the household budget and savings, the marriages of their children, and the taking of a co-wife. In addition, the Khmer woman is the most important person to her children, as the proverb "A father is worth a thousand friends, and a mother worth a thousand fathers" suggests.

Within the domestic unit in the Middle East, women are indispensable, since it is they who perform tasks it is impossible to have done by anyone else. Wives in high-ranking or chiefly households supervise various aspects of domestic production, while wives of peasants engage in physical labor such as fieldwork or weaving.

Decision making in a traditional Syrian or Lebanese household is arrived at by discussion and consensus of the whole family, with the oldest or most distinguished man serving as spokesman for the group. Thus instead of a patriarchal form of decision making, it is more likely to have been a consensual process.

Women of the Birom, although they have no formal legal rights in the wider society, have a position of power in the domestic sphere and by extension in the wider society because the household is the most important economic unit in the society. Women are essential to men because of the taboo on men's touching women's cooking pots. This makes it impossible for wifeless men to eat unless they live with kinsmen. When food is scarce, old widowers go hungry—since women feed their children first, next themselves and their husbands, and old men last. Older widows continue their household and farming activities longer than men and may live alone in old age or have grandchildren live with them. For this reason, they can be more independent than men. In addition, women know that they are able to disrupt the functioning of the household by leaving if they are dissatisfied with matters that affect them.

Rural Philippine families involve not only husband and wife but older adolescents in the process of decision-making within the family. Both rural and urban wives control the family resources by being family treasurer. In addition, rural women supplement the family income with small-scale trading and other entrepreneurial activities such as being folk healers, laundresses, midwives, or weavers. In the city, women have expanded their careers to include employment in both professional and service occupations. Both middle- and working-class urban wives exercise autonomy in running their households.

This brief examination of the domestic status of women in complementary societies has indicated that the economic contributions of women, as well as their centrality in the daily running of the family in general, give women a position of authority within the home even when they marry into the household from outside.

The domestic position of women and their general control of the family budget influences women's status within society. For example, if equality in domestic spheres were an important factor in North American society, then women in most regions of Mexico, the United States, and Canada would feel themselves to be treated equally with men.

However, in some societies the family is not as important an institution as it is in others. In many Western societies, prestige comes to those who have succeeded in economic or political life in nondomestic contexts. Women are excluded from these activities or have only recently been admitted.

On the other hand, women are very important in household and village affairs in the Philippines, the Middle East, and some parts of Africa. This authority spills over into the wider society and gives women as a group influence in the jural domain and a greater equality of status.

In her paper "The Position of Women: Appearance and Reality," Ernestine Friedl suggests that in many societies males have the appearance of higher prestige than women and that many societies have the appearance of being male-dominated. However, the actual situation may be quite different. In those societies in which the domestic unit is the most important social institution, having power in the household is more important than having prestige and power in outside contexts (Friedl, 1967, p. 97). Societies which are specifically of this type are found in the Middle East, Africa, Southeast Asia, and the Arctic as well as parts of Europe such as Greece and Portugal (Friedl, 1967; Riegelhaupt, 1967, p. 109).

The status of women in Africa has been summarized by Denise Paulme as being not inferior or superior "but different, and complementary" (Paulme, 1963, p. 6). As we have seen, Birom women do not have formal legal rights, but customary behavior has ensured that they achieve a status equal to though different from that of men and that they can manipulate men to achieve their own ends. Audrey Smedley argues that Birom has a system of noncompetition between men and women, with some roles reserved for men and others for women. Noncompetition assures that all tasks necessary to the maintenance of society are fulfilled and the fullest advantage to the whole society is achieved.

This contrasts with the Western ideology of the individual being free to pursue his own happiness. In many non-Western societies, of which the Birom and Middle Eastern societies are representative, both men and women are socialized to sacrifice their individual desires toward the collective goal of survival of their own group and of their society. Traditional Chinese values also emphasized duty, obedience, and preservation of the kin group at the expense of the individual. Modern China has shifted the individual's allegiance from his own family to the state. Westerners tend to look down on any system which submerges the individual to the interests of a larger group. It is often naïvely assumed that in any culture which submerges a woman's desires to that of her own or her husband's kin group, women will have an inferior status. In such societies, men also have their wishes subordinated to the needs of the larger group. Both the Middle East and China are examples of societies in which men are also subordinated to their lineages or the state.

There are a variety of other factors which influence the status of women in society in addition to the value society places on the domestic unit. No one factor operates by itself. Some other important factors are the kind and amount of economic production a woman contributes toward the maintenance of the household, the type of kinship system and residence pattern practiced by a society, the religious system, the educational opportunities available to women, and the political history of a society. In her excellent introduction to *Women in the New Asia,* Barbara Ward discusses some of these factors and the ways in which they apply to women in Southeast Asia (Ward, 1963).

Discussion of these factors is limited to those that effect women in the thirteen societies described in this book. Due to a lack of data in this volume, neither education or political history are discussed here.[1]

The manner in which kinship systems and rules of residence affect the status of women can be briefly summarized in this way. Ethnologists tend to assume that patrilineal descent systems emphasize the male line and may tend to introduce an element of male bias into a society (Ward, 1963, p. 84). Patrilocal residence, especially when it is coupled with patrilineal descent, can add a further degree of male bias to the society. An excellent example of this is the Lau of the Solomon Islands. Matrilineal descent emphasizes the female line and sometimes introduces a female bias into a society. Matrilocal residence may also add a further element of female bias to a society (Ward, 1963, p. 82). However, other factors seem to weigh more heavily than matrilineality and matrilocality in assessing the status of women. Judith Brown's comparison of the matrilocal and matrilineal Bemba of Africa with the Iroquois of New York State indicates that control of production and allocation of resources by women was the important determinant of the status of women in Iroquois society—rather than kinship organization and residence patterns (Brown, 1971, p. 164).

Societies that have patrilineal descent and patrilocal residence such as those of North and Central India, the Birom of Nigeria, the Arabs and Druses of Syria and Lebanon, the Arabs of Egypt, and traditional Chinese all have an ideal pattern of the three-generation household in which the father retains authority over all his sons and a mother over her daughters-in-law. In reality, this ideal is often not realized for several reasons. Aline Wong mentions that in traditional China only the wealthy class had the income to maintain a large household group. The majority of the peasants were landless. They survived by renting small plots of land which could feed only a few persons. To counteract the drain on the family income from excess mouths to feed and daughters' dowries to provide, peasants practiced female infanticide and the sale of young girls into slavery. The average family size in China appears to have been four to six persons.

In addition, the ties binding a three-generation household are extremely fragile. Property rivalry between the sons and personal clashes among the women of the household are prime causes of the breakup of extended families into smaller units. This is especially true of China in the traditional period and of families in North and Central India. (Michaelson and Goldschmidt, 1971, p. 341).

The relationships between members of patrilocal extended families also appears to have varied from the amiability within the household to the miseries of women, especially young daughters-in-law, mentioned by Aline Wong in her essay on traditional China. Both the Birom of Nigeria and the various caste and religious groups of North and Central India surround the new bride with taboos and restrictions to ease the transition from the natal home to that of the husband. A Birom bride may not speak openly to her mother-in-law until the onset of her first labor pains. A North Indian Hindu bride wears a veil in front of her father-in-law and husband's older brothers and speaks carefully when talking to her mother-in-law.

Louise Sweet demonstrates in her essay that women of the patrilineages of Syria and Lebanon are not controlled by men. While male dominance is a frequent characteristic of this type of family organization, it is variable in degree and mode of expression. In Syrian villages, males express idealized sentiments about women being weak creatures who have to be managed. In actual fact, women often manage themselves and their menfolk. This contrasts with the harsh reality of life in traditional China. In the Chinese extended family, a young woman suffered the miseries inflicted upon her by her mother-in-law in addition to those imposed on her by her husband or father-in-law.

Those societies described here that practice bilateral descent and inheritance tend to be flexible about rules of residence. Bilaterality is more often associated with individual choice of marriage partner than with arranged marriage. Strong male dominance is statistically more frequent in communities with patterns of patrilineality and patrilocal residence. However, Michaelson and Goldschmidt's analysis of peasant communities indicated that male dominance was reported in thirteen of twenty communities having bilateral inheritance (Michaelson and Goldschmidt, 1971, p. 334). Therefore inheritance of property by females and equal emphasis of ties to both male and female kinsmen does not automatically assure equal status of women within the society, although it may play a part in the higher status of women in societies such as the Khmer or Eskimo.

Religious sanctions also affect the position of women in the societies in the book. The effect of religious law on women is clearly apparant in Safia K. Mohsen's discussion of the status of Egyptian women. In Egypt, the practice of seclusion (which is found in other areas of the Islamic world) is made more restrictive by the right of detention or *habs*. In the Egyptian case, except for a weekly visit to the home of her parents, a woman must have her husband's permission to leave the house. She may not go out of the house to work or attend school without her husband's permission. A husband is allowed by Islamic law, as interpreted by Egyptian jurists, to keep a wife in his home against her will. Egypt is an extremely conservative area in the relationships between men and women. The Islamic right of detention is not practiced by Muslims either in Syria or India. Therefore, even in different areas observing the same religion, actual customs may differ.

According to Theravada Buddhism, women are religiously inferior to men. In order to be reincarnated favorably in the next life, therefore, Khmer women have to work harder to earn merit than men. They may not become monks, a role that earns much merit for men. However, this religious disadvantage has not been carried over into village social life and male-female relations, as Mohsen says it has in Egypt. May Ebihara points out that women in fact have considerable freedom and authority in Cambodian village life.

The effect of religion on Hindu women is much less obvious than its effect on Egyptian women. While Hindu women cannot become priests, goddesses are a very important part of Hindu belief. However, goddesses are both beneficial and threatening, both caring for people or bringing disease. Therefore the place of females in the Hindu religious system is somewhat ambiguous.

Economic productivity has an important effect on the position of women within a society. In those societies in which the main economic unit of production is the household, the amount of productive work contributed by the wife may be a factor in determining her relative status. In peasant villages, male dominance is strong where there is little female participation in agriculture and when agriculture is the primary economic activity. "Feminine control of such significant activities as agriculture, marketing, or collection and sale of shellfish does not appear to make a crack in the ideology of male dominance" (Michaelson and Goldschmidt, 1971, p. 333). North Indian villagers fall into this category of androcentric societies with male-dominated agriculture, as do Egyptian peasants and Guatemalan Indians. Syrian and Lebanese peasant women contribute heavily to the household unit's production and thus have considerable authority. However, an additional aspect of their domestic and village authority involves tending the home fires in those ethnic groups in which males emigrate to work elsewhere within the country or overseas. Especially in Christian and Druse communities, women are left behind as manageresses of the household for extended periods of time. Villages of these ethnic groups may be occupied by women, children, and only enough males to mount a defense in case of warfare.

Khmer and Philippine women who contribute heavily to the cultivation of the principal staple, rice, appear to have much more authority than peasant women did in the rice growing areas of traditional China. This may be due to two differences between the three cultures. First, Chinese peasant women did not assist their husbands with the planting, transplanting, weeding, and harvesting of rice on as regular a basis or on as large a scale as do both Cambodian and Filipino peasant women. Second, peasant women in the Philippines and Cambodia benefit from the inheritance of land and retain control over their land after marriage. Male dominance appears harder to maintain when women control scarce resources.

It also seems likely that women who contribute economically in a way which is valued by society have the basis for a higher status than women who may work just as hard and produce just as much but whose tasks are not as socially valued. Western society emphasizes the importance of work which earns a financial reward. Men's work assumes a greater importance in Western culture because of the monetary gain attached to it. As Helga Jacobson notes, women's work is valued both in the rural and urban areas of the Philippines. Women in the Philippine industrial sector do not experience discrimination except in those industries which have been developed by Western capital, employ Western managers, and follow an ideology that emphasizes the inferiority of women. The effect of this ideology is an important factor in controlling change in the status of women in a society.

Euro-American society and other manipulative societies have many subtle ways of expressing the inferior position of women and regulating the entrance of women into traditionally male preserves. One such technique is the myth—to which many men and women subscribe—of male superiority and female inferiority or male dominance and female submissiveness. This male-female relationship is assumed by many Westerners and even such diverse groups as the Lau to be a "natural" biological fact.

Societies as diverse as the Eskimo, the Arabs of the Middle East, and the Khmer of Cambodia all expect women to be modest in public. However, the etiquette of modesty in public places should not be confused with an attitude of meekness or obedience to males. The latter traits are those most closely associated with the myth of female submissiveness.

In actuality, a careful reading of the chapters in this volume will indicate that one quality that is lacking in most of the women described is submissiveness.

Submissiveness as a trait represents the idealized expectation of women's behavior in the Americas and Europe. It is the female opposite of *machismo* or male virility. In actual fact, not even Western women are submissive.

Eileen Maynard characterizes Guatemalan women as high-spirited and resourceful, with strength of character. As Woods puts it for Mexico, "The woman who is too submissive, even in Mexico, may be regarded more as a fool than as an ideal" (Woods, 1956, pp. 259–260).

The traditional Frenchwoman uses the appearance of submissiveness and "placation and tactical circumvention" of men to achieve her own ends. A minority of Frenchwomen have moved in the direction of those middle-class North American women who have assumed a greater control of their lives and their husbands than working-class women or women in traditional Western Europe.

MALE ATTITUDES TOWARD WOMEN

Men in many parts of Europe, Latin America, and North America verbally express their contempt for women as a group. Few quotations from the writings of male authors indicate approval of women. Women are commonly compared with the devil, hell, scolds, shrews, and are accused of having the qualities of fickleness, avarice, pride, and envy.[2] It is a common occurrence for women to hear derogatory comments by men about women.

Men in societies in which women have an equal status do not publically deprecate women. Jean Briggs observes that Eskimo men do not make the belittling comments that many Western men make, nor do the men of Syria or Lebanon engage in such talk. In both these areas women are valued and considered important members of the community, whereas women in Western societies are commonly forced to achieve their goals by manipulating men.

WOMEN'S ATTITUDES ABOUT THEMSELVES

The French are a classic example of a society in which women expect to be inferior and are not geared toward equality; therefore they remain inferior. Women may be politically and juridically equal, they may have equal education and an important share in the purchasing power of the family and the nation. However, if they do not feel that they are equal and if men continue to consider women inferior, women will not achieve equality. In all societies, women tend to perpetuate the status that they have. As Doranne Jacobson writes, "The system is that way because it works"; or as Audrey Smedley observes, "Women usually represent the conservative elements in the social system." In patrilineal societies such as the Lau and/ or the Birom, women are more careful than men to preserve their husbands' and sons' kin groups.

During the 1964 Presidential election campaign in the United States, Senator Margaret Chase Smith ran for President in several primary elections. The main criticism of her candidacy that I heard expressed by women did not involve the constitutional question of the legality of a woman candidate or the personal competence of Senator Smith. Her candidacy was criticized purely on the grounds of sex—on the grounds that, as a woman, she would be unable to be a competent President. Such criticism contrasts with comments made about the possibility of Imelda Marcos of the Philippines being a potential candidate for Philippine President or the achievements of Prime Ministers Gandhi of India, Bandaranaike of Ceylon, or Meir of Israel.

Militant Western feminists feel that women are universally oppressed by men. While this is obviously not the case, those societies in which women have inferior status will retain the status quo until women decide to change their own attitudes toward themselves and their abilities.

NOTES

1. Readers interested in an analysis of the effects of political history and education on the status of women would do well to read *Women in the New Asia*.

2. A random selection of thoughts by famous authors found under the subtitle "women" in *Bartlett's Familiar Quotations* (1955): "The venom clamors of a jealous woman poison more deadly than a mad dog's tooth," "Frailty, thy name is woman" (William Shakespeare); "Nor hell a fury like a woman scorned" (William Congreve); "A fickle and changeful thing is woman ever" (Virgil); "I expect that woman will be the last thing civilized by man" (George Meredith); "Dissimulation is innate in woman, and almost as much a quality of the stupid as of the clever" (Arthur Schopenhauer); "Where there is neither love nor hatred in the game, woman's play is mediocre" (Friedrich Wilhelm Nietzsche); "A woman is necessarily an evil, but he that gets the most tolerable one is lucky" (Menander); "A woman should be seen, not heard" (Sophocles).

BIBLIOGRAPHY

Aswad, Barbara: "Key and Peripheral Roles of Noble Women in a Middle Eastern Plains Village," *Anthropological Quarterly*, vol. 40, no. 1, pp. 144–149.

Bartlett, John: *Bartlett's Familiar Quotations*, 13th ed., Little, Brown and Company, Boston, 1955.

Brown, Judith K.: "Economic Organization and the Position of Women among the Iroquois," *Ethnohistory*, vol. 17, nos. 3–4, pp. 151–167, Summer-Fall 1970.

Covello, Leonard: *The Social Background of the Italo-American School Child*, E. J. Brill, Leiden, Holland.

Friedl, Ernestine: "The Position of Women: Appearance and Reality," *Anthropological Quarterly*, vol. 40, no. 1, pp. 97–108, 1967.

Gallaher, Art, Jr.: *Plainville Fifteen Years Later*, Columbia University Press, New York, 1961.

Grebler, Leo, Joan W. Moore, and Ralph C. Guzman: *The Mexican-American People*, The Free Press, New York, 1970.

Hollingshead, August B.: *Elmstown Youth*, John Wiley & Sons, Inc., New York, 1949.

Kitano, Harry H. L.: *Japanese Americans*, Prentice-Hall Inc., Englewood Cliffs, N.J., 1967.

Lantz, Herman P.: *People of Coal Town*, Columbia University Press, New York, 1958.

Lévi-Strauss, Claude: *The Elementary Structures of Kinship*, Beacon Press, Boston, 1969.

Matthiasson, Carolyn J. Weesner: "Acculturation of Mexican Americans in a Midwestern City," unpublished Ph.D. dissertation, Cornell University, 1968.

Michaelson, Evalyn Jacobson, and Walter Goldschmidt: "Female Roles and Male Dominance among Peasants," *Southwestern Journal of Anthropology*, vol. 27, no. 4, pp. 330–352, 1971.

"Executive Lib," *Newsweek*, vol 89, no. 15, April 10, 1972.

Paulme, Denise (ed.): *Women of Tropical Africa*, Routledge & Kegan Paul, Ltd., London, 1963.

Rainwater, Lee, Richard A. Coleman, and Gerald Handel: *Workingman's Wife,* McFadden-Bartell Corporation, New York, 1962.

Riegelhaupt, Joyce F.: "Saloio Women: An Analysis of Informal and Formal Political and Economic Roles of Portugese Peasant Women," *Anthropological Quarterly,* vol. 40, no. 1, pp. 109–123, 1967.

Swartz, Marc J., Victor W. Turner, and Arthur Tuden: *Political Anthropology,* Aldine Publishing Company, Chicago, 1966.

Ward, Barbara E. (ed.) : *Women in the New Asia,* UNESCO, Paris, 1963.

Warner, W. Lloyd: *American Life: Dream and Reality,* rev. ed., University of Chicago Press, Chicago, 1962.

"Women Must Change Attitudes to Get Equal Breaks," *University Affairs,* Association of Universities and Colleges of Canada, vol. 13, no. 4, April 1972.

Woods, Sister Frances Jerome, C.D.P.: *Cultural Values of American Ethnic Groups,* Harper & Row, Publishers, Incorporated, New York, 1956.

Index